Text Information Retrieval Systems
Second Edition

Library and Information Science

Consulting Editor: *Harold Borko*
Graduate School of Library and Information Science
University of California, Los Angeles

The list of books continues at the end of the volume.

Text Information Retrieval Systems
Second Edition

Charles T. Meadow
University of Toronto
Toronto, Ontario, Canada

Bert R. Boyce
Louisiana State University
Baton Rouge, Louisiana

Donald H. Kraft
Louisiana State University
Baton Rouge, Louisiana

ACADEMIC PRESS
A Harcourt Science and Technology Company

San Diego   San Francisco   New York   Boston   London   Sydney   Tokyo

Academic Press
An imprint of Elsevier Science
525 B Street, Suite 1900, San Diego, California 92101-4495, USA
http://www.academicpress.com

Academic Press
32 Jamestown Road, London NW1 7BY, UK
http://www.academicpress.com

Library of Congress Catalog Card Number: 99-62665

International Standard Book Number: 0-12-487405-3

PRINTED IN THE UNITED STATES OF AMERICA
02   03   04   05   06   07   SB   9   8   7   6   5   4   3   2

Contents

2

Data, Information, and Knowledge

3

Representation of Information

4

Attribute Content and Values

5

Models of Virtual Data Structure

6

The Physical Structure of Data

7

Querying the Information Retrieval System

8

Interpretation and Execution of Query Statements

9

Text Searching

13

Search Strategy

14

The Information Retrieval System Interface

15

A Sampling of Information Retrieval Systems

16

Measurement and Evaluation

Preface

Information retrieval is a communication process. It is a means by which users of an information system or service can find the documents, records, graphic images, or sound recordings that meet their needs or interests. We call all of these, collectively, *documents*. What characterizes this form of communication is that these documents, viewed as messages, are created before use, put into some kind of storage, and made available for people to search for and retrieve, possibly even years after their creation. Users must know how to make known their needs or interests. It is not always obvious how to do this.

With whom or with what must users communicate? The communication process will link the user to a librarian, museum curator, fingerprint identification specialist, or whoever is in charge of a collection of what we are calling documents. How is this done? It may be by direct communication with these intermediaries or by interaction with search tools the intermediaries have designed for that purpose. A library's catalog is one form of such a tool. A system of computer programs is another tool in our modern society. The communication will normally involve the processing of *text*, strings of words known to both parties in the process, that can be used to describe a document's content and other attributes and link it with a need expressed in similar terms.

This is not a trivial problem. It may require specialized knowledge. For example, to find whether a new invention has already been patented calls for technical knowledge in the field of the invention as well as knowledge of how patents are classified. It may require the use of a special language, called a *query language*, for expressing information needs to a computer.

Human beings often have difficulty understanding each other. Add to this that the conversation may be about a technical matter of which only one of the persons has any serious knowledge and we have the makings of a serious miscommunication. Make one of the parties a computer and we add considerably to the problem, especially if the machine invites users to communicate in natural language when it has, at best, a primitive ability to understand it.

When some information has been retrieved from its storage place, it becomes the user's task to evaluate it. We cannot accept just any patent; we cannot accept just any article about a company we are planning to invest in, or any match for a fingerprint. We have to be reasonably sure we have the best, or at least good enough, information. If we did not find what we really wanted, what do we do next? How do we improve the process? How do we evaluate the completeness, authoritativeness, or reliability of a document? Information retrieval systems do not answer these questions, but knowledge of their structure and operation can suggest alternative approaches to a search. There is a growing feeling among professionals in the retrieval field that users may be tending to settle for less than the best. Typically, a high school student will accept anything on his or her subject that is not too difficult to read. What if business managers, lawyers, or physicians did this? These professionals need to know how to search, retrieve, and evaluate information.

This book's purpose is not to teach readers how to become searchers, but to teach people who will be searching how the systems they use work. It is perhaps a "how to" book for retrieval system designers, in that it covers the problems they will face, and a review of the current available solutions. For the searcher, its purpose is to describe why such systems work as they do. The book is primarily about computer-based retrieval systems, but the principles apply to nonmechanized ones as well.

A typical reader will be a graduate student or advanced undergraduate in information, computer, or library science or in communication or journalism or a practitioner in the information services field. We assume a limited knowledge of mathematics and of computing. We have tried to explain all advanced mathematical concepts in nontechnical terms.

We begin the book with a general overview of information retrieval: how questions evolve from a lack of knowledge, how documents are created and entered into a storage and retrieval system, and what the main components of a retrieval system are. We go on to discuss the nature of information and such related terms as data, news, and knowledge. These are not idle abstractions. The differences matter because what may be news to one person is not to another, and what may be information to one is not to another. Users' reactions to systems that claim to provide information may reflect their varying senses of what information is. Information is not a tangible thing. It is represented by symbols. Our third chapter describes some of the means of representing information.

We then discuss how the symbols representing information are organized inside a computer and then how computers interpret and execute commands or process requests (*queries*). Following this we move into more advanced concepts such as ranking of output in order of likelihood of interest to a user, mapping the results of one search into another, and generating and using feedback about a search both from user to computer and from computer to user.

Although this is not primarily a book about how to search, we do include a chapter on search strategy. This is followed by a discussion of the interface between user and computer, how each party to human-computer communications goes about the task of communicating and helping the other achieve a mutual objective—a satisfactory search result. We then review several modern information retrieval systems to demonstrate their different approaches to solving retrieval problems, and conclude with a discussion of measurement and evaluation of information retrieval systems.

Some notes on typography. We use *italics* in the usual way, to denote emphasis or to indicate a word as a token rather than as one necessarily conveying meaning at the time it is used, as the token *word* is shown this way. Values of expressions assumed to be stored in or entered into a computer are shown in SMALL CAPITALS. So, if we want to show a command to a computer calling for retrieval of a text containing *word*, it will be written as SELECT WORD. Names of fields or attributes are indicated by use of arial type, as one value of the author field for this book is DONALD H. KRAFT.

Angle brackets indicate that their content describes the kind of value or the attribute whose value should occur in that position, as BEGIN <database name> means to follow the command BEGIN with the name of a database.

Three of us wrote this book but it takes many more people to create such a manuscript and find flaws with early drafts. Of course, there could still be flaws, but we are grateful to Professors Carol Barry and Stephanie Haas for much useful feedback. We also thank Joe Cox and the staff of the Inforum at the Faculty of Information Studies, University of Toronto, Dialog Corporation, Institute for Scientific Information, and Kaufman Consulting Services for information they found or provided and Detective Bruce Cadman of Metropolitan Toronto Police for his help with the material on fingerprinting. Naomi Henning, at Academic Press, handled all administrative arrangements quickly and smoothly.

Charles T. Meadow
Bert R. Boyce
Donald H. Kraft

1

Introduction

1.1

What Is Information?

To know what information retrieval is, we must first know what *information* is. There is no fully satisfactory definition. We examine the question in some detail in Chapter 2. Temporarily, consider the oversimplified characteristics that information is something that (1) is represented by a set of *symbols*, (2) which are *organized* or fit into some *structure*, and (3) can be read and to some extent understood by *users* of information.

Symbol, like *information*, is a word with many meanings. It can be any recognizable image, whether in print, paint, sound, or even odor. Little is lost if we insist that information can be represented only by symbols. Indeed, the computer scientist Edsger Dijkstra (1989, p. 1401) has stated that "when all is said and done, the only thing computers can do for us is to manipulate symbols." The symbols can be as simple as a single pulse of sound or electromagnetic energy, essentially a bit, or they can be as complex as a complete symphonic score or a novel. Between these extremes, and certainly the more common kinds of entity to which we normally apply this word, are a national flag, a word, a punctuation mark, and any string of printed characters. We leave for later discussion whether these symbols need such qualities as significance, novelty, truth, or authority to be *information*.

As soon as we get beyond the most elementary of symbols, such as A or π, then information, or its symbolic representation, must have structure to be understood. ACT, CAT, ATC, and TCA all have quite different meanings (including none, for some readers), as do FOOD FISH and FISH FOOD. The string 12345 can have any of several possible meanings, even if the reader knows it represents a date (is it JANUARY 23, 1945, or DECEMBER 3, 1945, American style, or 12 MARCH 1945, European style?).

To a large extent, information retrieval (IR) is concerned with three concepts: how to represent information, how to interpret the structure of its

1

symbols, and how to tell when one set of symbols has the same or a similar meaning as another. All present formidable problems for computers, and equally formidable challenges for the humans involved in the process, for it is the humans who give the symbols *meaning* and *significance*.

1.2

What Is Information Retrieval?

In brief, IR involves finding some desired information in a *store* of information or a database. Implicit in this view is the concept of *selectivity*; to exercise selectivity usually requires that a price be paid in effort, time, money, or all three. Information recovery is not the same as IR unless there has been a search and selection process. Copying a complete disk file is not retrieval in our sense. Watching the news on CNN all day with the viewer exercising no control over what is being shown, once the channel has been selected, is not retrieval either. A library is the best example of an institution devoted to selective retrieval. One does not go there to read the entire collection. One goes to look for something selectively, often something that will satisfy a set of highly individualized information needs.

Information retrieval is a communication process. In one sense it is a means by which authors or creators of records communicate with readers, but indirectly and with a possibly long time lag between creation of a message or text and its delivery to the IR system user. The records of a database are created and assembled without knowledge of exactly who will read them, or under what circumstances. The languages and channels of such a communication system are quite different from other well-known models, such as broadcasting and point-to-point communication.

Is information retrieval a computer activity? It is not strictly necessary that it be, but as a practical matter that is what we usually imply by the term, and that is what this book is primarily about. The computer system, consisting of both hardware and software, is what we call the *information retrieval system* (IRS). The term IRS may include the database, but whether it does may depend on the context in which the expression is used. However, all the important principles of information retrieval apply to purely nonmechanical IR as well. For example, a nonmechanized library functions as a retrieval system, in this case the staff or patrons being the instruments of search, decision making, and retrieval. King Henry II of England, in 1160, rode with his entourage from palace to palace, permanently on tour. Written records had to be carried along. Records, such as memos and letters, were stitched one to the previous one, creating an ever-growing scroll carried on the backs of mules. It grew so large it was called the

Great Roll of the Pipe. A new one was started on the first day of each year (Duggan, 1940, pp. 150–151).

We will primarily be discussing *interactive* IR. Today, this is found in three primary modes: (1) a central service, consisting of a number of databases with usually a single system for searching them, operated remotely from most users and requiring a telecommunications network for access; (2) a browsing service on the World Wide Web (WWW), which does not have its own databases but finds and searches "sites" owned by others; and (3) a local system operating in a single computer, in which are stored both retrieval software and a database, often on CD-ROMs. An example is an encyclopedia, stored on a disk together with its search software.

A remote retrieval service is operated through the medium of a computer in which the data are stored in files or databases and in which software interprets users' requests for information, finds it, and controls its transmission it to the requester. There is relatively little difference between local and remote systems in terms of operation from the user's point of view. Both are interactive in that there is almost continuous conversation between the user and the database computer. There is considerable difference in the cost. There tends to be a big difference between WWW browsers and other retrieval systems in terms of how deeply records are indexed and how specific searches may be. Any of them is a long way from King Henry's pipe.

Yet another view of the question of the mechanical nature of information retrieval is that we do not usually think of library catalogs, printed indexes, or encyclopedias as mechanical aids, but they are, even if they are older technologies. When first created, they may have seemed as strangely mechanical as today's computers do to some present-day information users. An encyclopedia is a collection of relatively small works bundled together with extensive indexes, citations, and cross references. It is not designed to be read from beginning to end, but to be used as a mechanism for finding articles of interest, often only after much searching.

While the selection of a record from an inventory file or a file of bank depositor accounts can be considered IR, the term is more commonly applied to the searching of files of text records or records descriptive of text or graphics. The uncertainty about how the content should be queried underlies much of the activity of IR. When querying is restricted to use of a single search key, such as a part or account number, there is not much challenge.

Blair (1990, p. vii) has stated that the "central problem of Information Retrieval is how to represent documents for retrieval." We are inclined to think that this is becoming less true as more and more databases consist of the complete texts of documents, while previously they consisted of index or classification terms that represented the documents' content.

Not only is the original, natural language of the text being used in the databases, but natural language is being used, increasingly, as the means of a user's telling the retrieval system what is wanted. This is called the *query*; whether it is written in natural language or any of the many artificial languages developed for the purpose, the trend is certainly toward more complex and expressive statements. The central problem is becoming how to match, compare, or relate the user's request for information with the texts stored in the database. As Liddy, Paik, Yu, and McKenna. (1995, p. 106) put it, "[A] successful retrieval system must retrieve on the basis of what people mean in their query, not just what they say."

On the other hand, the query might be considered a form of document representation, in that it represents characteristics of documents to be retrieved. If so, we can agree with Blair that it is a question of major importance how best to phrase this query, i.e., how to represent what we want to find in documents.

1.3

How Does Information Retrieval Work?

The process of selectively searching for information in a database can be viewed as starting from at least two different points. One starting point is the *user*, or prospective user, of information. We will henceforth consider *user* to mean a person who has an information need and who uses an IRS to attempt to satisfy that need. At the other starting point, a person or agency makes a decision to collect information and organize and store it for later search and retrieval. There are many complex steps before stored information and user come together.

We present here a model of the retrieval process and use it as a basis for all the more detailed discussions to come. The reader should be aware that there are other models and even other ideas about what is meant by a model of the IR process (Bookstein, 1983; Boyce and Kraft, 1985; Croft, 1982; Harter, 1986; Kochen, 1974; Korfhage, 1997; Lancaster, 1968; Maron and Kuhns, 1960; Salton and McGill, 1983; Soergel, 1985; van Rijsbergen, 1979, 1986). Generally, the purpose of any of these models is to set a framework within which the reader can interpret various aspects of the entire process.

The base model is illustrated in Fig. 1.1. This is an overall view of IR showing that it is a process that depends on separate actions of at least two groups. A user may be an individual or part of a community of some sort. It may be hard to tell from where a need for information arose. Some individual then develops a personal need, even though he or she may not know

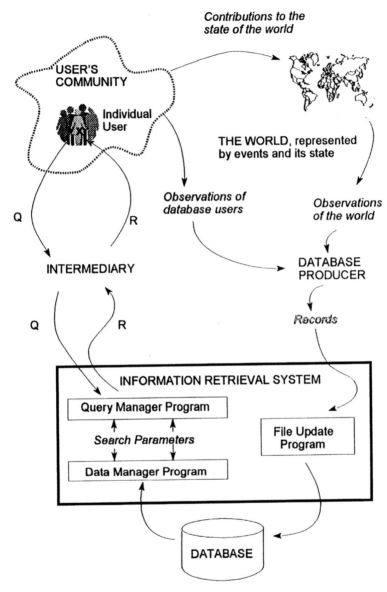

Figure 1.1

General view of an information retrieval system: The system is cyclic, with information generally flowing in a clockwise direction in this diagram. Information about the world comes from a community of users or potential users, who also represent the creators of information, and this is used, in turn, to affect the world, including the users.

exactly what is needed at this point. When, eventually, the information is found (or even found not to exist) typically some new information is created and contributed to the world. Database producers study what kind of information is available and what is needed. Then they collect and use it to create the records of a database. Now we go back to the user, whose information need may be conveyed to an intermediary, a person whose profession it is to assist users. The provision of information by the database producer and its search and retrieval by the user are asynchronous. Both will fare better if they have some understanding of each other. The user should know what producers' policies are, and the producers should know of users' general needs and characteristics. In the following sections, Figs. 1.2–1.4 show this three- or four-way interaction (user–intermediary–IRS production of new records) in more detail.

1.3.1 The User Sequence

The user does not exist in a vacuum. He or she is a member of a community or organization, has a job, mission, or interest, and interacts with other people to accomplish some goal, again not intending to exclude lone workers. The communication between a user and an IR system is illustrated in Fig. 1.2. Paragraphs below are keyed to numbers in the figure.

1. *The user's need for information*—Somehow and for some reason, such as being assigned to a new project or case, the user senses a lack of information. Belkin (1980) called this an *anomalous state of knowledge* (ASK), a gap or discontinuity in the person's knowledge. This term means nothing more than that the person recognizes the lack of or need for data, information, or knowledge. This is the start of the IR process.

Recognition that a lack of knowledge exists does not necessarily mean that the user knows *what* information is lacking. A physician or attorney working on a difficult case may know that information is needed, but may not know at the start what tests to run, questions to ask, obscure laws or journals to read, or precedents to examine.

In everything that is to follow about how to do information retrieval and to evaluate what is done, it is important to realize that *nothing in the entire process is more important to the outcome than the user's own understanding of his or her information need* and *ability to recognize what satisfies that need.*

Some people need information but get along without it. Others seek it out by going to some kind of information source, which may be a co-worker, a library, a fortune-teller, a stockbroker, or an online database search service.

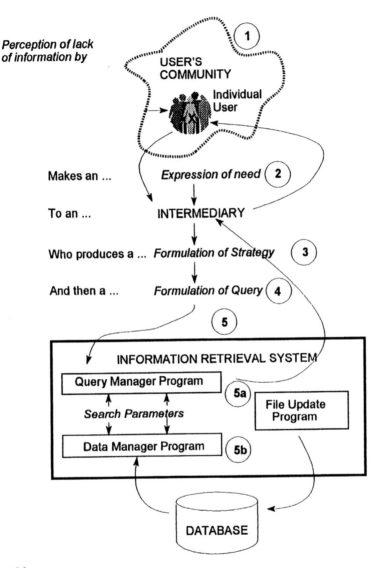

Figure 1.2
Communication between the user and the IRS: From the time a user perceives a lack of information until the receipt of an acceptable response from an IRS, there may be many steps, some involving intermediaries, and many repeated iteratively.

2. *Translating or expressing the needs*—The user's next step is to express the information need. The user typically goes to some information agency, where there is a person or machine to whom the need will be conveyed. If it is a person he or she is called a *search intermediary* or simply *intermediary*. Later (Chapter 9) we shall show that this function can be assisted to some extent by a computer program. The *expression* of need is a translation of the need, vague as it may be, into language the information agent can understand. The translation is not always going to work well, for a number of reasons.

An actual example is the case of an engineer who asked a librarian for information about "processing of jewelry." What he wanted, it turned out later, was information about use of laser technology to drill holes in diamonds. Did he not know the difference? Did he equate JEWELRY PROCESSING with DI-AMOND DRILLING in his own mind? Or did he phrase it this way because he thought the librarian would require a simpler explanation or that the jewelry industry would be the best source of information?

Another, not uncommon, example involves a search for an explanation of a disease in lay terms, from a database containing only research information. The request is likely to be worded along the lines of finding information about such and such a disease from the sufferer's point of view. The user's true goal, understanding the nature of the disease, rather than complex details of treatment or cause, may not be stated as a need because the user does not understand that it is necessary to say something so obvious. He or she is asked the subject and states it as the name of the disease. The physician looking for details of treatment information may well use the same terms as the layman—the name of the disease—and for the same reason, namely, that it is not clear anything else is required. Both will then get the same output from the IR process, but one will likely deem it satisfactory and the other, useless.

For a user to explain his or her information needs to the intermediary does not require that person to use library classification codes, thesaurus classes, or keywords. It involves one human being speaking to another, in natural language, although possibly laden with technical jargon. If this step is not done well, the retrieved results are almost inevitably going to be poor because the intermediary is likely to look for the wrong thing. The first two steps (recognition of an ASK and translation of it into a statement of information need) almost never are the subjects of formal training of end users.

3. *Formulating a search strategy*—The formal statement of need is not always uttered. Particularly if a user is going to do his or her own searching, say in the card catalog or even online, then he or she will probably not take the time to write down a formal statement of need. In a library, the user may even go directly to a known stack area and start browsing the books in the hope of finding what is wanted.

The search strategy is the general plan for finding the needed information. If a trained information specialist such as a reference librarian is involved, that person usually plans the strategy, but the very decision to go to that person may have resulted from a strategy conceived by the user.

There can be levels of strategy. Some writers use the term to refer to very explicit and detailed aspects of a search, such as whether the previously mentioned engineer with the drilling problem should have asked to retrieve records in a database containing the words (DIAMOND OR JEWELRY) AND DRILLING or just DIAMOND AND DRILLING. This level of detail fits the usual meaning of *tactic*, rather than strategy.

4. *Formulating a query*—This step in a typical retrieval process entails composing a formulation of the information need in terms suitable for the retrieval system to use. For a computer system, this may mean writing the equivalent of a computer program—a sequence of commands intended to produce the desired information. In a library, the query-formulation step involves selecting classification codes or journals and indexes to investigate.

The *query* is the precise formulation of the search, in terms appropriate to the retrieval mechanism. There are two important aspects of a query: (1) the terms, words, codes, or values used to describe records the user wants to retrieve, and (2) the logic relating different sets of values. In our example, DIAMOND and DRILLING are terms and they are linked by the operator AND. As we noted, in the early history of IR, the purpose of the query was to express the index terms or other surrogates for the desired documents. Today, the query is more likely to have to represent the relatively uncontrolled, actual set of words used in the documents, themselves. This change is both a help and a hindrance. To those who knew the various classification or subject heading systems, their nonuse creates ambiguities. To those who never knew them, there is no longer the need to struggle to find an appropriate code in order to do retrieval.

From this point on we concentrate on computer processing and remind the reader that it is most commonly the query, not the needs expression and certainly not the information need, that the computer must work with.

5. *Computer processing of the query*—The query is interpreted by the computer. This requires another translation process. In some computer systems the interpretation is straightforward. The computer acts upon the terms and operators that were in the query, no more, no less, barring only programming error. And, as noted above (the Liddy quote in Section 1.2) what is really wanted is the ability to act upon what was meant, regardless of expressions used. A number of research and a few commercial systems now have "intelligent" programs that improve on the literal text of a query in one way or another, the computer taking part in interpreting the user's need. We shall cover this in Chapter 9 and illustrate some systems working toward this end, in Chapter 15.

There are two distinct steps in computer processing:

a. Translation of the expression of the query into a set of *search parameters* that specify exactly what files are to be searched, what terms are to be looked up, and the conditions for retrieval. In most commercial retrieval systems, this translation is an uncomplicated one because the language in which the query is expressed is so precise. If natural language is used in stating the query, some degree of judgment is required in the translation, and the process is difficult and imperfect in execution. We call the program that does this translation the *query manager.*

b. Carrying out *search and retrieval operations* as specified by the search manager. However complex the translation, this part of computer processing is usually quite deterministic, and there is little or nothing that might be called judgment exercised by the computer. We call this the *data manager.*

Many readers will know that the results of a computer search are often not exactly what was wanted. The cause, in the kind of system we are now considering, is an imperfect query or imperfect records, i.e., one or both of these did not mean what they appeared to mean. More exactly, the meaning to the user, search intermediary, or author of a record (indexer, cataloger, reporter, etc.) all may have been different, and the computer restricted itself merely to matching strings of characters provided in a query with those in the records.

How can a record not mean what it appears to say? Let us start at the other end of our process model and see how records are typically formed.

1.3.2 The Database Producer Sequence

The user's information need arises from that person's organization or community. A different organization has made a decision to create an information store or database: perhaps it is a telephone directory, a file of citations and abstracts of articles published in medical journals, or a file of sales volumes and prices of shares on a stock exchange.

The decision to collect the information has to be followed by decisions on what the scope or coverage and the content of the record should be (Fidel, 1987; Harter, 1986; Marshall, 1990). For example, a designer has to specify which stocks or stock exchanges should be included, how up to date should the information be, and whether and how to represent such items of information as stock symbol, number of shares, price, journal title, abstract, or article title. These, of course, are not likely to occur in the same database, but database producers may have to deal with a wide variety of subject matter.

The steps at the database-creation end, shown in Fig. 1.3, are

1. *Decision to create a database*—For example, the decision is made to start a new newspaper.

2. *Decision on scope of the collection*—About what entities should information be collected? What kinds of stories or news coverage are wanted: general news, financial news, local news only, etc.

3. *Decision on design of the individual records*—What information is wanted about an entity (the traditional Who, What, Where, When, and Why of journalism)?

4. *Selection of the actual items for inclusion*—For today's issue, what stories are to be published?

5. *Creation of the content of individual records*—The news must be gathered and the stories written and edited. In the case of a stock market table, the data are generally considered *exact*. In the case of subject indexing or classification, much human judgment is required; hence differences of opinion on interpretation are to be expected. An inquiry for the latest price of a given stock will, barring a program error, yield the exact answer. The result of a request for all citations to published literature on a given subject will depend on a number of factors:

    a. Are all articles on the desired subject in the file? (Scope)

    b. What are the rules and language for describing subjects? How much narrative? What attributes of an entity should be described? (Record design)

    c. What specific decisions does a cataloguer make in each instance, e.g., is the article considered to be on drilling diamonds or on processing jewelry? (Record content)

    d. How is the query composed—how well does it represent the information need statement? (Query formulation)

    e. How well do the retrieved records match the needed information? (Output evaluation)

6. *Data entry*—At major newspapers today, stories are usually typed directly into a computer, having no paper embodiment until the newspaper is printed. For most kinds of databases, it is necessary to perform a keystroking operation of some sort in order to create the computer copy of a record. This is not actually part of information retrieval, but adds to the expense of the records created.

Regardless of how records are created, when they enter a computer there is work to be done to place them correctly in storage. The process is called *updating* or *database maintenance*. Entering the record may involve more than merely adding it to a file, for there are normally various indexes created

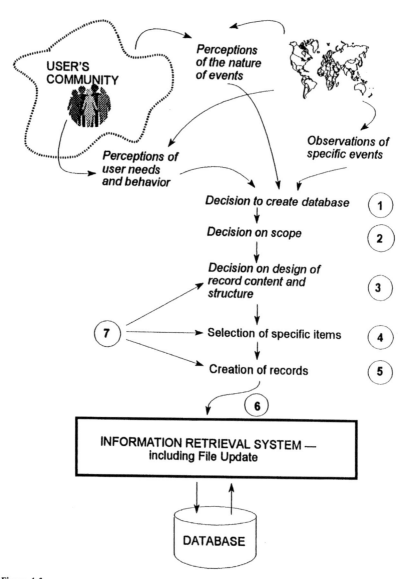

Figure 1.3

Role of the database producer: The producer must decide, in advance, what kinds of entities or events to record, and what information to record about them, and how to represent and organize them, and then must select the individual items to be included in a database, as they arrive at the production facility.

by and maintained within the computer to speed searching. These must be brought up to date whenever new information is added to or removed from a file.

7. *Quality control*—Both a part of the process of creating records and a *post hoc* process of review of database content, quality control is concerned with the correctness and consistency of entries. The work ranges from a review of the statements made or values entered into a record to handling cases of errors detected after the record enters the database.

1.3.3 Query Processing

Inside the computer (Fig. 1.4), at the simple level we are discussing here, the following steps are taken: (1) the query is interpreted, (2) terms are extracted and looked up in indexes, and (3) records that satisfy the query are identified. Then (4) the user is told how many were identified, and he or she is permitted to browse through them, to look in the indexes to help find other search terms, or to revise the query. Messages, including retrieved records, are (5) formatted for display and (6) transmitted to the user, or they may be (7) printed and later mailed. In a fee-based system, users (8) must be appraised of costs. In a separate sequence of actions (9) new records are constantly being added to the database or existing ones are corrected or deleted.

1.3.4 Why the Process Is Not Perfect

If the records of the database contain natural-language text, graphics, or other complex patterns, or if they contain codified interpretations of the text or images, such as subject classification codes, then it is expected that users will not be able to identify exactly those records sought at the first try.

Consider first a query to a stock market or a factory's parts inventory file. The file would have one entry for each company listed on the exchange or for each part normally kept in inventory by the organization. Each record would have a well-established set of information elements descriptive of the stock or the part. These might be the stock symbol or part number, latest price, or number on hand. One does not expect the stock tables to include information about the quality of food at McDonald's or the current price of Ford automobiles. Users tend to know, at least generally, what is available. The meanings of the names of the data elements present will be well established, at least among the

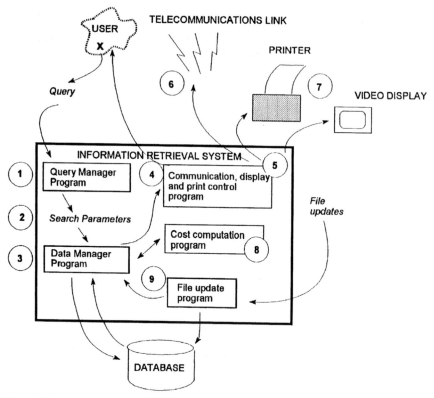

Figure 1.4

Major components of the IRS: The complete retrieval system has five major program components, indicated by small rectangles: a *query manager* to interpret queries, a *data manager* to search for and retrieve specific records, a *communication program* to handle all output to users, a *cost computation program* (for those IRSs whose users are charged per use), and a *file modification program* to update the files.

community of users of the database. The codes or values of the data elements will be unambiguous.

By contrast, a file consisting of the text of a newspaper or of catalog descriptions of books in a library or of pictures in an art gallery may have data elements that not every user is familiar with, such as the names of sections of the newspaper, the classification schedule for books, the often arcane terms used to describe a painting. The user may not know what to ask for, even when he or she knows, mentally, exactly what is wanted, but the user of the stock table knows there is only one latest price for General Motors stock.

So the user may not know exactly what he or she wants or may not know what attributes or values are used in the database. Finally, a user dealing with an unfamiliar system may miss the serendipity that comes with browsing in *approximately* the right part of an information collection. Browsing may yield new terms to use and may open entirely new paths of search and discovery.

The user interested in the history of the IBM Corporation, of the computer industry, or of IBM's role in the computer industry does not necessarily know what words or codes to use to describe the topic "history of the computer industry, especially of IBM." In this case, there has to be some probing to see what is in the file, what terms seem to bring the best results, and, finally, which of the records retrieved are the most promising. This user is interested in retrieving not the character string HISTORY OF IBM, but records descriptive of books about the people, devices, and events that make up that history. These books, in turn, contain the history. The bibliographic records are called *surrogate records*—they represent other records. They do, of course, also contain information in their own right: *information* about what books a library owns, who the authors are, when published, etc. These are facts, not just surrogates for facts. It is also a fact that an indexer assigned a certain descriptor to a document surrogate record. The descriptor is a surrogate. It describes what the indexer thinks the document is about. Its presence in the record is a fact. The fact that the descriptor has been assigned does not guarantee that the user will agree that the document represented is on the topic designated. The uncertainty of the process is compounded if the surrogate retrieved by the IRS meets the formal requirement but does not answer the user's need for information. In other words, the surrogates do not usually convey the information searchers really want. Their intent is to point to the containers of the desired information.

1.4

Who Uses Information Retrieval?

Although anyone can be a user of an IRS, there are three primary classes: (1) information specialists or reference librarians; (2) professional persons or end users with both information needs and considerable subject-matter knowledge, such as physicians, lawyers, chemists, or teachers; and (3) others, essentially novices, differing from the second group in that they lack subject-matter expertise. This group includes students and casual system users. Many high schools are now teaching their students to use IRSs, and some public libraries make the services available to their users, regardless of background. Online computer services such as are now found on the World Wide Web offer retrieval service to anyone, with only minimal access costs and little user skill required. The distinctions among these groups are often based upon experience in various aspects of computer use or information content, but this very term *experience* can be hard to operationalize (Meadow, Marchionini, and Cherry, 1994).

1.4.1 Information Specialists

An information specialist or librarian is a person who assists others to find information (Auster, 1990). Job titles vary considerably. Many people play the role, but perhaps do not devote themselves exclusively to providing information service. A county agricultural agent falls into this category. There are those who do it as a business, typically identifying themselves as information brokers (Sawyer, 1995; Warner, 1987; Warnken, 1981) in that they do not create information for their clients, but find it and perhaps interpret it for them.

The information specialists were previously identified as intermediaries between users and the retrieval systems. Whatever specific roles they may play, they are generally expected to know the following:

1. The kinds of information available in a discipline or specialty served (e.g., law, medicine, or banking) or available in a library or other institution in which the specialists serve
2. The mechanics of using information systems relevant to the subject or institution (including how to load a database on CD-ROM into a computer and how to access a remote database service)
3. The terminology of the specialty served (again such as medicine, law, or chemistry)
4. The methods of interviewing users to draw out their information needs—the expressions of their ASKs

1.4.2 End Users

For many years, IR was seen by those offering the service as a means of serving end users, but only through an intermediary. With the invention and wide distribution of personal computers, the end users began to be a significant force in the market for two reasons: the personal computer made it practical for them to make direct use of online retrieval services, and the library market had been just about saturated so service companies were looking for new markets. By the early 1980s few libraries of significance were not already customers of online services. To increase the number of users, IR services had to find new customers, and the end users were there, with their personal computers, ready to expand the market.

The typical end user is a member of a heavily information-dependent profession, discipline, or industry (Levy, 1987; Ojala, 1986). We have mentioned physicians, lawyers, and chemists, but research scientists or technologists of all disciplines need to search their respective literatures, and business people need to research market changes, company history, or credit worthiness. News reporters need to find background material on persons, institutions, or events mentioned in current stories. Students are beginning to find that there is enough material in online databases to justify an expense that is perhaps the equivalent of a restaurant meal.

Members of professional or trade groups are skilled at interpreting the information in their own fields. They can do what many intermediaries cannot do—immediately recognize and evaluate new information or make serendipitous associations between their information needs and seemingly unrelated information they may stumble on during a search. Typically, they are not expected to know the mechanics of searching and retrieval.

While many end users will be experienced at using computers, others will not be. Those who do know computers well constitute almost a separate user class, because of their (assumed) ability to learn search mechanics easily and quickly owing to the similarity of searches to other computer processes. There is a difference between knowing the language and knowing what to say, in any language, to an IRS.

1.4.3 Novices

The novice class consists mainly of students, currently at the high school and undergraduate levels. In time, use of IRSs will penetrate elementary school curricula. We usually pay graduate students the compliment of placing them in the professional end-user class. Of course, all these boundaries are fuzzy. It is important to recognize that the novice group cannot be counted on to have any great degree of subject matter knowledge or knowledge of search mechanics. Moreover, they probably do not have well-developed information-evaluation skills.

1.5
What Are the Problems in IRS Design and Use?

We have tried to make the following list of problems independent of time and the status of technological development, but that goal cannot be met entirely. We have separated design problems from behavioral problems as much as possible. Even this cannot be done completely, because many design problems depend on an understanding of user behavior and on our ability to train users in skillful use of the systems.

Here are some of the problems outstanding in the design of information retrieval systems, or in their use.

1.5.1 Design

In Chapter 16 we shall discuss measurement and evaluation. Unless we know well how to measure and evaluate IRSs, we cannot know the exact contribution of any one component or technique to the ultimate success of the system. Hence, we are still in a collective state of uncertainty about how to design a retrieval system. Some of the major considerations are

1. *Representation of information in the database*—If information is represented by symbols, users of the information must know and understand the symbols used. As well, there are technical factors governing use of symbols and the syntax that interrelates them. How can a system be designed to minimize the time and effort required of users to learn what they need to know about representation?

2. *Organization of information within a computer*—The trend in the computer industry for years, probably a good one, is to relieve the end user of the need to know, in detail, how information is organized inside the computer. Designers must know, because lack of understanding can cause excessive delays in computer processing. New organization and search techniques are still being developed.

3. *User interface*—We can relieve users of the need for knowledge of the interior intricacies of the system if we design the interface well enough. The user communicates directly with the interface. The objective should be to make best use of the user's own perceptions and understanding of what is being dealt with.

4. *Query management programs*—These programs interpret what the user says, whether in natural language or in any of the many approaches to artificial languages. The ideal seems to be to make the language the one most meaningful to the user and let the program determine what additional information it needs to do the retrieval job effectively. The program can then ask for that information from the user.

5. *Data management programs*—These programs are part of the technical intricacy we hope to screen users from, but they are of critical importance to system functioning. Whenever we can speed the search process, we can reduce the cost.

6. *Presentation (display) of information to the user*—There are both technical and behavioral problems in display: what to display, using what symbols, how arranged on a screen, and how they interrelate with each other.

1.5.2 Understanding User Behavior

These are the aspects of information retrieval we have the most difficulty anticipating for design purposes.

1. *Understanding information representation and organization*—We have mentioned the question of representation of information. The complementary question is what is the best way to bring the user to understand it.

2. *Understanding how to communicate information needs*—Earlier, we pointed out that the success of the entire process depends on how well users can express their own needs. This skill is not commonly taught in school until the graduate level, and then only in a limited number of subjects, notably library science, law, and chemistry. Information systems can help, to some extent, if they can be designed to elicit information from users, rather than expecting users to volunteer it.

3. *Understanding how to formulate queries and evaluate results*—We have also pointed out that understanding and expressing need is not the same as translating that need into the formal expressions to be given to a computer. This is a complex training problem, especially for end users who typically do not wish to devote much time or energy to this kind of training.

4. *Understanding how to evaluate information and systems*—If needs are well understood, then the ability to evaluate the contribution of individual records or pieces of information comes readily. Even so, evaluating the contribution to overall user performance of an IRS remains an unsolved problem. Users need to be taught not only how to evaluate records, and to recognize what in them is useful in reformulating a query, but also how to evaluate a complete system to make, for example, a procurement decision about a new information retrieval service.

1.6

A Brief History of Information Retrieval

The oldest and conceptually simplest way to do information retrieval is to look at every item in a collection to determine if it satisfies the information need, a method often, with justification, referred to as *brute force*. This is a tried-and-true method that is as old as collections of information-bearing items. It requires no equipment and no preordering, and remains useful today in some circumstances. Unfortunately, the amount of effort involved is directly proportional to the number of items in the collection, and today's collections are often very large indeed. If, however, the collection is small and is unlikely to be used very often, brute force may be an efficient strategy.

If a collection has any size and is expected to be often searched, then putting the collection or some surrogate of it into a useful order becomes time and cost effective. This may mean sorting the file or creating an *index*, a separate file that serves as a systematic guide to the items in the collection. There are several kinds of indexes and they are of great importance to information retrieval. The early history of IR is largely a history of how indexes were created and searched. More recently, emphasis has shifted to other factors, such as how language is interpreted and how users interact with systems.

1.6.1 Traditional Information Retrieval Methods

Before the now heavy use of the computer as a tool to search text for the purposes of retrieval, attempts to locate material by, say, author, title, or subject in large files depended on the search of *surrogate records* that represented the items in the collection. The surrogates contained only what was deemed necessary for finding the item in a search; hence they could be much smaller than the collection. It was and is, of course, possible to search the items themselves, and indeed items, such as books on library shelves, are usually arranged according to a systematic scheme which places like material together. This creates a form of index whose entries are the items themselves. The method has limitations, however, since only one criterion for ordering the items can be used to create the primary order of the file, and most books and data records cover multiple topics and often have multiple authors. Also, if an item is in use, and thus absent from the file, the item's potential availability is not apparent to the user.

The very earliest libraries seem to have arisen out of Greek culture, both in Greece and in the famous Greek-sponsored library at Alexandria, Egypt. Of course, any collection of several clay tablets could be said to have constituted a library. The early Greeks used what we now call a bibliography as the basic tool for finding books. The most famous of these, the *pinakes* of Callimachus, lists works at Alexandria in eight categories: oratory, history, laws, philosophy, medicine, lyric poetry, tragedy, and miscellaneous. These were recorded on scrolls, hardly easy to use in searching, but there was little else available (Johnson, 1970, p. 57).

This is how Vannevar Bush commented on early search systems:

> The real heart of the matter of selection, however, goes deeper than a lag in the adaption of mechanisms by libraries, or a lack of development of devices for their use. Our ineptitude in getting at the record is largely caused by the artificiality

of systems of indexing. When data of any sort are placed in storage, they are filed alphabetically or numerically, and information is found (when it is) by tracing it down from subclass to subclass. It can be in only one place, unless duplicates are used; one has to have rules as to which path will locate it, and the rules are cumbersome. Having found one item, moreover, one has to emerge from the system and re-enter on a new path. (Bush, 1945, p. 106)

Therefore, standard practice has been to create surrogate records for the items which incorporated all the elements believed to be required to represent predicted information needs. The surrogates could then be arranged with multiple entries so that an item representation appeared at each point in the file where the ordering scheme (usually alphabetical) would require it to appear. We could have author records interspersed with subject records, all pointing to books on a shelf. This ordered list of multiple item surrogates could be printed as a book catalog, another form of index for the item collection. However, since most collections are dynamic, in the sense that they are constantly growing and changing, such a printed form is not an ideal means of storage. Thus, cards came to be used as a storage medium, since they could easily be removed, and new material inserted in the proper places in the ordering scheme. Such a file, the familiar *card catalog*, provides a systematic guide to a collection and is another example of an index.

The card catalog, like many inventions, did not spring full-blown into existence. It evolved. In the immediate aftermath of the French Revolution, the new government confiscated many book collections and had them cataloged, the information recorded on cards or slips of paper which were then sorted and fastened together. Card catalogs, more or less as we now know them, came into use in the mid-19th century. (Kent and Lancour, 1970, pp. 261–265).

If we consider an index to an unchanging collection, such as the content of a book, the ordered surrogate file is permanent, i.e., never changes because the text does not change. An index entry of this sort need not be a complete surrogate record of the portion of text referred to. All that is required is that the entry concept be present in the text, with an indication of its physical location— a page number. If several text items are represented by the same index entry, only one record is required, which now represents a retrievable concept, to which are appended (posted) the page numbers of the items to which the concept applies. This process, the conversion of multifiled document records to concept records, is known as *inversion*, and the ordered list of concept records as an *inverted file*.

It soon became clear that if we were willing to update the appropriate concept records whenever a document was removed or added, the order of the item file became irrelevant as long as it was consistent. We could have a file of individually unique item records, organized by any criterion, and a file of concept records, organized by any other criterion (an index), that provided access to the first file.

1.6.2 Pre-computer IR Systems

Until the 1950s, the means used to describe the content of documents was almost universally to apply subject headings or classification codes. A subject heading is a short description of a subject, such as *France, History, Middle Ages*. Mortimer Taube, founder of the company Documentation Incorporated, is generally credited with adapting an idea that dated back to the 1930s (Taube 1953–1957) of using a set of single words or short phrases, which he called *Uniterms*, to describe the document's content. Instead of the subject heading given above, we might have indexed a document by the separate terms *France, History*, and *Middle Ages*. The difference is that the subject heading is one syntactic expression and someone searching on *France in the middle ages*, or *History of the middle ages*, might not find that heading. Taube saw that the subject heading contained three separate concepts, *France, History*, and *Middle Ages* precoordinated, preformed into a syntactic unit. His idea of entering each term separately into an index allowed the searcher to look for any combination of the terms of interest. This came to be known as *postcoordination*, where the terms are associated after indexing, at search time, as the needs of the search dictated. The older method of combining index terms in a syntactic statement came to be known as *precoordination*.

Two methods of mechanical searching of cards soon became popular (Casey, Perry, Berry, and Kent, 1958). Taube used cards, each with a single subject heading, called a *Uniterm*, as shown in Fig. 1.5. The cards were arranged in 10 columns for the posting of item numbers by their rightmost digit.

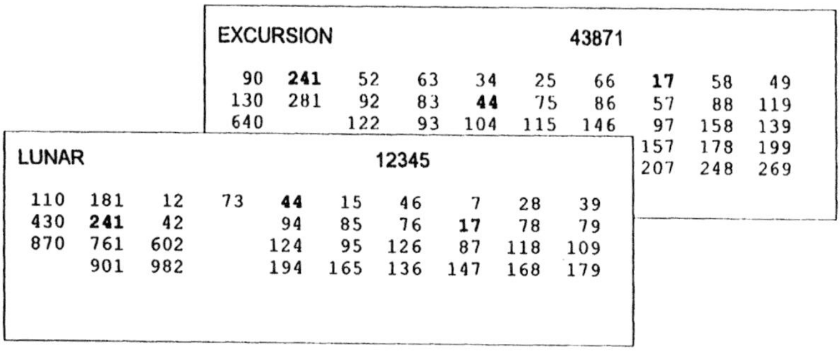

```
  EXCURSION                                    43871

     90   241    52    63    34    25    66    17    58    49
    130   281    92    83    44    75    86    57    88   119
    640         122    93   104   115   146    97   158   139
                                               157   178   199
  LUNAR                         12345          207   248   269

    110   181    12    73    44    15    46     7    28    39
    430   241    42          94    85    76    17    78    79
    870   761   602         124    95   126    87   118   109
          901   982         194   165   136   147   168   179
```

Figure 1.5
Cards used with the Uniterm system: Each card represents one term, shown as both a word or phrase and a number, and the accession numbers of all documents to which that Uniterm pertains. The document numbers are listed in 10 columns, according to the low-order digit of the number. This facilitates manual scanning. The boldface numbers indicate those in common to both terms.

This facilitated manual comparisons. In a serial file of document records, to search for multiple concepts, say the subject LUNAR and the subject EXCUR-SION, we would find the cards corresponding to these two concepts. We would then compare the record numbers listed to see if there were any in common. If so, the corresponding documents satisfied the request. In the figure, it can be seen that documents numbered 241, 44, and 17 are found in both cards; hence these satisfy the search requirements. Finding these document numbers was a manual task using postcoordinate indexing and a method of mechanical searching.

W. E. Batten reported a similar method in in 1948 at the Royal Society's Scientific Information Conference, which may have influenced Taube. Again there was a card for each term, but the document numbers were represented by coordinates of a point on the card, rather than written explicitly. The Batten card was a carefully laid out grid, rather like a piece of graph paper on card stock. If a term appeared in that document, a hole would be drilled at an appropriate location to represent that document's accession or serial number. If we wished to search for DOCUMENT and RETRIEVAL we pulled those two concept cards and placed them over one another on a light box. The numbers corresponding to the positions where light shone through indicated documents indexed on both concepts. See Fig. 1.6. Thus, the number of concepts that could be represented was very large, but even with very large cards and very fine grids, the system was limited in the file size it could handle. Such an approach came to be called an *optical coincidence system*.

The second type of card device was the edge-notched punch card, first reported by Calvin Mooers (1951) as the core of his *Zatocode* system. The card took the opposite approach to that of Taube and Batten. It represented a document, not a term. A description of the item was typed on the body of the card. This edge of the card had a series of holes, each labeled with a number which could represent a single *descriptor*. This was Mooers' word for a multiword precoordinated phrase describing an indexed concept. The holes for the numbers were notched out with a punch to carry out the coding of the assigned concepts, as in Fig. 1.7. The first part of the figure shows details of a similar card system. The presence of a value was indicated by punching out the edge of the card. A needle was then run through a deck of such cards in the hole position representing the concept sought, and the deck vibrated. This caused cards that had been notched to represent the desired concepts to drop out. It is from this action that the expression *false drop* originated. A card that dropped but was not really relevant, was a false drop. The second part of Fig. 1.7 shows Mooers' Zatocard (Perry, Kent, and Berry, 1956, pp. 52–53). Descriptors were encoded, using several numeric hole positions each. Logically, this process is similar to Batten's light coincidence. Taube's method used the human eye to

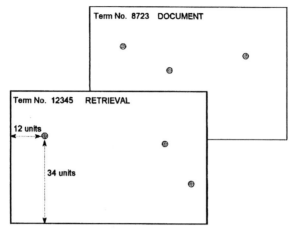

Figure 1.6

Optical coincidence system: This method inverts the logic of the Uniterm system, by having a card for each document and showing, with it, the numbers corresponding to index terms that pertain to the document. The numbers are represented as small holes in the card or surface at coordinates corresponding to the term number, e.g., term number 1234 with be represented as a hole at a location 12 units to the right of the left edge and 34 units up from the bottom.

detect coincidence. If a request were for information about the composition of stars and a document were retrieved about composition, in the printing sense, of the *Star* newspaper, that would be a false drop. This demonstrates the value of terms that describe context. The occurrence of false drops is probably the greatest weakness of postcoordinated indexing systems.

Both these systems and Taube's Uniterm cards were intended to effectuate the coordination of concepts at the time a search was carried out, rather than at the time of indexing. Each requires significant effort at the time of indexing so that greater speed and flexibility will be available at the time of search. Each uses the algebra of sets, developed by George Boole (1854) to create sets of items during a search, and they are clear precursors of the automated retrieval systems that followed.

1.6.3 Special Purpose Computer Systems

It was clear in the early 1950s to those who considered the problem that if Boolean logic was the underlying model of information retrieval, then the general purpose computer which could carry out such operations might have retrieval potential. The likely first experiment in this area was reported in

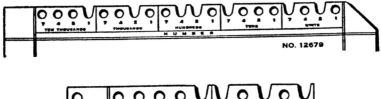

a.

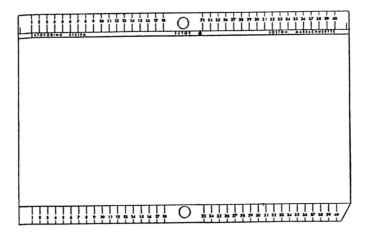

b.

Figure 1.7
Edge-notched cards: The card shown in (a) illustrates the basic method of encoding using edge-notched cards. Part (b) shows the card used for Zatocoding, a particular and advanced method. (Illustration from Perry *et al.*, 1956.) (a) The basic method of edge-notching cards: If a needle were run through one of the hole positions, and the deck of cards then lifted, those cards for which the position had been punched, indicating the corresponding code was present, would drop out. The first method encodes numbers; the second, letters. The position marked NZ denotes letters from n to z. If not notched, the range a–m is indicated. A number, indicated by a combination of the numerals 1, 2, 4, or 7 identifies a letter within the range. (b) The Zatocard: This card was used together with a numeric coding scheme to indicate which descriptors were present in a document. The center of the card was reserved for a typed description of the document.

Phillip Bagley's (1951) MIT Master's thesis. His analysis indicated that a search of 50 million item records, each containing 30 index terms, would take 41,700 hours, primarily because of the need to move and shift text in memory while carrying out the comparisons. His solution was to recommend the construction of a special purpose machine designed for the simultaneous comparison of large blocks of data. We will briefly discuss examples of such machines before returning to the uses of the general purpose computer whose evolution soon overcame the problems Bagley identified.

Perhaps the most interesting example is the Western Reserve Rapid Searching Selector, reported on by Shera, Kent, and Berry (1957). James W. Perry and Allen Kent, working in the Center for Documentation and Communication Research at Western Reserve University, were particularly concerned with the number of false drops that occurred in Uniterm and edge-notched card systems and wished to construct a system of semantic coding which would take into account the context of term usage. They developed the *telegraphic abstract* which consisted of phrases containing *role operators* that indicated the context of term use. Terms were also classified into semantic factors which were rather like facets and provided a further context. This method of describing documents was intended for highly technical documents. A code might represent products or materials, processes or tests, properties of materials, persons, or organizations named. It might distinguish between an organization identified as involved in some process or test or one simply named in a document.

Figure 1.8a shows an abstract in conventional style and Fig. 1.8b shows its telegraphic version with explicit tags for the various objects and concepts. Queries were similarly encoded (Perry *et al.* 1956, pp. 103–104). The selector was a machine designed specifically to match these codes efficiently. While these devices appeared to have the desired effects, the complexity of creating the telegraphic abstract and the fact that multiple abstractors would produce often quite different abstracts of the same item led to the abandonment of the system and the selector along with it.

A second device, the *minicard* selector, combined digital and photographic technology (Kessel and DeLucia, 1959). The minicard was a positive photographic transparency that contained microimages of a document as well as rectangular patterns that represented digital codes for index terms. The digital portion was scanned into a special purpose computer which could carry out a process to determine if the document was a match to a query.

General Electric (Mallery, 1987) later produced a device for scanning full text on magnetic tape. The GESCAN Rapid Search Machine allowed entry of terms, phrases, and boolean operators on a console. A magnetic tape was then scanned and occurrences matching the query were reported on a screen. These were stored and could later be printed.

Alterations in Cast-Iron Properties Accompanying Use of a Strong Inoculant of the Si-Mn-Zrtype. C. 0. Burgess and R. W. Bishop. Trans. Am. Foundrymens' Assoc. Preprint No. 44-16, 35 pp. (1944).
 A study of the effect of ladle treatment on the Brinell hardness, tensile strength, transverse strength and chill depth of C 2.5%, C 3.0%, and C 3.5% unalloyed gray irons, each group varying in Si content from 1 to 2.5%. A total of 48 heats was melted in a 35 lb. induction furnace. The max. heating temp. was 2800°F. The heats were poured at 2600°F. A uniform ladle addn. of 0.25% Si-W-Zr alloy was made to some of the irons. Ladle inoculation produced cast irons having high mech. properties and low depth of chill. Improvement in strength after inoculation was most marked in irons having a low total sum of C and Si. The ladle inoculation acted to compensate for minor variations in the melting materials and in the melting operations. It would appear that the ladle treatment of cast iron will eventually be considered as essential as final deoxidizing treatments with steel. C. W. Schuck

Serial No. 00190190 Authors C. 0. Burgess and R. W. Bishop. Trans. Am. Foundrymens'l Assoc. Preprint No. 44-16, 35 pp (1944). *Field*, Ferrous metallurgy *Starting material*, *Material processed*, *Properties given* for Gray iron *containing* 2.5-3.5% C and 1-2.5% Si. *Properties* Tensile strength, transverse strength, Brinell hardness, chill depth. *Process* Ladle treatment *By means of* Si-Mn-Zr alloy; 35 lb induction furnace. *Condition* Temperature 2800°F (max) *Process* Casting *Condition* Temperature 2600°F (max) *Product*, *Properties given for* Gray iron containing C, Si, Mn, Zr in small amounts *Properties* (improved) Tensile strength, transverse strength, depth of chill. *Discussion* Ladle treatment; Gray iron composition; Casting processing.

Figure 1.8
Conventional and telegraphic abstracts: A conventional abstract is presented above, with its telegraphic version below, for comparison. The latter would be harder for the nonspecialist to compose and read but contain more information for the knowing person. These are taken from Perry *et al.* (1956). (a) A conventional abstract from *Chemical Abstracts*: Technical language is used, but the syntax is conventional, not subject to rigid rules of expression. (Reproduced with permission of the American Chemical Society.) (b) Telegraphio-style abstract: The syntax is not that of conventional English, in that various role indicators are italicized and punctuation is unusual in, for example, the lack of periods in the paragraph. However, there is more, and more precise, information here for those able to read it.

Perhaps the most modern special purpose system is the Fast Data Finder, originally built by TRW and now distributed by Parcel. This special purpose device is used in selective dissemination of information (SDI) systems to hold queries and process them against document files at 3.5 megabytes per second (Mettler and Norby, 1995; Yu, Hsu, and Otsubo, 1984).

1.6.4 General Purpose Computer Systems

The special purpose digital devices, in general, have been supplanted by general purpose machines. By the middle 1960s references to special purpose devices were rare, and the long-term trend of increasing power and memory capacity coupled with decreasing cost for the general purpose computer had become apparent. Quite likely the first operational general purpose computer information retrieval system was developed at the U.S. Naval Ordnance Test Station at China Lake, California, by Bracken and Tillit (1957). They used index term concept records serially arranged on magnetic tape. Queries were entered on 80-column electronic accounting machine cards ("IBM cards"), and these were sorted by index term and matched once with the master tape. Records containing any query terms were copied to another tape. The Boolean logic was then carried out on this record subset, and the resultant document numbers were printed. Several others followed suit, making minor improvements.

In the same time period interest in automatic indexing by computer, rather than simply using the machine as a matching device for retrieval, began with Hans Peter Luhn at IBM, who designed a means of automatically extracting from the text of documents sentences that contained occurrences of those words that were of high enough frequency to be considered significant, but not those of the very highest frequency whose number was thought to indicate a structural rather than semantic purpose (Luhn 1958). Bar Hillel (1959) soon suggested selection on the basis of the ratio of word frequency in the document to word frequency in the language as a whole, and thus originated the basis of *inverse document frequency*, the most common modern term selection method, which uses term occurrence in the document and the number of documents in the file to which the term has been assigned, to identify important discriminating terms.

The retrieval processes were to be greatly improved with the advent of disk storage and the useful random access file structures that followed. We have now reached a point, however, where we have sufficient background to discuss the movement toward the modern commercial online information retrieval system which dominated the scene in the seventies, eighties, and early nineties.

1.6.5 Online Database Services

During and after World War II a considerable expansion occurred in the literature of science and technology. The traditional means of access to this literature was through the use of abstracting and indexing services. These agencies, some governmental, some for-profit, and some sponsored by learned societies, serially published indexes which covered the recent production of scientific literature which they then provided to libraries, laboratories, and even individuals. These printed indexes were sometimes in the form of multientry book catalogs and sometimes in a two-file format with the full citation and often an abstract and an index to it. To handle the problem of searching over both old and new material, cumulations were regularly created, at considerable expense.

The publishers in the late 1950s and early 1960s saw that such a process was quite suitable for automation, since editing and cumulation were far easier in an electronic medium than with paper files. In 1961 the Chemical Abstracts Service produced *Chemical Titles*, a computer-produced and -printed subject index to 600 important journals that they covered. Other secondary journal publishers soon followed, perhaps most notably the U.S. National Library of Medicine with its *Abridged Index Medicus* (AIM) database. The normal process for producing such databases included a human analysis to create an indexed and abstracted document surrogate which was then used by computer programs to produce the needed publications. A by-product was the creation of an archival database of machine-readable document records. By 1970 the automated production of the secondary publication was the normal state of the art.

As had been demonstrated at China Lake and other specialized collections, databases could clearly be searched by a computer program which could sort out records that contained specific data in specific fields. Thus if a service acquired a set of indexed concepts from a system user, in which this user had a continuing interest, these could be matched against the indexing of each new update to the database by passing the request file against the surrogate file in a batch process, with the matching citations extracted for use. This is called *selective dissemination of information* (SDI). If the requested concepts were passed against the whole archive file, a retrospective batch search could be performed. Such a search approximated the sort of literature search normally performed by a researcher prior to initiating a project and had the potential to replace the manual search through the cumulated printed issues of a secondary publisher.

In the early 1960s, retrospective searches were not entirely satisfactory because the turnaround times were necessarily long (measured in days) and any desired feedback based upon results would necessitate repeating the entire process. By the middle 1960s mainframe computers had enough speed and memory to carry out their regular batch jobs while reserving resources to handle a small number of interactive terminals using random access disk files. This made the interactive information retrieval system a possibility, and project MAC demonstrated its feasibility at MIT in 1963 (Lee, Fano, Scherr, Corbato, and Vyssotsky, 1992). The Systems Development Corporation (SDC) began development of such a system for commercial purposes soon thereafter (Nance and Lathrope, 1968).

The National Library of Medicine, which had been running batch searches on its AIM (Abridged *Index Medicus*) files since 1963, contracted in 1967 with SDC to install the ORBIT system on an experimental database. In 1970 the medical institutions throughout the United States had access to the AIM file on SDC's IBM 360/67 computer through the Teletypewriter Exchange Network (TWX), yielding a system called AIM/TWX. By late 1971 the 1200 journals of *Index Medicus* were available in a single file, and in 1973 the AIM/TWX system became MEDLINE and was using software patterned after the original ORBIT system but maintained by the Lister Hill Center for Biomedical Communication.

At about the same time a second interactive software retrieval package called RECON was under development in the Lockheed Palo Alto Research Laboratory. This became operational in 1966 using a collection of NASA citations. It later became the DIALOG system (Wente, 1971). Both Lockheed and SDC maintained proprietary versions of their software and, as storage capacities and operational speed increased, they contracted with secondary publishers to provide databases, access to which could be sold to the general public as a new source of revenue to the database supplier as well as the fledgling information retrieval services who now became database vendors. The two separately developed systems "went commercial" at about the same time in 1972.

The growth of both systems and of MEDLINE was greatly stimulated by the advent of packet switching networks which came to be called *value added networks* (VANs), precursors of today's Internet. Since the services made their retrieval systems available on a central computer and the potential users were widely distributed, a long-distance telephone call was necessary to connect the user with the system. By 1972, TYMSHARE, the first commercial VAN, was supplementing the Medline backbone and a competitor, TELENET, was soon on the scene. TYMSHARE, through a series of mergers and acquisitions, became part of the MCI domain and TELENET part of SPRINT.

These services connected local computers nationwide with leased telephone lines, which they kept very busy by breaking up data sent between remote sources into small packets, adding a final destination address and reassembly data to the packet, and keeping it in local storage until space was available on a line to send it to another machine nearer its destination. At the machine nearest the destination the transmission would be reassembled and transmitted to the destination device. Thus only a local call from a computer or terminal to the nearest node was required to enter the network, and the very efficient use of the leased lines allowed the network to charge a rate well below that of a normal long-distance call. Such relatively cheap communication technology made wide use a possibility and led to the creation of the Internet.

A system developed in 1972 by the Data Central Corporation, and later acquired by Mead Paper Corporation, was the ancestor of the present

LEXIS/NEXIS law and newspaper retrieval system, still active today. It was the first commercial system to allow searching of the full text of documents, rather than surrogates only.

1.6.6 Modern Experiments (SMART and Other Systems)

Retrieval experimentation began with projects conducted in Cranfield, England, starting in 1957, although an inconclusive study was carried out by Documentation Inc., reported by Gull (1956), and Cleverdon and Thorne (1954) performed a small test that might be considered a precursor of Cranfield. The first Cranfield Project compared the performance of four indexing languages, Universal Decimal Classification (UDC), alphabetical subject headings, Uniterms, and a special faceted classification. While little difference was demonstrated in the performance of the languages, a model methodology was established which has dominated retrieval experimentation since that time, and a great deal of discussion and interaction was generated. After Cranfield the components of a retrieval study were a collection, a series of questions, a retrieval system, an evaluation procedure that allowed a determination of what documents in the collection were relevant to what questions, and performance measures based upon these relevance judgments. Relevance, then, was measured on a binary scale, although as early as 1960 Maron and Kuhns pointed out that the relationship is much less certain.

In the 1970s and beyond, the single most influential test bed for information retrieval experimentation was certainly Gerard Salton's SMART system, developed first at Harvard, then operated at Cornell University. Salton (1980) reviewed SMART and synthesized the knowledge gained in the extensive published experimental work using the system. SMART uses terms automatically extracted from documents or abstracts of documents and appends weights to terms, based on their frequency of occurrence. It thus can provide a list of retrieved records in order by a function of their total term weights and can accept as queries term lists without boolean operators. It allows the evaluation of a great many factors that influence retrieval performance and has been used with a great many collections of items; much of the information provided later in this book will have some relationship to SMART experiments.

The most recent ongoing evaluation effort is TREC, the Text Retrieval Conference (Spark Jones, 1995). TREC is an extended evaluation project, which meets annually and distributes textual data and topics (queries) from the National Institute of Standards and Technology (NIST). Promotion is by the U.S. Advanced Research Projects Agency (ARPA), which has added and deleted "Defense" in its name several times. Participating researchers run the topics against the data using their systems, and their top-ranked documents are merged into a single list and evaluated for relevance by NIST assessors (Robertson *et al.*, 1977). The evaluated sets are then available for further research. TREC is having a major stimulating effect on text retrieval experimentation.

1.6.7 The World Wide Web

We will begin our discussion of the Web with a second quotation from Vannevar Bush, who, speaking of traditional retrieval structures, suggested in 1945 that a model for retrieval closer to that of the human brain might be most effective.

> The human mind does not work in this way. It operates by association. With one item in its grasp, it snaps instantly to the next that is suggested by the association of thoughts, in accordance with some intricate web of trails carried by the cells of the brain. It has other characteristics, of course, trails that are not frequently followed are prone to fade, items that are not fully permanent, memory that is transitory. Yet the speed of action, the intricacy of trails, the detail of mental pictures, is awe-inspiring beyond all else in nature. (Bush, 1945, p. 106)

The World Wide Web (WWW or "Web") is an attempt to use a hypertext model, an approach not unlike that suggested by Bush. The simplest definition of hypertext, "nonsequential writing," is that by Nelson (1988). The thought is that as we pursue a text we find topics in need of expansion or explanation. The author can provide links or pointers to the location of related material and these will appear with the material, not separately, as in a bibliography at the end of the work. The reader may then proceed forward sequentially or move to the linked location for further information. These links are like citations embedded in a text but the difference is that the reader of hypertext may "go to" the cited work immediately, at any time.

At the completion of a review of this material the reader may return to the initial text or follow further links in other directions. The model can be used in a conventional book, but is more effective in automated files where the physical page shuffling can be handled automatically. The resulting linking structure is weblike. If we assume items of information on computers at widely separated locations with such a linking structure in place, as well as a telecommunication network that allows interaction among the various computers, we extend the hypertext model worldwide and approach the associative structure that Bush suggested.

The Internet provides the telecommunication network upon which such a structure can be implemented. The initial work was carried out by the Advanced Research Projects Agency of the U.S. Department of Defense (ARPA/DARPA). The first recorded description of what might be achieved was in a series of memos written in 1962 by J. C. R. Licklider of MIT, the first head of the computer research program at DARPA. He envisioned a "Galactic Network," a globally interconnected set of networks through which anyone could access data and programs from any site. Such an entity would allow use of computer resources physically remote from the person with the need, and not require the costly duplication of such resources locally. The first paper on packet switching theory was published by Leonard Kleinrock (1961). He convinced DARPA of the theoretical feasibility of communications using packets rather than circuits.

In 1967, DARPA produced a plan for the ARPANET, and, by the end of 1969, four host computers were connected together into the initial network. ARPANET was demonstrated in 1972, the same year that electronic mail was introduced over the network.

In Geneva, Switzerland, Tim Berners-Lee, a physicist at the Centre Européen de Recherche Nucléair (CERN) created the World Wide Web in 1991 by using a hypertext model. (Berners-Lee, 1996) Using an existing document markup language called the *Standard Generalized Markup Language* (SGML) with some extensions, he was able to code documents with embedded Internet addresses that could be read by a program called a *browser* which copied the hypertext documents from servers with Internet addresses. Not only text but embedded graphics could be transmitted and viewed at any site with a browser.

From the original four hosts in 1967, the Internet has grown to over 100 in 1977, to over 28,000 in 1987, to nearly 20,000,000 in 1997 (Zakon, 1997). This is impressive growth indeed. The Web is rapidly becoming a mainstream communication channel, with significant advertising, news, and commercial sales enterprises making use of a medium originally thought to be for the exchange of scientific information among scholars. The growing use of broadband cable connections in homes and offices can only improve the speed of transmission and the growth of the medium. We thus have an interactive retrieval system whose boundaries have no predictable limits, rapidly becoming part of the economics and culture of the modern world. We have come a long way from China Lake, in terms of computer power and communications technology, but the basic principles of retrieval system design and operation have not significantly changed; rather they have adapted to the new environment. It is our hope to set forth these principles in the following chapters.

2

Data, Information, and Knowledge

Introduction

Most people seem to feel that there is a difference between data and information, but careful, reasoned distinctions are far less common than are assertions of the existence or nature of differences. It is probably also true that most people do not feel the need for careful, reasoned definitions of the words they use in day-to-day conversation. Besides *data* and *information*, there are other terms such as *intelligence, news, meaning,* and *wisdom* that we sometimes use synonymously. At other times, we may recognize differences among them.

But there are practical reasons, in information retrieval (IR), for considering some of the philological or philosophical concepts underlying these words. At the heart of most of it is this axiom:

For any given message or text, the determination of whether it is data or information, or contains news or wisdom, is in the mind of the beholder and not in the recorded symbols.

Consider these questions: Will we accept uncertainty regarding the truth or validity of information we retrieve? Will we modify the manner in which we ask a question if we are unsure of the validity of the outcome? Will we take action on the basis of the content of the information retrieved, if we are unsure of its truth or validity?

What steps are creators of a record willing to take to ensure that users will agree that the record is "true"? Unless all people will answer these questions the same, for every text, we have to assume it is a person, not a text, that determines the wisdom, etc., of that text.

2.2 _____

Definitions

It will not matter a great deal whether readers accept these definitions in their entirety. In fact, there has been considerable attention in the literature to this topic—the meaning of the various words that relate to data and information. A few of the many works on the subject are Belkin and Robertson (1976), Brookes (1980), Meadow and Yuan (1997), Menou (1995), Nitecki (1985), and Teskey (1989). We present one view primarily to bring out some necessary distinctions rather than to insist that these are the only correct definitions.

2.2.1 Data

A *datum* is a string of elementary symbols, such as digits or letters. It is the value of an attribute. It need not have meaning to everyone, but it must be clear what attribute a datum is a value of. Fox, Frakes, and Gandel (1988) point out that data can be not only something such as a collection of numeric readings from a pressure gauge, the usual view, but an observational report in text form from an anthropologist in the field, although the report may be the result of very careful scrutiny or analysis. Both examples also represent the use of symbols that are identified but may not have much or any meaning to a given reader.

2.2.2 Information

This word has no universally accepted meaning, but generally it carries the connotation of evaluated, validated, or useful data. Information, to most of us, has meaning, but whatever it is that makes a set of data into information exists *outside the data* and *in the interpreter*, be that a person or computer program.

A very formal definition of information comes from the field of engineering. Claude Shannon (Shannon and Weaver, 1959, p. 19) defined it as essentially a measure of the absence of uncertainty or, mathematically,

$$\text{Information} = H = -\sum_{i=1}^{n} p_i \log p_i, \tag{2.1}$$

where p_i is the probability of occurrence of a symbol in a message system, and the summation is over the number n of all possible symbols in a language or system of codes in use. For example, the symbols may be letters and numbers.

In a given natural language, each character has an associated probability of occurrence, and these probabilities are not all equal. If two languages use the same alphabet, which is close to the case with English and French, the letter frequencies may be quite different, as they are in this case. Consider just the frequencies of q, z, and k in these languages. Then, for a communication system transmitting messages in a language, H measures the information content of the *system* consisting of the codes and their probabilities, a selection mechanism (perhaps a person composing messages), and a transmission system. H tells how much information is inherent in that system, over a period of observation. There will be more information in the system of a telegraph company that will transmit whatever messages its clients bring them than in a telemetering system that transmits the temperature at one place once every hour. H does *not* measure the information content of an individual letter, word, or message. But Shannon's work does represent the beginning of a formal science of measuring information.

A note of caution in interpreting this measure comes from Shannon's coauthor, Warren Weaver:

> To be sure, this word information in communication theory relates not so much to what you *do* say, as to what you *could* say. That is, information is a measure of one's freedom of choice when one selects a message. If one is confronted with a very elementary situation where he has to choose one of two alternative messages, then it is arbitrarily said that the information, associated with this situation, is unity. Note that it is misleading (although often convenient) to say that one or the other message conveys unit information. The concept of information applies not to individual messages (as the concept of meaning would), but rather to the situation as a whole, the unit of information indicating that in this situation one has an amount of freedom of choice, in selecting a message, which it is convenient to regard as a standard or unit amount (Shannon and Weaver, 1959, p. 100; emphasis added).

Shannon was interested in measuring the amount of information that could be sent over a given communications channel. If we use a language in which all words have equal probability of occurrence, then we can send more information per word than if the language has (as does any natural language) a very wide range of probabilities of word occurrence. The word *the*, for example, usually conveys very little information. Hence, much of the time spent transmitting it is wasted. That is why the telegraphic or newspaper headline style of writing often does not use such common words as *the* or *a*, but a full text needs these articles both for precision of meaning and for style.

If all but one of the words of a language had probability 0, and the remaining one had probability 1, then the information content of the system is zero—there is no uncertainty what message will be sent; it is always the same—it conveys no information.

The statement "1 + 2 = 3," taken by itself, has no information content for most of us because "everyone" knows it; it brings nothing new or unexpected to us. The statement that horse number five won a race is information, if the race was honest, but might not be information to a person who had "fixed" the race because, for that person, the message had a probability of occurrence equal to 1.

An operational definition is that *information is data that changes the state of a system that perceives it,* whether a computer or a brain; hence, a stream of data that does not change the state of its receiver is not information. Such a definition was proposed by Shreider (1970). Following the Shannon definition, he defined a *guide* to a person's or entity's knowledge as the set of possible events with their associated probabilities, both as perceived by the observer. Events are messages that might be or have been received. Then information coming to this recipient is anything that changes the guide, i.e., changes the destination's knowledge of the external world. A student who carefully listens to a lecture and hears and believes something new has had the state of his or her mind changed by information. The student who daydreamed through the same lecture, who physiologically heard the same message but absorbed nothing, was not changed by it, so did not perceive any new information.

A related definition has it that *information is what is used to affect a decision.* Yovits, Foulk, and Rase (1981, p. 189) stated, "We treat information as data of value in decision-making." This version also ties in the concept of reduction of uncertainty. A decision maker is faced with a set of alternatives, is uncertain which to select, and needs information to make the choice. If the person were not uncertain, i.e., knew for certain what to do, then we would not call it a decision situation. There have to be alternatives for there to be uncertainty.

Some of this sense is implied in this quotation, from the comic strip character Andy Capp's caustic comment on his wife's drawing of conclusions from rumor: "information is the intelligent interpretation of facts before they ever occur" ("Andy Capp," 1989). Rumor, whether true or not, can change the state of a system.

2.2.3 News

While not a term of conceptual importance in understanding IR, news is usually defined similarly to *information.* News is a message, unexpected to some extent, that is believed to be true. Even a statement that serves only to verify an earlier news statement may be, to some extent, unexpected; hence, it is itself news. If we had heard an allegation on a news report, and hear a confirmation later, the confirmation is news about the earlier report.

A statement or datum is not news if we already know its content. It is only news if we did not know it, therefore did not expect it. Otherwise put, the probability of receipt of the message was less than 1 for the recipient but greater than 0; i.e., it is a possible statement but not a certain one. There is the old dictum: *Dog bites man is not news. Man bites dog—that's news.*

2.2.4 Knowledge

In general usage, knowledge seems to represent a higher degree of certainty or validity than information. A typical desk-top dictionary suggests that information is a set of facts, while knowledge connotes understanding, with the implication that not all information is necessarily understood. It is possible to insist that data and information are the same, but hardly anyone would equate knowledge with data. Knowledge also has the characteristic of information shared and agreed upon within a community. Fox *et al.* (1988) refer to knowledge as *justified true belief*, if X knows that a given proposition is true if and only if

> The proposition is *true*
> X believes that it is true

and

> X is *justified* in believing the proposition is true

Of course, for most of us, most of the time, there is no way to be sure what is true and what is justified. Justification of belief tends to be community based. Some communities accept revelation. Some political activists believe certain *truths to be self-evident.* Some communities believe in *proof.* Science generally accepts that what is true and what is justified depend on current paradigms, but these are subject to change. Thus, an earth-centered universe was once a justified, true view of the universe, but we have had a paradigm change since then, and the old view is no longer accepted as valid in the science of astronomy. The dispute between creationism and evolution as the basis for teaching biology seems to be gaining heat. Similarly, we once accepted Newtonian physics, but it has been replaced by relativity and quantum mechanics.

If a physician asks a database for the value of a patient's temperature at 12:00 noon today, he or she will tend to accept the number provided it is within a believable range. It will generally be understood that all the user expected the database to tell is the *value* of the temperature reading, not its *significance,* and hence would show no disappointment at not being apprised of its significance. Thus, it is information because it is understood and becomes knowledge as it enters the physician's personal store of perception and understanding.

Another aspect of the question of what is information or knowledge is this: If a database can provide the value of the attribute subject in a record about a book or article, is that value a correct one? Is the article really "on" that subject? This often turns out to be a matter of opinion. If a community of users agrees with the assessment of value given by the cataloger, then it is "true." If not, it is "false."

In recent times a new concept called a *knowledge base* has been introduced; this is different from a database. We shall pursue this point in Section 2.3.

2.2.5 Intelligence

One meaning of intelligence is a measure of reasoning capacity. Of more relevance here is the usage that intelligence is information. We use the term in the context of the results in the military, diplomatic, or industrial worlds of gathering information about adversaries. People in the intelligence world sometimes differentiate between information and intelligence just as we have between data and information. For any practical purpose, then, in this context intelligence is information.

2.2.6 Meaning

This is the most difficult of all the information-related descriptors to define. Here are some quotations that express the conundrum:

> The suggestion that words are symbols for things, actions, qualities, relationships, *et cetera*, is naive, a gross simplification. Words are slippery customers. The full meaning of a word does not appear until it is placed in its context, and the context may serve an extremely subtle function—as with puns, or *double entendre*. And even then the "meaning" will depend upon the listener, upon the speaker, upon their entire experience of the language, upon their knowledge of one another, and upon the whole situation.
>
> Everyone, of course, who has ever given any thought to the meanings of words has noticed that they are always shifting and changing in meaning. Usually, people regard this as a misfortune, because it "leads to sloppy thinking" and "mental confusion." To remedy this condition, they are likely to suggest that we should all agree on "one meaning" for each word and use it only with that meaning. Thereupon it will occur to them that we simply cannot make people agree in this way, even if we could set up an ironclad dictatorship under a committee of lexicographers who would place censors in every newspaper office and microphones in every home. The situation, therefore, appears hopeless. (Cherry, 1957, p. 10)

> [N]o word ever has exactly the same meaning twice. (Hayakawa, 1939, p. 60)

> Relative to the broad subject of communication, there seem to be problems at three levels. Thus it seems reasonable to ask, serially:

> Level A. How accurately can the symbols of communication be transmitted? (The technical problem)

Level B.   How precisely do the transmitted symbols convey the desired meaning?
(The semantic problem)

Level C.   How effectively does the received meaning affect conduct in the desired
way? (The effectiveness problem) (Shannon and Weaver, 1959, pp. 95–96)

Suffice it to say, IR would probably be easier if every word had its own
unique meaning. But, as Hayakawa pointed out, the real world is not that way.
People reading the same text may interpret it differently, and hence act upon
it differently. This action may range from selecting a bibliographic descriptor
to declaring war. Similarly, people visualizing the same subject on which they
want information may express what they want differently.

2.2.7 Wisdom

A person who has wisdom does not necessarily have more data or facts
than others, but the wise person's utterances are more likely to be accepted by a
community of users and to provide insight into matters of importance. Insight
may be recognizing relationships among observations that have not previously
been recognized as related. A person whose utterances are not accepted as true is
hardly likely to be considered wise. Again, we find that commonality of opinion
is important—justified true belief.

The poet T. S. Eliot (1937, p. 157) expressed the sense of difference
among wisdom, knowledge, and information this way:

> Where is the wisdom we have lost in knowledge?
>
> Where is the knowledge we have lost in information?

We may gain some insight from the ancient Book of Job. The question
is asked, "Whence cometh wisdom? and where is the place of understanding?"
(Job 28:20). It does not come from an information retrieval system. It may come
from that which is retrieved, but much depends on the attitude of the reader or
hearer toward the writer or speaker.

In summary, to paraphrase Shakespeare, nothing is either true or false,
but thinking makes it so. While some of the definitions and distinctions we
have made will have no practical effect on the creation of or search of records,
the concept of validity (or justified belief, consensus, or credence) is a practical
one. Those who create records strive, or should strive, to create records whose
content is acceptable by or credible to users. Readers value records as they seem
to bear true or useful information. *Useful* can mean *true, valuable,* or even just
entertaining.

2.3

Metadata

Metadata refers to data about data or information about information. Typically, metadata are descriptive of the organization or content of a body of data, such as a record or database. One of the oldest forms is a library catalog, an entry in which tells its reader where another information item is found (location) and something of its content and source. Location information is typically in the form of a classification and an author code indicating where on a shelf a book is stored. The card may also tell in which portion of the library the book is to be found. Content is described by the same subject classification, possibly additional subject classification codes (perhaps both Library of Congress and Dewey codes) and subject headings. Source information includes such attributes as publisher, date, and author name. If the item described is a mathematical table, relevant metadata may tell about the format of the data, number of significant digits, source of information, perhaps even the mathematical formula used to caluculate the values and the value ranges in which the formula provides certain levels of precision. There is no ordained set of metadata. Whatever will help a user know how to find, use, or interpret the indicated information may be included.

As libraries have increasingly become depositories for large numbers of computer databases as well as conventional books, periodicals, and graphic images it becomes increasingly important for them to be able to tell prospective users what is in these databases, what the data look like, and even what they mean. Hence, the equivalent of the old card catalog has grown in size and comprehensiveness.

In a sense, as simple a device as the thumb index of a dictionary constitutes metadata. Where does it begin and end? A library catalog card entry describing a book's location or subject content clearly qualify. Is a review of that book also metadata? Is biblical exegesis? Each is a discussion about some other information item. But they may be original items in themselves. Later in this volume we describe data structures that use indexes, then indexes to the indexes, possibly continuing for several levels. These, collectively, are metadata.

The U.S. Library of Congress developed a method for describing the structure of data records to enable libraries to exchange catalog records among institutions which may have different software and file structures. Called Machine Readable Cataloging (MARC) it was a standard for creating files that could be translated from or to almost any database system (MARC citation). Much of the information in a MARC record is metadata. Actually, it combines metadata with the data content.

In summary, metadata tells about an information item. It may tell what elements are present, such as author or title. It may give descriptive information that is not explicitly present in the item, such as the language of a text. Texts rarely say, "The language herein is English." Or, as noted above, metadata may describe mathematical properties of data, such as precision of elements.

The answer to the question raised earlier about where metadata begins and ends is that it does not matter. There is no need to make hard-and-fast rules about whether book reviews are data or metadata. What is important is that we recognize the need for metadata and learn how to use it effectively. In the new world of electronic publishing, files are stored in a server and transmitted to a client computer. These files may contain text, representations of sound, or graphics. The file will contain information about layout, type fonts, and colors. All this is needed by a receiving computer for it to be able to display the records appropriately, possibly with different software than the sending computer used. A language called the *Standard Generalized Markup Language* (SGML) was developed to aid in exchanging text files (Goldfarb, 1990). It allows a user to define various elements of a document and these definitions can then be used to locate information or decide how to display them. A derivative of SGML has been developed for use with World Wide Web files, called the *Hypertext Markup Language* (HTML) (Graham, 1995). HTML is primarily used to control displays.

Figure 2.1 shows a small sample of text marked up with HTML. The metadata is the set of tags, which denote the role of an information element, its display color, type size, or other such facts. The figure shows the beginning of a bibliography that appeared in a home page on the Web. Some of the tags are standard. Users can create their own. For example, there is a tag for title that instructs an interpreting program how to display the text that follows. It could also be used by a search program to identify words that occur in the title of an article. The author of a text is not tagged as such in this example, but any using organization could create such a tag, specify how authors' names are to displayed, and make authors' names available to search programs. This sample shows only a limited number of usages and is intended only to provide a sense of what the language is like.

Attempts are being made to develop metadata standards, that is, to specify what attributes of a document should be made explicit. One such is called the Dublin Core (after Dublin, Ohio, where it was mainly developed). This is a continuing attempt to develop a standard set of metadata attributes to be used for describing a document in a library context (Weibel, 1997). The core consists of 15 data elements, not all of which are going to have a value for each document (*Dublin Core*, 1998). They are shown in Table 2.1. Other contexts might want to emphasize somewhat different attributes, such as reliability of source, security classification, or type of paper or binding.

```
<html>
<head>
<title>Charles T. Meadow Personal Bibliography</title></head>

<body bgcolor="#ffffff" text="#000000" link="#008080"
vlink="#ff0000"
alink="#ffff00">

<font size=3 color="ff0000"><strong>PUBLICATIONS,
BOOKS:</strong></font><p>

<ul><li>Boyce, Bert R.; Meadow, Charles T., and Kraft, Donald H.
<em>Measurement in Information Science.</em> San Diego: <a
href="http://www.apnet.com">Academic Press</a>, 1994.<p>

<li>Meadow, Charles T. <em>Text Information Retrieval
Systems.</em> San Diego: <a
href="http://www.apnet.com">Academic
Press</a>, 1992.<p>
```

Figure 2.1
Sample of html-marked text: <html> starts the html text. <head> indicates
the start of a text element called header and </head> ends that element. <li>
starts a new line, <p> ends a paragraph, and <a href=> introduces a link to a
related Web site, in this case that of the publisher of the book cited.

2.4

Knowledge Base

A database, however true or valid its content, is *a collection of data that can
be searched by a retrieval program as directed by a user.* A knowledge base (KB) in
this context is a set of information *used by a person or program to perform a function.*
In IR, a KB may be used (Teskey, 1989) by the retrieval software to

Table 2.1
Elements of the Dublin Core[a]

title	other contributor	source
author/creator	date	language
subject/key words	resource type	relation
description	format	coverage
publisher	resource identification	rights management

[a]The core consists of 15 data elements used to describe a document expected
to be stored and retrieved electonically. Not all are of equal value for each
document (*Dublin Core*, 1998).

Select the database to be searched

Assist users in composition or modification of a search

Parse data (messages) received from the database, meaning to decompose
a message into its components and identify the syntactic role of each

Interpret, or assist the user to interpret, output

Make decisions or assist in deciding whether to accept retrieved output or
revise a query

Information retrieved from the database or provided directly by the user
can be used by the system as knowledge. If a user places high weight or importance on certain subject-describing terms, then this information can be used
by a program to improve retrieval results. Note that the knowledge in this case
is knowledge of *importance* of terms, not of the *existence* of the terms. It is also
possible for a program, given a set of search terms, to find other terms likely
to be useful. This could be based on enough knowledge of a subject field to
be able to make word associations within the context of that field, to know, for
example, that *file* and *database* are closely related terms in the context of IR or
computer science and either could be used for the other, but not so in the context of carpentry. Alternatively, relatedness can be based entirely on statistical
characteristics of a text or set of texts.

In brief, when a program retrieves data or information from a database
or an online user and uses that information as the basis for a subsequent query,
then that information is *knowledge* by our usual definition. It changes the state
of a system (the information retrieval system [IRS]), or it is the basis for action (terminating a search or revising and continuing it). A query might ask for
the name of the CEO of each company marketing a given type product, and
earning revenues of at least $X. The next query can use the retrieved names
in a request for information on their addresses, or universities attended, or di-
rectorships held. (Such a search might be done by a fund-raising group within
a university.) In this second query, the names are now treated as factual information or knowledge, i.e., we are no longer questioning whether these are the
names of CEOs because the database has told us they are.

There is no special form or structure of a KB. It can have any form that
can be used by an interpreting program. The list of names of CEOs we just
postulated would have acquired, at least temporarily, the status of a "model of
the world," which has been proposed (Teskey, 1989) as the distinction between
information and knowledge. Probably the most common forms are *frames* and
rules. A frame is essentially a record that describes a context or entity. Rules are
typically stated as in programming languages: IF TITLE CONTAINS "EXECU-
TIVE" THEN RELEVANCE(RECORD_NUMBER) = 1.

Where does the knowledge in a KB come from? People who build these
are coming to be called *knowledge engineers*. The content of a KB may come
from experts in a field in which the program operates (e.g., epidemiology or

securities investing). It is the knowledge engineer's task to find the information and put it in a form useful to the software. At times, software designers and producers do not seek expert knowledge of a subject domain or of user behavior. Probably all readers have seen examples of software in which the developing programmer's assumptions about its use have been substituted for knowledge of how the intended users will react to it.

The term *knowledge base* is relatively new, but "smart" programs have been in existence for some time. Programs that can play chess or checkers (Samuelson, 1959) were available as early as the 1950s, the first decade in which computers were a commercial product. "Intelligent" information retrieval dates to the 1960s (Salton, 1980). In these early days the knowledge used by the programs tended to be incorporated into the program, not maintained as a separate database for use by the program.

Suppose a company wants to find its most valuable employees for a management development program. It could take any of several approaches. Before it can find these people, or, more accurately, before it can find their records in the personnel database, the company must define its meaning of *valuable*. Here are some approaches to the combined problem of defining and finding records.

1. Look for all those earning more than $100,000 per year in salary. This is very easy but overly simplistic. The decision to pay the person that much has already been made. Now, you are in effect looking for those who deserve it or who do not yet earn at that level but have the potential to do so.

2. Look for all those earning a salary above $90,000, having a title including the term MANAGER or VICE PRESIDENT or, if in the SALES DEPARTMENT, recently exceeded sales quota by at least 10%. This begins to suggest that the selection criteria are not easily fixed, that perhaps it would be worth having a separate program or set of rules to define the current meaning of *most valuable employees*.

3. Maintain a copy of the corporate organizational structure, coded in such a way that the x% highest ranking people can be readily identified, *and* maintain a payroll file so that the top y% of earners in all categories can be identified, *and* maintain a list of accomplishments such as patents or management performance awards, *and* maintain a history of each employee from which the speed of promotion can be computed, and so on. By this time, we are recognizing that selection is a complex process, likely to change with time, and is something we may want personnel specialists, not programmers, to be in charge of defining. So we separate the set of rules for finding valuable people, the knowledge base, from the programming of software that will use the knowledge base to search the database. When these more complex criteria are used, the data are not likely to be available in neat, well-tagged files, but scattered through many text fields.

2.5 _____

Credence, Justified Belief, and Point of View

It seems clear that, in everyday use of the words, "higher" appellations like *information, knowledge, meaningful,* and *wisdom* are used for texts that we understand and find useful, while *data* implies some degree of lack of proof of validity or value or that some processing is needed to bring out the information, like developing photographic film. It also seems clear that these higher designations are not inherent in the data but are a function of the beholder, because surely different people will understand and trust messages differently. What is data to one may be wisdom to another. What is wisdom to one may be a falsehood to another. If a program, rather than a human, is the beholder, and if it has been designed to "believe" certain data, then those data become its knowledge. Do computers believe? Most of us might say no, but they do accept some data and act upon or reject others. Practitioners of propaganda, whether of the commercial advertising or political persuasion type, know well that people can be conditioned to believe certain messages regardless of the content of the messages.

Why does it matter? There are still those who believe that any computer output is "right." Others will say that errors in output are the fault of the computer, not the person who provided the data or who wrote the program. In information retrieval, users must understand what can be considered true, correct, or valid and what merely contains words that were requested.

When a program retrieves a record because it contains a particular key word, there is no implication that the program values the record for any reason other than the simple fact that it contains the specified word. When a program uses a record of its own KB to learn how to parse a database attribute, it "believes" this record—bases its actions on the record's content without further verification. That is credence, even for a machine.

Similarly, a user searching in a library catalog, having found a card for a book on the desired subject, really knows only that the book's classification code as assigned by the library matches the desired one. Using his or her personal KB, the KB user is able to make use of words in the title, the name of author or publisher, citations, published book reviews, or friends' recommendations to establish a higher level of potential value than is implied by the subject code.

Perhaps the user will accept the information in the classification schedule, or apply specialized knowledge to reject it. A user not familiar with the subject field being searched is probably more likely to accept this authority than is an expert in the field whose more detailed knowledge may lead him or her to question the classification. Experienced library users come to learn that catalogers do differ among themselves, and hence that a subject classification perhaps should not be treated as knowledge; it is data, subject to verification of its truth to each user.

It has been reported (this may be apocryphal, but the story makes an interesting point) that during the Cold War computers at the U.S.-Canadian North American Air Defense Command had more than once indicated a ballistic missile attack to be in progress against North America. The human operators of the information systems did not credit this computer-evaluated data. They would not act on it as if it were established, justified truth, because it did not coincide with their perception of world conditions. In other words, a world war is unlikely to start in the absence of high international tension. This kind of tension is not readily measurable by a computer, but can be perceived by intelligent, informed people. There was the possibility, of course, that there was an attack, but it was unintended. At any rate, the information system users were reputedly unwilling to take action on the basis of computer messages in which they could not place much credence.

A common criticism of early bibliographic IRSs among inexperienced users was that they did not retrieve *information*—they only retrieved *citations* to information. Citations are metadata. This complaint had some validity because the bibliographic records are not usually what the searcher is ultimately looking for. On the other hand, if the searcher is looking for the correct spelling of an author's name, the proper citation for a known book, or its location in the library, then the record does have *information*, not merely data, and will usually be believed.

If the object of a search is to find out how to produce room-temperature nuclear fusion, then the searcher has to resolve two questions *after* retrieving citation records: (1) Are the articles "pointed to" really on the desired subject, i.e., do they purport to tell *how*? (2) Are the articles pointed to reliable, credible, or true? (Can fusion actually occur at room temperature?) The mechanical retrieval system usually does nothing to help with the credibility issue, but credibility affects the retrieval process. Credibility has to do with the relationship among the searcher, the creators of the catalog record, and the books or articles cataloged. Credibility, therefore, does affect user behavior (looking further, finding information about the author, taking out the book, perhaps even deciding to read it).

Thus, we return to an earlier point: the need for communication among record creators and users. We can see that not only must they share an understanding of the meaning of words and other symbols, but they must also share an understanding of the truth, validity, or credibility of the information. Neither area of understanding need be perfect, and the IRS can be used to help resolve some degree of uncertainty. For example, is this author's name really spelled correctly in this record? Is this the way it is spelled in records of other books we know he wrote? (A publisher's advertisement for the books of Prof. Charles

H. Davis of Indiana University showed a different rendering of his name with each one: Charles Hargis Davis, Charles H. Davis, and Charles Davis. Davis is a common name. What is the correct form with which to find other information by or about this particular Davis?) If a user believes subject descriptors are accurate, then retrieved citations can be acted upon in one way: withdrawing books or making an effort to read them. But if the user cannot believe subject descriptors are accurate, then references or citations merely trigger a different action—a search for more, corroborating evidence—and the retrieved records are seen as a long way from the ultimate goal.

We do not mean to suggest that there is no truth or that there are no absolute values. We do mean to suggest that information retrieval outcome can suffer if users insist that there is one and only one way to express a concept or that any document on a given subject is as valuable as any other. We do mean to say that successful retrieval requires that users, intermediaries, or computer programs designed to help users recognize that there may be different ways of expressing a concept and that common use of a few key words does not guarantee that two documents mean the same thing.

2.6

Summary

The essence of this chapter has been to point out that information, when acquired by a person, leads to some kind of action. The action may be internal (making up one's mind or making a decision), or it may be externally manifested by moving, buying, shooting, or some such act. These may also be viewed as the result of the act of deciding. It is also true that the nature of the action will be determined by the recipient's degree of belief in the information or understanding of its meaning.

3

Representation of Information

Information to Be Represented

There are so many kinds of information structures, ranging from a bit or pixel, at one extreme, to an encyclopedia or complete library at the other, that it is difficult to suggest there is a base unit of information. In one sense, the base is the *bit*, or binary digit, representing either of the values 0 or 1, and not being further subdividable. It could also be the *letter*, as the base unit of text, or the *phoneme*, the base sound unit of spoken language. A *pixel* can be the base unit of a picture, typified by the dot in a newspaper photograph. A pixel has coordinates, and either color or shade of grey. It is not restricted to the binary choices, black or white. The basic unit of sound could be a single cycle of sound of a given wavelength and amplitude. For us to hear a monotonic sound, such as from striking a single piano key once, requires a sequence of cycles of the same wavelength. Other sounds are made up of combinations of such elementary tones. Whatever the elementary form, a datum is made up of elementary symbols combined according to some rule, depending on the type of symbol. For letters being grouped into words, that structure is called *morphology*. Individual data are then combined into higher-order structures that may range from arrays of numbers to book-length texts or motion pictures. The higher order groupings are also governed by rules called, in written language and increasingly in other forms of language, *syntax*.

This is a rather technical view of data. Another view, more oriented toward content and meaning, is to assume that the basis of information is an *entity* about which we have information. The entity may be an event described in a news article, or a scene portrayed in a painting, or a person about whom we have medical observations. Each type of information we have about an entity is called an *attribute*, which has a *value*. In the case of a medical record, the attributes will be well defined: name, date of birth, date of visit, blood type, complaint, diagnosis, etc. The corresponding values may be JOHN Q. CITIZEN, 15 MARCH 1966, 13 JULY 1989, A POS, etc. Note that the nature of the patient's complaint or the physician's diagnosis may be poorly defined, but the meaning or intent of an attribute called complaint or diagnosis is usually expressed more clearly. In the case of the news article, the attributes are less clearly defined, and the exact attributes to be represented will depend on the nature of the event, but the classic ones are the five W's: who, what, where, when, and why. The descriptions of these attributes are values in the form of strings of text, and they will vary widely from article to article.

A painting is so complex an entity that its attributes are not completely defined. Artists, critics, and viewers may all perceive different attributes. In one sense, we may say that they are a set of pixels, each of which has a location and a color. This view breaks the painting down too far for most viewers, who cannot get the sense of the overall entity from this sort of mechanical description, while they can get the sense of the news event from the five W's.

We give the name *record* to the set of information about an entity. A record was once a precisely defined concept in data processing, when it might have referred to all the information contained in a physical subdivision of memory, such as a punched card, a fixed-length set of characters on a magnetic tape, or a segment of random access memory. This view is no longer current with modern developments in hardware and software, but it probably is current in most people's thinking. Today, the set of information about an entity may be dispersed among several locations, with the different pieces being assembled as needed into an *ad hoc* record. Modern records need not be of uniform size for all entities. At least temporarily, we refer to records in a somewhat imprecise way as the complete *set of recorded values of attributes* of an *entity*. The entity may be another record (a library catalog record referring to a book, itself a record) but it is more likely to be something outside the information system, such as a person, event, or painting.

A collection of records constitutes a *file* or *database*. In some cases it is important that the database contain records about all the entities in some population, say all the patients in a hospital or all the employees of a company. In other cases, we know this is not possible. In spite of the *New York Times'* motto, "All the news that's fit to print," it cannot print all the news, unless there is a very narrow interpretation of what is fit to print. One of the bases of the *Times'* readers' respect for the paper is the manner in which stories are selected for printing from among all those that could have printed. *File* tends to have a precise meaning in modern computer science, such as a set of data assigned a name and storage location by the computer's operating system or to a set of records, while *database* may be used as a synonym for file or to mean a set of related files.

In future chapters we shall reconsider the question of the structure of information. For now, we turn our attention to the question of what information to represent in a record, and how. We should point out at this time, however, that we must not be too dogmatic about what is an entity and what an attribute. An entity can be a person. A person has attended a school, which fact is then used as an attribute of the person. Information (a set of attributes) about that school refers to the school as the entity, not to the person. But this is conceptually no different from saying that there is a subject of an essay, expressed by a paragraph within it, that there is a subject of that paragraph expressed by a sentence within it, and a subject of that sentence expressed by a clause within it. So an entity may be the subject of a record, and another entity may be part of the description of the first.

It is easy to decide to represent a person's name. It is another question to decide exactly *how* to represent the person variously identified as

John Fitzgerald Kennedy
Kennedy, John F.
Kennedy JF
The 35th President of the United States of America

These are just a few of the possibilities. To the human reader the first three are virtually identical. To a typical computer program searching for a particular string of symbols, they are not. The fourth version, not a name at all, nevertheless uniquely identifies the person named John F. Kennedy.

Dates are another example of how complexity can come out of apparent simplicity. The strings

October 14, 1988
14 October 1988
10/14/88
14/10/88
881014

can all mean the same thing, but even to the human reader there is some ambiguity here. European usage for October 14, 1988, is 14/10/88 and the American is 10/14/88. The date 000704 is the cause of great anxiety as the 20th century ends because it could refer either to the year 1900 or 2000 and we have no basis for deciding which without some contextual information.

Most users of libraries know that it is one thing to have a well-defined attribute called subject, but that it is quite another for the user to figure out how the library has classified the subject being searched for. There may also be more than one value for the subject attribute for any given book. How many descriptions to use and how to represent them are database design decisions. The book *The Expedition of Humphry Clinker* by Tobias Smollet was classified in the following Library of Congress classes by different libraries: PR3694, PR3690, PR3691, PR3693, and PZ3. The first four of these codes all refer to different aspects of Tobias, himself. The PZ3 code seems to have been an error, since it refers to authors in the period 1750–1950 who did not publish after 1750. It is easy to see how differences can arise. There is no right or wrong here, except for the PZ code, only differences of opinion. The incidence of such differences is decreasing since shared cataloging systems have come into use.

As we noted in connection with the attributes of a painting, we have no well-established, general method of determining the attributes of a graphic image comparable to the fairly standardized set of attributes we have developed over time to describe a body of text. Whether books in a library or letters in a law office, we tend to describe text in terms of title, subject, date, and author. Then, depending on who are the expected users, there may be such attributes as author's affiliation, case number, or publisher. While it is possible to describe a graphic image in terms of pixel placement and color, and sometimes possible to find the various shapes represented, we cannot expect any database that contains only representations of pixels to tell us what picture in a collection contains the image of a dog or shows the use of broad brush strokes.

The situation with regard to sound is similar. It is possible to record sound digitally and store it along with some descriptive text. There are indexing methods for music, but these tend to represent only the opening bars of a piece. If the searcher remembers only a passage in the middle, it is unlikely to be found by an automatic procedure. In Chapter 4 we show a few rather elemental methods of representing sound in an index. We can, to some extent, convert spoken words to characters representing words, but no known information retrieval system (IRS) would search for word occurrences in an unconverted file of sound recordings. The time required would be prohibitive.

The designer of a record has to decide what information (attributes) ideally should be represented about each entity in a database. He or she must also decide what entities are to be represented: "All the news," a selection of the news referring to certain people, a selection of the news about certain types of events, or a selection that presents those events meeting the local criteria for political correctness. Selecting the books to include in a library's collection presents a similar decision problem. Finally, the designer must decide how each attribute is to be represented: as codes, numbers, text, digitized pictures, etc.

In the first round of decision making, prime consideration must be given to the information the users of the database will probably want. What they want is conditioned by what they know about the subjects of the database, and what they may come to learn from using it. For example, although a corporate personnel department might be content to identify employees by name, programmers and accountants might insist on a unique identifying number so that changes of name or multiple occurrences of the same name do not lead to errors in payroll and tax accounting.

Technical computer and communications considerations may then come into play. Perhaps users of a library's catalog would like the entire table of contents of each book to be represented in the catalog card or its computer equivalent. Many would like the complete text of every book and article in a library to be computer searchable. Even storage of the table of contents is not yet a practical reality, and the full text on a searchable medium is unlikely to be seen for years to come, because of both technical and copyright considerations. However, memories are now large enough and we are seeing more and more large texts on the World Wide Web, which may encourage publishers to venture into new forms of publishing.

3.2
Types of Representation

Information must be represented as symbols. Within a computer, the symbols representing the words of a text are bytes made up of strings of bits. Most bytes have graphical representations for printing. While the set of 7-bit bytes is fully adequate for representing English language text, if we are interested also in other languages, more than 26 letters, and upper and lower cases of each, are needed (e.g., the non-English characters ä, á, λ, ñ). Then there are musical notes and mathematical symbols. Because the total is limited, not all symbols of interest to all users can appear. Because the number of characters is limited, the selection of a means of representation is critically important. The representation must be comprehensible both to computer programs and to human users.

A database designer must decide how each attribute will be represented, as numbers, letter strings, codes, or text strings (which usually imply use of upper- and lowercase letters, numbers, and punctuation). Codes, measures, or text can range from precisely selective to indicative of a broad class of values. The choice should be up to the designer, but what matters is how the codes or values function in practice—do they separate nonidentical entities and bring together similar ones?

There is virtually a continuum of methods for representing information, from natural-language text to highly compact, previously defined codes, and to pictures and sounds. The methods vary mainly in terms of discriminating power, identification of similarity, descriptiveness, ambiguity, and conciseness, which we shall discuss at greater length in Section 3.4. A different approach, altogether, is to represent the *words* not the information, itself, on the assumption that the words constitute a fair representation of the information. We heard confirmation, in the many hearings concerning President Clinton, that simple-sounding phrases may mean different things to different people. But, when we are trying to find documents that discuss certain topics, the mere occurrence of certain words is a strong indicator that the topic was discussed.

3.2.1 Natural Language

Natural language is the language we "naturally" speak. It is contrasted with artificial languages, such as BASIC or JAVA, that are consciously designed and usually highly restrictive in vocabulary and syntax. Natural language has no limit to its vocabulary and no complete set of rules to describe its syntax, or grammar. While we have some generally accepted vocabularies, it is also true that many words have more than one meaning, and several different words can have the same meaning. An author (anyone who creates a text, even an oral one, not just one who writes books) is free to define new words or temporarily change the meaning of established ones, or to switch from one natural language to another with or without explicit warning to readers, as in these examples:

A device that modulates outgoing signals and demodulates incoming signals is called a *modem*. (Defining a new word)

Henceforth, we shall use the term *text* to be synonymous with *natural language message*. (Redefining an existing word)

As they say in French, *c'est la vie*, and there are similar expressions in Spanish, Italian, *et cetera*. (Using different languages in a single text, only one of which is explicitly identified)

The primary advantages of natural language as a means of communication are that (1) it can be understandable to large groups of users without special training and (2) just about any nuance of meaning can be expressed. This does not mean that untrained people can read chemical journals any more than they can read medical X-ray pictures. It does mean that any user familiar with the vocabulary of chemistry can read the text, but if there is a reference within it to a particular *Chemical Abstracts* Registry Number, even many chemists will not know what that code means.

Another advantage is that natural language and its users are fault tolerant. The song title *Yes, We Have No Bananas*, the common expression that inverts its own literal meaning, "I could care less," or the just plain ungrammatical, "I ain't got none," are all readily understood by most native speakers of English.

The disadvantages of text are primarily (1) the lack of conciseness, (2) ambiguity, the possibility that the text will not yield a single meaning to all readers, and (3) the difficulty of interpretation of text by a computer. Can a computer understand the topic of the sentence "To be or not to be, that is the question"? Probably not, but it can do some text interpretation. If the text is of a fairly straightforward, explanatory nature, whose author has not used unusual imagery or metaphor, computers have been fairly successful at "understanding" what the subject is. This usually means selecting the words most important to the subject, or recognizing that two or more texts are on the same or similar subjects. When computers can do this, they can relieve human users of much work in retrieving information. It may be precisely by the use of unexpected images, as in poetry, that an author is best able to convey a meaning, but such information is likely to be missed by a computer.

3.2.2 Restricted Natural Language

When it is necessary for a computer as well as humans to interpret a text, restricting the vocabulary or syntax can alleviate many problems. Like natural language, restricted natural language is not well defined. It can be any sublanguage for which the vocabulary or syntax or both are significantly limited, yet for which the meanings remain more or less as in natural language. Reasonably descriptive texts can be written if all sentences are of the form *noun, simple verb, noun*, and we can easily allow an optional adjective before either noun, giving, for example:

Computers understand restricted language.
People understand complex language.
Computers misinterpret natural text.*
Most humans comprehend natural language.

The asterisked sentence is an example of how a restricted language can be misleading. Computers do not always misunderstand natural text, but they may do so and will probably do so more often than people will. This is actually a conditional sentence, but we cannot express such a subtle conditional or probabilistic concept in this primitive language.

The restricted natural language technique is used with command languages for computer software. A common form of language for use with a database search system permits such sentences as PRINT NAME AND ADDRESS FOR SALARY >= 35000.

The program that recognizes this might allow variation in the order of occurrence of clauses: FOR SALARY >= 35000 PRINT NAME AND ADDRESS, but might probably not recognize the meaning of GIVE ME THE NAMES AND ADDRESSES OF EMPLOYEES WHO MAKE AT LEAST 35K.

Human users seem to like the flexibility of being able to write clauses in any order. Many like the fact that the resulting sentence reads like an English sentence. If there were a syntactic error, a computer program might be quite adept at identifying where the error lay, something it probably could not do unless a restrictive syntax were in force.

The Association européenne des constructeurs de matériel aérospatial has developed a form of "simplified English" for use in aircraft maintenance documentation (AECMA, 1995). Commercial airplanes are manufactured in only a few countries, but used and serviced in many. A guide was developed to reduce the complexities of English for non-native speakers. It is not a new language. It is an attempt to reduce ambiguity. For example, we commonly use an expression such as "follow the instructions." But *follow* is formally defined as meaning only "to come after." Or, instead of "This regulation *extends* to all units," say "This regulation *is applicable* to all units." Basically, the guide simply urges good English usage, yet it could only help, hardly hurt, text-based information retrieval. On the other hand, it does restrict expressiveness somewhat.

3.2.3 Artificial Language

user & advantages

When the information to be represented is limited in variability, it can be represented in highly compact and unambiguous form, cutting storage requirements and vastly simplifying the computer programs that must interpret it. While user training in the use of the language is required, the chance of usage errors can be minimized.

An example is a command language for a computer system, whether for general purpose computing, as C++ or BASIC, or specialized use, as with the database systems PARADOX or DIALOG. Command languages have a syntax, and there is usually at least some degree of context dependence. This means that a symbol does not always carry the same meaning, wherever or however it occurs, but that context can determine meaning. For example, many such languages use quotation marks, as we do in natural language, to alter interpretation. WRITE ("X + Y") in a computer programming language typically means to write the symbols "X", "+", and "Y", while WRITE (X + Y) means to write the sum of the values of variables X and Y.

In the DIALOG IR command language, SELECT COMPUTER means to retrieve all records containing the word COMPUTER as a value in any of several tacitly understood attributes. The command EXPAND COMPUTER means to look up COMPUTER in a dictionary and display some of the words that precede and follow it alphabetically. The command EXPAND SELECT COMPUTER is ambiguous in English because it could either consist of a phrase with two commands (an error) or a request to EXPAND the phrase SELECT COMPUTER, which is syntactically acceptable even if not very meaningful. DIALOG would sense only the latter meaning and would look in its dictionary for the phrase SELECT COMPUTER. If a mistake had been made (the first interpretation) DIALOG would not catch it, and the user might be baffled by the system's response, which is meaningless in this assumed context. It is something like what happens when a wrong number is dialed on the telephone, but the caller does not immediately recognize the initial response and believes the connection is correct. Then, the question, "Is Ms. So-and-so in?" can receive a baffling response when the answerer denies that this person, who is expected to be well known, is even to be found at that number.

The very precision of meaning of artificial language may require expenditure of great effort by users to learn error-free usage. It is characteristic that small errors are not tolerated. In effect, the use of artificial language tends to represent a shift of responsibility from computer software and records designers to users.

3.2.4 Codes, Measures, and Descriptors

These are individual strings of symbols such as a Dewey Classification Code (used to identify the subject matter of a library book), a single word (descriptive of a book's subject), a color code (for describing an automobile), or a real number (patient's temperature). Some other examples are:

A *bit map* is an array of bits. Outside the field of computer graphics it means that each bit has an assigned meaning that can be represented by the value 0 or 1. In graphics, it refers to a means of representing a picture. The map 011100 in a personnel file might compactly indicate a person who is Not a Union Member (first 0); Salaried (1); In the Savings Bond Program (1); In the Retirement Program (1); Not in the Stock Purchase Program (0); and Not a Full-Time Employee (0).

A *menu*, in computer terms, more or less as it is in restaurant terms, is a list of options offered to a user. Selection of an option is often done by entry of a code, typically the line number of the choice or the first character of the text describing the choice, or pointing to the choice with a mouse. It is almost unheard of to require that a user type in the entire text of a choice instead of a code representing that choice (but it has been done).

A list of frequently used phrases is used in voice radio communications, to be transmitted as codes in order to speed transmission and reduce error, for example, ROGER, OVER, or 10-4. Each of these has a precise, assigned meaning within a community of users.

Descriptors, in the sense of words or phrases used to describe the subject content of a text or graphic, are discussed in Chapter 4. They are usually drawn from a list of allowable terms, as are codes.

The advantage of strictly limited attribute values is that they tend to be unambiguous and concise. If we ask for the number on hand of a particular item in the warehouse, both the number and the item description will be well identified and unambiguous in meaning, although, in fact, the information could be wrong. For example, 1.21 divided by 0.31 gives a quotient of 3.903225. . . . But as data this is misleading. If the first two numbers are known only to two decimal places, the quotient cannot be known to six or more, even though there is the appearance of greater precision. Similarly, a linear measurement made with a tape measure subject to stretching or heat-caused expansion may not be as accurate as it appears.

It is possible that the appearance of precision of value or definition could lure users into asking the wrong question, say for number sold when the real goal is to find rate of demand or projected sales. The difference, which can be critical, is that what is actually sold may not be what the customers initially wanted, but agreed to accept if what they wanted was not available. It could result in restocking second-choice items and not reordering what was really wanted. Classification codes may represent little more than the opinion of one classifier, not "truth." Knowledgeable users, in such cases, learn that errors and ambiguities do occur, and they look for alternate possibilities.

When records are designed to appear well defined and structured, and something goes wrong with the data, there may be more confusion than if the data did not *appear* to be so precise. What is an air traveler to think when an incoming flight is posted on a display board as due to arrive one hour *after* that same flight is shown as scheduled to depart the airport? Or what does a department store customer do when an automated store directory gives directions such as, "Go down two flights, then turn right" that are all wrong because the machine is located on the wrong floor? These may appear far fetched, but they have been encountered by the authors.

3.2.5 Mathematical Models of Text

Another approach to document representation is to focus on what words or other symbols are present on the assumption that these represent the meaning. The simplest method is simply to list the attributes of the document and the values of these attributes. Then this list is searched instead of the document. When an attribute may contain more than one word or string of nonblank characters, it is useful to record the relative position of each word within the text. This way, if the words NEW and ORLEANS are in a text, we can quickly determine whether they constitute the phrase NEW ORLEANS or are merely part of a discussion about something new in the city of Orleans.

A frequently used model is called the *vector space model* (Salton and McGill, 1983, pp. 120–123). It represents a *text* rather than a complete document, in that it normally does not recognize attributes, only words occurring in one attribute that contains text. The model assumes an n-dimensional space, one dimension for each possible word or term. This means that, in general usage, n would have a value in the thousands or hundreds of thousands, the number of words

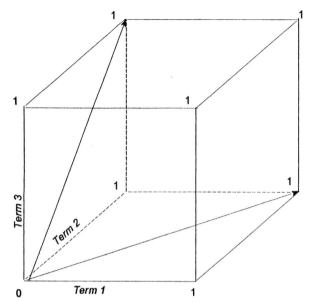

Figure 3.1
Document vectors on the vertices of the unit hypercube: each text is represented by a vector whose component, along each term axis, is either 0 or 1. Thus, all vectors must terminate only at one of the corners of the cube. In real life the number of dimensions is far greater than can be illustrated on a two-dimensional page.

in a natural language. Each text is represented as a vector in this space. Each component of the vector (distance along one axis) is either 0 or 1, depending on whether the corresponding term is absent from or present in the text. In its simplest form each text vector terminates at a point in the vector space within the unit *hypercube*, as shown in Fig. 3.1. A hypercube is simply a geometric construct analogous to a three-dimensional cube, but having *n* dimensions. Since each possible term is either present or absent, all vectors reach a point at a vertex of the hypercube, as shown in the figure.

A variation permits the use of a measure of significance or importance of the term to the text instead of the binary present–absent value. In this case, a vector can terminate at any point within the hypercube. See Fig. 3.2.

In either case, the use of text vectors allows us to compute a measure of similarity of one text to another. Similarity, here, means similarity of vocabulary, which is a reasonable approximation to similarity of meaning. The measure is based on the angle between two vectors. The smaller the angle, the greater the similarity. This will be discussed at greater length in Chapters 9 and 10.

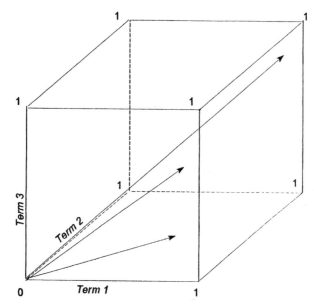

Figure 3.2
Document vectors in the unit hypercube: each document is again represented by a vector whose components may be anywhere in the range 0.0 to 1.0. Therefore, the vectors may terminate anywhere within the hypercube.

3.3

Characteristics of Information Representations

When we select a mode of representation of an attribute, such as natural language or a code, we are selecting a tool, albeit an information tool. We want it to perform certain tasks: (1) to discriminate between different entities, (2) to identify similarity among entities, (3) to allow accurate description of entities, and (4) to minimize ambiguity in interpretation. These desiderata may conflict with one another.   (5) Conciseness

3.3.1 Discriminating Power

The ultimate in discriminating or resolving power is a unique code value, one that applies to one and only one entity in a database, thereby clearly separating the one entity from all others. Because a person's name cannot be relied on to have this characteristic, large employers, schools, prisons, and tax authorities issue numbers that are unique in the community in which they are used. By mistake or fraud such codes are occasionally not unique, but the effort is made, and the instance of error is usually low. The U.S. social security number, intended as a unique identifier, does not always function as such. When, early in the history of Social Security, a facsimile of a social security card was included in a line of men's wallets, over 5000 people reported the number thereon as their own. Also, the Social Security Administration has reported that over four million people have two or more numbers (*Records*, 1973, p. 112). Hence, with probability about as high as we can get in information systems design, we can accept that different values imply different entities, that equal values in different records imply that the records refer to the same entity, *and* that some errors will be made. A well-designed, complete information system should have some procedures for recognizing errors and for handling them when they do occur.

3.3.2 Identification of Similarity

Classification codes can show both similarity and dissimilarity. When entities are not truly unique, we would like to be able to tell when there are differences among them. Dewey Decimal Classification codes show both the similarity and difference among entities. If two code values are 004.692 (electronic mail) and 004.693 (electronic bulletin boards), then we can see at a glance that the entities are alike, in that they share the attribute of being in classes 004 (data processing), 004.6 (interfacing and communication), and 004.69 (specific kinds of computer communication), yet are not identical because they are in different subdivisions of the 004.69 class.

3.3.3 Descriptiveness

This is a characteristic related to uniqueness. We use descriptive power to show how one entity differs from others, but at the same time to show similarities. Of importance, then, is completeness of description, describing accurately all the important information about an entity. Of course, importance will vary with the beholder. A language with great descriptive power gives its user the choice of what aspects to stress. Natural language, as we have noted, offers the ultimate in expressiveness in words and enables us to avoid the problems caused by overly simplistic classifications or codes. Library classification codes may or may not be highly descriptive of book content; it depends on whether users understand them.

3.3.4 Ambiguity

The partner of descriptiveness is often ambiguity. Novelists and poets can be descriptive in ways many of us cannot approach, but they can also be easily misunderstood. Where a community of users shares a common understanding of a set of symbols (a hospital's operating room team, pilots and air traffic controllers, waiters and cooks in a restaurant) terse language can be used with little probability of error. Where there is no prior basis for common understanding, meanings must somehow be established within the text of the communication, and here is where the poet surpasses and the inarticulate writer simply fails to communicate.

Ambiguity refers to lack of uniqueness of meaning. Precise writing is not necessarily concise, but it is unambiguous. "The temperature is five degrees Celsius" is ambiguous to some extent because the reader does not know whether "five" means "5" an integer between 4 and 6, or "5.00," a number between 4.995 and 5.005. Codes have the capacity for precision, but do not always attain it, as color codes often really identify a dye lot rather than describing a color in a way that conveys a visual image to readers of the words in a file.

3.3.5 Conciseness

This refers to the number of symbols used to represent a value: "2" is more concise than "two." Also, "Mt." is a concise and common representation of "Mount" but this conciseness comes at a cost when the abbreviation is used for sorting, as in a telephone directory. In that case, the publishers must recognize the abbreviation, temporarily replace it with the full word, sort, then go back to the abbreviation for printing. People not fluent in English may find it difficult to find Mt. Sinai Hospital in the directory because it is not listed as spelled. Further, highly concise codes may not be particularly useful for expressing fine points of variability. The value of conciseness is mostly economic, but it also affects how well a message holds a reader's attention.

3.4
Relationships among Entities and Attribute Values

The composition of symbols can be used to make clear the relationship between attribute values and the entities to which they refer.

3.4.1 Hierarchical Codes

A hierarchical code identifies a node in a hierarchical or tree-like structure (Fig. 3.3), in this case a portion of the Dewey Decimal Classification. Such a strictly hierarchical structure allows each node to have one and only one "parent" or superordinate (except for the highest node in the structure) and any number of "children" or subordinates. Records or nodes sharing a common parent are known as "siblings."

If the reader or user knows the structure, then identifying a node means that its relationship with all other nodes is understood. In a geographic context, identifying the Province of Ontario implies that it is included within the nation of Canada and the continent of North America, and that it contains the cities of Toronto, Kingston, and Hamilton. If the term *Ontario* were not part of a hierarchy, then we would not know if, standing alone, it indicated the province in Canada, the town in New York, the city in California, or the Great Lake.

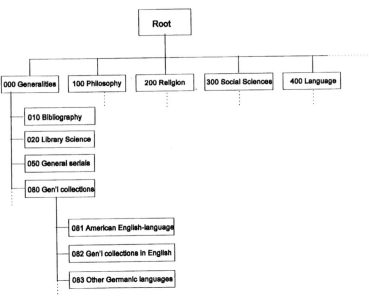

Figure 3.3

Basic hierarchical structure: perhaps the most common organizational method in use, each element has a single "parent," or superordinate element, except for the first element. Any element may have any number of subordinate elements. This is a segment of the Dewey Decimal Classification structure, the entirety of which would not fit on a single page. Some titles have been shortened. Any given subject is expected to fit into one and only one category and then all superordinate categories are implied.

3.4.2 Measurements

A measurement is a comparison of some attribute with a reference point or scale (Boyce, Meadow, and Kraft, 1994). There are, of course, internationally accepted standards for measuring length, time, and mass. To measure the height of a person is to make a statement of the ratio of the person's height to the standard of length. Such *ratio measures* can be highly exact in the sense that they can record the finest degree of variation.

Sometimes we can measure only nearness to distinct points, such as the integral number of feet of a person's height or the letter scale (A, B, etc.) used as a grade in school, where it is understood that the intervals between points on the scale are supposed to be all alike, i.e., that the difference between the grades A and B is the same magnitude as the difference between B and C. This is called *interval scale measurement*.

"Measures" like GOOD and BAD in behavior, LEFT and RIGHT in politics, or GOOD, BETTER, BEST as often found in mail order catalogs, imply an ordering of the values but no precise indication of the distance between them; hence, such measures are called *ordinal*.

A fourth class of measurement is called *nominal*. It refers to the use of values that have no ordering among them. Typical examples are the terms used to describe a person's race, gender, or religion. In a typical data form, there will be a set of possible values for each of these attributes, but there is no established meaning, for example, to relative distance or ordering among Baptists, Anglicans, and Roman Catholics or between males and females. Usually, we simply resort to alphabetic ordering in such cases.

Measures are used to achieve uniqueness in description, to discriminate, to identify similarity, and to minimize ambiguity. How descriptive they are depends on the scales used. A common procedure in restaurants is to invite patrons to evaluate service using an ordinal scale containing the points FAIR, GOOD, and EXCELLENT. The absence of POOR quite limits descriptiveness.

3.4.3 Nominal Descriptors

Nominal descriptors are often used to describe the content of bodies of natural-language text to make it easier for searchers to discriminate between records on their subject and others. These may be individual words selected from the text, called *key words*, or phrases with some hierarchical relationships among them, called *subject headings*. Their use makes writing a query easier for searchers because there are fewer ways to represent a subject in this "language" than in natural language. Typically, subject-describing terms are limited within any database, i.e., there is a defined vocabulary, and both the creators of records and searchers are expected to use these terms only. That requirement imposes the further requirement that all users learn the language or face the likelihood of unsatisfactory search results.

Nominal values are often limited by a published list of allowable values, as in the classification schedules for book cataloging or the model types in automobile inventories. An attribute such as a person's name is also a nominal descriptor. It would hardly be possible to devise a complete list of permissible names to be held by employees in a large company or students at a university. Nonetheless, each name is a valid descriptor of the person, and almost any combination of letters might be used in some part of the world as a name. Although we could maintain a list of authorized bibliographic descriptors, and a computer can assist users by rejecting invalid ones, we cannot use any kind of authority list to validate a name, unless we are dealing with a limited entity population, such as the set of authors of books cataloged by the Library of Congress or of persons listed in the Manhattan telephone directory.

One rule that is normally imposed is that only one form of any given term will be used as a nominal descriptor. We might specify the singular form for nouns and the participle form for verbs, e.g., use WORD, but not WORDS, WORD'S, WORDING, WORDED, etc. More important, in cases such as the spelling of authors' names, it may be necessary to establish an *authority file* showing the form deemed correct within a community. This would overcome variations in transliteration of non-English names, use or nonuse of first name or initials, or pseudonyms.

3.4.4 Inflected Language

The use of prefixes and suffixes, even when not using full natural language, creates many problems for information systems, at both the record creation stage and the search stage. Inflections show similarities and differences and can add to ambiguity. The usual method of control over this form of ambiguity is to impose rigid controls, such as:

Alphabetize all names using MC or MAC prefixes as if spelled MAC.

Alphabetize names beginning with VON, VAN, or VAN DER by what follows, i.e., do not include the prefixes in the name for this purpose (or *always* use the prefix for alphabetizing).

Omit punctuation: O'MALLEY becomes OMALLEY or the separate words O and MALLEY.

Use only one form of a word with multiple endings (see the WORD example above).

3.4.5 Full Text

As we pointed out earlier, if the content of an attribute is represented in unrestricted natural language, there are many ways to say the same thing, and any given word may have more than one meaning. Relationships between records can be well established if word usage is similar. Dictionaries and thesauri can be used to establish a link between different words or phrases having similar meaning.

Long ago, H. P. Luhn (1958) recognized that words occurring frequently in a text, apart from the "common" words like A, THE, OF, etc., characterize the subject matter and can be used to relate similar texts. This basic notion has been expanded on and refined by such researchers as Salton (1989), Croft and Thompson (1987), and Liddy *et al.* (1995), now giving us reliable ways to relate a natural-language question to records stored in a database, or to relate one database record to another. Both relationships are established through similarity in the pattern of frequency of use of words or word families, i.e., a word and its synonyms or other words frequently co-occurring with it. We shall pursue this at greater length in Chapter 9 and show a practical example in Chapter 15.

3.4.6 Explicit Pointers and Links

The final means of recording a relationship between records is to establish an attribute of each record that "points" explicitly to related records. This means that the author of the record, or some computer program, has recognized the nature of relationships that could exist and has set up something like a "see also" pointer. In this case, each record indicates the location of the next record in order (whatever the ordering basis may be): the next closest record in meaning, a subordinate record, a superordinate record, a record cited by the entity of this record, etc.

This is the basis for the design of a database using one of the newest (Nelson, 1981; Parsaye, Chigell, Khashafran, and Wong, pp. 223–291; Shneiderman and Kearsely, 1989) and yet oldest techniques of database ordering, now called *hypertext* (Englebart, 1963; Englebart and English, 1968; Nelson, 1965). Essentially this means of ordering was called *linked lists, threaded lists,* or simply *list structures* (Lefkovitz, 1969, pp. 127–129). In hypertext a series of records is linked by multiple chains or pointers. The reader or searcher may follow any pointer at any time. If the text of this book were written in hypertext, a reader might choose to follow this paragraph with the next one mentioning the word *Hypertext,* or the first paragraph in the next chapter, or the bibliographic entry for the third reference, or for the next paragraph in the order written by the author. A bibliographic citation is a form of pointer. Most commonly it means, "The source of the information just stated is _____." It can also indicate a source for more information than was presented in the citing work.

3.5

Summary

In all of IR, we are continually trying (1) to find records with unique attributes, (2) to separate one set of records from others, based on attribute values, and (3) to bring together those records with similar attributes, i.e., to create sets of similar records. The success of the mechanics of these activities depends heavily on the manner in which attributes are represented. If one record identifies the color of an object as GREEN and another identifies the same object as RED, because the two humans who created these records disagreed in their perceptions owing to color blindness in one of them, there is almost no way to relate the records on the attribute color. We can, however, relate the records if we can refer to another source that establishes RED and GREEN as synonyms for one particular record author, or if we can find other attributes that may have values in common. It is in this search for alternatives that we sometimes find the greatest creativity exhibited by searchers or by the designers of computer programs to assist users.

4

Attribute Content and Values

Types of Attribute Symbols

An attribute of an entity has a *name* and a *value* or *content*. Content may be the entire value of an attribute or only part of it, as when we refer to a part of a text, say the introduction to a politician's speech, which may it turn contain several hundred words. The entire text or value is contained in a *field* of a record or *attribute* of an entity. The field is the container of the value. It may be sub-divided, say into paragraphs, then sentences, then individual words—anything that has a physical definition, such as ending with a period or a tab character. *Value* is the mathematical meaning, not the economic meaning. The value of an attribute named date of birth might be 590217 (17 February 1959). An attribute named author might have the value TEDESCO, ALBERT S. In neither case are we attributing preference; we are merely recognizing that a symbol, or value, identifies a particular date or person. The complete text of a news article may be considered a single attribute of the news item, along with date, by-line, headline, and page number.

Value is a concept of importance to those concerned either with computer programs that process data or with computation of the amount of storage space required. *Meaning, reliability, credibility,* and like concepts are equally important, but not in the same sense as the value chosen to represent an attribute. To a large extent, but not totally, database designers have control over the symbols used to represent attributes. One way to look at this is in terms of the alphabet or basic symbol set used to construct individual attribute values. Among the common types are *integer* (a string of bytes using only the characters $0, 1, 2, \ldots, 9$ plus an optional sign byte) or *alphanumeric* or *character* values, usually a string of any characters that have a print equivalent, such as $0, 1, 2, a, b, c, \ldots, (, @, !, \ldots$.

Specifying the basic types, together with some syntactic or morphological rules, gives the following types.

4.1.1 Numbers

Most commonly, we deal with *integers* (or whole numbers) or *real numbers* (whose meaning in the computer world is a number that may have a fractional part). Real numbers, as the term is used in computing, consist of a set of numeric digits with one and only one decimal point and a sign. They are commonly represented in computer storage as two numbers plus a sign: a *mantissa* between 0 and 1, and an *exponent*, understood to be applied to 10. The number 12.34 might be represented as 01234002, where:

> The initial zero is taken as a plus sign.
> 1234 is the mantissa, representing 0.1234.
> 002 is the exponent, implying that 0.1234 is to be multiplied by
> 10^2 or 100, giving 12.34.

Another example of a numeric form, of less interest to information retrieval, is currency, represented as a number preceded by the sign \$ (or £ or ¥), with optional commas between every three digits and with data to two decimal places, as \$12,345.67. Commas may be optional. In Europe, 12,345.67 may be written 12.345,67 or 12 345,67. The storage representation can be the same as a real number, but somewhere there must be stored the notation on how to represent the value in a display.

4.1.2 Character Strings—Names

These are represented, unhappily, in many different ways. An author's name in a bibliographic file might follow the pattern last name, comma, space, first initial, period, second initial, period, as TEDESCO, A.S. One of the difficulties caused by the many different standards in use is that a searcher looking for TEDESCO AS (no punctuation) may fail to retrieve the name, because a program tends to declare the search string to have been exactly matched or not matched at all. Usually, names the world over consist of or are transliterated into strings of alphabetic characters and blank spaces. Numerals, as part of a name, are represented in Roman form, as Elizabeth II or John Smith III. Such a rule can help in checking the validity of spelling. If "?" shows up in a name, it implies an error.

Once we have selected a means of representing an attribute, it becomes possible to determine the similarity or other relationships among entities by virtue of the values assigned. For example, we can measure the similarity of one real number to another by computing their difference or ratio. If the height of one person is 180 cm and another is 181.2 cm then, for many purposes, we would probably like to consider these values to be equivalent, or at least similar, the difference being well less than 1%. We have no established *metric* for the measurement of similarity of names as we do for numbers, although metrics exist. How similar are SMITH and SMYTHE or TSCHAIKOWSKY and CZAJKOWSKI? One possible answer is achieved by counting the number of letters in common. SMITH and SMYTHE share 4 out of 5 or 6, depending on which count is used as denominator. The other names share 7 out of 10 or 12. Another approach is the use of digrams, or letter pairs, that are in common. SMITH has the digrams SM, MI, IT, TH, and SMYTHE has SM, MY, YT, TH, HE. This gives only two in common out of four or five, but if we recognize the similarity of I and Y, the count goes to four of five. TSCHAIKOWSKY and CZAJKOWSKI share 4 out of 11 or 9 digrams, but if we can equate Y and I or I and J, which look different but are pronounced similarly, the count goes to 7 of 11 or 9. Again, the method is sensitive to language and transliteration variations, but it gives a reasonable measure quickly.

Much of the effort of database design goes into selecting symbol systems or means of representing attributes to fit the needs of database users, including adhering to existing standards and customs. For example, it is usually more convenient for data processors always to refer to employees by number to avoid error. But this is socially unacceptable. Custom dictates that names may be augmented by numbers for more positive identification, but not replaced. Another custom, in the form of a U.S. federal government standard, but not mandatory for nongovernmental use, is the set of state abbreviations such as AK, AL, AZ, ... The remainder of this chapter is devoted to various ways to achieve uniqueness in attribute representation, or its opposite—using value systems that assign similar values to similar entities. We conclude with an examination of some of the problems of ambiguity in attribute value systems and methods of controlling them.

4.1.3 Other Character Strings

When it comes to ways of representing part numbers, classification codes, automobile license plate numbers, etc., there may be no limit to the characters set used. Certainly, there is no general rule. Therefore, we do not have generalized means of recognizing subfields or of morphological correctness. If the string is limited to words then it is possible to check spelling, as with word processors, or to find related words. Further, standard programs for truncation or classification by sound (see Section 4.3) may be used.

4.2 ⎯⎯⎯⎯⎯⎯⎯⎯⎯⎯⎯⎯⎯⎯⎯⎯⎯⎯⎯⎯⎯⎯⎯⎯⎯⎯⎯⎯

Class Relationships

aggregate

A common need in database usage is to group together records that share an attribute value, which means to create a subset of the database consisting of all records having a common (or similar) value of some attribute. The phrase DESERT SAND may conjure up different images to different people. In the manufacture of automobiles or household appliances, it might denote a color. Whether the color it is applied to is the color of the sand in any actual desert is not the point. The point is that any two products to which this value is attributed may be assumed to be colored alike. Two products with only slightly dissimilar colors may have quite different-appearing color names.

A major league baseball team might search its own and other teams' rosters for a first baseman who is over 6 ft tall, over 190 lb in weight, under 25 years of age, and has a batting average of at least .275. On the other hand, having set all these specifications, the team's manager might like to ask for a tolerance of 5–10% on all values, to avoid missing someone who bats well at .300 but is one year overage at 26. Both these examples illustrate that true precision is not achieved merely by writing down precise-looking values, and that overly precise values may not be what is wanted in a search.

4.2.1 Hierarchical Classification

The classification of the subject matter of books or of journal, magazine, or news articles is a major application of attribute design in which the values must show the degree to which entities are subject related. The most common way to do this is to use a hierarchical classification system. Biology, perhaps more than any other science, makes use of such classification systems for identifying plants and animals or their internal structures as well as for writing about them. The basic concept is that all subjects (or all living things) constitute a universe to be divided into a series of mutually exclusive subdivisions. *Mutually exclusive* means that an entity, assigned to one category, cannot also be assigned to another at the same level of detail; the one assignment excludes any others. This notion is extremely convenient but does not always correspond to reality or to everyone's perceptions. Few books will be seen by all readers to be on one and only one subject; hence, to belong in one and only one class.

Hierarchical classification also implies that, when a subclass has been assigned, the entity is identified as being a member of every superordinate, or higher, class in the structure. The superordinate class is often called a *parent*; a subordinate class, a *child*; and children of the same parent, *siblings*.

Figure 3.2 showed a segment of the classification schedule, or hierarchy of values, for the Dewey Decimal Classification, used mainly for books. Table 4.1 shows part of the system used in biology for living things.

Given a particular book, a library cataloger using the guidance provided in the classification schedule and other supporting documentation, as well as his or her experience with how similar books were previously classified, decides in which subclass to put the book. Also to be considered in this decision is how the users may perceive the subject. Whether a book on information retrieval or on database structure should be subordinated to library science or computer science may depend on which user group the book is intended for. The appropriate choice of classification is not a constant. Thus, the convenient assumption that a single classification value for each book is appropriate and will satisfy all user needs breaks down if we do not understand how the users will perceive the subject.

On the other hand, within a given user community the use of hierarchical classification does give an approximate measure of closeness (see Section 3.3.2) that can be of great value when the user is not sure in exactly what category the information being sought *should* be. So, as with much of information retrieval, the issue is not whether classification is "good" or "bad" but how well users understand what it means and what its limits are. It generally has to be recognized that when either a user or a cataloger assigns a classification code to an information entity, there is only a certain probability that this assigned

Table 4.1

Hierarchy in Biology[a]

Taxonomic group	Name
Kingdom	Animalia
Phylum	Chordata
Subphylum	Vertebrata
Class	Mammalia
Order	Primate
Family	Hominidae
Genus	*Homo*
Species	*sapiens*

[a]The taxonomic groups for animals, starting from the highest level, the kingdom Animalia, to the most specific, usually combining genus and species, and showing the hierarchy above *Homo sapiens*, our own species.

value is "right." By "right" is meant that this is the code value usually assigned to such information; hence, it will probably be used when searching for the item—another example of the community of users and the justified true belief issue.

4.2.2 Network Relationships

Sometimes a set of entities is related in a way that appears hierarchical at first glance, but does not have the characteristic that each entity belongs to one and only one superordinate entity. For example, a doctor in a hospital may have more than one patient, so the doctor–patient relationship may be viewed as a hierarchy of one level. But a patient may be treated by, hence in a sense be subordinated to, more than one doctor. In some communications networks, station or node A may talk with $A1$, $A2$, ..., but each of them may talk only with A. Station A, in turn, may be similarly subordinated to another station X, but other network configurations might permit $A1$ to talk directly with $A2$, or with B, a member of another branch of the hierarchy. In these cases, we use a structure called a *network*, although the other forms are also networks—an unfortunate multiple meaning of the term. These network concepts are illustrated in Fig. 4.1.

Basically, the concept of parent, as used in a hierarchy, is generalized in a network. A record in a network may have more than one parent and must somehow identify the parents of the entity and also the children and perhaps the other siblings.

4.2.3 Class Membership—Binary, Probabilistic, or Fuzzy

In Section 4.2.1 we introduced the complex question of uncertainty in the degree to which an entity has a particular attribute value (such as that it falls in subject class C). The reality is that we must consider the extent to which members of a particular user group *agree* that it has the attribute, or the extent to which it *measurably* has the attribute. For example, we can assert that the home language of a family in the Province of Québec is French, with probability 0.83, according to *Canadian Markets 1986*, and the melting point of copper is $1083.0 \pm 0.1°C$ according to the *McGraw-Hill Encyclopedia of Science and Technology*. Both these variables may have different values if measured under different circumstances. Subject classification is based on group concurrence. Demographic values are based on measurement by survey. Physical measurement under controlled laboratory conditions, using universal standards for units

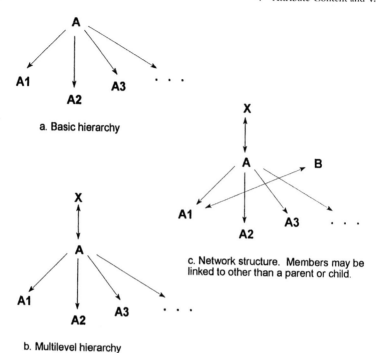

a. Basic hierarchy

c. Network structure. Members may be
linked to other than a parent or child.

b. Multilevel hierarchy

Figure 4.1

Forms of networks and hierarchies: The basic hierarchy (a) consists of a single "parent" with several subordinates. In a multilevel hierarchy (b) the parent of one element may be a subordinate of another. In a network structure (c), any element may "belong" to or be related to any other element.

and for methods of measuring, is generally accorded the highest level of acceptance by scientists. But, even slight variations in materials used or test conditions can result in different values. Scientists must learn to cope with these differences in reports. A vivid example of this is a famous graph showing the thermal conductivity of tungsten, at different temperatures, as measured by a large number of observers. The individual values were all plotted (Fig. 4.2) on a single set of axes and a smooth curve fitted to the data. The smooth curve is very smooth and suggests that values along it are the most reliable. But there are dozens of points *not* on the curve that someone, under some circumstances, thought reliable.

Binary Membership

When a person has been awarded a university degree, he or she may thereafter be classified as a graduate at the level of bachelor, master, or doctor.

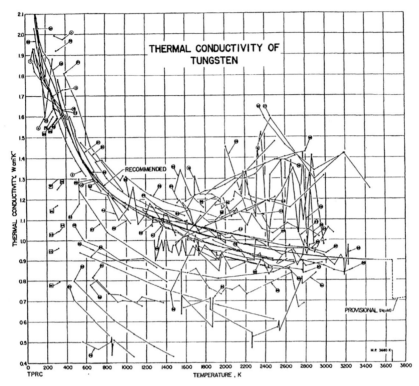

Figure 4.2
A graph of physical measurements showing variations around a smooth average: this chart portrays a number of individual measurements of the thermal conductivity of tungsten, indicating how many variations there can be of even so well-defined an attribute. (First published in *Journal of Physical and Chemical Reference Data.*)

Barring fraudulent credentials, there is no doubt about the *degree obtained*, which is a different matter from that of what the person *knows*, although the former is often used as a measure of the latter. When a bank opens an account for a customer, it may be a demand savings account, checking account, or time deposit. The bank will determine the classification with the customer's concurrence, and that is that. The decision may subsequently be changed but is not subject to evaluation or review; the customer may have meant to open a different type account, but there is no question about what type *was* opened. In these cases, we have examples of *binary membership* in a class or set. An entity is in a class or not. These are the only possibilities; there is no in-between possibility. Most bibliographic classification and indexing is of this form.

Fuzzy or Probabilistic Membership

When a library cataloger reads a 300-page book about information retrieval (IR), a decision has to be made about which class to place it in. There are at least two choices in the Library of Congress classification system: Z699 K37 and QA76. The choice is a matter of opinion, or the choice may be stated as a matter of probabilities. We could say that the book is in class Z699 K37 with probability 0.7 and in QA76 54 with probability 0.8. The probabilities are independent of each other and do not need to sum to 1.

Multiple classification is inconvenient as the basis for shelving books, since a given book can only be in one place at a time, and all of it, not seven-tenths of it, must be there. But the use of probabilities with subject headings might be quite helpful to a library user browsing in a catalog. The user would see that the cataloger was uncertain, and this provides the user with *more*, not *less*, information. While the book *cannot* be physically in two places at once, it *can* simultaneously have two applicable subject headings or classifications. Catalogers and users may have different opinions as to the probability or strength of membership of an entity in a class.

When we are uncertain whether or not an entity belongs in a particular set, we can create a *fuzzy set* (Kraft and Buell, 1983; Zadeh, 1965), one whose boundaries, content, or definition are incompletely specified, or fuzzy. This is an extension of the concept of probabilistic membership. We can do this by assigning the entity to the set and assigning a measure of strength of membership explicitly stated as an additional attribute.

If all book classifications were accompanied by probabilities, then we might do library searching by asking such questions as the following:

> "Get me all books that are in class C with probability greater than 0.5." Such a statement means the user will accept books with even a somewhat tenuous relation with the given class.
>
> "Get me all books in class $C1$ with probability greater than 0.9 or in class $C2$ with probability greater than 0.6." This means we want to be quite sure about $C1$ but are willing to accept a relatively obscure connection with subject $C2$.

If we list the possible classes in which an entity falls without assigning a probability *and* without implying certainty of membership, this is binary membership. The method is commonly used in assigning descriptors to articles in bibliographic files. As many as 10–20 terms may be used to describe the article, but there is no implication beyond the fact that the article is concerned with this term to some degree; no weights or degrees of certainty are assigned. In other words, the indexer may be implicitly acknowledging that variation in strength of association exists but no attempt was made to quantify its extent.

Yet another variation is to have a multilevel indicator, or weight, showing the extent to which an article belongs in a subject class, e.g., that the term describes the article to a major or minor extent. We shall meet fuzzy sets again, when we discuss the logic of searching in Chapter 10.

4.3

Transformations of Values

Earlier, we posed the question of how similar are such names as SMITH and SMYTHE or TSCHAIKOWSKY and CZAJKOWSKI. Similar questions are those of determining how close one numeric measure or one fingerprint is to another. Some kinds of symbols may have so much variation that, as is the case with fingerprints, even two records of the same finger, taken at different times, may show some differences if we consider all detail. One way to compare or match them is to transform the original symbol into a higher-order or more general one, that is, to abstract the important characteristics, which is what we do with the subject matter of a text when preparing an abstract or catalog record.

With numeric data we most commonly do this by establishing a series of value ranges, or class intervals, such as reporting taxpayer incomes in such ranges as $0–9999, $10,000–19,999, etc. Hierarchic codes that represent a sequence of nodes in a hierarchical structure can be truncated for comparison. This is commonly done in libraries that use a truncated version of the classification code to inform users where to find books in the various classes.

4.3.1 Transformation of Words by Stemming

Truncation can be used with words to achieve a quick approximation to the word root. A word for which we want to find an exact or near match may be written as a stem or root word, and the retrieval system asked to find words in storage that match the root. For example, the root ELECTR can be said to match the complete words ELECTRIC, ELECTRICAL, ELECTRICITY, ELEC-TROMAGNETIC, ELECTRON, and ELECTRONIC. It will also, unfortunately, match ELECTRA, the name of a character from Greek mythology, a play based on that character, and a now-obsolete airplane. Logically, we are saying that we wish to create a set of all records containing the word root in any context. Two types of procedures are commonly used to determine the root of a word. The first determines the semantic root and would equate BOX with BOXES and perhaps, depending on the rules in use, equate RECEIPT with RECEIVE. The second (Section 4.3.2) is to spell words alike (usually names) that *sound* alike.

There is no single procedure for determining the root of a word. Rather, a set of rules and procedures is established and each word to be stemmed is tested by all the rules to see if they apply. We briefly review two sets of rules and procedures devised by Lovins (1968) and Paice (1990).

Lovins' Method

This involves a two-step operation: first, the removal of an ending, then the possible transformation of the ending of the remaining word. Note that the result is not always the best possible root, but in such cases consistency may be more important than elegance.

A list of endings is compiled, and for each a condition code is specified governing conditions under which the ending is removed. The list is in descending order of length of the ending, and then alphabetical. This means that a longer ending containing a shorter one (as ARIZABILITY contains ABILITY) would be eliminated first. Examples are shown in Table 4.2.

Condition code A in the table specifies no restrictions on stemming. Condition code B specifies that the remaining stem, after removal of the ending, must be at least three letters long; C requires the remaining stem to be at least four characters or more.

Table 4.2
Endings in Lovins' Stemming Algorithm[a]

Length	Ending	Condition code
11	ALISTICALLY	B
	ARIZABILITY	A
	IZATIONALLY	B
10	ANTIALNESS	A
	ARISATIONS	A
	ARIZATIONS	A
	ENTIALNESS	A
9	ALLICALLY	C
	ANTANEOUS	A
4	ABLE	A
	ABLY	A
	AGES	B
	ALLY	B
3	ISM	B
1	E	A

[a]This is a sample of word endings or suffixes arranged in descending order of length and alphabetically within a length group. This way, the longest suffix match is made first.

Using Table 4.2, the word REALISTICALLY would be reduced to RE by removal of ALISTICALLY, but for the rule for condition code B. This says not to remove the ending if the remaining word would have fewer than three letters. Instead, a shorter ending would be sought, such as ISTICALLY, giving the preferred root REAL. The word BELIEVE becomes BELIEV, by truncation, and this would later be transformed to BELIEF by a rule not in our abbreviated table, but see the following list of rules. The word ISOMETRIC would first become ISOMETR and then ISOMETER. CONSTABLE would become CONST, and TABLE become T because condition code A specifies no minimal remaining stem, although another rule might have specified that no word should be shortened to a single letter.

A set of transformational rules modifies the ending of a word after a stem is removed.

a. If a potential stem ends with a consonant other than S, followed by the letter S, then delete the S:

STEMS → STEM

but

STRESS → STRESS

b. If a word ends in ES, drop the terminal S. (This rule has difficulty with plural words of Greek origin for which the singular ends in IS, as THESIS → THESES.) Other rules could be written specifically to deal with these Greek words. Some examples are

PLACES → PLACE

LIKES → LIKE

INDICES → INDICE (This would be an error unless
    further processing were used to recognize the Latin morphology.)

SYNTHESES → SYNTHESE (Similar error, this time with Greek morphology.)

c. As endings, IEV → IEF and METR → METER. This works well with English words, not with Russian, such as PROKOFIEV.

d. If a word ends in ING, delete the ING unless the remaining word after deletion consists only of one letter or of TH. Thus

THINKING → THINK

SINGING → SING

SING → SING (No change.)

THING → THING (No change.)

PRECEDING → PRECED (Error—not a meaningful word; needs further
processing.)

SLING → SL (Error—not a meaningful word,)

Note that the computed root of PRECEDING would be the nonword PRECED.
The E could be restored by another rule calling for adding E if, after stemming,
a word ends in ED, ET, or ES, but then MEETING → MEET → MEETE, which
we do not want but could eliminate with a rule about double vowels preceding
the terminal consonant. It is easy to see how rules can proliferate.

e. If a word ends with ED, preceded by a consonant, delete the ED unless
this leaves only a single letter:

ENDED → END
RED → RED
PROCEED → PROCEED (ED not preceded by a consonant.)
PROCEEDED → PROCEED

f. If, after removal of an ending, a word now ends in BB, DD, . . . , TT,
remove one of the doubled letters. Thus, EMBEDDED → EMBEDD by removal
of an ending, then EMBEDD → EMBED by this rule.

g. If a word ends in ION, remove the ION unless the remaining word has
two or fewer letters. If the last letter of the stem is a consonant and the letter
preceding it is a vowel, add an E:

DIRECTION → DIRECT
POLLUTION → POLLUTE
PLANTATION → PLANTATE (Error?)
ZION → ZION
SCION → SCION
ANION → ANION
CATION → CATE (Error.)

Note that CATION is a made-up word, the combination of CATHODE and
ION, and so does not have the usual kind of semantic root.

A workable stemming program would probably require at least 10–
20 rules (hundreds are possible), including large numbers of provisions for special cases and irregular words. The program would probably also have logic for
iterative application of some of the rules, such as transforming DIRECTIONS to
DIRECTION to DIRECT. Programs to remove prefixes are possible but tend to
be not very productive for search purposes. ACCEPTS, DECEPTION, and RE-
CEPTION can be easily stemmed to ACCEPT, DECEPT, and RECEPT. Then,
removal of the prefixes would yield a common stem of CEPT. All three words

are derived from a Latin root meaning *to take*, but the modern meanings are lost in these transformations.

The Paice and Husk Method

This is a more modern stemming procedure which "is iterative, and uses just one table of rules; each [of which] may specify either deletion or replacement of an ending" (Paice, 1990, p. 56). A simple example is a rule written as SEI3Y>, which states that if the ending IES (written backwards in the rule statement for easier detection by a program) is found, replace the last three letters with the letter Y. A later rule states that if the detected string (form is the actual Paice–Husk term) starts with a vowel, then at least two letters must remain after stemming, e.g., by rule GNI3 we convert OWING → OW, but SING → SING.

There have been many stemming algorithms, none perfect. In general, the more rules of the types illustrated, the greater the probability of correctly stemming a word. But, inevitably, mistakes will be made, as often as not owing to the vagaries of natural language, especially English. For example, as noted above, English words taken more or less directly from Greek, like THESES, do not follow the usual rules for removing terminal ES. Using English rules, we would probably convert THESES into THESE, instead of THESIS. We can readily transform DIRECTION to DIRECT and POLLUTION to POLLUTE (add the E after stemming because the next-to-last letter is a vowel), but the same rule gives the transformation PLANTATION → PLANTATE, a word that while nonexistent seems reasonable. Also, the more rules, the more expensive it is to do stemming, so perfection is rarely sought. Paice states (1990, p. 59) "there *are* people who tinker with rules, but they do so in an *ad hoc* fashion; no systematic work on stemmer optimisation seems to have appeared in the literature."

4.3.2 Sound-Based Transformation of Words

A different approach is to transform the spelling of words so that words that *sound alike* can be made to *look alike* typographically to a computer or human reader. This would be particularly useful when names are translated or transliterated from one language to another. A system called *Soundex* (Steuart, 1990, pp. xii–xv) is commonly used by police and motor vehicle agencies in North America to encode names, and is used in some database software as well. While it deals with the expected sounds of the letters, it deals with only the letters, not the actual sounds. Thus, it really encodes more what the names *look* like than what they *sound* like. The transformation is culturally biased because of different pronunciations by people of different national origins.

Soundex is a mapping of many onto a few values. The original version reduces any name to one alphabetic character followed by three numeric digits, although it can be varied both in length of code and technique of mapping. The basic rules are simple. Retain the first initial of the name. Then convert subsequent letters according to the rules shown in Table 4.3. Use no more than three digits and fill with zeroes if the name does not otherwise require three. MORAN translates into M650: initial M, O not coded, R maps to 6, A not coded, and N maps to 5. Then fill with one zero to make three digits. The similar names MARAN, MARIN, MOREN, and MORRIN all map to the same value.

SMITH maps to S530 as does SMYTHE, but under these rules SCHMIDT becomes S253. The German form, SCHMIDT, calls for recognition that SCH often indicates an alternate sound for S. If SCH were coded as S, then since D and T are treated alike in Soundex, SCHMIDT would be equated with SMITH. The word SCHOOL, also derived from the German, is pronounced in English by S followed by the K sound for CH. SCHEDULE uses the SK sound in American English, but the SH sound in England. TSCHAIKOWSKY (Russian transliteration) maps to T222 and CZAJKOWSKI (Polish) to C222. The system is imperfect, mainly because it does not recognize these differences in the way names from languages other than English are treated. Soundex does work often, is easy to use, and can be modified to eliminate or reduce some of the problems illustrated. It could be used as a technique for encoding or compacting ordinary words used as descriptors in a record. The code is not unique, but the mem-

Table 4.3
Transformation of Letters in Soundex[a]

Letter	Numeric equivalent
B, F, P, V	1
C, G, J, K, Q, S, X, Z	2
D, T	3
L	4
M, N	5
R	6
A, E, H, I, O, U, W, Y	Not coded

[a]Individual letters are given the numeric equivalents shown. Note that vowels are not coded and that several consonants may have the same numeric value. Thus, many names can be transformed into the same code. If there are not enough consonants to fill three positions in the code, fill with zeros. Hence, SKY becomes S2000, LEDGER becomes L326. Code double consonants as one occurrence.

ory saved might be enough to overcome this defect. See also the discussion of signatures in Chapter 9.

4.3.3 Transformation of Words by Meaning

The more or less mechanical transformations of words by stemming or sound-based encoding are just that—mechanical. They are based on structure or sound, not meaning. Another approach to transforming words so that they can be matched with similar ones is by use of dictionaries or thesauri that explicitly state the relationship of one word to another. For example, a document might mention HOSTILITIES, and a query ARMED CONFLICT, both meaning essentially the same thing. A dictionary or thesaurus might declare that the official or canonical term is WAR, which is treated as a synonym of these others and is the preferred or even required term in the context of a given database or publication.

An "ordinary" dictionary has definitions of words, that is, other words or phrases that try to convey the meaning of the entry word. It may also explicitly identify synonyms or antonyms, as well as other, related words which it identifies by such uses as "See..." or "More under...." A thesaurus for ordinary use would tend to be specialized, listing words that are synonymous, antonymous, even rhyming with an entry word, but not giving definitions. Thesauri intended for computer use are normally highly structured, giving for each entry word other words related in any or a combination of the following ways, each relationship followed by one or more other words:

- *Broader term*—TERM1 is a broader term than TERM2 if the meaning of TERM2 is included in that of TERM1. In common usage, SCIENCE is a broader term than PHYSICS.
- *Narrower term*—if TERM1 is broader than TERM2, then TERM2 is narrower than TERM1. PHYSICS is a narrower term under SCIENCE.
- *Related term*—most commonly used to indicate a possible near synonym in some contexts and could be used to indicate siblings (terms sharing the same immediately broader term). DATABASE and RETRIEVAL are related terms in the context of COMPUTER SCIENCE, but RETRIEVAL has other, unrelated meanings as well. PHYSICS and CHEMISTRY are siblings, under the common broader term SCIENCE.
- *Use*—sometimes words included in a thesaurus are not, or are no longer, official controlled terms, but they may be listed for the convenience of users. We might have an entry such as "PERSONAL COMPUTER: use MICROCOMPUTER," simply to indicate that the former, however commonly used in natural language, is not the approved term in

the database. Or "RADIO ENGINEERING: use ELECTRONIC ENGI-
NEERING" to reflect a change in usage.

Used for—the converse of *use*. If MICROCOMPUTER is shown as the
preferred term instead of PERSONAL COMPUTER, then there would
be a thesaurus entry showing "microcomputer: used for PERSONAL
COMPUTER."

What happens if a word appears in a text but is not in the thesaurus? Such
a word could not be used in an index that was restricted to canonical terms
only. Too rigid a rule prevents new terms from gaining currency in indexes.
A solution by the ERIC database is to allow only canonical terms in an attribute
called descriptor but any term an indexer chooses in a separate attribute called
identifier.

A very large thesaurus called WordNet has been created at Princeton University (Miller, 1995) specifically for use with computer systems, not necessarily
restricted to information retrieval applications. WordNet provides information
about relationships among words, not definitions of meaning. It is not a printed
work. Its intent is to provide information on current, not historical, usage. This
implies a need for frequent updating.

WordNet consists of a large number (over 166,000 in 1995) of word pairs,
consisting of an entry and a related word, plus, of course, the relationship or syntactic category. Words listed as entries are nouns, verbs, adjectives, and adverbs.
The semantic relationships noted are the following:

Synonymy—the related word is similar to the entry, as (PIPE, TUBE).

Antonymy—the terms are opposite in meaning, as (WET, DRY).

Hyponymy—one term is under or subordinate to the other, as (MAPLE,
TREE).

Meronymy—one term is a part of the other, as (TWIG, TREE).

Troponymy—one term describes a manner of the other, as (WHISPER,
SPEAK).

Entailment—one term implies the other, as (DIVORCE, MARRY).

Such a work could include the entire hierarchical structure of a machine,
sometimes called a parts explosion, as (KEY, KEYBOARD), (KEYBOARD, COM-
PUTER) or (VALVE, TIRE), (TIRE, WHEEL), (WHEEL, AXLE ASSEMBLY), . . . ,
which are much oversimplified. WordNet could also be set up to recognize different relationships in different contexts, such as that *leaf* has a different meaning
in printing than in furniture design or botany. This calls for highly skilled development and use. Will information retrieval system users take full advantage
of such a resource, if offered? Will they insist on its being offered? It is too early
to tell.

4.3.4 Transformation of Graphics

We can search text for the occurrence of words, codes, or phrases, or can determine subject matter from word occurrences. But with today's technology, we are not that far along in determining the content of graphic images. Pictures can be digitized in the sense that color or grey scale at specific positions within the picture can be represented digitally. Thus, we have a digital set of coordinates, x, y, and the color or grey scale represented as a number from 0 to n. But what do these pixels represent?

There are two ways of processing text that are far ahead of what can be done with graphics. In one, a searcher provides words and the search system converts these to related words by stemming, looking up in a thesaurus, or finding others that frequently co-occur. In the second, the system can form an abstract of the contents of the text. In graphics, we can do some of the first but not the second, except in very limited domains. In general, we must first describe content by use of text, and then search the text. Since different indexers may see quite different images, especially in nonrepresentational art, the limitations are severe. A review of indexing methods for images is found in Rasmussen (1997).

In a few specialized applications, however, successful storage, search, and retrieval of graphic images is possible. It is possible to prepare a generalized representation of some object, then search a graphic file for occurrences of this pattern. For example, we could describe a cow graphically, then search for a match. But no standardized example of a cow exists to match every artist's vision of one.

Fingerprinting is probably the outstanding example of successful graphic IR. Fingerprints are made up of a series of ridge lines in that portion of the skin called *friction skin*, occurring on the hands and feet. These ridge lines tend to form into general patterns known as arches, loops, and whorls as in Fig. 4.3a. In addition to the general pattern, there are many fine details, called *minutiae*, that can be recorded, digitized, and used as the basis for information retrieval, i.e., for finding a matching print in a file, given a print to use as the basis for a search. The print used for searching might come from a recently arrested person charged with a crime or from an accident victim for whom identification is sought. It also might come from a *latent print* found at the scene of a crime.

The minutiae recorded consist of such features as *ridge endings*, *bifurcations* (splitting of a ridge into two), *islands*, or *lakes*, illustrated in Fig. 4.3b (*Science of Fingerprints*, 1979, p. 29). Islands are ridges of very short length, and lakes are formed when a ridge bifurcates, then rejoins. The original fingerprint filing and search systems concentrated on the overall patterns. The more modern systems

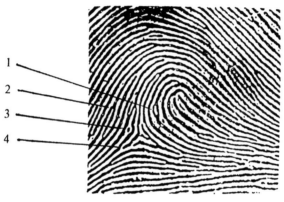

Figure 4.3

Characteristics of fingerprints: (a) Some of the common general forms: arch, loop, and whorl.
(b) Minutiae within a pattern in which can be seen examples of (1) *a lake* (a small white space
surrounded by ridges), (2) a *bifurcation*, (3) an *island* (a short ridge, surrounded by white space), and
(4) a *ridge ending*. (Photos courtesy of U.S. Federal Bureau of Investigation.)

also use minutiae. By plotting the location and type of the minutiae of a print,
enough information can be recorded to distinguish it from almost all other
prints. It is not necessary that the mechanical search retrieve a unique match. It
is good enough, even preferable, for the search to retrieve a modest number of
possibly matching prints, so that a human expert can make and testify in court
to the final decision about whether or not a match has occurred. We do about
the same in text searching. We do not expect a retrieval system to get exactly
the one item we are searching for; we are normally content to retrieve a small
set from which we select the best.

Minutiae will vary, even on prints of the same person, taken at different times and under different circumstances. The skill of the technician in inking and impressing the hand, or scratches and the like on the fingers can cause minor variations. Thus, the algorithm used by a computer for matching prints must be one that looks for a degree of match, not an exact match, between prints. Essentially, it looks for a fuzzy set of matching prints.

This type of system works because, in spite of the complexity of the image, users are able to identify exactly what aspects of the image they are interested in, and then to devise a means of measuring and recording those aspects, namely, minutiae and ridge patterns. With something like news photographs we can, at best, describe in words the principal object in view or the place and date of the photograph. We cannot identify everything of possible future interest, such as an interesting (as determined later) background object.

There are other examples of the need for searching and matching of graphic images. Again in police work, it would help to be able to match descriptions of a face with stored photographs. While police artists are sometimes successful in depicting a face based on eyewitness accounts, such descriptions are often unreliable. Is there a method of automatically scanning a photograph to record features objectively that can later be used to search for a match, from a new photo or a description? Work is being done, but no solution is readily at hand at this time.

In trademark law it would help to be able to find any trademark matching an existing or potential one. When a company wishes to create and register a new trademark, it must conduct a search of previously registered marks to assure that no duplicate or near duplicate exists. Further, it is the responsibility of trademark owners to protect their rights from infringement by others. There are no trademark police impartially looking for violations; hence, many companies, in addition to verifying the lack of a match for a proposed new mark, routinely search for near matches to their existing marks, looking for possible violations. But, again, there is no way at this time for a computer to match the graphics. The searcher must be content with a search of a verbal or encoded *description* of a trademark, with the final matching being done by the searcher.

4.3.5 Transformation of Sound

In Section 4.3.1 we described the Soundex system for encoding letters according to their sounds. This is basically the transformation of one alphabetic symbol into another. But there are problems caused by multiple possible sounds for some letters and the same sound generated by more than one letter. In music the original symbols, the musical notes, are less ambiguous auditory

Figure 4.4
The Barlow–Morgenstern music indexing method: the musical notes for a line of a Smetana opera are shown. Its encoding would be EEBBCC#.

symbols. The conventional musical notation is itself but an encoding of the sound. Still, this notation can be quite complex, and the same piece may be represented differently to suit different instruments or concepts of the arranger. A common problem in musical IR is that a searcher knows or can hum a few bars of a theme or opening line and wishes to find the name and composer of the work.

Two somewhat similar methods have been devised for providing an index to first lines of music. In one (Barlow and Morgenstern, 1976) notes are represented in print by letters corresponding to the lettered positions on the musical scale, but the timing of the notes is not represented. Further, the transformation is based on the assumption that the music has first been transposed into the key of C. Then, an index of approximately the first 12–16 notes is prepared. It is easily possible for more than one composition to produce the same notation, but the assumption is, as with graphics, there will be so few matches that coupling the notation with additional information such as the type of composition (operatic aria or popular song) or the name of the composer will quickly narrow the possibilities. Figure 4.4 shows the encoding of the first line of an aria from Smetana's *The Two Widows*.

A second indexing system (Parsons, 1975) was designed to minimize the musical knowledge required for its use. No transcribing of keys is required and, if only a mental image of the melody is available, the exact notes are not needed. In this method, the first note of a line is always represented by the symbol *. Thereafter, all that is recorded is whether the next note goes up or down the scale or repeats the previous one. Thus the symbols used are *, U, D, and R. Again, this method does not give unique retrieval, but is intended to enable a searcher to find a small number of possibilities quickly. Figure 4.5 shows the encoding of the opening bars of *God Save the Queen* (or *America*).

Figure 4.5
The Parsons music indexing method: the musical notes for *God Save the Queen* (or *America*). Their encoding would be *RUDUU URUDDD.

Downie (1997) has an experimental system that allows for indexing of the entire work, treating a sequence of notes, an *n-gram*, essentially as a word, then using a text retrieval system to find any indexed work that includes an n-gram the searcher can supply, which may occur anywhere in the musical piece. The length of the n-gram and the detailed nature of the coding of a note can vary.

Both these methods illustrate the same central point, which also applies to graphics and, less obviously, to all other forms of retrieval. Retrieval does not require that a unique match be found for a query. A surrogate record may be used instead of the original—as fingerprint minutiae instead of the complete print image, up or down coding instead of the original notes, or title, author, or subject heading instead of a text. If the use of these surrogates saves enough storage space and search time and produces few enough output records, then they are adequate.

4.4

Uniqueness of Values

While we often want attribute values to reflect membership in a set or class, so as to associate entities with like attributes, we also sometimes have the opposite need: to separate each entity from all others. Particularly when the entities of a file are people, it is convenient, important, and may even be legally necessary to clearly distinguish each person from all others. In the United States and Canada there is no universal identifying number, a number such that each citizen or resident has one and only one number, which no one else has. There is the U.S. social security number and the Canadian social insurance number, but these were not intended as universal identifiers and their issuing agencies prefer that they not be so used. If we had such a system then it could be used to advantage by anyone with a database of people, whether employers' personnel files, bank deposit records, credit card accounts, or school, police, medical, or tax records. There would be no need for each database owner to create a new numbering system for the people represented, and, if necessary, it would be quite easy to find information about a person in someone else's database, because the one necessary key would be known.

The very universality that would be so convenient for record keepers is found abhorrent by many people in North America because it takes away some degree of anonymity and therefore of protection from prying or from errors in interpretation. We all make mistakes, whether it be an unpaid bill, a poor grade in school, or a youthful scrape with the police. The inability of such seekers after personal history as future employers or motor vehicle agencies to readily find this embarrassing information is a protection for us. As long as this is so, the opportunity exists to start over. Not every case is so dramatic as that of Benjamin Franklin, who ran away from an indentured apprenticeship in Boston to a spectacularly productive new life in Philadelphia. But most of us, if we have had a dispute with a department store over a bill, do not want an allegation of credit unreliability to be made available to every other business we might wish to deal with. This is essentially the reason behind laws that prohibit release of the names of juveniles arrested by the police or even convicted in the courts.

If there is going to be an identifying number, even for use within one organization (a student or employee number), it is worth some effort to prevent duplicate assignments and to reduce the likelihood of error in transcribing or transmitting the number. One way to do this is to include in the number a *check digit*. A simple example is to decide on, say, a 10-digit number, add together the first 9 individual digits, then use the units digit of the sum as the 10th digit of the identifier. The U.S. social security number (ssn) consists of 9 digits, usually written in the form 123-45-6789. The sum of this sample of digits is 45 and the units (rightmost) digit of the sum is 5. Hence, we might use the 10-digit number 123-45-6789-5 as a more reliable ssn. If a single digit is misread or mistyped, say as 124-45-6789-5 then the check digit is wrong (it would be computed as 6 here), and the existence (but not the location) of an error would be detected. We could also include the year of birth, or a code for it, as part of the identifying number, as done in Sweden (Westin, p. 261). This would reduce the likelihood of mistakenly using a 2-year-old's number for a 60-year-old person. Date of birth is less useful in a military or school setting, because the ages of most of the people involved tend to fall within a relatively narrow range. However, one of the issues in identifier design (Secretary's, 1973, pp. 109–113) is whether or not the number or code should include any personal information at all about the identified person.

The simplest method of assigning numbers is sequentially: the next entity for which we create a record gets the next number in numerical sequence. This is conventional when there are no privacy issues involved and no severe penalty for error in transcription (hence no need for redundancy). Libraries do this with acquisition numbers for books. The acquisition number contains no information about subject matter or author identification. It serves solely to distinguish one book from another, even two copies of the same work, and is used largely in accounting and inventory operations. This is contrasted with a call number used as the basis for placing a book on a shelf and composed of an indicator of subject matter and of the author's last initial.

4.5 ——————————————————————————

Ambiguity of Attribute Values

While unique identifiers are used for some applications and indicators of class membership, for others, in yet other cases there is uncertainty about values or meanings, causing confusion to a human reader or a computer program, or both. One source of ambiguity is semantic—the meaning of symbols. *Synonyms* are two or more different symbols having essentially the same meaning. *Homonyms* or *homographs* are two or more symbols that either sound or appear alike but have different meanings. *Anaphora* (Liddy, 1990) are words, such as *it*, whose function it is to represent other words.

Synonymy is often context dependent. In general usage the verbs *counsel* and *advise* mean essentially the same thing, as do *street* and *road*. But we do not ask which street to take to get from Indianapolis to Chicago, and we retain legal counsel, not advice when in trouble with the law.

Examples of homonyms are *red* (the color) and *read* (the past tense of the verb *to read*), and of homographs, *pound* (the verb) and *pound* (the monetary unit of Great Britain).

Consider the color word *red* and some related words: *cerise, scarlet,* and *crimson.* To an artist these may have quite different, or at least differentiable, denotations, which are well understood and can be readily communicated to other artists. To the average person, these words may all have the same denotation, or we may understand that there are "supposed" to be differences, but we really do not know what they are. Similarly, a news article might describe a person as *imposing*, which will not bring up the same image to all readers. Worse, if a user tries to retrieve news articles about imposing people he may not find any, or may find very few and be unable to comprehend the commonality of meaning of *imposing* in this set of articles. For this reason, in describing the content of books or of journal articles or the like, libraries try to use standardized phrases or a controlled vocabulary to do so.

A *controlled vocabulary* is one for which some authority decides which words or codes are to be used and defines the meanings of these terms or the relationships among them. Although use of a controlled vocabulary cannot guarantee that each reader or cataloger will select the same terms to describe an item, at least each term *can* be explained as to assumed meaning and differentiated from other terms; hence, a controlled vocabulary causes each term to be unique in meaning, for those who understand the vocabulary and its documentation. We shall discuss means of achieving vocabulary control and some implications of its use later in this chapter.

The homonym or homograph problem is generally worse for computers than for humans because humans rely heavily on context to resolve ambiguity.

The very word *mean* has a number of different, unrelated meanings in common usage: it is a noun in statistics (average), a verb in linguistics (to denote or connote), and an adjective in describing an unpleasant personality ("a mean junkyard dog").

In IR, the existence of homographs suggests that the occurrence of a symbol in an attribute value may not mean that the entity actually has the attribute that could be inferred—a person of mean character versus a person of mean height versus a person whose example can mean much to us. Homographs, therefore, force us to consider different ways that (1) a concept or attribute we wish to search for might have been expressed in the records to be searched and (2) a value might occur that could appear to be what is wanted, but is not. In the first case, we would search for alternative values, e.g., AVERAGE, MEDIAN, or MODE. In the second, we would be aware that MEAN could retrieve completely irrelevant records. We might have to use other terms to establish context. If we want material about mean heights of people, we might want to look as well for such words as AVERAGE, STATISTICAL, or WEIGHT. Only AVERAGE is a synonym in this group. The other words help establish a context of statistics about persons' bodies.

Although simplistic rules for use of pronouns make them appear unambiguous, such is often not the case, and the resolution of anaphora is a problem of great difficulty in information retrieval. In the sentence, "The dog wagged its tail," the meaning of *its* is clear, and its use here is grammatically correct—it refers to the most recent noun. In, "Will everyone remove their hats," the meaning of *their* is clear to most readers, but grammatically incorrect because it does not agree in number with the noun it actually represents. This could make it difficult to form a correct association by computer. In the sentence, "Books have illustrations, but their meanings may be unclear," it is not at all clear whether *their* refers to *books* or *illustrations*. Information retrieval systems permitting natural-language queries tend to ignore anaphora.

Another form of ambiguity arises from syntax. The fact that a word occurs in a text, even aside from homographic considerations, does not mean that the text is *about* that word. For example, the word *earthquake* occurs in this book. It has just been used in an example. This does not mean that the book should be said to be about that subject.

In summary, uncertainty can creep into recorded information or its interpretation, however carefully we design or edit. There can always be someone who interprets words differently or who does not read instructions. There can always be typographical errors, even if we do devise error-detecting techniques to find most of them. As we shall point out later, ambiguity in language can be a great *benefit*, although achieved at a *cost*. We cannot eliminate it. We must learn to live with it and even to take advantage of it.

4.6 _____

Indexing of Text

In mathematics and computer science, *indexing* is a procedure or method for accessing information. In mathematics the notation x_i tells us that there is a sequence of values of the variable x—a one-dimensional array. The value of i identifies a specific element, and i is called an *index*. In computer science the concept of indexing is more general. An index may also be an array or a file whose elements point to elements of another file. If there is a file whose records are in order by ssn, there may be a separate file (see inverted files in Section 6.4.2), each record of which contains a name and a ssn and is in order by name. This, too, is an index.

Most professional books or textbooks have a subject index at the end and may have a separate author index as well, listing each author cited and the page on which the citation occurs. Even the table of contents of a book is, in a sense, an index. It lists the numbers and names of chapters and sections and the pages on which they begin, giving a good general sense of subject content.

In library science an index has a still broader meaning, as discussed in Section 1.6. To index a book, journal article, or technical report is to record the values of various attributes expected to be used as a basis for searching. If the attribute is subject, then this form of index functions like a book's subject index. If the attribute is the author or a named person in the text, then the index functions like a book's author index. Traditionally, a great deal of effort has gone into subject indexing, especially of journal literature and technical reports.

There are three types of subject-describing attributes: *classification codes* (Section 4.2), *subject headings*, and individual words descriptive of a subject, often called *key words*. The term *descriptor* can be applied to any of these but is most often used for the latter two.

Subject headings are taken from a prepared list of headings. In North America the most common such list, for books, is the *Library of Congress Subject Headings* (1998). Typically, two or three headings from this collection are made a part of a library catalog record for a book. For a journal article or report, there are usually separate sets of subject headings for each discipline or profession. There is the *Thesaurus of ERIC Descriptors* (1995) in education, *Medical Subject Headings (MESH)* (1987) in medicine, and the *Ei Thesaurus* (1993) in engineering. The vocabulary and needs of each discipline may be so different that these sets of subject headings may bear little resemblance to each other, except structurally. An article on the effect of asbestos materials on the health of children in school buildings may be indexed from totally different points of view in the separate professions of medicine, education, and architecture.

At the end of World War II, a great quantity of scientific literature (produced as part of the war effort) had never been made public. In the 1950s the Cold War triggered a spurt of scientific and technological activity, and documentation. During the period from 1945 to the 1960s, attention began to be paid to the needs of *subject control*, or indexing of the literature (Becker and Hayes, 1963; Bourne, 1963; Committee on Government Operations, 1960; Herner, 1984; Weinberg, 1963). By some definitions, *information science* was equated with *documentation*, which, in turn, was largely devoted to methods of indexing.

Gradually, the emphasis began to shift from indexing toward *retrieval*, as the volume of material required not just the creation of descriptive records that could be published in book form (such as *Chemical Abstracts* or *Index Medicus*) but mechanical assistance in retrieval, as well. There is no sharp delineation in time between these emphases. Indeed, one of the landmark publications in information retrieval was published in 1945 (Bush, 1945); but, on the other hand, not everyone agrees that the shift in emphasis has ever occurred.

As computers became faster and less expensive, it has become feasible, successively, to include a natural-language abstract as part of a bibliographic record (for display only); then to permit search of the abstract for any word or combination of words occurring in its text; then to allow use of word roots and specific sequences of words in a search; and to find words that are related to but not equal to words used in a query. Now we have many databases that contain the full text of books, journals, or newspapers. In a retrieval system such as the WWW, where information can be added by anyone at any time, it would be possible to employ previous users' evaluations of records as index terms. These might not have any of the terms the user originally specified as necessary.

Further, today the complete texts of written works are likely to be included in a database that once might have had only a catalog or index record. This, of course, means that every word used by the author, every combination of words and pattern of frequency of use of the words is available to the searcher or to a program operating on the searcher's behalf. These—the more complete information plus the intelligence that can be built into a computer program—make it less and less important for the searcher to rely on formal index terms.

We have, then, a change in the basic paradigm of IR. Earlier, retrieval largely involved the user seeking the terms that had previously been assigned to the text as the means to associate his or her query with stored records. More recently, the work of association is done at the time of the search, not beforehand. Indexing is still important, because if a user *does* understand how the index works, a great deal of time can be saved.

4.7
Control of Vocabulary

We use a controlled vocabulary to reduce ambiguity in indexing or describing an entity, whether at the time of creating a record, of searching, or both. Controlling a vocabulary means to limit the number of possible values that can be used for attributes. Reducing the number of words or codes available for description and providing comments, hints, or instructions for their use can, and should, reduce "error." "Error" here may simply mean that two different people may select different terms to describe the same entity. It is not a matter of attributing fault or failure to either party. Lack of consistency among indexers has been a traditional problem, in IR, long before computers came upon the scene.

4.7.1 Elements of Control

To achieve a controlled vocabulary, the following elements are necessary.

1. *The vocabulary*—this could be a list of words to be used, classification codes, subject headings, names of colors, etc. The list must be limited. In natural language, the language, itself, can be used to define new words, or words can simply be used in new ways on the assumption that people will understand. Terms from the 1950s or 1960s, such as MCCARTHYISM or STALINISM are still in use and generally understood, while HOOVERVILLE from the 1930s is probably lost on many modern readers. Of importance is that the vocabulary be able to describe the domain of entities and attributes and that it avoid or come close to avoiding having more than one term with a common meaning.

2. *Explanatory notes*—these are guides to help with users' term selection. They are necessary. We cannot rely solely on the users' knowledge of subject matter or skill in natural language because the controlled language is *not* natural, and controlled usages may reflect the jargon of a narrow discipline or industry. The controlled language certainly limits vocabulary and almost always limits syntax as well. The whole point is that, in natural language, there is almost always more than one way to express a concept, but, in a controlled language, there is not *supposed* to be more than one way to do so; hence, users may need help in finding that way. The most common forms of help are dictionaries or thesauri that list the words in use, relationships among them, and explanations to help in term selection.

3. *Communication*—a vocabulary and thesaurus are not enough. Language is a tool of communication. There must be communication among the users of a language to evolve a common understanding of usage and interpretation.

It is not enough for a group of record creators to use a language skillfully. The searchers must also be able to use it skillfully.

A thesaurus displays the word list, relationships among terms, and scope notes or guides to usage. Controlled languages change, as do any other languages, but not so quickly or readily. New terms must be added; archaic ones discarded; perhaps others redefined. The changes are relatively easy for a record creator to adapt to, since it is necessary only to keep up to date on the changes and begin new usage as soon as it is official. Usually, all changes to a thesaurus are rapidly disseminated to record creators.

It is not common for a database to be retroactively changed whenever its thesaurus is changed. Therefore a searcher has to consider which terms were appropriate for the date of all records to be considered for retrieval. For example, in *Medical Subject Headings* a particular condition was indexed from 1969 to 1980 as *Nominal Brain Dysfunction* and from 1981 to 1983 as *Hyperactive Syndrome*, and since 1984 as *Attention Deficit Disorder with Hyperactivity*. A search for information about this condition over the period 1965–1985 would have to contend with three different index terms.

4. Procedure for change—while we want to limit change in controlled languages, we do not want to stifle it. Normally, an official body is established with the authority to modify a controlled vocabulary when necessary, and with the obligation to communicate changes to users.

4.7.2 Relationships among Terms

Controlled vocabularies are usually created as hierarchic structures, although they may vary considerably in the number of levels of depth of the hierarchy. The typical relationships used are those described in Section 4.3.3. There can be other relationships and certainly other names for those illustrated there. It is necessary to have the relationships among terms defined and explained and as well-disseminated among the potential user group as possible. Until relatively recently, it was not common for libraries to make the book *Library of Congress Subject Headings* available to patrons. Generations of users may have been told in school or in library tours that "you can look it up by subject," but were never told what subjects they could look "it" up under or how to find these subjects. This book of subject headings is a thesaurus for a controlled language, although the "language" consists not of individual words but largely of short phrases. If users do not know what is in it, they must guess, and the poor retrieval outcome that is likely to follow on guesswork is caused neither by the catalogers nor by the retrieval system, but by lack of communication among the community of users.

4.8

The Importance of Point of View

In Section 4.5 we discussed several aspects of the ambiguity of attribute values based upon the characteristics of natural language, and illustrated by some of the vagaries of English. These quirks, caused by the relationships of signs to one another in a linguistic context, are on the level of meaning analysis referred to by Morris (1946, p. 3) as syntactic meaning, which goes beyond the basic *semantic meaning*, the relationship of signs to their significants. Morris suggests, however, that there is a third level that deserves mention, *pragmatic meaning*. This is the relation of signs to situations and behaviors in a sociological or psychological context.

Pragmatic meaning distinctions often occur in natural language. We have previously (Boyce *et al.*, 1994, p. 101) used the example that shows the phrase "Baton Rouge" stated at an airline ticket counter in Toronto could mean that a passenger wanted a ticket to go to Baton Rouge, while the same phrase stated to a flight attendant who is announcing that the plane is about to land could mean the passenger wants to know if the plane is landing in Baton Rouge. (It is a good example because the basic context is airline travel in both examples, there is no syntactical difference in the expression, the sign and the significant are the same in both examples, and yet within that context the viewpoint of both the speaker and the listener change with the sociological situation.

This would indicate that we might well need to consider such ambiguity in any study of the meaning of natural language, and that we might wish to control for it, should we be designing a controlled vocabulary. Since a search on BATON ROUGE would find items where the phrase was used as a potential destination, and where it was used as a current location, those who wanted only to retrieve the current location usage might find a large number of false drops.

It is possible to attempt to control for this problem by the use of the precision device known as the *role indicator*. This requires that the designers of a vocabulary decide prior to its publication what potential points of view might cause ambiguity in searching, list these points of view, and assign a code to each of them. The indexer is then required to append such a code to each term assigned, and it may then be used by the searcher to limit the pragmatic meaning of the term (e.g., BATON ROUGE as a destination for ticketing or as the name of the next destination of a particular flight). The assumption is that there is a set of points of view that can be identified that will apply to all the terms of the vocabulary, and that indexers can apply them consistently. The *role* is related to the idea of a *facet* in classification theory, and to some extent to the idea of a *scope note*, which is used in a controlled vocabulary to distinguish homographs. Scope notes are unique to the terms to which they are assigned, whereas *roles* are assumed to be applicable to all vocabulary terms. In a sense roles may be considered a restricted set of subheadings that may be applied to any term.

The first use of roles appears to have been in the telegraphic abstracts discussed in Section 1.5.2. There seems to be little doubt that roles can improve the percentage of useful records and reduce false drops. Unfortunately they may also reduce the number of relevant records retrieved, add complexity to both the indexing and searching processes, and have an adverse effect on indexer consistency. As Lancaster (1968, p. 233) has said, "A cost-effectiveness analysis may well reveal that it is more economical not to use role indicators, thereby saving indexing and searching time, to allow some incorrect term relations to occur, and to eliminate the irrelevant citations thus retrieved through a post search screening operation. . . ." Certainly the device is little used today.

While the difficulties of pragmatic meaning are real, their effect on retrieval may not be terribly great. They are one more element to be considered in text-based retrieval. This is not to say that there are not other sociological or psychological factors that affect how the user of an information retrieval system judges the results of a search. These factors are not topical, however, and are not related to the interpretation of a term's meaning but rather to factors affecting relevance judgments (Barry, 1994). We will discuss these in Section 16.2.

4.9

Summary

The essence of this chapter has been that attributes in databases are represented by symbols whose values must be generally understood among the users of the databases. In particular, the authors or composers of records and of codes and controlled languages must consider the users. In some cases, such as sound and graphic records, the encoding of an attribute may be so complex that simplifying transformations are necessary.

5

Models of Virtual Data Structure

The Concept of Models of Data

Just as we have symbols to represent the content of information, we need a means of representing its *structure*. A data structure is a collection of data elements or objects and relationships among them. These relationships concern the physical layout of the data objects or the semantic relations among them. There are many kinds of semantic relations, e.g., that one element is the color of another or that one record is subordinate to another.

A *model of data* is a particular type of structure or manner of visualizing a data structure. One way of modelling gives consideration only to the constituent elements and sequencing or placement of data elements within other elements. The most common example is to state that records consist of name, address, and telephone number and that these records are sequenced alphabetically by name. Another kind of structural description considers only linkages among data elements, for example, to state that a linkage exists between elements *a* and *b*. Another might state that element *b* is subordinated to *a*, without defining the exact nature of the subordination. Another level of interpretation of data structure concerns the semantics or meaning of the linkages. For example, for a given employee (the entity of a record), it could be stated that address is not merely a subordinate element but that it identifies where the person lives (Cardenas, 1985; Date, 1985; Korth and Silberschatz, 1986; Parsaye *et al.*, 1989; Standish, 1980; Wiederhold, 1987). That may seem an obvious meaning of the word *address* but there are others, such as a location in computer memory.

In optics there is a concept called a *virtual image*. It is created when light reaches the eye after being reflected from a mirror in such a way that an object appears to emanate from within or behind the mirror. The point is that the eye perceives light rays just as if they were coming directly from the object, but in fact the object may be hidden from direct view, as in Fig. 5.1, with only the mirror directly visible. It is not a conjurer's trick, although interesting games can be played with the phenomenon.

Computer science has borrowed the term *virtual* and applied it to data structure. The term *structure* here has two meanings, just as it does in civil engineering. The Golden Gate Bridge is a structure—a combination of various steel and concrete members assembled with specific relationships among them. This is an instance of a structure. The Golden Gate Bridge is also a suspension bridge. A suspension bridge is a generic type of structure, an abstraction. In a similar way there is the distinction between the structure—specific or abstract—that is used with any given computer or software system and that which is assumed by a programmer. The one assumed is an abstraction, a virtual image of the real structure.

An example occurs in hypertext (described in Section 5.4.1). A user views a display that offers a choice of several possible next displays, or next pages. The intent is to give the user the sense of continuity along any path that is meaningful to him or her. Each path becomes a virtual document. Actually, the sequence in which the hypertext frames are stored in random access memory (RAM) may be unrelated to their sequence in disk memory or in use.

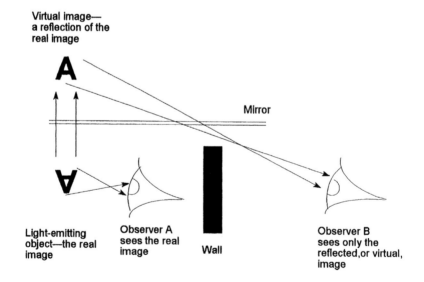

Figure 5.1

Virtual image in optics: in optics observer A directly sees the image, but observer B sees only a virtual image of the same object. To observer B, the image appears just as real as the one A sees.

A more complex example is *virtual memory*. Under this concept a computer programmer may write an application program as if that program and all of its data were stored in a large random access memory (RAM). The programmer need not be concerned with running out of space, which may actually be quite limited, and may, therefore, seem to exceed the physical amount of RAM capacity available. Nor is the programmer concerned with the mechanics of making a change to a file. A new value is simply presented to the appropriate program.

In a virtual memory, the *address space* is the memory structure a programmer may refer to in the text of a program. It is not infinite but may be limited in extent only by the magnitude of a number used as an index or subscript. The operating system would break up a large program or its data into smaller units, usually called *pages*. Only a relatively few pages can fit in RAM at any one time. The point is to insure that these are the ones needed, the ones containing the data or program segments currently in use. Then the total amount of space needed is much less than what the programmer assumes it to be. The operating system would shuffle pages between RAM and disk storage, using the same physical space over and over again, each time for a differently addressed body of data. This shuffling, or *paging*, takes time and requires that the program doing it find the pages needed and, when bringing a new one into RAM, decide which currently RAM-resident page to erase in order to make room for the new one. In Fig. 5.2 when a segment of a program currently operating in RAM wants another segment, say number 18, a message is sent to the operating system asking for the segment. The operating system (1) checks to see if the segment is already in RAM, (2) if not, retrieves it from disk, (3) decides which page in RAM to overwrite, and (4) writes the new page over it. Without going into any more detail, it should be obvious that such a program can be extremely complex. By using virtual memory, the application programmer can ignore this difficult problem and concentrate on the logical processing of data, not the finding or moving of it.

The terms *virtual structure* or *logical structure* refer to any virtual data organization, as distinguished from a physical organization. *Data independence* is said to exist if users can deal directly with the virtual structures, thereby avoiding the complexity of the actual structures.

In this chapter we are primarily concerned with the user's mental image of the logical or virtual structure of data. A word processor may break a document into storage segments that have no relation to the author's perceived virtual view of the document's structure. It might use a series of 128-character strings, ignoring paragraph, sentence, and even word boundaries, and storing these strings in a sequence different from that in which they occur in the text.

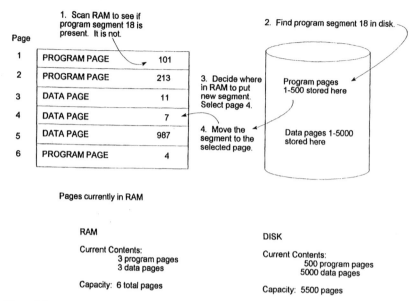

Figure 5.2

Paging: the main memory of a computer is usually limited. Segments of data or programs are brought in as needed from a larger memory. Shown is the sequence of events when a new segment of a program is needed. The RAM is searched to see if that segment is already present (1). If not, it is found in disk storage (2). It must then be decided where to put it in RAM, which may require overwriting another page, calling for a decision of which page to remove (3). Finally, the move is made (4). The efficiency of these operations has a great effect on the speed of execution of programs.

The user does not see the computer break up text into segments and reassemble them. The difference between the user's view and the physical reality is of little or no consequence to the user. Unless the author has to go through the painful process of recovering an accidentally deleted file, he or she will never see the physical structure.

5.2

Basic Data Elements and Structures

Before going on to other models, let us consider more of the basic terminology of data structures. A data structure begins with a single attribute and then is built up by combining attributes into larger elements.

5.2.1 Scalar Variables and Constants

A *variable* is a data element that is a representation of an attribute and can take on differing values, i.e., whose value can vary. A *scalar variable* is a single instance of a variable. This is sometimes referred to as a *field* or *item* in computer programming terms. The variable is used to represent an attribute, and sometimes the words are used interchangeably. A *constant*, in computer terms, is the same as a variable, but its value may not change once the program using it has been compiled; hence, not during execution of the program. If we were using the value of π in a calculation, we would store it as a constant (3.14159. . .). If we were using the conversion factor between U.S. and Canadian dollars, we would normally make it a variable, asking the operator of a program to supply the current value when the program was run or querying another file for the current value, because such a value changes continually.

Scalars may typically be of the type *integer* (a whole number), *real* (a number with a possible fractional part), or *string* or *character* (a sequence of bytes, as a word).

5.2.2 Vector Variables

A *vector* is a variable that consists of a *set of scalars*, each representing an instance of the same attribute, such as a series of temperature readings for a hospital patient, or a series of subject headings descriptive of a book in a library catalog.

5.2.3 Structures

A *structure* is a set of data elements, not necessarily all of the same attribute type. This narrow definition has little to do with the broader concept that is part of the title of this chapter—*data structure*. The term is used often in the narrow sense in computer science, as well as in the broader one. Context usually makes clear which is meant.

A structure called Address might consist of the scalars street, city, state, zipcode. The key characteristic of a structure is that it can have depth; it need not be flat. Elements may contain other elements. An element of a structure might be another structure or a vector, as a student record called Student might consist of name, address (another structure), and Courses Taken (a vector).

5.2.4 Arrays

In mathematics, *array* simply means a rectangular arrangement of data. A vector is a one-dimensional array. A list of delinquent credit card numbers is one-dimensional. An airline time table is a two-dimensional array. The columns represent different flights, and the rows, different airports. A numeric value within the array represents the time at which a given flight will arrive at or depart from a given airport. In data processing, an element of an array can be any kind of data element. Thus, a file is an array of records. A byte is an array of bits. An array could contain structures, as an array of Former Address, each of which is defined as above.

5.2.5 Tuples

The word *tuple* is a noun made out of a suffix, as in *triple* or *quadruple*, and which in turn comes from *ply*, meaning *layer*. A tuple is a one-layer structure. It represents one occurrence of what is typically a flat structure. It could be defined also as a structure whose constituent elements must be scalars—it cannot contain an array or subordinate structure. The term tuple has generally been used only in the context of *relational* databases, which we shall describe in Section 5.3.2. In that context a tuple has the interesting characteristic that it need not permanently exist as an element of any existing file. A tuple could be made up of variables taken from more than one file and combined into a virtual file, one that may not physically exist, but that the user may address as if it did exist.

As an example of a tuple, consider two separate files, one describing materials on hand and one describing dealers from whom the items were purchased. They might have the structures illustrated in Fig. 5.3.

Suppose our company anticipates a general transportation strike in Centreville and wants to see what items that we stock originate there and how close we are to needing resupply. (What to do about the strike would be a subsequent question. Now we just want to see what position it might leave us in.) The computer can enter the Supplier File to find records with CITY = SUPPLIER CODE. From these records, extract supplier code. Then search the Materials File for records of those suppliers and use the results to create a temporary series of tuples, each containing supplier code, item, type, number on hand, and reorder level. These will only be for Centreville suppliers. The resulting tuples are not permanently stored. They are created as needed, may be displayed or used for computations, and then discarded when no longer in use. The user has only to

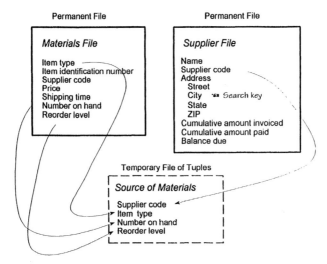

Figure 5.3

Creation of a temporary tuple: there are a permanent Materials File and a Dealer File. From these can be created a temporary set of tuples showing from what city each item in inventory comes. This particular combination of elements is not normally needed, so the temporary file is discarded when its information has been examined.

define the desired content of the tuples, then address questions as if the tuples existed. The user plays no role in physically assembling them.

5.2.6 Relations

A *relation*, in brief, is the set of all the tuples that exist for a given set of variables. In our previous example, if we name the five variables supplier code, item type, number on hand, reorder level, and city, then form all the tuples for which there are values of these variables, we have the relation. In other words, a relation, in the database sense, empirically defines the content or semantic relationships among the variables constituting the tuples. In the world of the database, there can be no semantic relationship not explicitly represented by a set of attribute values: an attribute value, such as grade in a school, by definition, may range over the theoretical interval 0 through 100, but in reality, it ranges from the smallest to the largest actually occurring values, which in an era of grade escalation may only span 72 to 98. Thus, the pragmatic value of the range is determined by the relation, not by a theoretical statement.

By analogy, the attribute **salary** of employees of a company can be described by giving the set of salaries that are actually paid each month. Alternatively, the salaries could be defined statistically by giving the mean, mode, median, and other measures of the distribution, but not the individual data values, themselves.

5.2.7 Text

It is not clear how to classify a data element consisting of natural-language text, such as an abstract in a bibliographic record, the text of an article in a full-text newspaper file, or even the response to a questionnaire item that adds, at the end of the list of choices: "Other (specify)."

Text could be considered a scalar string variable of very great length. While this is not very practical, there are information systems, particularly older ones, in which the text component could be displayed but not searched. Thus, large as it is, the entire text is treated as a single variable or field. More modern systems will allow searching within a text variable for a particular substring of characters, say the occurrence of STEROID within a text assumed to be dealing with athletics.

A text could also be considered an array of words. This means we would ignore the syntax connecting them, but doing so considerably simplifies the mechanics of searching. Most retrieval systems, in effect, do this, by making a separate file (array of tuples) of words that occur in records of the database and the numbers of the records in which they occur. The new file is sorted alphabetically and, as noted in Chapter 1, is called an *inverted file*. One is illustrated in Fig. 5.4. It is now quite easy to find where (in which records) a particular word occurred. This approach does not take any of the syntax of the original text into consideration. Expanding on an earlier example, suppose a text were to include the statement "This text is about bicycles rather than automobiles," which denies that *automobiles* is the subject. If we were to search for all records "about" automobiles, by which we literally mean all that contain the word AUTOMO-BILES in any context, we would retrieve this text. This is the most commonly used method in commercial database operations today.

Finally, we could treat a text as a structure, made up of a series of words with a syntax relating them to each other or to the entity they describe. This would be a great advantage to the searcher, because he or she could then use the meaning conveyed by the combination of syntax and vocabulary. The problem, of course, is that the syntax of natural language is too complex and variable for this purpose. We would have to considerably restrict the syntax or the interpretation of the text, to use this method.

Text

> Fourscore and seven years ago, our fathers
> brought forth on this continent a new nation,
> conceived in liberty and dedicated to the
> proposition that all men are created equal.

Words and position number   Words and position
in order of appearance   numbers in alphabetic
                                   order

fourscore	1
and	2
seven	3
years	4
ago	5
our	6
fathers	7
brought	8
forth	9
on	10
this	11
continent	12
a	13
new	14
nation	15
conceived	16
in	17
liberty	18
and	19
dedicated	20
to	21
the	22
proposition	23
that	24
all	25
men	26
are	27
created	28
equal	29

a	13
ago	5
all	25
and	2,19
are	27
brought	8
conceived	16
continent	12
created	28
dedicated	20
equal	29
fathers	7
forth	9
fourscore	1
in	17
liberty	18
men	26
nation	15
new	14
on	10
our	6
proposition	23
seven	3
that	24
the	22
this	11
to	21
years	4

Figure 5.4
An inverted file: shown are a short text, the list of words in order of occurrence, with the sequential
word number appended, and the same word list sorted into alphabetic order.

The uncertainty about how to search text, and how to interpret it if we do
search it, represents the principal difference between *database management systems*,
such as Paradox or Access and *information retrieval systems*, such as Alta Vista,
LEXIS, or MEDLINE. The latter three systems use a great deal of text. Their
design is based on two assumptions. The first is that users will not know exactly
how to phrase a question because they cannot know how words were used in
every text to be searched; hence, they will not know exactly how to phrase
a particular topic. The second assumption is that the users will not know how
much information on the desired topic is in the file; therefore, they do not know
how much is likely to be found—possibly more or less than desired. Probing,

analysis, and revision are necessary. By contrast, searching for the number of red sedans on hand at an automobile agency means using a precise syntax and vocabulary, knowing that this information will be explicitly represented in the file and once only, whether the inventory level is 0 or 100.

5.3
The Common Structural Models

A data model, in our usage, is primarily a mental construct. It is descriptive of the structure of data, not necessarily its meaning, although the two concepts are not entirely separable because both involve the relationship of information elements to each other. We present here a review of the four major data models currently in use. They represent data structures as visualized by a user, who may be a person querying a database, or an applications programmer writing a program to process data in a database. Both must understand the logical structure and the relationships among data elements. They do not necessarily need to know the physical structure used inside the computer, so long as programs exist that can access data using the structures these users visualize. The values of the data elements and the rules governing them are also separate, but not entirely so. We discuss physical data structure in Chapter 6.

Record location and sequence are almost invariably based upon a *key* which consists of one or more attribute values that are within the record. Sorting a file of student records by last name alone would result in many records with the same key. Therefore, a secondary key of first name is almost always used and perhaps even a tertiary key of date of birth to get as close as possible to having a unique key for each record. If there should be more than one student with the same last name, first name, and date of birth, their records would be in random order.

5.3.1 The Linear Sequential Model

The *linear sequential model*, another very common data structure, is also called a *flat structure*. It is simply a list or table of elements, with no hierarchical structure other than the accumulation of records within the file—a straight line, no branching. An example is the list of students registered for a given course—the class list. There may be no information except the student number and name. The numbers are in numerical order. Such a structure could be considered hierarchical, consisting of a trunk with a large set of leaves emanating directly from it, but what is most important is that it is always clear where the next and previous elements are.

In this model, the data are organized so that the next element in alphanumerical order after the current one follows the current one immediately. The method is simple and compact. It makes for simple searching. This model of data is the oldest we have and it can be described as a special, limiting case of each of the models to follow. The commands or operations available for use with the structure vary considerably with individual implementations. Typically, retrieval commands are limited to some variation on a command such as SELECT IF ATTRIBUTE = VALUE. For example, we might ask a system to SELECT IF NAME = 'SMITH, A.B.'

Most of white pages telephone directories are files of this sort—they are listings of name, address, and telephone number, ordered by name. Yellow pages, and actually some parts of white pages, may have considerable variation in the amount of information per entry. The ordering is by business category, then alphabetical within a category. The category is not explicitly represented as an attribute of the individual entry.

5.3.2 The Relational Model

A relational database consists of a set of relations (in the sense of Section 5.2.6) or files of tuples. Typically, there is considerable semantic interrelationship among the data elements in these databases; and a powerful set of operations may be performed upon the data. Users may define tuples, combinations of individual attributes, to suit their own needs, and assemble tuples to build relations (Codd, 1970; Korth and Silberschatz, 1986, pp. 45–106).

A number of operations can be performed on relations. Let us create a small database of three relations (Fig. 5.5) to illustrate the operators, or symbols for the operations. Call the relations Transcript (student's name and number and listing of courses taken and grades received), Identification (listing of personal information, such as address), and Resources (listing of instructors and classrooms assigned to courses). Typical operations are:

1. *SELECT*—The SELECT operator creates a subset of the tuples of a relation that includes only those meeting the criteria stated in the command. For example, SELECT COURSE = 'PHYS 101'(TRANSCRIPT) means to create a new relation containing all those tuples of Transcript that have the value PHYS 101 in the course attribute. Different implementations of a relational database system can allow of different syntaxes for commands. The one we have illustrated has command name, followed by selection criteria, followed by the name of the relation to be operated upon, in parentheses. An easier syntax might allow this to be said as SELECT FROM TRANSCRIPT IF COURSE = 'PHYS 101.'

In both cases, it is implicit that what is selected is each complete tuple meeting the stated criterion.

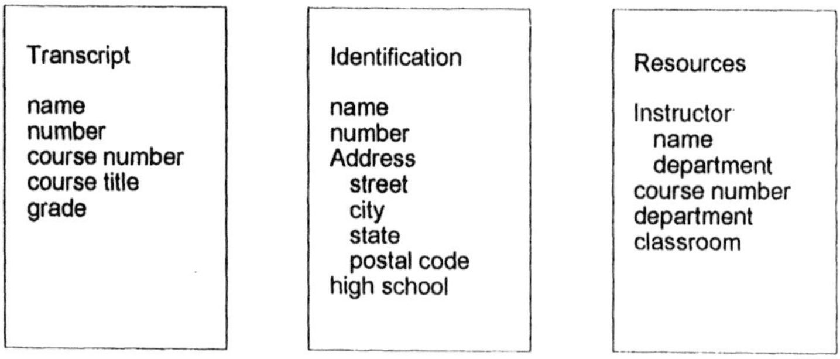

Transcript	Identification	Resources

name
number
course number
course title
grade
	name
	number
	Address
	  street
	  city
	  state
	  postal code
	high school
		Instructor
		  name
		  department
		course number
		  department
		  classroom

Figure 5.5

A set of relations: the contents of relations that make up the history of a student's record are shown. The first, Transcript, shows the student's name and number, course number, and grade, for each course taken. The second, Identification, contains personal information about the student, and the third, Resources, information about courses.

2. *PROJECT*—The PROJECT operator selects the attributes of a tuple meeting the stated criteria. The subset is defined in the example that follows by an embedded select command. The command PROJECT STUDENT, STUDENT NUMBER (SELECT COURSE = 'PHYS 101') (TRANSCRIPT) creates a new relation consisting of two attributes, the student's name and number for those students registered in course PHYS 101 (specified by the parenthetical operation). While, again, we recognize that the symbolism may bother those not used to mathematics, we can also see that quite complex operations or sets of operations can be defined upon data in a very compact form. We see that operations can be nested, one being embedded within another.

3. *CROSS*—The CROSS operator allows expansion of a relation by adding to it information from another relation. Suppose we want to know what secondary schools provide our university with its best students. Using the cross operation, PROJECT STUDENT GRADE (TRANSCRIPT) CROSS PROJECT STUDENT, SCHOOL(IDENTIFICATION), all student names and their average grades are collected from Transcript; then, for each student, the name of each student's high school attended is found in Identification, and the two sets of data are combined. This yields a new relation containing student, grade, and school. These three attributes have not been together in one relation before. The original goal of forming a new relation identifying the best students (defined here as those with a B average or better) and the schools from which they came is achieved using the command PROJECT STUDENT, GRADE (SELECT GRADE >= 'B' (TRANSCRIPT))CROSS PROJECT STUDENT, SCHOOL(IDENTIFICATION).

4. *UNION*—The UNION operator brings together two sets of tuples, as in SELECT COURSE = 'PHYS 101'(TRANSCRIPT) UNION SELECT COURSE = 'CHEM 101'(TRANSCRIPT), which produces a list of tuples containing either one of the two courses. This is equivalent to the Boolean OR operator.

The same result could have been obtained by the usage SELECT COURSE = 'PHYS 101','CHEM 101'(TRANSCRIPT), where the comma (or other symbol, depending on implementation) indicates the operator OR or UNION.

5. *INTERSECT*—The operator INTERSECT, if used instead of UNION in the preceding example, would give those students who have taken *both* Physics 101 and Chemistry 101. It is, of course, the Boolean AND operator.

5.3.3 The Hierarchical Model

In a *hierarchical model*, also known as a *tree structure*, each element of data except one "belongs" to one and only one higher or superordinate data element. The sole exception is the highest element. In an organization chart, the highest position might be that of Chief Executive Officer. Metaphors for these structures abound. They are often called trees, but relationships may be named after family relationships (parents, children, siblings; or even hens and chicks).

Tree structures have a *root* element, although this is something of a mixed metaphor because the root of a tree has a branching structure like its crown. It might be more accurate to use *trunk* as the name of the starting element. From the trunk emanate *branches* and *limbs* or *twigs*, any of which can lead to the final element, a *leaf*, which can have no subordinates within this metaphor. A hierarchical file might have a structure as in Fig. 5.6.

A hierarchical structure is usually easy to understand. Relationships are precisely defined. If we are told we are dealing with the degree attribute (i.e., BA, MS, PhD, etc.) we know precisely where it lies in the scheme of things (subordinated to level, which has subordinates inst name and degree). Probably (no one keeps statistics on such matters) this is still the most commonly used data structure model, especially if we include noncomputer files. To store a set of previous addresses in an employee file, create a data element called previous addresses. It would contain an array of address structures, each of which contains the scalars street, city, state, and zip.

Hierarchy seems an almost natural organization, or perhaps it seems natural because it is so common. It is by far the most common form in which to structure an organization of people—a corporation, football team, or social club. It is frequently used and established by persons who may not even be aware that a formal definition exists. The overall structure can be complex, but the

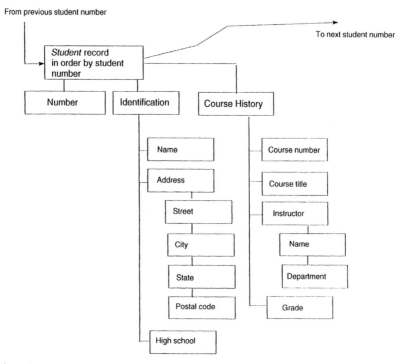

Figure 5.6
A graphic representation of a hierarchical student record.

individual relationships are relatively straightforward. At one level of generality, we can describe a complete structure of an organization of people entirely in terms of the hierarchical relationships. Those with any amount of experience in organizations know that the organization chart does not begin to tell all about where power really lies and who communicates with whom. Nonetheless, we repeatedly use the structure, probably because of its apparent simplicity. In other words, the reality often is that the hierarchical model is not capable of describing the real organization, but it is used for simplicity.

The elements of a record may be of any of the structural types described. For example (Fig. 5.7), there might be an array **Previous Address**, which consists of structures or tuples containing **street, city,** and **state.** This is common. It is interesting that there are usually some limitations on searching within subordinate elements. While it is technically possible for a user to specify the retrieval of the *third* value of **Previous Address**, this capability is not commonly available when using hierarchical database software. The languages simply do not permit

```
┌─────────────────────────────────────────────────────┐
│                                                       │
│   Previous Addresses                                  │
│                                                       │
│   street              city            state          │
│                                                       │
│   123 4TH STREET      ALTOONA         PA              │
│   66 ILLINOIS AVE     CHICAGO         IL              │
│   43 BISCAYNE BLVD    MIAMI           FL              │
│   RR 2                SMALLTOWN       IN              │
│                                                       │
└─────────────────────────────────────────────────────┘
```

Figure 5.7
An array of structures or tuples: it is not normally possible to search for occurrences of MIAMI following CHICAGO. A searcher usually must be content with finding whether or not the terms appear at all, then checking the sequence manually.

expressing this concept. To find those cities to which people moved next, after having lived in Chicago, we usually have to be content with finding whether or not the person (the entity) has ever lived in Chicago, and then finding all cities in which the person lived subsequently. The order of occurrence would have to be checked by manually viewing the records. Other limitations of query languages are discussed in Chapter 8.

Retrieval commands will be essentially the same as for the linear sequential model, but must allow for more than one value of a given attribute within a record and for the possibility that a given name may be used for more than one attribute. For example, in the relations illustrated in Fig. 5.5, we have the attribute name occurring in all three relations. A convention for referring to similarly named data elements is to precede the name of the variable with the element that contains it, as Identification.name in this context refers to the student's name in the Identification relation. This method shows the hierarchical relationship and avoids ambiguity in use of attribute names.

5.3.4 The Network Model

The network model differs from the hierarchical one by the removal of two constraints. First, we no longer necessarily speak in terms of subordinates and superordinates, but replace these with a more generalized relationship that indicates only that one node is connected to another, and the direction of the link. We still do not identify the nature of the relationship, as part of the definition; we merely note that the link exists. A second constraint removed is the limit on number of superordinate nodes. Any given element or node may now have any number of related nodes of any kind. In the hierarchical model, a node could have at most one superordinate and any number of subordinate nodes (Korth and Silberschatz, 1986, pp. 107–142).

In a typical university database, students and instructors have different relationships: teacher–student; research manager–employee; teacher–teaching assistant. They may each be associated with a course, but in a different way. Rather than repeat basic information about the instructors, students, and courses again and again, a course file can refer to an instructor and to a list of students. An instructor file can refer to a list of courses taught. A student file can refer to a list of courses in which enrolled, a faculty advisor, a research supervisor, etc. The World Wide Web abounds with links, not necessarily having any other meaning than that "here is another, related, record."

The commands associated with a network data model would be the same as for hierarchical data, but there should be a means of making use of pointers. If the same university record data were organized as shown in Fig. 5.6, we might want to retrieve the names of all students who were ever taught by a particular instructor. The command might be of the form SELECT IDENTIFI-CATION.NAME FOR INSTRUCTOR.NAME = 'OLSON, L.R.', which would be interpreted as asking the program to follow pointers between instructor entries, then within a record selected by the Instructor.name = <criterion> clause, follow pointers within the record to the student's name, and retrieve the value of name from the selected records.

5.4
Applications of the Basic Models

Two modern types of databases are not themselves models of data, but are types of databases built using one or more of the models just described. We introduce them here to point out that not every type of database application requires a different structural model and also to illustrate that there are different levels of database structure. It is important in communicating with others to be sure that all parties are referring to the same level.

5.4.1 Hypertext

This model is interesting partly because both the underlying software concepts and the application were conceived three decades ago (Englebart and English, 1968; Nelson, 1965; Lefkovitz, 1969) but it has become popular only recently. Essentially, a hypertext file is a series of records or nodes connected by multiple relationships to other records or nodes. Recall that, in a linear sequential file, there would always (except for the last one) be a single *next* record, and the meaning of *next* would be well understood by users. In a hierarchical file, there could be any number of next records but at most one record preceding any given one. The next records would all be *next* in the same sense, i.e., all would represent different values of the same attributes of an entity, such as one of several courses for which a student is registered.

In hypertext, a node may be related to any other node in any way defined by the database designer. In this sense it is a network-model database. A user who is reading a record on a computer monitor could ask for, as a next record, any of the records for which a connection has been defined. If the file were a textbook, it might be presented as shown in Fig. 5.8; a single text record, be it chapter, section, or paragraph, might have multiple connections to other segments of the book.

At the top of the figure is information about navigation through the complete text. Under this is identification data about the the reader's current location: chapter, section, and paragraph numbers, and titles. Since a paragraph of text may need more than the meager space available in a computer display, the page number refers to the display page within a paragraph. A well-designed system would allow more than one way for the user to indicate what to do next: move a cursor to the choice (e.g., **B**ack) or type B. Going back can have more than one meaning: back one page, one paragraph, etc.; hence, a second

Path:	Next §	Back	Table of Contents	Index	Word	Help
	Page	§	Section	Chapter	▲	▼

Chapter: 5 Models of Virtual Data Structure
Section: 4 Applications of the Basic Models
§:   1 Hypertext
Page: #
Next §:   5.4.2 Spreadsheet files

Text:

> This model is interesting partly because both the underlying software concepts and the application were conceived nearly three decades ago (Englebart and English, 1968; Nelson, 1965; Lefkovitz, 1969) but it has become popular only recently. Essentially, a hypertext file is a series of records or nodes. Recall that, in a linear sequential file, there would always (except for the last one) be a single *next* record, and the meaning of *next* would be well understood by users. In a hierarchical file,

Figure 5.8
A hypertext presentation of a textbook: a hypothetical display shows a portion of a page displayed (at bottom), its position within the book (middle), and a number of choices for what to see next (at top). The user could move about quickly and follow links to other sources, but could not see much text at any one time.

menu, shown below the path line, might be brought into use if the user indicates only B. Another option is for the user to place the cursor on one of the highlighted words in the text, which would instruct the system to go to the next record (or the previous one) containing that word. "Word" in the path indicates that the user wants to follow a word path, rather than the chapter–section–paragraph numbering system. "Word" in the heading would show what word was being followed if a word path had been previously selected. This means that every word in a text is potentially a link to other occurrences of that word. There are other ways to organize a page, with more or fewer options. For any of them to be useful, users would have to learn the system and become comfortable with its use.

Hypertext can be a method of information retrieval. In a hypertext, links have been predefined by the author, giving some selectivity to the user, although generally restricted to these predetermined paths. The user can also go to a general index and use it to retrieve new records or to start on a new path at any time. These selection criteria are not necessarily based on an explicit link to the most recently displayed record. The hypertext technique can be used in IR by allowing a user to point to any component element of a record, whether a word in a text or an author's name, and ask to see other records with the same element value. This is contrasted with the more conventional requirement that a user state explicitly the selection criteria for the next node.

5.4.2 Spreadsheet Files

Spreadsheets have become a popular tool. Although they are called matrices, they are more strictly an array of structures or tuples, or a structure of arrays. That is, every element does not represent the same attribute and may have considerably different characteristics from others in the same tuple. A spreadsheet is a set of data organized into rows and columns, and may contain accounting data as in Fig. 5.9, showing information about items sold in a retail store: product, price, number sold, tax rate, gross receipts, and sales tax owed. The last item is the amount of sales tax collected and to be paid to the government. The tax rate is 8% on accessories, 5% on clothing.

Spreadsheet software makes it quite simple to enter data into the array and to change it once there. Spreadsheet systems differ from almost any other file structure in that a data element (cell of a matrix) may contain values or mathematical formulas for computing the values. Values, in turn, may be data or labels, which might be the names of the attributes.

Figure 5.10 shows some of the content of this spreadsheet, cell by cell. Note that cell A7 is a label or the name of an attribute. Cell E7 has a conditional

```
        A           B         C        D        E       F          G
  1                           ABC Company, Inc.
  2                  Sales, Receipts, and Sales Tax Due
  3
  4  Product      Product   Price   Number    Tax     Gross      Sales
  5               Class             Sold      Rate    Receipts   Tax Due
  6
  7  Shirts       CL        23.50     112     0.05    2763.60    131.60
  8  Ties         CL        18.75      23     0.05     452.81     21.56
  9  Hosiery      CL         5.98     437     0.05    2743.92    130.66
 10  Shoes, pr    CL        83.00      26     0.05    2265.90    107.90
 11  Wallets      AC        15.00      14     0.08     226.80     16.80
 12
 13  TOTALS                                           8453.04    408.53
```

Figure 5.9

A spreadsheet file: this array shows type of product sold, class, price, number sold, tax rate, gross receipts, and sales tax due. Letters across the top identify columns, and numbers on the left identify rows. These may be used in algebraic formulas. The sales tax rate is computed as a function of product class. Gross receipts are computed as price times no.sold times (1 + tax rate). Sales tax owed is the amount collected as tax and due the government.

value: it is 0.05 if the item is clothing, and 0.08 otherwise. The content of F7 is a formula, the definition of a relationship among values. When the values are shown, as in Fig. 5.9, the formula is replaced with its value. Because the formulas usually take up more space than the values, the formula version of the spreadsheet is typically printed as a sequential file, as shown here.

In effect, a spreadsheet is two files, one representing attribute relationships and one representing attribute values. The first file, which is logically structured the same as the second, contains instructions on computing values, such as just illustrated, or it could simply provide a value and instructions to copy the given value. The second file contains the values, whether directly provided by a user or computed by formula. A spreadsheet is the only commonly used data structure that contains, as an integral component, instructions for changing its own values, although word processors also embed commands in the text—for example, to change type font.

5.5

The Entity–Relationship Model

The term *entity–relationship (E-R) model* is used to convey semantic information about the interrelationships among data elements, as part of the definition of the containing information structure. Here we depart from formalisms of hierarchies, which can, in simplest form, describe relationships only in terms of ownership or inclusion, or relations that might describe only the attributes

```
A7:     [W10]   'Shirts
B7:     'CL
C7:     (F2)    [W7]    23.50
D7:     (F0)    [W6]    112
E7:     (F2)    [W6]    @IF (B7="CL",0.05,0.80)
F7:     (F2)    (C7*D7)*(1+E7)
G7:     (F2)    (C7*D7)*E7
A8:     [W10]   'Ties
B8:     'CL
C8:     (F2)    [W8]    18.75
D8:     (F0)    [W6]    23
E8:     (F2)    [W6]    @IF (B8="CL",0.05,0.80)
F8:     (F2)    (C8*D8)*(1+E8)
G8:     (F2)    (C8*D8)*E8
A9:     [W10]   'Hosiery
B9:     'CL
C9:     (F2)    [W8]    5.98
D9:     (F0)    [W6]    437
E9:     (F2)    [W6]    @IF (B9="CL",0.05,0.08)
F9:     (F2)    (C9*D9)*(1+E9)
G9:     (F2)    (C9*D9)*E9
A10:    [W10]   'Shoes, pr
B10:    'CL
C10:    (F2)    [W8]    83.00
D10:    (F0)    [W6]    26
E10:    (F2)    [W6]    @IF (B10="CL",0.05,0.08)
F10:    (F2)    (C10*D10)*(1+E10)
G10:    (F2)    (C10*D10)*E10
A11:    [W10]   'Wallets
B11:    'CL
C11:    (F2)    [W8]    15.00
D11:    (F0)    [W6]    14
E11:    (F2)    [W6]    @IF (B11="CL",0.05,0.08)
F11:    (F2)    (C11*D11)*(1+E11)
G11:    (F2)    (C11*D11)*E11
A13:    [W10]   'TOTALS
F13:    (F2)    @SUM(F7..F11)
G13:    (F2)    @SUM(G7..G11)
```

Figure 5.10
Actual content of a spreadsheet's cells: note that cells F7, F8,... contain a formula in essentially algebraic language, using cell names as variables. Cells E7,... contain a conditional statement, yielding the value 0.05 if product type is CL, and 0.08 otherwise. Cells F13 and G13 contain a function that computes the sum of a column of numbers. Cells in column A are labels, such as SHIRTS.

grouped together in a tuple. The E-R model will allow us to describe the relationships in semantic terms, i.e., tell us what these relationships mean (Chen, 1976; Fidel, 1987; Korth and Silberschatz, 1986, pp. 21–44).

The model is portrayed graphically and uses four basic symbols, shown in Fig. 5.11. The rectangle represents an entity; the oval, an attribute of an

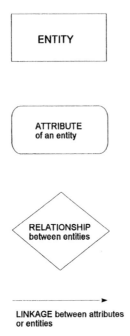

Figure 5.11

Symbols used in an entity–relation map: the rectangle represents an entity, the oval an attribute of an entity, the diamond a relationship between entities. A line or arrow represents a linkage between an attribute and an entity or between an entity and a relationship.

entity; and the diamond, a relationship among entities. The line or arrow represents a linkage between an attribute and an entity or between and entity and a relationship.

Figure 5.12 shows the record of Fig. 5.6 in E-R form. This uses a simplified version of the notation, which could be expanded to show such information as whether a relation is one-to-many or many-to-one. Many students enroll in a course. Only one instructor teaches a given course (also simplified to omit multiple sections of a course).

A course entity has attributes name, number, number of credits, and grade for any particular student. An instructor entity has attributes name and city. The number of attributes for all entities is simplified, or the page would be quite full.

A student is *identified* by name and number, and *lives at* address. A student is *enrolled in* a course, which is identified by course number and title, and it is *scheduled* at a meeting time and in a classroom, which is in a building and has a room

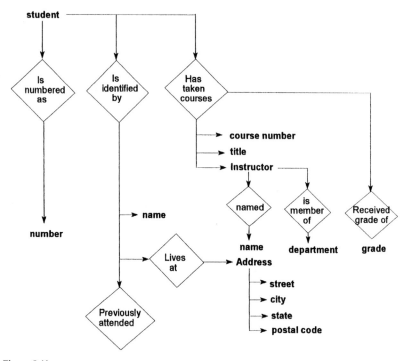

Figure 5.12
An entity–relation map: this maps shows two principal entities, student and course, and the various entities and attributes linked to them.

number. Both course and classroom are attributes and indicate a relationship to another attribute. Each record of this database shows an instance of a student, enrolled in a course, which is scheduled for a classroom.

A *relationship set* is formed, for example, by combining all instances of a student number being enrolled in a course. Another is all instances of a course being scheduled in a classroom at a meeting time. Note that, unless there is some degree of standardization in naming and defining relationships, the model may not convey a great deal of information.

Although this is not necessarily an easy diagram to read, it is possible to trace a connection between a student's name and the name of each of the student's instructors. It is also possible to tell whether one can find out whether any student lives in the same city as an instructor. The diagram does not answer the questions about who lives in the same city, but it does indicate that there are data relationships and connections that will yield this information. Whether the software is capable of using them is another question, of course.

The purposes of constructing an entity–relation model are to help plan a database and to enable users to understand what can be done with it.

5.6
Summary

End users of IR systems often have little patience for dealing with such esoteric concepts as the structure of a record. Some IR systems encourage this attitude by essentially treating a record as simply a set of words, not distinguished as to field or attribute. As databases get larger, as is happening on the Web, and as more people use and learn to understand IR systems, we can expect a return to the use of record structure in searching, for those who have abandoned it or never learned it.

6

The Physical Structure of Data

6.1

Introduction to Physical Structures

The structures introduced in Chapter 5 were virtual ones. In this chapter we shall see how data are actually stored in a computer's memory. The physical organization of data in memory is a complex and highly technical subject (Batory and Gotlieb, 1982; Cardenas, 1985; Date, 1985; Frakes and Baeza-Yates, 1992; Korth and Silberschatz, 1986; Standish, 1980; Tremblay and Sorenson, 1985; Wiederhold, 1987). Our intent is to give an overview of the subject, not a detailed exposition. Since users or application programmers may not "see" data at the detailed, physical level, it is reasonable to ask why it is necessary to know about it at all. We all know that it is possible to drive an automobile without knowing the thermodynamics of internal combustion engines. Yet, to be skillful, a driver must understand something of the limitations of the engine and such phenomena as moisture in fuel lines or the effect of reduced road friction on braking. The benefits of understanding physical structures are that it enables us to

Evaluate retrieval software, whose cost and performance may depend on its physical structures

Estimate or perhaps just understand the timing of a computer program and why certain functions take so much time (see, for example, the discussion of left-hand truncation in Sections 8.2.5 and 7.4.5)

Comprehend the effects of errors, either made by the IRS software or in the formulation of a query

For example, in competitive bidding to supply software for an information retrieval service, one bidder may claim its product requires only half the amount of disk storage space as most others. If true, and if there were no consequent costs (such as slower search times), then this would be a significant advantage. The evaluators would have to be able to understand the importance of this claim, its likelihood of being true, and its impact on performance.

We have pointed out previously that in modern computing the distinction between records and files is not so clear as it was in the days of punched card records or magnetic tape files. Perhaps we should redefine a *record* as a set of contiguously stored data elements. In other words, a record is not all the information we have about an entity; it is a set of data about an entity that we choose to store together in one unit. The complete description of the entity may require several records, and different kinds of records might be assembled, according to the needs of the moment.

We shall first consider the structure of data within a record and then the larger, more complex, and more economically important issue of the structure of files or sets of records. There are important economic implications, for physical structures govern cost in time and money.

6.2
Record Structures and Their Effects

The main structural elements of a physical record are essentially the same as those of a virtual record: the individual data elements or attributes and their relationships. But at the physical level we have to know *where* the elements are in memory and what is the actual basis for their positioning. It is not enough merely to know that they exist or to know what assumptions we are permitted to make about them.

6.2.1 Basic Structures

The simplest record structure consists of a set of attribute values, stored one after the other, each of a predetermined size in number of bits or bytes. A record, if stored on disk, will normally be read into RAM as a unit, or as part of a larger unit. Sometimes a logical record will be stored as a number of smaller parts for the purpose of input–output operations. This is done with some word processors whose users see a document as a single record, but the physical reality may be a large number of smaller records.

To find any particular attribute within such a record, we must know, for each attribute, the location in memory of the first bit or byte, and the length of each attribute value or the location of its last bit or byte. There are other, equivalent ways of describing the same structural features.

If a record consists of name, address, telephone number, and date of last change, and if the length of each attribute value is fixed in advance, the program

‍

Attribute	Number of Bytes	Content
name	11	SMITH, JOHN
address	32	1287 MAPLE ...
telephone	10	8085551234
date_of_last_change	6	991228
name	14	STEINBERG, MAE
address	27	327 MAIN ST ...
telephone	10	8085554321
date_of_last_change	6	000116

Figure 6.1
Variable-length record: in this form, each attribute value carries with it an explicit tag showing its length. The name and address attributes vary widely; date and telephone do not.

can easily find where the address or telephone number is located. This is called a *fixed-length record.* Complications set in when attribute values have a large range in terms of number of characters. For example, a person's last or family name can range from two (NG) to many (IPPOLITOV-IVANOV). The abstract of a bibliographic record can range from a few bytes (ABSTRACT MISSING) to several thousand. Although it is convenient to make each attribute value of fixed length, it can waste a great deal of memory to do so. One among many methods to permit variable-length attribute values, hence *variable-length records*, is to append to each attribute an explicit statement of its length as in Fig. 6.1. Here, the record is of variable length, but if we know the starting location and have these length tags or a table of lengths, it is easy to find any element within the record.

The same basic technique can be used if there may be more than one value of an attribute. Bank depositors may vary widely on number of transactions during a month, each of which must be represented in a record. A depositor record might be organized as shown in Fig. 6.2. Here, because the Transactions array has subordinate elements, we need another attribute showing the number of occurrences of a transaction, each of which consists of date, type, and amount, each of which is shown with its length. Alternatively, we might show the total number of bytes used by the array of transactions or show both the number of array elements and their cumulative byte count. While the attributes of a bank transaction do not vary much in terms of length (most of us need distressingly fewer than eight digits to record the amounts of our deposits), in other kinds of records they could vary more. Variable-length arrays might contain variable-length fields. Technically, a variable-length structure within a variable-length structure introduces nothing new, although it can make finding the date of a deposit of $12,450 time consuming. (Why would one want to search a file using

Attribute	Content	Length (bytes)
name	SMITH, JOHN	10
account number	1234 567 890	12
no_transactions	3	1
Transactions		
date	990624	6
type	2	1
amount	000005.45	8
date	000113	6
type	2	1
amount	000237.00	8
date	000115	6
type	3	1
amount	000100.00	8

Figure 6.2
Variable-length record: each field or attribute is of fixed length, but there can be a variable number of occurrences of the structure Transactions. The number of bytes for each field is explicitly given in the table and the number of transactions is given.

amount as a key? One of the largest banking transactions one of us ever took part in involved an international transfer of funds "by wire." Something went wrong with the transfer, and he was told by the bank staff the only way to trace it was by amount, and not account number, name of depositor, or name of recipient. A rather strange retrieval technique but one geared to a highly specialized application.)

Yet another organizational method, although logically equivalent, is to use *pointers* instead of counts of length. A pointer tells where the next element begins or the current one ends, as shown in Fig. 6.3.

A weakness of this structure is that we must follow chains of pointers from the beginning. We cannot jump into the middle of such a record structure, because we could not know what attribute we were dealing with. In this example, if a program found itself looking in location 163, it would not know the next two bytes contained a transaction type, but if it started at location 41 and had reference to a table of attributes in this record, it would know, at each pointer, what the next attribute was going to be.

6.2.2 Space–Time and Transaction Rate

It takes time to find the length attributes, interpret them, and access the location of the next element. The pointer or list approach is one of many ex-

Content of a record assumed to be stored beginning at location 41.	Comment
(41) name/SMITH, JOHN/61	(41) indicates the storage address of the first byte of the attribute, containing, first, its name, then its value, then a pointer to the next attribute value. A separator is necessary.
(61) address/287 MAPLE AVENUE, AKRON, OH, 44444/109	
(109) Transactions/1/290	Transactions is a structure, consisting of several attributes, and there may be more than one set of them. The 1 following its name shows the number of occurrences, the 290 shows the address of the first one. Note that the next attribute need not be contiguous to this one.
(290) date/990217/163	
(163) type/2/312	
(312) amount/00000545,116	The last attribute points to the start of the next record.

Figure 6.3
Variable-length record with pointers: pointers are used throughout to show where the next attribute or record begins, and separators are used to show where the names of attribute, value, and pointer begin or end.

amples of a data structure in which there is a trade-off between space and time. Typically, a saving in one is compensated for by extra payments in the other. Unfortunately, there is no standard way to measure the value of space or time consumed or saved. It is not the purchase cost of memory that is paramount; it is usually the effect on time. Almost any lack of memory can be overcome by some form of programming, such as use of virtual memory. The problem is that the time cost of implementing a virtual memory may be excessive but will depend on the specific application at hand.

The factor of greatest importance in assessing the need for memory or the press of time is the rate at which transactions must be carried out. And this, in turn, depends not only on how long the file searching and computation take, but the number of users who may be connected and waiting in a queue for service. Again, this is so dependent on the specific application that not much can be said generally.

One facet of transaction rate is *volatility*, the rate at which a file or database changes. A file of stock market transactions or of positions of aircraft in an air traffic control system is going to change frequently and in both cases it is essential that the computer keep up with what can be very high volatility. A bibliographic information retrieval system does not have a high change rate. Changes to files may, in fact be posted during low usage times of day or days of the week to avoid slowing search transactions during prime time. Search transactions do not necessarily require high speed of execution, but there can be a great many pending at any one time and user satisfaction is going to depend on the elapsed time required to respond to any given query. Consequently, *query rate* is the other major factor in determining a system's time performance.

6.3

Basic Concepts of File Structure

This section is concerned with the organization of records within files. A primary consideration is the assumption that records will be stored on disks or in some auxiliary memory that is larger in capacity and slower in read–write speed than RAM. Access time is critical. We do not *want* the auxiliary memory to be slower, but will tolerate it because of the high cost of speed and because, with good organization and program design, we can do without some of the speed. A major consideration is how to organize data to minimize the time it takes to find the records wanted and read them into RAM.

6.3.1 The Order of Records

If the records of a file were stored in random order, then there would be no way to learn where a given record is, in advance of searching. A program would have to start at the beginning of a memory block and look at every record until it found the one wanted. For a file of n records, this requires that an average of $n/2$ records be examined, and possibly as many disk accessions carried out. A disk accession (i.e., reading a record stored at a specified location) takes on the order of milliseconds, while commands to operate on data in RAM are executed at speeds measured in microseconds or nanoseconds.

Since the time it takes to access one record and then to read it takes time equivalent to thousands of RAM-directed computer commands, it is important to try to minimize the number of accessions. While the computer is waiting for a record to be read, it may not be able to do anything else with the program that called for the record. *Time-sharing* or *multitasking* are modes of computer operation in which the computer can make use of input and output (I/O) delay times to operate other programs. A disk accession is begun and, while waiting for it to be completed, part of another program is run, possibly parts of several programs. This kind of internal traffic management within the computer is itself time-consuming but less so than waiting for I/O commands to be completed before starting the next command. This mode of operation is only minimally available in small personal computers, common in larger workstations, and standard in mainframe computers.

If records are placed in sequence based on the values of an attribute, the *sort key*, then we can predict approximately where a record with a given key value is located and thereby save much search time in finding and reading that record.

6.3.2 Finding Records

There are four basic ways to find the location of a record: (1) examining each in turn until a desired record is found; (2) using an index that tells the location or approximate location; (3) using a pointer in each record to point to the location of the next record; (4) using the value of the *search key* to compute the location of the record corresponding to the key value. A search key is an attribute value that identifies a record, such as SMITH, A.B. in the name attribute. The first method, examining each record, takes or can take a great deal of time, but conserves memory because no space need be devoted to indexes or pointers. The second can be fast but can tie up a great deal of memory for storing the index. The third is not particularly fast in searching, but is so in adding new records to or deleting from a file. The fourth can be the fastest of all but, as we shall see, it introduces complications that can slow it down. This is another example of the space–time trade-off mentioned in Section 6.2.2.

There are five organizational methods based on these location devices: (1) *sequential files*, in which records are stored contiguously, and usually in order according to content; (2) *indexed files*, in which a separate index provides information about the location of records in the main file; (3) *lists*, in which pointers tell the location of the next record, obviating the need for putting records physically in order; (4) *tree structures*, which combine some of the best features of sequential files and lists; and (5) *direct access structures*, which provide the fastest means of determining the location of a record.

6.4

Organizational Methods

Each of the methods described here has variations on how it is implemented by any given computer operating system. It may be difficult to learn exactly how a favorite retrieval or database system organizes records and it may not matter until a file grows very large and has a high level of activity. By then, changing software may be expensive.

6.4.1 Sequential Files

In a sequential file, records are stored contiguously and are normally in order based on a sort key. New records are added to a sequential file only by appending them to the end of the file. That means that if the file consists of records with key values 12, 15, and 18, and we want to add a record with key 14, it would go at the end of the file, which is then no longer in key sequence. This is illustrated in Fig. 6.4. Or, we can copy the entire file, first copying the record with key 12, then reading in the new one, with key 14, then copying the rest of the original records in order. An alternative is to append the record, then sort the entire file, and yet another alternative is to leave the file with some records out of sequence and to sort it only every now and then. This last approach is fast when adding records but can slow searching drastically, especially for a highly volatile file. To delete a record can require a complete recopying of the file.

Although the sequential method may sound terribly inefficient because it is slow, it is efficient in its use of memory because no space need be devoted to storage of anything but the records, themselves, i.e., no indexes or pointers.

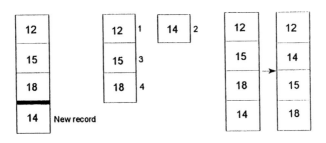

a. Append the new record (14) to the end of the file. This is the fastest method, but it destroys order among records.

b. Recopy the entire file, inserting the new record in its proper position. Time-consuming, but preserves order.

c. Append the new record as in a, then sort the file. This also preserves order but is very time-consuming.

Figure 6.4
Adding records to a sequential file: the execution time for methods *b* and *c* is nearly independent of the number of new records added, if that number is small compared with the number already in the file.

If there is a high ratio of search transactions to record addition or deletion transactions, then the method may also be reasonably efficient in use of time.

To search for a record sequentially means that each record must be examined in sequence, starting with the first, until the desired record is found. This requires an average of $n/2$ records to be examined. If the search key is not the sort key, or if values are not unique (e.g., searching a file ordered on employee number for all persons whose place of birth is CHICAGO), then we have to examine every record (n of them) of the file to be sure to find all the matching records.

If the file is in order, and we use the sort key as the search key, then there is a faster way to search, called a *binary search* (Salton, 1989, pp. 173–175). A binary search program would begin searching in the middle of the file. If the middle record is not the one wanted, then only half the remaining half of the file need be further searched (Fig. 6.5), because the program would know whether the desired record's key were higher or lower then the key tested. Then it would go to the middle of the remaining half, and then to the middle of *that* half, and so on. This logic gives, on average, the procedure with the fewest record accessions for finding records, if it is necessary to look at the records to find the keys. The maximum number of accessions required is $\log_2 n + 1$. If the record or memory design is such that the computer must deal with larger addressable units than the individual record, the efficiency of the method is degraded. That means we must first find the sector or element containing a group of records, read it, then search within it for the desired record.

When magnetic tape was the only computer auxiliary memory, all files were sequential, because the only way to access a record was to start at the beginning of the tape and read each record sequentially until the desired one was found. When disk memories were introduced, it became possible for a read mechanism to go more or less directly to a known record location, bypassing all others. With these memories, binary searches of sequential files can be carried

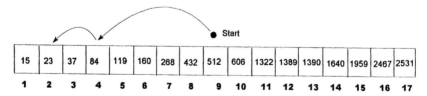

Figure 6.5

Binary search logic: to find the record with key 23 (if it exists in the file, which is not known when the search starts) start at the center. If the desired record key is lower than the center key (512) look further only in the first half of the file. Then find the center of the remaining half, etc., until only one record, or none, remains.

out, or other organizations can be used that allow faster searching than that possible with a linear sequential search.

6.4.2 Index–File Structures

Within RAM, a record can be accessed directly if its location is known. With a disk memory, we can go directly to only the track or sector (portion of a track) that contains the record. One method of finding the location in terms of track or sector is to create an index—a separate file that tells where records are in the first file. For example, as shown in Fig. 6.6, if we have a file, called the Main File, of rather large records, using ssn as a sort key, we might create a second file that consists only of ssn and the location of the corresponding record in the main file. This second file would have as many records as the first, but use many fewer bytes, only enough for an ssn and a location.

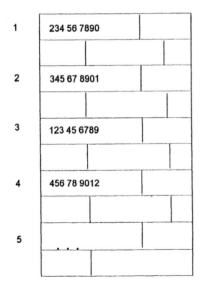

Main File	Inverted File

Figure 6.6
Inverted file or index: to find a record with a given key, look first in the inverted file and retrieve the record number. Then look in the Main File for that record. If the Inverted File can be stored in RAM, then finding a Main File record requires only one disk access.

Many more index records can be read into RAM than main file records.
A batch of index records can be searched in RAM at high speed, continuing
to read successive batches until the desired ssn is found. When it is found, the
location of the corresponding full record is extracted, and access can be gained
directly to the corresponding record.

There can be more than one index for a given main file. An index to
the personnel file can be created by occupation or employee name. In these cases,
we would again create one index record for each main file record, append a
location, and then sort the resulting index file by its key. A library's card catalog
is an example. Its records are sequenced by title, author, or subject heading, but
the books these records refer to, the components of the main file, are in order
by a call number, a combination of subject classification code and an author code.
A user must search the catalog on one of the other keys, find the appropriate
card, then retrieve the book's call number in order to locate the book, itself.

By using a number of inverted indexes to one main file, as in Fig. 6.7, we
can search the latter on any of several keys, at high speed. A considerable price
is paid, however, for the storage space required as additional indexes are added.
It adds to the cost in time to make a change to a file. Adding a new record to
the main file also requires adding one to each index file.

The advantage of the indexed file is the speed of search. Disadvantages
are the amount of memory consumed and the time required to change the files.
Index files work best under conditions in which there is relatively little change
action compared with search action. An example of a good application of this
method is an online database search service that updates its files only once a day,
week, or even month, but searches them thousands of times a day.

6.4.3 Lists

Some file applications may call for the opposite of the ideal indexed structure. Consider a hospital with a relatively rapidly changing population of patients, each of whom is likely to have a different medical history, set of laboratory tests, drugs prescribed, and therapies. There are likely to be several changes
to each record daily, but relatively little searching. Because of the large number
of possible attributes of any patient, a desirable file structure would allow entry
of only those laboratory and therapy reports that are needed for each individual
patient. This is preferable to reserving a fixed number of storage locations for
each patient, held for possible future use. The laboratory-type data would be
entered as separate records, linked to the appropriate patient.

One method of linking is to use pointers between records. Figure 6.8
shows a sequential file to which has been added a pointer to the next record as
an attribute of each record. *Next*, in this case, means the record with the next

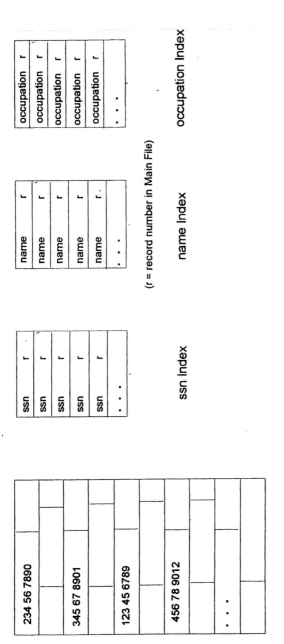

Main File

Figure 6.7 Use of multiple indexes: an inverted file or index can be created for as many attributes as desired. To search the main file on an attribute for which there is no index means a lengthy sequential search. If there is an index, using it to retrieve record number (r) means there need be only one accession of a record in the main file.

Record No.

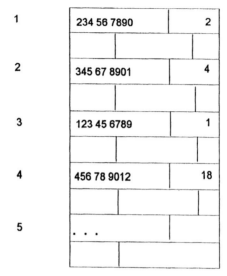

Figure 6.8
Pointers as a means of indicating record order: the records of this file are sequentially organized, i.e., attributes within the records are stored in the "conventional" way. One of the attributes is a pointer to the record with the next higher key value.

higher value of the sort key. If this is done, then there is no longer a need to keep records in physical order by sort key, because the physical order of storage no longer indicates the logical order of key values.

In some applications it may be useful to know what record pointed *to* any given record. For this purpose, a second series of pointers can be established, so that one series points forward to the next higher key value and one points backward to the previous, or next smaller, key value. These are then called *forward* and *backward* pointers, respectively.

This is the general structure of a *list*. In computer science the term has a special meaning and does not denote simply an array. Typically, two or more lists are maintained simultaneously. One contains the data, and one contains information about empty or unused space in the area of memory set aside for future additions to the file. Here is a brief example of how it might work.

To start with, before any data are put into the file, set aside an area such as shown in Fig. 6.9, here containing 10 record positions, each with an address $(1, 2, \ldots, 10)$ and initially set up each with a pointer to the next sequential record position, except for the last, whose zero value is a code indicating the

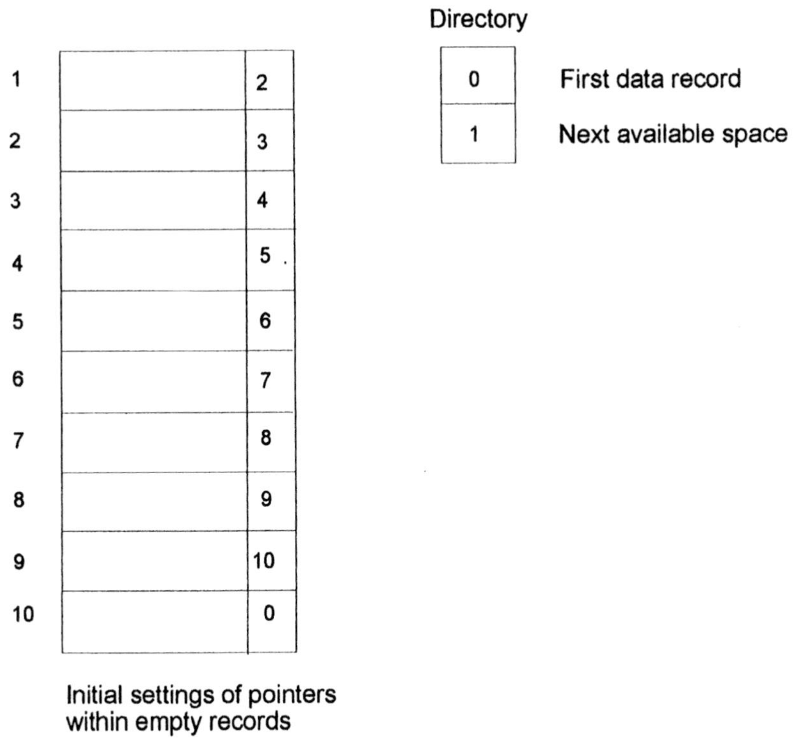

Directory

1		2
2		3
3		4
4		5 .
5		6
6		7
7		8
8		9
9		10
10		0

0	First data record
1	Next available space

**Initial settings of pointers
within empty records**

Figure 6.9
Initial setup of a list structure: each record position, except the last, has a pointer to the next physical record, all being initially empty. The directory shows, by the 0, that there is no first data record and that position 1 is the first available space.

end of the list. A *directory*, a small file outside the main file space, tells where the first data record is to be found and where the next free record space is to be found. Initially, there are no data records, so this condition is designated by a 0 in the data directory and a 1 in the empty space directory to point to the first record as the first available space.

Now, add the first data record (Fig. 6.10). It has a key of 324. We put it (a) in position 1, indicated by the pointer in the free-space directory, take the pointer from that record and put it (b) in the free-space directory (c). We also record the address of the first record in the data directory (d) and change the pointer in the first data record (e) to 0, indicating that there is no next data record. So far, this has been a great deal of work to place a single record in a file.

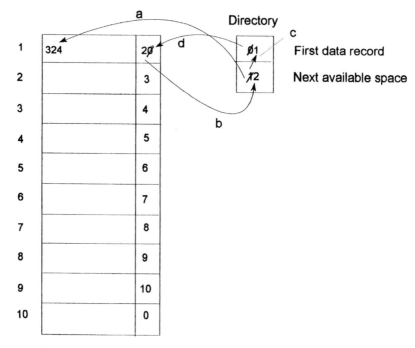

State of the file after adding one
new record, in position 1.

Figure 6.10
Adding a record to a list: a record with key 324 has been added in the record space indicated by
the directory as being next available. The new record's pointer is set to the previous value of first
data record. The next available space pointer gets the value previously used as pointer in the record
in position 1. The 0 in the pointer of record 1 indicates that there is no next data record.

Now (Fig. 6.11) we add a second record. It has a key of 287 which
means it logically *precedes* number 324. So we want to put the new record first
logically, but since the first physical record position is now in use, we do not
want to have to move the incumbent. So, we look (a) to the data directory,
which points to physical record position 1, in which is found a key of 324.
The new record is smaller so we take the pointer from the free-space directory
and place it (b) in the data directory, indicating that the current next free space
is to be the logically first data record. Then put the new record (c) in position 2, formerly pointed to by the free-space directory. This new record should
point to the record with key value 324, so the old first record pointer (1) is
placed (d) in the pointer of record 2. The old pointer to the next free space,

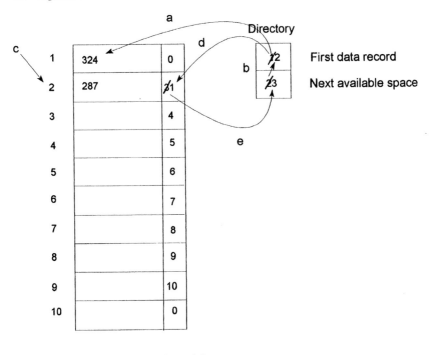

State of the file after adding
a second new record, in
position 2.

Figure 6.11
Adding another record to a list: now, add a second record with key 287, less than the first record's key of 324, so it must logically precede that record. The new record goes in position 2, as indicated by next available space. It is now the logically first record, hence it points to record 1 as the next record.

in record position 2, goes to the next available space pointer (e). And that is all there is. No changing of record positions, but we have a file that is "in order" by key.

We can keep adding new records, in any order, but the work required is essentially the same as for the second record. Perhaps now the advantage of the method is becoming apparent. To delete a record, which is shown in Fig. 6.12, move the pointer value of the deleted record (a) to the pointer of the preceding record, move the pointer value (b) in the free-space directory into the deleted record, and place the pointer to the deleted record address (c) from record 2 into the free-space directory. That is all—no moving of records. The space deleted by this procedure will be reused when the next record is added to the file.

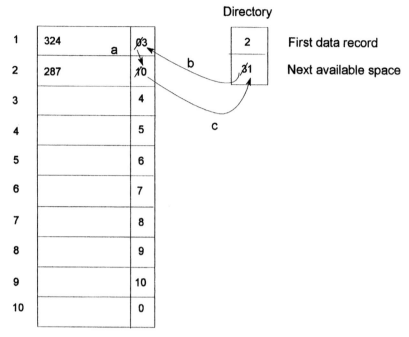

State of the file after deleting
the record, in position 1.

Figure 6.12
Deleting a record from a list: to delete the record with key 324, follow the chain of pointers until
that key is reached. Set its pointer to show the next available empty record (3). The first data record
value remains 2, but the next available space, in the directory, is set to 1. It is not necessary to remove
the data from record 1; when a new record arrives, the old information will simply be written over.

By using multiple pointers in a record, any record can point to several
next ones, each using a different sense of "next." This is the essence of the
multilist file structure (Lefkovitz, 1969). It is the physical analog of hypertext.
When considering any record, there may be a variety of "next" records to go
to. There might be a basic patient record, as in Fig. 6.13, containing primarily
identification data, then a series of pointers to laboratory results, drugs prescribed, therapy prescribed and taken, etc. The first laboratory record might
point to a second, and so on. The result is a file with a completely variable
number of components of each patient's logical record, with new component
entries being added as needed and older ones dropped when no longer needed.

The advantages of this method are its flexibility and comparatively modest
space requirements. We can not only change the content of such a file with rel-

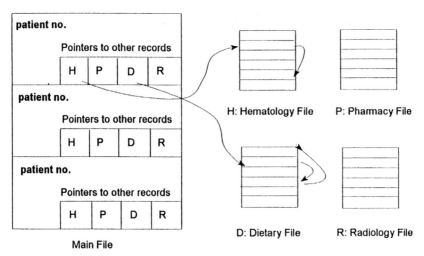

Main File

Figure 6.13

Multilist structure: there is a main file record for each hospital patient. Each points to the first relevant record in one of the other files, and that to the next relevant record, and so on. All these records could be interfiled in one large file. The number of attributes in use and the number of values occurring for patients may vary considerably from person to person.

ative ease and speed, but we can even change its logical structure (variable numbers of subordinate records, such as the lab reports referred to above). Pointers individually do not take up much space, but if we use many of them, the space cost can become significant. The disadvantage is that search speed may be quite slow. This is another space–time trade-off.

6.4.4   Trees

A tree structure is a set of records linked by two or more pointers. Each points to succeeding records whose keys are "above" or "below" the current one. A directory points the search program to the location of the initial record, which is the one having the median key value, i.e., half the other keys are below, and half, above (see Fig. 6.14). A search is done by starting at the initial, trunk, or root record and following the pointer in the appropriate direction. Then, at the next record, make a similar decision, and so on until the sought-for record is found, or it becomes clear it will not be found (Korth and Silberschatz, 1986, pp. 275–282).

By *balanced* is meant that, when following a tree from its root, at any point half the remaining branches or twigs are to one side of the current one,

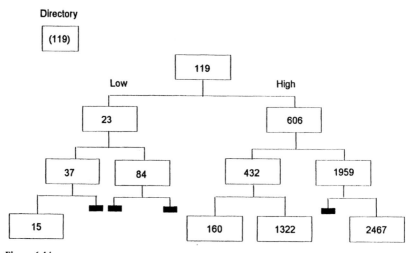

Figure 6.14

A balanced binary tree: the directory points to the record holding key value 119. Thereafter, each record has two pointers, one to the next lower valued key, one to the next higher valued key. A horizontal line indicates an end of the tree. Shown here are only keys, not other record content.

and half are to the other side. If a tree were not balanced, a point might be hit where there were 60 remaining tree elements below that point, 50 on one side and 10 on the other, requiring considerably more search time down one branch than the other. In a balanced tree, it would always be close to 30 and 30. A balanced tree structure is a special case of a list. The intent is to provide a fast method of searching a sorted file while retaining the advantage of a list structure. It allows for use of binary search logic, traditionally associated with sequential files. The concept can be generalized to an n-ary tree with n (> 2) pointers, giving faster searching as n increases, but with more space devoted to pointer storage as in Fig. 6.15.

The advantage of this method is fast searching compared with both sequential file and conventional list searching. The main disadvantage is the space required for storing pointers.

The same tree could accommodate sets of pointers based on many different keys, so that it performs like a multilist structure.

6.4.5 Direct-Access Structures

The single most common disadvantage of all the other methods considered thus far is the time it takes to find where a record with a known key is

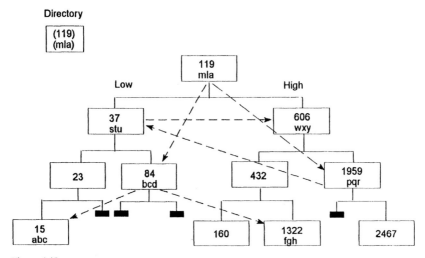

Figure 6.15
Two trees combined: a second set of pointers in each record enables the tree to serve to connect records based on two different keys, one shown as numeric, one alphabetic. The dashed-line arrows represent alphabetic pointers. Note that the records are not in the same sequence in the alphabetic tree as the numeric.

stored. A direct-access structure permits making use of a family of techniques known as *hashing* or *mapping* (Knott, 1975; Knuth, 1973, pp. 550–567) to transform a key value into an address.

Figure 6.16 shows the basic method. A common method of address computation is to divide the key by a prime number and use the remainder as an address. If the key is alphanumeric it can be treated as a binary number, or the nonnumeric characters can be converted first and then the division carried out. For example, if a key were 12,345 and the prime number, 31, then the result of a division is 398 with a remainder of 7. The 7 is used as the address or relative address. Note that the address computed uses fewer digits than the key, else we would not need the computation. This method can map any set of keys into 31 address locations. In another method, square the key and extract the required number of digits from the middle of the product. For example, the square of 12,345 is 152,389,025. One might extract digits 4 and 5 (counting from the right), yielding an address of 89. The number of digits used must be consistent with the size of the memory into which the keys are mapped.

In some cases it would be possible to set aside a location for every possible key value; then the key instantly translates into a location. It could be done with a social security number by setting aside "only" a billion locations (ssn is a nine-digit number). For an employer with 9000 employees whose records are

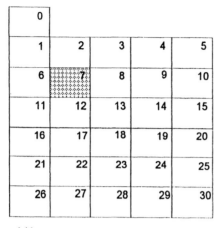

Search key = 12345

Divisor = 31

12345 / 31 = 398 7/31

Hashed address = 7

Figure 6.16
Hashing or address mapping: the key of a record being searched for, or to be stored, is divided by a prime number equal to the amount of addressing space. The remainder is the actual or relative storage location.

to be sorted on this key, this is an impractical solution. Instead, this employer would surely prefer to be able to do a simple computation on the ssn and compute a four-digit address from it, thereby limiting required memory to locations numbered 0 to 9999. An employer with 100 employees could afford to use a sequential search, simplifying the search program.

Hashing or mapping can be used to decide both where to store a new record and where to find one already stored. It is extremely fast. It uses high-speed computation instead of slow disk access to an index. If used for a file that needs only one search key and has relatively low volatility it is probably the best of methods. But it has two major drawbacks. First, note that key 76, with a divisor of 13, hashes to 11, key 77 hashes to 12, and 78, to 0. Thus, successively occurring keys (76, 77, 78) will not normally be stored in adjacent locations; hence, in doing a sequential search of the file, it cannot be known where a record identified only as "next" will be stored. We must have the key. Variations have been developed to alleviate this problem (Garg and Gotlieb, 1986).

The second and usually more important disadvantage of hashing is that more than one key can hash to the same value. Key 76 with a divisor of 13 hashes to 11, as do 89, 167, etc. Since two records cannot be placed at the same location, this attractive method of finding locations seems flawed. The reader is invited to ponder this problem. A solution is discussed in Section 6.6.2.

6.5

Parsing of Data Elements

In a personnel file for which an index is to be created on the attribute ssn, we would expect to include in this index each ssn and the number of the record in which it occurred. If, on the other hand, there were a text attribute in the record, say a narrative summary of the employee's job history, then we would hardly expect to index this by including the complete text of the summary in the index. That would be useless, because we would never expect a searcher to use a complete summary as one long search key.

With the key-word method of indexing text, the question arises of which words to use. In this chapter we are not so concerned about which actual words to choose as about deciding how to organize them. One possible selection rule is to select every word in the text. This has the advantage of mechanical simplicity, but results in selection of many words that common sense suggests cannot make a meaningful contribution to a good index and, of course, fills memory with useless entries. We can improve on this approach by omitting those words found on a *stop list*, typically a list of very common words generally deemed to lend no significance to identification of the subject matter of a text (Fox, 1990). Such words, in English, include *the, of, an,* and the like. The Dialog Corporation, with perhaps the largest collection of online files in the world, uses only AN, AND, BY, FOR, FROM, OF, THE, TO, and WITH in its stop list, because so many seemingly innocuous words may have meaning to some users. The word A, for example, would be dropped by most of us, but it identifies a vitamin of importance to others.

Another approach altogether is for a human indexer to read the text and select the most meaningful words that describe the subject. This method can be counted on to give good descriptive material, but adds to the cost of preparing the index. Automatic selection of key words by computer is possible but has never worked well enough to be successfully used commercially. By this we mean selection of key words as an index to be used as a surrogate for searching. This is different from using user-supplied key words to find relevant documents. Also, indexers do not always agree on which words are most meaningful (Sievert and Andrews, 1991). Searchers, then, have some guessing to do.

Indexing may use the complete content of an attribute whose value requires relatively little memory (such as ssn), or it may *not* use the complete content if the attribute value takes up a great deal of space and is such that no user is ever likely to use the entire value as a search key.

Consider a person's name when used in an author field of a bibliographic record. Certainly it seems clear that it is desirable to index bibliographic records by author, but in what form should the name appear in the index? Should we list only the last names? Also list the first names if we have them? Should the names be indexed in some strict format? If using only initials, is it necessary to use periods after each?

Subject headings also raise problems because these are usually syntactic statements of several words, and there are several for each bibliographic record. Should the index entry consist of the complete set of subject headings used in a record, as a unit, together with record number? Should each subject heading be separately entered? Should each word in each subject heading be indexed separately?

There are two basic mechanical ways of parsing a syntactic expression to create an index, by word or by phrase. There can also be a combination of the two or, of course, no index at all.

6.5.1 Phrase Parsing

Phrase parsing means to treat the entirety of an attribute value as a single phrase, or single entity for indexing purposes. The ssn is of this type, because the entire value of the attribute is used as the index element. An attribute like author is conventionally recognized as a phrase, consisting typically of last name, a comma, a space, first name, comma, space, middle name. Since there are often multiple authors for a published work, each of these name phrases is indexed, but each author's name is treated as a whole, i.e., we do not put the last name in an index separate from that containing first name, but we do keep the first author separate from the second. Similarly, if a document is described by the subject headings EUROPEAN HISTORY and FRENCH REVOLUTION, then each of these phrases might be included in the index, as an entity, but not the individual words HISTORY or REVOLUTION.

6.5.2 Word Parsing

This means to break up the content of an attribute value into its individual words, possibly deleting "stop" words. In this case, the original syntax may be lost *within the index*. This method is used with relatively large bodies of text, in which inclusion of the entirety in an index would be meaningless.

If an author's name were word parsed then we could search on first or last name or even a single initial, but information retrieval system (IRS) operators do not usually consider such options worth the cost. However, an institutional name might benefit from word parsing because it is more likely users will remember individual words in the title, but not the exact name. Is the insurance company called MASSACHUSETTS MUTUAL or MUTUAL OF

MASSACHUSETTS? Word parsing eliminates the problem. We search for MAS-SACHUSETTS near (within two words of) MUTUAL, in either direction.

6.5.3 Word and Phrase Parsing

Both word and phrase parsing might be used with such attributes as sub-ject headings, job titles, or names of inventoried items. This allows those who know the correct phrase to find it quickly. It also allows browsers wider lati-tude for searching. Someone who wants to look for material on revolutions in Europe, could ask for EUROPEAN HISTORY or FRENCH REVOLUTION and might also find material indexed simply under REVOLUTION and EUROPE. This condescension to the user can add considerably to the size and cost of an index, but also to its utility.

The form of parsing used to create indexes is of critical importance to the success of an IRS. Economically, an error in judgment can result in memory's being allocated to the storage of useless data. Unless users understand parsing and the specific parsing techniques used with each attribute, they may be unable to find the information they want. Because author is likely to be phrase parsed, it is not possible to search on an author's first name. If title is only word parsed, as is often the case, then it is cumbersome to browse an alphabetically ordered list of titles of works in the file. To do so would require accessing the main file to retrieve only titles from records, rather than finding the titles, already in order, in an index.

Figure 6.17 shows some examples of the methods.

6.6
Combination Structures

There is almost no limit to the number and type of combinations of the basic methods of organizing information. Indeed, most methods used in practical settings are combinations. Here are a few.

6.6.1 Nested Indexes

In a sequential file consisting of a large number of large records, so that only a small fraction can fit in RAM, there is an advantage to creating a sec-ond, index file consisting of the main file record keys and locations. The index can be searched faster because we can bring more of its records at one time from disk storage into RAM than we can main file records; hence, we can

Field	Content	Parsing
AU	MEADOW, CHARLES T.; COCHRANE, PAULINE A.	PHRASE*
TI	INFORMATION RETRIEVAL AND THE HUMAN CONDITION	WORD
DE	INFORMATION RETRIEVAL;	
	IMPACT OF INFORMATION RETRIEVAL	BOTH*
JN	INFORMATION RETRIEVAL	PHRASE

* Parsing recognizes subfield boundaries denoted by a semi-colon

Terms extracted for the <u>Inverted File</u>

au=meadow, charles t.
au=cochrane, pauline a.
information/ti
retrieval/ti
[and] **
[the] **
human/ti
retrieval/de
condition/ti
information retrieval/de
information/de
retrieval/de
impact of information retrieval/de
impact/de
[of] **
information/de
retrieval/de
jn=information retrieval

Terms as they will appear in the <u>Inverted File</u>

au=cochrane, pauline
au=meadow, charles t.
condition/ti
effects/de
human/ti
impact/de
impact of information

information/de,ti
information retrieval/de
jn=information retrieval
retrieval/de,ti

Notes: ** These words are normally dropped by use of a stop list.

Figure 6.17
Word and phrase parsing: the left-hand column shows words and phrases in the order they are extracted from the text. The right-hand column shows how they would be filed in the inverted file.

more quickly find the key wanted. If the file is to be searched on the basis of n keys (say a sort key and any of $n - 1$ other attributes found in the record), then the index is necessary to avoid searching the entire main file each time a search is done. The combined indexes in this case will have n times the

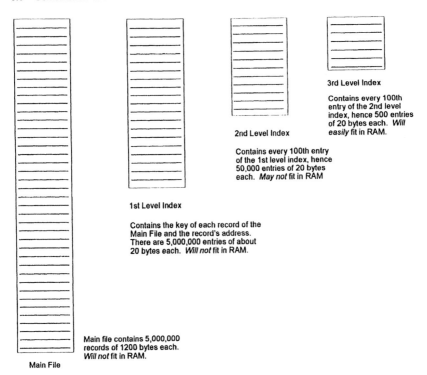

3rd Level Index

Contains every 100th
entry of the 2nd level
index, hence 500 entries
of 20 bytes each. *Will
easily* fit in RAM.

2nd Level Index

Contains every 100th entry
of the 1st level index, hence
50,000 entries of 20 bytes
each. *May not* fit in RAM

1st Level Index

Contains the key of each record of the
Main File and the record's address.
There are 5,000,000 entries of about
20 bytes each. *Will not* fit in RAM.

Main file contains 5,000,000
records of 1200 bytes each.
Will not fit in RAM.

Main File

Figure 6.18
Nested indexes: this example shows a hypothetical file of five million records, with three levels of
indexing. Only the third index is sure to fit in RAM in its entirety.

number of records as the main file and, although they will be smaller records,
the totality becomes a burden to search. The n indexes can be treated as n
different files or combined into a large, single file. Dialog does this. Their inverted file consists of words extracted from fields to constitute what they call the
basic index plus words or values extracted from other fields, prefixed by a field
code. For example, a record about a journal article published in the year 1999
would have an entry PY = 1999 interfiled with words taken from the body
of the text or title, and placed alphabetically among them, followed perhaps
by PYRITE.

To speed the searching of such a large, combined index, we can create an
index to *it*, as in Fig. 6.18. An effective way to do this is to determine how many
index records can fit in RAM at one time. Suppose this to be 100. Then, in a
third file, enter the 1st, 101st, ... keys in the index and their locations within
the index file area.

With any luck, the index to the index will now fit in RAM. This means that to find any record we would need only two disk accessions: one for the portion of the main index, pointed to by the in-RAM index, and one for the record, itself. If the entire second-level index does not fit into RAM, then create a third-level index, and so on. Note that files of one million or more records are now common and files of 100 million or more are in use. If each successive index level reduces the number by a factor of 100, a one-million-record file would have one million records in the first index, 10,000 entries in the second-level index, and 100 entries in a third-level index. Perhaps only the third would fit in RAM.

6.6.2 Direct Structure with Chains

The common solution to the problem of more than one key hashing to the same value or address is to create a list of all those records that have the same hashed value, as we see in Fig. 6.19. The first record assigned a given hash value is placed in the computed location. The next record is placed in a vacant location and a pointer links the record stored at the hashed location to the second record at its new location. If a third record with the same hash value arrives, it is linked by pointer from the second record, and so on. In each record

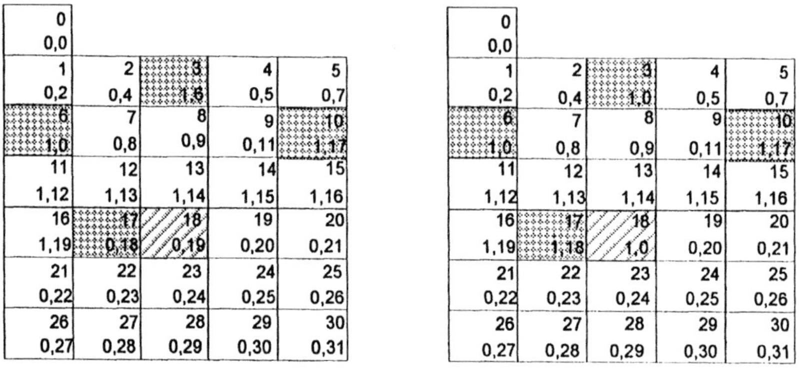

Figure 6.19

Direct file structure with pointers: the figure on the left shows the status of a file to which a new record, whose key hashes to 10, is to be added. That location is in use, but points to 17, which is also in use but is the end of the chain. Hence, put the new record in the next free space (18), the pointer in 17 will still point to 18, but the status code shows 17 is not the end of the chain. The new record is now in location 18 and its status indicator shows it as the end of a chain of records that originally hashed to 10. Note a second chain going from 3 to 6.

a 1 indicates the record position is in use—contains data. A zero indicates the space is available. This code is followed by a pointer to the next record, whether data or unused. A zero here indicates the end of a chain.

When more than one key value produces the same address location, this is called a *collision*. Collision probability can be reduced by increasing the amount of space devoted to file storage or by varying the hashing algorithm. But complete elimination of collisions is virtually impossible with hashing unless the range of key values is quite limited, relative to available memory. The method we have suggested, using any available empty location to store the next record that collides with an existing one, makes finding the space fast and easy, but increases the possibility of a collision because it uses up a space that might be directly assigned to another record. An alternative is to maintain a separate file dedicated to records that caused a collision in the main file.

No variation on hashing is likely to be perfect, but it can be fast. It may, in actual application, require frequent adjustment in expanse of memory allocated and in choice of the hashing divisor if the file is highly volatile.

6.6.3 Indexed Sequential Access Method

Like the previous organizations, the indexed sequential access method (ISAM) is a family of methods. The essence of all ISAM variations (Fig. 6.20) is that a *main file* is created whose records are in order on a key and stored on disks such that the disk sector containing a given record can be directly accessed if the sector number is known (Korth and Silberschatz, 1986, pp. 266–274). An *index*, possibly nested, provides the location of the appropriate sector. The specific record will then have to be found within the sector by a sequential search, but this process takes little time if the number of records per sector is small. When the main file is created, it may have empty space built in, to allow for the later addition of records without the need to recopy the file. In case all the empty space in a sector is used up, *overflow areas* are set aside, and a list method is used to connect the main file with the overflow area, and individual records with one another within the overflow area.

Thus, there are three major parts of an ISAM file, actually three or more interrelated files—Main, Index, and Overflow. Because of the nests of indexes and overflow areas in the main file, more space has to be devoted to directories than in other organizations. These point to the beginning of files and subdivisions of files. They add to the overhead cost of the method. But, on average, ISAM is a reasonably efficient use of storage and effective in terms of speed. It is a commonly used method for these reasons.

Nested indexes point to
segments of the Main File

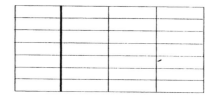

The Main File. Each sector (a row in this illustration)
contains an index, to the left of the heavy line, and a
set of records. The index gives the highest key value
of records in its sector and the address of the first of
any overflow records.

Overflow area. Records that logically belong
in the Main File, but for which there is no room,
are placed here in any of several arrangements.
They may all be in one structure, chained together,
or there may be a separate list for each sector
from which they overflow.

Figure 6.20
The indexed sequential file structure: such a structure has, at its heart, a sequential file, an index or
nest of indexes, and an area for storing overflow records from the main file.

6.7 _____

Summary

For any file, we have a choice between placing records in random order (or arrival order) and putting them in order according to a key. Random order means that the location of the record is not determined by the
value of an attribute in the record. Such a method is fast at placing the
record in memory, but may render searching impractically slow. Think of
a library with random ordering of the books on its shelves. This could
work for a small, personal library where the owner knows every book and
its location by heart, but it would be impossible for a major library. It is,
therefore, a technique almost unheard of in practical use for large computer
files.

It is far more common to order or sequence records on the basis of the value of one or more attributes, collectively known as the sort key. This gives two advantages: if we know the key, we can usually quickly find at least the approximate location of the record, thus saving considerable search time compared with having to search every record. Also we can make use of sequential searching when it is to our advantage. Sometimes, we might like to start at a given key, such as a fragment of an author's name, and then search in sequence until a name is reached that does not contain the fragment. For example, we might want to look for an author whose name begins with TCHAI. To do this, find the first name that begins with this string, then search sequentially until a name is reached that does not begin with this string.

We have established the concept that the "next record" may not necessarily be the next one in physical position in memory, but the next one in terms of key value.

In order to find records, given a key, we can use either an index or a computational method. The latter method is faster, by far, but the former preserves the ability to search sequentially when we want to search on the basis of more than one key.

The file structures in use with most database software make use of combinations of the various methods we have surveyed. Largely, this is because different files and usage patterns place different demands on file structures. To avoid a different structure for each file, we tend to compromise on some aspects in order to achieve good performance on most of them.

7

Querying the Information Retrieval System

7.1

Introduction

Recall from Chapter 1 that subsequent to the creation or recognition of an information gap or anomalous state of knowledge (ASK), there may be several different expressions of what information is needed. One may be the expression made to an intermediary or person whose profession it is to assist in carrying out information searches. A second form of statement may be the need as expressed *after* consultation with the intermediary. And a third—the one required statement—is the query presented to the information retrieval system (IRS). This last statement is the one interpreted by the IRS.

If the query is in natural language, then the IRS interpreter must exercise a great deal of "judgment" to be able to translate accurately into the target command language. If the query is written in a typical command language, little or no judgment may be required for the IRS to do faithfully what was asked. The word *judgment* is in quotation marks because some readers may object to the notion of a computer's showing judgment, but judgment by computer may mean merely that it uses complex, context-dependent logic to interpret statements. Natural-language statements may be ambiguous in syntax and meaning. Command-language statements, on the other hand, are likely to have been designed to be unambiguous to the software that interprets them, requiring little resolution of ambiguity. The command language may not permit the statement of the user's true interest to be given in subtle language, but the IRS is asked to interpret queries, *not* the intent behind them. *Judgment* then is the logical ability to disambiguate an expression to convert it into command language.

We will continue to use the term *query* to refer to the user's or intermediary's statement to the IRS. A query is a statement or series of statements made by a user to a retrieval system for the purpose of specifying what information is to be retrieved and in what form. Most commonly, it is stated in the formal, artificial language called a *query language*. The other main language possibility is natural language.

Almost any IRS feeds back certain information to a user about the progress of a search, such as how many records were found meeting the specified criteria. On the basis of this information, the user decides what, if any, query statements to issue next and frequently also decides whether to proceed with the search as initially conceived, to modify it, or to start entirely over again. While IRSs vary considerably in the appearance of their languages, feedback procedures, and record formats, the essence of the information passed in either direction between user and system tends to be much the same from system to system.

The hardest part of learning to write queries that succeed is learning how to describe the information. Successful queries (1) retrieve the information wanted with (2) only a tolerable amount of unwanted information and (3) at a reasonable cost. Although studies of users and their behavior are sparse on this topic, it appears that the problem is not so much learning and using a new (command) language as knowing what to say—in any language. If a user is looking for information on the decay of plastics in a landfill, is it necessary to describe the chemical transformation? Is it sufficient to use a few generic terms such as DECAY or BIODEGRADABLE, together with PLASTIC? There are too many options, variations in user needs, databases, and IRSs to be able to make a general suggestion about how this query should be stated.

In this chapter we concentrate more on describing tools available (IRS functions, languages, and commands) than on how to use them. Chapter 8 covers how commands are *interpreted* and executed. Chapter 13 has some material on how to *use* commands, but teaching effective use of an IRS is quite different from our goal of describing system function and structure. Our approach is to present the basic functional logic that can be called upon, then review a sample of the commercial systems available.

7.2
Language Types

A query language is the means by which the user tells the IRS what to do or what is wanted. There are two broad types: *procedural*; and *nonprocedural* or *descriptive*. A procedural language involves the use of *commands*. A procedural IR language is much like a traditional computer programming language. The user makes such imperative statements as SELECT <records meeting certain criteria>, PRINT <certain records from a designated set of the database>, or LOGOFF from the current online session and break the communication link.

A nonprocedural language is used to tell the IRS what result is wanted, and the IRS then works out how to produce it. The same information is conveyed as with a command or procedural language, but imperative verbs are not used and often the IRS prompts the user: What subjects should be selected? In what order should records be displayed?

Some descriptive languages use a graphic format. The user fills in values in a table. The placement of these values conveys the logic, and the whole then becomes a form of graphic representation of the search logic.

Figure 7.1 shows an example of a *graphic query representation* or *concept map*. The query represented is for a search on earthquake-resistant construction techniques used in California, with a date restriction. There are three subject facets, one for the concept EARTHQUAKES, one for CONSTRUCTION, and one for CALIFORNIA. Then there is a date facet. TECHNIQUES is not the sort of term that helps much because an article on a new building material or method of construction may never mention the word. The date facet simply shows a range of acceptable publication dates, 1990–1999. The Boolean logic of this query is an understood OR between terms of any one facet and an AND between facets.

Languages or user interfaces are often referred to as *menu-based*. This means that a list of options is presented to the user, who selects one or more rather than typing the entire value indicated. Selection can be by moving a cursor to the choice and double clicking a mouse button, striking one key, or typing the number or first letter of the choice. This method saves much typing time and probably eliminates many typographical errors. It is, of course, still possible to make the wrong selection. Clearly, the menu method is useful only when the number of choices is limited. Finally, the menu method is a means of *entering* information into a computer, or conveying elements of a language;

Query: Information about earthquake resistant construction
techniques used in California, published between 1990 and 1999.

EARTHQUAKES	CONSTRUCTION	CALIFORNIA	1990-1999
earthquakes tremor shock	construction building	california san andreas	1990-1999

Figure 7.1

A concept map: the query is at top. Terms in the first line of the map are taken directly from the query. Those below are deemed to be related to the terms in the query.

it is not really a type of language. Either commands or data descriptions can be entered this way. Some World Wide Web search engines provide menu type options that can be used to broadly restrict a search prior to entry of the query, for example, by requiring a term to be in a certain part of a document. Web site indexing is rarely as detailed as is that associated with bibliographic retrieval systems.

Occasionally, writers refer to a menu language as a contrast to a command-based Boolean language. This is a misnomer. The *language* is not Boolean, the detailed logic is. We can use menus to form sets and combine them according to Boolean algebraic laws, or we can use a command language to implement fuzzy-set logic.

7.3
Query Logic

In most retrieval systems, users are asked to consider the database as a set of records about a set of entities. The retrieval procedure is to describe characteristics of subsets of the database in which the user is interested. Indeed, one definition of IR is that it is a method of partitioning a database such that one partition holds only the records of interest.

If a query results in retrieval of a record that meets the formal specifications of the query, but clearly is not relevant to the question, such a record is called a *false drop*. If a query language permits only individual words as query terms, without consideration of their proximity or order of occurrence in the record, then a user interested in FOOD FISH would have to ask for FOOD AND FISH. The user interested in FISH FOOD would ask for FISH AND FOOD, logically the same thing. The two concepts do not differ to this assumed query interpreter. Any false drops in this case are the consequence of limited query language.

False drops are also a natural consequence of a conscious attempt by the searcher to compose a broad query, maximizing *recall*, the percentage of relevant material found, in order to be sure little or nothing is missed. The opposite strategy, maximizing *precision*, aiming for a high assurance of relevance, probably causes the system to fail to retrieve some records that are at least marginally relevant. The trade-off between these two strategies is discussed in Chapter 13.

There are several approaches to the manner of expressing the logic of a query. Whatever the language, a query statement results in the creation of a subset of the database, which we shall call the *retrieved set* (or sometimes the *retrieval set*) or simply the *set*. There are two meanings of *logic* to contend with. One, which can be called *macro logic*, is concerned with the system of principles underlying an activity or science... [describing a] necessary connection or outcome *(Webster's,* 1962, p. 862) and refers to what a query asks an IRS to find—the *what*. The second meaning, *micro logic,* refers to operation on sets that might be specified within a query as a part of its overall logic—the *how*.

One approach to query formulation involves defining sets in such a way that any given record is either in the set or not in it. Another approach is for the user to describe the desired output in terms of the likelihood of certain characteristics being present and asking the system to tell which records *best match* the query statement. In this form of querying, records are not treated as in or out of a set; they are in it to a variable degree. Sets so defined are *fuzzy sets* (Kraft and Buell, 1983; Sachs, 1976; Zadeh, 1965). Proponents argue that this is the more "natural" way for people to describe their needs or to understand what was found.

Yet another approach, really a variant on the second one, is for user and system to converse about the similarity of one record to another, about one set of records being like another, or about the relevance or utility of some records compared with others. For example, a user having retrieved a record may ask for others similar to it or may tell the IRS which records were most relevant and expect it to use this information to revise the query automatically to find more records like these or exclude more that are unlike these.

7.3.1 Sets and Subsets

The design of most text-oriented retrieval systems, until very recently, anticipated frequent revision of the query statements and called for the IRS to create a set for each query or even for each attribute-value specification or Boolean combination within the query. Each such set represented a subset of the database, but the word *set* is the common usage. Its physical manifestation is not seen by the user. It is a list of identifying numbers of records satisfying the query or component statement. The user is typically informed only of the set number assigned by the IRS and the number of records in the set. A set with no members is called a *null set*.

7.3.2 Relational Statements

These specify the characteristics of records in a set to be formed or, equiv-alently, the characteristics of records that compose a subset of the database. Sets are defined by specifying an attribute, a relationship, and a value, for exam-ple, publication date = 1987, author = KRAFT, DONALD H., or salary > 45000. Unfortunately, a different meaning of *relational* is used than in the context of relational databases. Each record whose named attribute has a value conforming to the stated requirement is included (has its number or pointer included) in the set. The basis is binary; the statement is either true or false; hence, a record is in the set or not. Note that equality is not the only relationship that may be expressed. The list usually includes:

Equality (=)—e.g., subject = TENNIS

Inequality (>, <, <=, <>, >=)—e.g., date > 881014 or subject <> TENNIS
  (The symbol <> is used for *not equal* in most computer languages.)

String containment (CONTAINS)—e.g., chemical name *contains* ETHYL
  (A record will be in the set if ETHYL occurs anywhere in the chemical name attribute value, such as in ETHYLENE or METHYL or TETRAETHYL LEAD, ...)

Range—e.g., 20,000 < salary < 100,000 (combination of inequalities)

7.3.3 Boolean Query Logic

Historically the first and still the most common method used for expressing micro logic in query statements is Boolean algebra. This involves specifying the operations to be performed on sets that have been defined by relationship statements or previous set operations. The sets are all subsets of a *universe of discourse*, which in this case is the database being searched. Sets within this universe of discourse are combined using the *Boolean operators* defined next and illustrated in Fig. 7.2.

1. *AND*—given sets 1 and 2, a third set can be defined that includes only records that are in *both* sets 1 and 2. Set 1 may contain records with date > 881014, and set 2, those with subject = TENNIS. Then if set 3 is defined as SET 1 AND SET 2, it would contain records with both the desired date and the desired subject. This is called the *logical product, intersection,* or *conjunction* of the first two sets.

2. *OR*—given two sets a third can be formed from records that are in either the first or the second or both. This is written SET 1 OR SET 2, and is called the *logical sum, union,* or *disjunction* of the first two sets. or is almost always used in the *inclusive* sense, meaning records that are in set 1 or set 2 *or both*.

3. *NOT*—while AND and OR are binary operators in the sense that their operations require at least two sets within the universe of discourse, NOT is a unary operator, meaning that it can be applied to a single set within the universe of discourse to specify all elements other than those in the set to which it is applied. If the single set is A, then NOT A is known as the *complement* of A. Normally, in a retrieval context, NOT is considered to mean AND NOT and is treated as a binary operator. Thus if records are wanted about WIMBLEDON

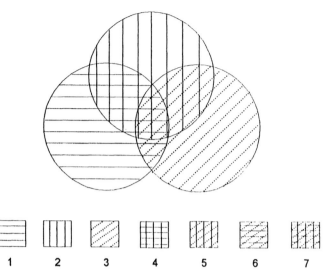

Figure 7.2
Venn diagram showing meanings of Boolean operators: regions 1, 2, and 3 represent three sets, or concepts. Regions 4, 5, and 6 are the intersections of sets 1 and 2, sets 2 and 3, and sets 1 and 3, respectively. Region 7 is the intersection of all sets 1, 2, and 3. Set 1 OR 2 is anything in region 1 or 2 or both. Set 1 NOT 2 is region 1 less region 4. Set 2 EXCLUSIVE OR 3 is regions 2 and 3 but not anything in region 6.

but not about TENNIS, the logic is that set 1 is to contain records with WIM-BLEDON; set 2, records without TENNIS; and set 3, their intersection, records containing WIMBLEDON but not TENNIS. Symbolically, SET 3 = SET 1 AND NOT SET 2. Set 3 is called the *logical difference* of sets 1 and 2.

4. *EXCLUSIVE OR*—found only occasionally in operational systems, this operator forms a new set containing members that are in one set or another, but *not both*. It may be expressed as the union of two sets from which the intersection has been excluded, or (S1 OR S2) NOT (S1 AND S2). An example of its use might be a search for medical patients who are taking drug A or drug B but not both, because a research project wants statistics on side effects, but wants to exclude the complications of interaction between these two drugs. If allowed in a query language, its symbol is likely to be XOR.

The not operator is easily misused. A record does not really have to be about Wimbledon to mention that name. (*She played better in the U.S. Open than last year at Wimbledon.*) The use of NOT logic can subtle. The searcher may be interested in the sociology of the Wimbledon area of London and not the sport of tennis, but refusal to accept occurrence of the word TENNIS in a record would also exclude one that says something like, "But Wimbledon is not just the home of a tennis stadium, it also...." NOT is practical to use where the values of the attributes are controlled and thus have very low ambiguity for the records under consideration. If a record has a language field, NOT might be used to exclude certain languages. Symbolically, SET 1 NOT LA = JAPANESE.

There are two major schools of thought about the logic used in a series of set definitions. One is to make the best definition possible and aim for an immediate solution to the problem of finding the information. Normally, experienced searchers do not expect to get the exact results they want on the first try, especially when searching records on the basis of words contained in a natural-language text. Therefore, their approach is to use a series of search statements or queries, beginning as probes and gradually improving on earlier results. Let users define sets, find out their size, perhaps browse through their contents, and then define a new set based on a modification of an earlier one. Sometimes it is necessary to back up, to return to a set other than the most recent one. To accommodate this approach to searching, the set number may be stated in a set definition statement, as if it were an attribute-value statement.

For example, suppose we are looking for information about the nutritional value of prepared foods for pet cats and dogs. It is worth a diversion here to point out that use of *and* in the preceding sentence has the meaning of *or* in Boolean logic. "Cats and dogs" in colloquial usage means, "either cats or dogs or both," but a rigidly literal interpretation might be "what is in common to, or a member of both sets of, cats and dogs." This is one of the reasons it can be difficult to teach Boolean logic applied to natural language. Now, the search might start with

SELECT PET OR PETS (creating Set 1, say, of 12,000 records)

Next, try

SELECT DOGS OR CATS (creating Set 2 of 8000 records)
SELECT FOOD AND NUTRITION (set 3, 5000 records)
SELECT S2 AND S3 (set 4, 3 records)

But this last may seem too small, so the searcher goes back to the more general

SELECT S1 AND S3 (set 5, 27 records)

Of course, using fictitious set sizes is quite artificial, but this example does convey the value of being able to return to any previously defined set and resume the search from that point.

Some IRSs use the logic of automatically ANDing a subsequent query statement to the most recent one. Searchers using such a system would start with a broad set definition, and then successively reduce its size by adding more restrictive criteria. It is not necessary to name the set being reduced, because it is always the last one created, nor is it necessary to write the Boolean AND because it is understood. For the search illustrated previously, the searcher might have started with an even broader term, ANIMALS, reduced this to PETS (assumed to mean ANIMALS AND PETS), then to CATS OR DOGS (now giving us ANIMALS AND PETS AND (CATS OR DOGS)). Under this approach, if a user wants to take another path, say CANINE NUTRITION, it is necessary to start the search again. There is no objective measure of which approach is better. Searchers tend to learn one method then to prefer that one thereafter.

The advantages of the Boolean query logic are that it is easy to write interpretive programs for it and that the logic is crisp and decisive: records are in a set or they are not. The disadvantage is a "soft" one: most people do not naturally think in Boolean terms; hence, the logic seems artificial, and it is sometimes difficult for users to express what they want or to understand what they get. Even though we may not know exactly how people think, the sense among researchers in the field tends to be that forcing users to work in terms of binary set-defining functions is not a popular approach (Bookstein, 1985; Croft and Thompson, 1987; Hildreth, 1983; Salton and McGill, 1983, pp. 118–155; Salton, 1989, pp. 345–361).

7.3.4 Ranked and Fuzzy Sets

Ranking means to assign to each record a measure of the closeness of the record's content to the query, or the extent to which the record matches the query. If ranking logic is used, Boolean operations can still be used to define a set, but we shall not be satisfied to say that any record is either in the set or not. It should be possible to rank all the records of a set on this measure and present them to the user in something like the order of probability of satisfying the information need. The point of ranking is to acknowledge that there is uncertainty (the definition of the set is fuzzy) as to whether the query exactly expressed the user's needs. If the user knows the question is imperfect, there is little to be gained in getting back an answer that claims, in effect, "Here is the exact information you wanted."

Mathematically, we can define a binary set membership function S such that, for any record R_i and query Q, the functional value is either 1 or 0, depending on whether R_i satisfies Q or not. A record satisfies a query if the attribute values and combinations of values requested in the query are found in the record. A notation can be

$$S(R_i \times Q) \rightarrow \{0, 1\},$$

which says that S maps the combination of a record and a query into a set of values, each either 0 or 1. The curly brackets indicate a set whose members are selected from the values shown within. Then the retrieval set for Q is all the records R_i such that $S(R_i \times Q) = 1$. This is a *crisply* defined set, each record of the database being clearly in the set or not in it.

If the function could take any value in the range between 0 and 1, then the set is *fuzzy* and the membership function can be written as

$$S(R_i \times Q) \rightarrow [0, 1],$$

which maps the records and query into the set of numbers lying between 0 and 1, inclusive. Then no record (except those for which S is exactly 0 or 1) can be said to be clearly in or not in the retrieval set. Effectively, S no longer expresses whether or not R_i is in the set, but the degree or strength of the association of R_i with the set. Otherwise put, the boundaries of the set are fuzzy. Any users, at any time, can set a threshold value for S, which could determine the set membership. Each record has a rank S, and the membership consists of all records of rank $\geq S$.

The use of ranking or measurement of the probability of a match, instead of binary Boolean logic, is receiving a great deal of attention in IR research (Noreault, Koll, and McGill, 1977; Noreault, McGill, and Koll, 1981; Ro, 1988; Robertson, Thompson, Macaskill, and Bovey, 1986; Salton and McGill, 1983, pp. 146–151). Some of the most common ways of achieving ranking of records are described next:

Weighted Terms

Membership in the set is not precisely defined. A user's query might include a weight for each term, showing its relative importance. Then the user can select the n records with the highest total weight. For example, the query might state (TENNIS(.8) OR GOLF(.4)) AND CHAMPION(.6). Probably, an IRS executing such a command would treat it first as an unweighted statement for formation of an initial set, then use the assigned weights to compute a rank for each record. Since CHAMPION is required here by the Boolean logic, the assignment of a weight to it is actually superfluous and represents one of the complications of this method. But if TENNIS and CHAMPION both appeared in a record, it would have a weight of $0.8 + 0.6 = 1.4$. If the combination GOLF and CHAMPION appeared, the record would have a weight of $0.4 + 0.6 = 1.0$. If both TENNIS and GOLF appeared with CHAMPION, the record might be construed to have either the weight $0.8 + 0.4 + 0.6 = 1.8$ or $0.8 + 0.6 = 1.4$ if we use only the higher weight in the OR expression. A variant is to add the weight each time a word appeared, so if GOLF appeared six times in a record, its total contribution to record weight would be 2.4.

This method has the apparent advantage of allowing users to express variations in the relative importance of terms used, but the same criticism applies as to Boolean logic: it is not a "natural" way to communicate. Users would have to learn how to assign weights, by experience, and until they became adept results might be worse than without weights.

Word Lists

To avoid the requirement for the precision of weights, a user can simply be allowed to use a list of words as a query statement. A record's score would be computed by adding 1 for each time any of the words appears in the record. The query could be TENNIS, GOLF, CHAMPION, CUT, TOURNAMENT, WINNER.

An article about the winner of a golf or tennis tournament is likely to have most of these words in it, probably some of them repeated several times. An article that mentions a *champion* of a political cause might have but a single instance of this one word, and few if any of the others, and so is unlikely to be highly ranked with respect to this query. This method can be used with weightings, also. Actually, the word list is simply a set of words with an implied OR between each pair, with equal weights. The method does not allow expression of the concept AND. Users are thereby saved the trouble of learning to express the logic but lose some precision of expression. A natural-language query can be interpreted this way, by ignoring all syntax, perhaps eliminating common words, leaving only a list of unconnected words.

Both these techniques can be interpreted as using fuzzy sets. In both cases, a large number of records might have a score greater than zero, and these form an initial set, but they may vary considerably on total score. Hence, the user makes the choice of a cutoff level.

Ranking Boolean Sets

Ranking is not the same as set formation, and there is no reason why ranking must be based only on information contained in the command used to define the set. A set could be formed in a conventional manner, using a binary set membership function. Then a separate command could define the basis for ranking members of the set, such as providing a list of terms of particular interest to the user. Records could also be ordered on the frequency of occurrence of attribute values within a set, such as ranking in order by frequency of occurrence of an author's name. (See Sections 7.4.6 and 8.3.1.) For example, a set might be formed based on the name of an author or institution and then the records ranked on the basis of relevance to some subject-defining terms.

7.3.5 Similarity Measures

In a sense, nothing could be easier for a user than to have found at least one record that is highly valued and to be able to say, "Get me more like that."

That first record would have to be found by use of other logic. If a user finds a bibliographic record or newspaper article on the desired subject and wants more, he or she can simply ask for more (Noreault, Koll, and McGill, 1977). Rather than reformulating the query, the query interpreter could treat the text of the record (or selected attributes of it) as an unweighted list of words, and the system could then proceed as described. The mathematics of some methods of similarity measurement are described in Section 9.6.1.

Another variation is *relevance feedback* (Salton and McGill, 1983, pp. 140–145, 236–243), about which we shall say more in Section 11.5. Briefly, the user provides a query statement, then rates some of the retrieved records on relevance. Using this rating, the IRS can increase or decrease the weighting of terms, select new ones, or delete unproductive ones in the original query on the basis of frequency of occurrence of terms in records. Even if the user has not rated individual terms in a retrieved record, the combination of user record ratings and IRS record analysis can result in a sharper definition for the next iteration of the search.

These methods have great appeal to users—they take so little effort. The main difficulty is that the query interpreter does not necessarily know exactly what aspects of the initial record were attractive to the user. It might base its measure on the largest text attribute of a record, while the user was interested in the combination of author and corporate source. There may not be any means in the language by which the user can specify what about the record is wanted.

7.4
Functions Performed

Although there is some variation from system to system, the functions performed by an IRS do not vary greatly. Much of what variation existed among the older online retrieval services was in terms of appearance or the name of a function, not its essence. Newer systems, operating locally, usually from a CD-ROM, or Web-based, may be significantly different. The following is a basic list.

7.4.1 Connect to a Remote IRS

This function links a user's computer to a remote IRS. It may not be required in local systems. It is also called *logging on* or *logging in* and is generally taken to include:

The user making the telephone connection with a telecommunications network, which includes dialing the telephone, telling the network computer what remote service is wanted, and explicitly or implicitly identifying such parameters as transmission speed, mode (duplex, half duplex), byte configuration, and parity mode

The user making the initial connection with the IRS, which requires identification of the user, typically by both an account number and a secret password

The system sending the user a series of messages containing news of the IRS, such as information on new databases, price changes, or new system features

The user then being put "into" a default database, i.e., some database that is selected automatically by the system as the one to be searched, with charges beginning to accrue based on this selection

Note that remote IR systems today are likely to be accessible through the Internet, whether or not they retain their older access mechanisms. This lowers the cost to users and changes the details on how to connect, but still involves some form of connection-making.

7.4.2 Select Database

The user selects the database or databases to work with. Some systems allow only one to be *open*, or in use, at a time, although multidatabase searching is possible and is becoming more common.

7.4.3 Search the Inverted File or Thesaurus

This function initiates a search in which the user browses through values of attributes, not complete records. For example, the user might be uncertain of the spelling of a person's name and want to scan a list of names beginning with a known string of letters. Then, based on this reconnaissance, a choice will be made, and a set created, using the selected value or values of the name attribute. Searchers may request such a search to find out what terms are there, what similar terms might be found (i.e., similarly spelled terms), *and* in how many records a specific value of an attribute occurs. Obviously, the entire inverted file cannot be displayed at once. The common practice is to display a window on the file, of anywhere from about 6 to 20 terms, the system allowing the user to step through the file, one page at a time. Oddly, having a command for backward paging is less common than for forward paging.

A thesaurus is stored as a structure similar to that of an inverted file, as a series of entries for terms, each entry showing other terms to which the entry is related and the nature of the relationship. Searching it is much like searching the inverted file. There is not necessarily a thesaurus for every database. If there is one, it is searched in the same manner as an inverted file, but the display includes references to related terms. Then, if the user asks, the list of related terms with the nature of their relationships is displayed. Either all related terms or a page of thesaurus data is displayed. The user may then go on to another base word, or follow the chain of relationships. The sequence might be to ask for the inverted file display for PHYSICS, see that there are *n* related terms for PHYSICS, and then ask to see them. This might be followed by asking for the display for the subordinate term BIOPHYSICS, then one of *its* related terms, and so on. Figure 7.3 shows some typical pages from an online thesaurus.

7.4.4 Create a Subset of the Database

Mentally, when a subset is created, searchers usually envision that the records meeting the specifications are put aside, and the sets numbered. In fact, it is normally a set of record numbers or other pointers that is recorded, not complete records. The specifications are usually given by a series of statements or Boolean combinations. Records having these values or combinations are selected for inclusion in the set.

7.4.5 Search for Strings

It is common for searchers to know how to begin the spelling of a word or name, but not know the entire spelling. They may know many words that have the same root, with different endings, but all conveying essentially the same information about the subject of a text that uses the word. Two examples are

> FIND GREEN—As a name, should this be spelled GREEN or GREENE?
> FIND ELECTRIC AND AUTOMOBILE—Should the first word have been
>   ELECTRIC, ELECTRICAL, ELECTRICITY, . . .?

A convenient way to express this uncertainty is to tell the IRS that the word must *begin* with ELECTRI, but that it does not matter with what it *ends*. This is indicated by using a specified character in the position where the variable ending would begin, such as ELECTRI*. Other languages may use # or # ? as the truncation symbol. This usage would retrieve the variations of the word ELECTRIC but would not retrieve variations of ELECTRONIC, unless the root

```
?expand testing
```

Ref	Items	RT	Index-term
E1	1		TESTIMONY CONGRESS 97TH
E2	1		TESTINESS
E3	42054	68	*TESTING (GATHERING AND PROCESSING ...
E4	1		TESTING ALTERNATIVES
E5	2		TESTING APPARATUS
E6	7		TESTING CENTERS
E7	25		TESTING CONDITIONS
E8	1		TESTING CONTEXT
E9	1		TESTING CORRELATION
E10	1		TESTING EDUCATIONAL POLICY
E11	51		TESTING EFFECTS
E12	4		TESTING FOR ESSENTIAL LEARNING AND ...

```
Enter P or E for more

?e e3
```

Ref	Items	Type	RT	Index-term
R1	33725		68	*TESTING (GATHERING AND PROCESSING ...
R2	0	U	1	TEST ADMINISTRATION
R3	0	U	1	TESTING METHODS
R4	0	U	1	TESTING TECHNIQUES
R5	405	N	15	ADAPTIVE TESTING
R6	1352	N	15	COMPARATIVE TESTING
R7	1433	N	11	COMPUTER ASSISTED TESTING
R8	132	N	11	CONFIDENCE TESTING
R9	2720	N	12	EDUCATIONAL TESTING
R10	389	N	6	GROUP TESTING
R11	305	N	4	INDIVIDUAL TESTING
R12	1691	N	12	MINIMUM COMPETENCY TESTING

```
Enter P or E for more

?e r7
```

Ref	Items	Type	RT	Index-term
R1	1433		11	*COMPUTER ASSISTED TESTING (USE OF ...
R2	0	U		COMPUTERIZED ADAPTIVE TESTING
R3	0	U		COMPUTERIZED TAILORED TESTING
R4	6901	B	13	COMPUTER USES IN EDUCATION
R5	42054	B	68	TESTING
R6	405	R	15	ADAPTIVE TESTING
R7	2226	R	19	COMPUTER SCIENCE
...	...			...

Figure 7.3

Thesaurus searching in ERIC, through Dialog: the first display shows terms in the inverted file, in alphabetical order. In the second, the user has asked to see information about terms related to TESTING (by typing E E3). The display shows related terms and the nature of the relationship. In the third panel, the user has selected one related term, COMPUTER ASSISTED TESTING, and sees the terms related to it. The * simply reminds the user what term had been entered. (Reproduction by courtesy of the Dialog Corporation.)

used was ELECTR*. These symbols (*, #, ?) are available for such use because punctuation is normally deleted from terms as they are placed in an inverted file, so there can be no ambiguity by this usage. There *is* sometimes ambiguity created by dropping the punctuation.

Truncating an author's name avoids problems of uncertainty of the author's first name or middle initial, or of correct format of the name. However, a very common stem such as GREEN* could retrieve many false drops, such as GREENE, GREENLEAF, GREENSPAN, ... Usually, an author field could be truncated as GREEN,? The comma will be part of the text of the field because this punctuation is usually retained in the author field, in effect as a subfield separator, between last name and first or initials. This usage would find all people named GREEN but none named GREENE. Some systems allow for user specification of the exact maximal number of letters that may follow a root, as ELECTRI?3 in Dialog would allow ELECTRICAL but not ELECTRICIAN.

Another common need is to allow for variation within a word, to search for WOMAN or WOMEN, DEFENSE or DEFENCE. The purpose here is not truncation but to indicate that any single letter or character is acceptable in the indicated position. The symbol used is often called a wild-card character. WOM*N might then be taken to call for a word with any letter in the position indicated by *. Were there a word WOMUN, with unrelated meaning, that would be retrieved, too.

Yet another search problem is to indicate that an extra letter might be present. This arises in trying to accommodate both British and American spellings, as LABOR and LABOUR. A technique occasionally found is to allow use of a different symbol here. LABO#R, where # is *not* being used as the symbol used for "any letter here," but could indicate that either *no letter* or any *one* letter is acceptable here.

To allow truncation on the left-hand side of a term is an altogether different operation. If we want to search on *SULPHATE, the alphabetical ordering of the inverted file is of no help in finding words that *end* in SULPHATE. There are two methods of handling the increasing need of users for this kind of logic.

The first is historically an old one, implemented in MEDLINE, the National Library of Medicine's online service. Called by various names, most commonly *string searching*, it uses the *contains* relationship by another name, allowing a user to specify any substring of an attribute value. A sequential search is done in every record *in a predefined set*, not the entire database, to see if that string exists in the stated attribute of the record. Searching the entire database in this manner would be prohibitively expensive. The method works if the user has the good sense and skill to define a *small* set before using this feature. With this method, it does not matter if we are looking for a sequence of full words (FIND ICH BIN EIN BERLINER IN S3 in a database of the speeches of J. F. Kennedy) or a word fragment, which might be truncated on both ends (FIND SULPH

IN S4). Again, the logic is simple, and the execution speed is reasonable *if* the defined set is small enough.

The second approach is to use truncation on the left-hand side of a word. Logically, this works the same as right-hand truncation; the symbol can be replaced by any number of any letters, so that *PHONE matches MICRO-PHONE, TELEPHONE, MEGAPHONE, FRANCOPHONE, etc. This feature is not commonly found in commercial systems and is treated in more detail in Section 8.2.5.

Multiple-word phrases that occur in text may also be considered as strings. Since the inverted file contains only single words and pre-coordinated phrases, there is no access to such a phrase unless it has been established in the thesaurus or an authority file ahead of time, or it is searched by the word-for-word scanning of specified attributes as explained previously. However, by using *proximity operators*, which are discussed in detail in Section 9.3.3, multiple words adjacent to one another may be specified in a query and used to search for multiple-word strings. This requires that the document numbers linked to inverted file entries carry word position numbers relative to the beginning of the attribute field for that document record.

7.4.6 Analyze a Set

Since we are always assuming that a query addressed to a text file may retrieve unwanted records, and may miss some of what was wanted, a tool for analyzing what was retrieved is useful. A relatively inexpensive way to analyze a set is to provide a frequency distribution of the values of selected attributes. For example, if a query retrieved 300 records, the searcher is not likely to want to browse all 300. But the IRS could provide a list of the 10 most frequent subject headings, in order of decreasing frequency, or of authors, corporate sources, or even year of publication. These can give the searcher ideas on what to include in or exclude from the next version of the query. Statistics on a combination of author and year of publication can, without need to look further, show the rise or waning of an author's career or of attention to an area of research.

The European Space Agency's Information Retrieval Service was the first to offer a command called ZOOM (Ingwerson, 1984) that provides such a frequency analysis once a set is created and the user specifies the attribute to be used, and similar capabilities were included in CITE (Doszkocs, 1983a, 1983b). One use of ZOOM is to see what the most frequent subject headings were in a set, perhaps a set originally defined by use of key words in the title. Then, looking at records that have the most appealing-looking subject headings, the user might decide to create a new set based only on those headings. ZOOM, or any similar set analysis, could also be used to find not just the authors in a field, but also the most prolific authors, publishers, corporate sources, or dominant patent assignees in an area of technology. It is a command that can be used for direct problem solving or question answering, as well as for finding citations to documents. The sort of information derived by set analysis is what is used in some IRSs to make automatic revisions to a query, but is rarely shown to the user.

This capability is not found in most Web-based systems. One reason is that the documents on the Web rarely have attributes tagged as such. (Another may be lack of user interest.)

7.4.7   Sort, Display, and Format Records

Once a set is created, users usually want to see what is in the records, to be sure that they do, in fact, reflect the meanings intended. Usually, a user is offered options of which records to display and the format in which to display them.

Selection of records is the first option with which to be concerned. It is usually expressed as a list of record numbers or a stated or implicit *all*. Format is the next consideration. Some retrieval services offer only a limited number of formats (data layouts) but make their selection simple. The layouts themselves may be complex. Others allow the user to specify the content and format of records. Doing so can be tedious, especially if the user has to specify an entire page layout, which requires answering such questions as where page numbers go, exactly where the title goes, how many characters to allow for it, whether multiple authors should be listed across one line or one per line, etc. The compromise is usually to allow the user to specify which attributes are to be printed or displayed and in what order, but not exactly where on the page an attribute is to appear, or what to do with multiple occurrences of values.

Sorting changes the order of presentation of records. Bibliographic or news records are usually placed in the database in order of date of receipt by the database producer. Actually, an accession number might be assigned by the search service, highly correlated with publication date. For viewing purposes, the records are usually shown in the order of most recent first, or descending order of date, but a user might want to see them by author. This option is available from most services.

The command to display records of a set must identify the set, the format, and the records to be used. If sorting is to be done, it usually requires a separate command issued before the display command. Dialog allows the usage PRINT S1/TI, AU/1–5,7 to indicate that the user wants to print offline records 1, 2, 3, 4, 5, and 7 of set S1, and from each set to see only the title and author attributes, in that order. Their command DISPLAY S1/3/1-5,7 calls for the same records from the same set, but using predefined, standard format number 3. DISPLAY causes the IRS to stop after each record and await a user's go-ahead signal, while the similar command TYPE displays the records in sequence without interruption. TYPE and DISPLAY create displays at the user's computer; PRINT causes a printout at Dialog and subsequent transmission to the user.

7.4.8 Handling the Unstructured Record

The previous section discussed the display and formatting of records with a large number of well-defined attachments, typical of bibliographic or business records. However, in World Wide Web records, while they may be coded in HTML (see Section 1.5.7), may have no predictable structure as to attributes contained, or control of attribute values. These are all provided by diverse and uncontrolled Web page designers. The index may be created from the whole text of the Web page, or only certain HTML designated heading material. Thus, sorting such records, or modifying the display, itself is not normally an option.

Efforts are underway to standardize the use of HTML labels which would provide more controlled access. None have yet reached the stage of wide consensus or use. Most prominent so far is the Dublin Core Metadata Element Set (Section 2.3). This set of elements provides a structure for discovery of Web-based resources established by an interdisciplinary, international consensus of many stakeholders in the document description arena. "The Dublin Core is intended to be usable by noncatalogers as well as by those with experience with formal document description models" (*Dublin Core*, 1998). Its 15 elements meet the needs for basic bibliographic description for electronic documents. The elements were shown in Table 2.1.

7.4.9 Download

This refers to a capability to move a set from the control of the ROM-oriented IRS to accessibility by other software. Downloading is done to enable searchers to edit and print results, perhaps for delivery to clients, or to create or add to a locally maintained database. Copyright law (databases for public searching usually claim copyright protection) prohibits the resale of retrieved, copyrighted records. For example, a large company is not supposed to have its library retrieve some records, then make multiple copies and distribute them around the company without permission, any more than it can photocopy portions of a book for similar usage. Even more so, a searcher is not supposed to sell the retrieved sets. Enforcement of such prohibitions is difficult, as it is with photocopying. Evidence of what users are actually doing in this regard is difficult to acquire, but there seems to be no evidence of large-scale abuse of the law. Downloading to a reusable file is now common as is transmission by electronic mail, the latter involving a slight delay but not nearly as much as conventional mail.

Copyright law, and particularly the concept of what sort of exceptions come under the doctrine of fair use, is subject to varied interpretations resolved only by case law, and varies from country to country. There is some debate as to whether databases are subject to copyright law in the United States. If they contain only factual material without significant creative expression, they may well not be. However, World Wide Web pages, and the full text of documents found in databases are certainly protected. Viewing such output online is clearly permitted since there is an implied contract generated by the posting of the material on the IRS. Downloading or printing a single copy for personal use is very likely fair use, but that is less clear. The production of multiple copies of such material for any purpose but face-to-face classroom instruction is almost surely infringement (Gassaway, 1997; Litman, 1997).

7.4.10 Order Documents

This is generally not applicable to local systems. In many cases, online database records contain references to documents, such as books in a library's collection, or patents. One of the early criticisms of IRSs was that they did not present the user with these documents, the ultimate goal of the search, but merely with the references. The user might have had to wait weeks before seeing the documents, perhaps procured through interlibrary loan. Many retrieval services, therefore, have initiated a service whereby a user's request for "hard copy" is transmitted to a service that will provide it. Usually, it is not the database search service that provides the documents. The number of full-text databases online is increasing, and these may now include complex or high-resolution graphics, an economic impracticality a decade ago. Also, the print quality of a computer printout is now gaining on that of a printing press. Hence, we are moving toward a day when perhaps any document could be downloaded in full and in high resolution. Many World Wide Web sites permit the display of documents in their files using software like *Adobe Acrobat* that permits such high-quality display.

7.4.11 Save, Recall, and Edit Searches

The composition and editing of a query can be very time consuming, and because charges in the traditional IRS are still made for online connect time, it can be expensive as well. It is possible in these traditional IRSs to save the query statements locally, as a file in the user's personal computer. Retrieval services commonly also offer the option to save a search in the IRS computer. Then, if it is to be run again, say next month, or if a similar one with only a few changes is to be run, the saved search can be retrieved, edited slightly if necessary, and run again. Clearly, this implies not only a *save* function, but also a *recall* one, and some form of edit facility enabling the user to change the query without retyping it entirely. Because some queries are long and difficult to type, the save, edit, and recall functions are useful with local as well as remote systems.

The normal World Wide Web search engine will provide an entry box for a single set of search terms or a Boolean statement. The functions *save* or *recall* are not usually offered, nor can one normally refer to previously formed sets. An entered search statement can be edited to change its form and resubmitted, but previous sets are not retained.

7.4.12 Current Awareness Search

In remote systems which handle large databases, the latter are frequently updated, while CD-ROM users are supplied periodically with a completely new file. Much database searching is *retrospective*, going back in time, looking for old records as well as new. A way to do searching that is both less expensive and less immediate is to set up a search to be done in a noninteractive, offline mode.

Also known as *selective dissemination of information* (SDI), and more recently as *push technology*, the usual implementation calls for the user to compose and store a query, which is then run only when a particular database is updated and only against the new records, not the entire file. The original use of the idea was to enable a library or central information office to disseminate new information within an organization. With the Web and its penchant for new terminology, this technique acquired the name *push technology* because the system is visualized as pushing new information toward a user, rather than the user specifically asking for it (*pulling*) in each instance of use. An SDI query is often called a *profile* because it is a relatively permanent description of a user's interests. Since it is applied only to new records, the profile is going to retrieve only those that satisfy the query and are new; hence, the term *current awareness*. The frequency of updates varies considerably among databases, from the almost continuously changing of stock market files to the once per month updating of the average bibliographic file. Clearly, if the updates are moment by moment, the concept of SDI has less meaning than for the less frequently updated files.

Because current awareness queries are directed against new records only, there are going to be far fewer hits, so the searcher can cast the logical net over a wider area. Of course, the user is, or should be, free to modify the stored query whenever it seems not to be retrieving what is wanted or retrieves too much. A common problem among SDI users is to accumulate a seeming mountain of citations and, as a result, to stop reading them, defeating the purpose of the search. Narrowing the search to the point where it retrieves the number the user will take the time to read calls for concentration and skill by the user.

Some Web sites, such as the Custom News Service of the National Science Foundation, permit the user to create a Web page which will automatically collect new foundation publications that fit a profile entered on the Service-provided profile options page, and then to display their citations. These citations are hyperlinks to the publications themselves, which are maintained on the site. For a publisher without interest in charging for access such an SDI can be most effective.

A relatively brief appearance on the scene was made by PointCast, a company offering push service on the Internet. One feature was that searching was done while the computer was otherwise occupied or idle. A disadvantage, at least from the point of view of this author, was that it seemed to be aimed at users who wanted to track specific companies, not subjects. Subject searches gave results that were too broad, too voluminous. Auleta (1998) put it that, "... the demand for 'push' was diminishing. The difference between 'push' and 'pull' blurs when one sets aside, say twenty favorite Web sites with 'bookmarks'. ..."

Many learned journals also make their full issues available on Web sites and may provide their own retrieval system for this database. Such sites normally require a password received on some contractual basis. A person who subscribes is expressing his or her interest in being made aware of the new publications of such journals. Other journals make only their tables of contents or abstracts available, usually at no cost. The use of such a site is again a current awareness mechanism.

7.4.13 Cost Summary

This is generally not applicable to local systems or sites on the Web. Most public Web search engines are free for the user and cover their costs through advertising. But for the more traditional systems, when the user is paying for the service, in the course of searching and browsing among retrieved records, they can easily lose track of accrued costs. It is therefore necessary for searchers to keep track of their budgets. Since many searches are done on behalf of clients in a library or information center, there may be a need to know the cost in order to bill the client for the service. In response to this need, search services provide cost information during the course of a search. At any time, a user can request an estimate of costs incurred, covering charges for connect time, search terms used, records retrieved or displayed, and telecommunications. A similar display is usually provided automatically whenever the user changes databases or terminates a search.

7.4.14 Terminate a Session

For purposes of correct rendering of invoices, control over telecommunications, and efficient operation of a fee-based IRS, it helps to have a positive statement from the user that the search session is over: the bill can be tallied; the communication lines broken; and internal computer memory devoted to other users. A session may also be terminated if a certain amount of time elapses since the last user input, typically 5–10 minutes. A temporary logoff command may be available to ask the IRS to suspend billing, disconnect from the communications network, make the communications port and memory space available to others, but retain a record of the search so that sets need not be recreated when the search resumes.

7.5
The Basis for Charging for Searches

Historically, the cost of online searching was entirely a function of connect time, plus modest charges for storage of saved searches. The connect charges included telecommunication costs as well as use of the IR system. Today, much has changed, as Web-based users may have quite powerful systems in their own computers, or libraries may provide services free of charge. What "free of charge" means in most cases is that someone other than the direct user is paying. Our discussion here is concerned with online services that do charge their users.

Cost computation was once a simple matter of subtracting the time at which a connection was made from the time at which it was broken. By contrast, the cost of a local search is largely a matter of recovery of the capital cost of hardware, IRS software, and the data disks. Most libraries do not place an hourly charge on individual users for the service.

Today, remote pricing is based on more complex formulae, which may involve connect time, number of records printed or displayed, number searched through, age of the records, or the format of display. There is even a movement to begin charging according to the number of terms in a query, whether or not they retrieve anything, on the grounds that the service sold is a *search service*, not strictly a *retrieval service*. Online, fee-based services are now usually accessible through the Internet, but this changes only the cost of communications, not the cost of database searching.

The issue of how to charge for online retrieval is in something of a turmoil as this is written and may not settle for some time (Hawkins, 1989). Changing technology and user patterns of behavior have their effects on pricing. As online storage, search, and distribution services replace print publication for many databases, data distribution on compact disks threatens online services, and the ease of downloading affects the number of online searches performed (although that point is still uncertain) entrepreneurs will look for price modes that at least keep up their level of net income. Users will always look for a way to reduce costs and for any flaw in the pricing scheme that enables them to lower their own costs.

There is little new or different about the behavior of suppliers and customers in this industry compared with any other, and no reason to expect any change in the constant struggle for relative advantage. One difference, however, and an important one, is that users of information are not used to paying for some kinds of services. Libraries have traditionally been free in modern times. Web service has largely been free. Further, many users have become convinced that "everything" is available free on the Web. This is not true. In addition, the cost of putting material on the Web and the possible loss of revenue from print versions will probably cause price increases in what we have so far had for free. User attitudes will have to change.

8

Interpretation and Execution of Query Statements

8.1

Problems of Query Language Interpretation

In Chapter 7 we described the languages and logic of information retrieval systems (IRSs) from the point of view of a user. Here, we begin our look inside the IRS to understand how commands are interpreted and executed.

Earlier, in Chapter 2, we discussed some of the problems of language in general and the opinions of scholars in the field that words do not have fixed meanings, established before use. Meaning is to some extent determined by context, even to some extent with artificial languages, but the problems attendant upon imprecise meanings are much worse in natural language. Natural language, moreover, has inexact syntax, and this adds to the ambiguity of words. The process of analyzing a statement in a language and breaking it into its constituent elements or roles is known as *parsing*, some aspects of which were discussed in Chapter 6.

Knowing the role of a word helps us understand its meaning. For example, here are some almost classic, ambiguous sentences in English. In each, it is *not possible* to know the exact meaning of all the words because there is more than one possible way to parse the sentence, hence more than one possible meaning. These are presented without the context usually needed to help resolve the ambiguity.

> *At the physics conference, she gave her paper on time.* Was this a paper about the subject of time or a paper on an unstated subject that was delivered as scheduled?
>
> *Time flies like an arrow.* On first reading this seems to be unambiguously saying that time passes quickly. That interpretation makes *time* the subject and *flies* the verb. But, suppose a computer, lacking human ex-

perience, is interpreting the sentence. It could decide that *flies* is the subject, in which case *time* could be an adjective, denoting a kind of fly. Now, one need not be an entomologist to know (or suspect) that there is no such thing as a time fly. This ambiguity might be resolved with the aid of a thesaurus, but a thesaurus of the general language is hardly likely to list every species of every insect. Can the computer know what kinds of flies exist? At any rate, if the subject is *flies*, then the verb could be *like*, and the whole thing could mean that this kind of fly likes to eat arrows. Yet a third interpretation is that the sentence says one should measure the speed of flies in the same manner as one measures the speed of arrows.

He ate the cake. Here is a sentence without much apparent variation in syntax, but the meaning can vary according to emphasis placed on the spoken words. As the emphasis shifts to different words of the sentence, the meanings may vary in these ways:

> **He** *ate the cake.* That male person, or animal, is the one who ate the cake.
>
> *He* **ate** *the cake.* Among the many possible things that male might do with cake, he chose to consume it.
>
> *He ate the* **cake**. Of all things that he might have eaten, he chose the cake.

Emphasis can be shown in print with italics or quotation marks, but at least as often it is not shown typographically. Then, of course, there are idiomatic expressions that have meaning that bear no apparent relation to the meanings of the individual words. *That takes the cake* means that some thing or activity is highly rated and has nothing to do with food, although this expression apparently has it origin in the awarding of a cake as a contest prize.

These, then, are some of the problems. Let us examine some of the procedures for handling them.

8.1.1 Parsing Command Language

The usual parsing method is to make a left-to-right scan of a statement, looking at each word or code for occurrences of strings of characters that can "legally" occur in a given position. For example, most command language syntax calls for a command to be followed by one or more arguments, attributes, or parameters. The command is stated as an imperative verb, such as SELECT. The parsing program would begin at the left end of the statement and look for a substring that constitutes a valid command in the language. The arguments may be meaningful only in the context of a specific command. TYPE 1/5/8 tells Dialog to type record 8 of set 1, using format 5, but EXPAND 1/5/8 will cause Dialog to look for the string 1/5/8 in its inverted file. The language of BRS (founded in the United States, now operated in the United Kingdom) uses *modes*. A command causes the IRS to enter a mode, and thereafter query statements are interpreted in the context of that mode. The set-forming command FIND needs no verb because it is understood. This causes the system to enter search mode, and the string PRINT following the mode statement would be interpreted as a search term, not a command. It is as if a full command FIND PRINT had been issued. A new mode statement, prefaced by "..." would change the mode, hence the default command.

Recognizing the command can be done by looking for the first blank character following the first nonblank or for the end of the command string (code for the ENTER key), then treating everything between as the potential command. However, many languages "forgive" the absence of a space between the command and its argument. Therefore, the most likely way to locate the command in the input string of characters is to start at the beginning and look for any substring that matches a legal command. Search in descending order of command or abbreviation length: SELECT (6 characters), EXPAND (6), print (5), TYPE (4), PAGE (4), PR (2), E (1), T, P, ... This assures that an initial substring of PR, if not followed by INT, will be matched with the abbreviation PR, rather than P. The list must always be so constructed that the full command precedes its abbreviation, not normally much of a problem.

Once the command is identified, the program would use a table (part of a knowledge base) to tell it what kind of argument or parameter list follows this particular command. Following SELECT, for example, the rest of the statement might be AUTHOR = SMITH, J.C. One of the next elements in a SELECT statement, then, could be the name of a data attribute (AUTHOR or the abbreviation AU). Another sequence following SELECT could be S1 OR AUTHOR = SMITH, J.C., where S1 denotes a previously defined set number. Yet another possibility is that the first character after the command SELECT is a left parenthesis, as SELECT (SUBJECT = CAT OR SUBJECT = DOG) AND AUTHOR = TERHUNE, A.P. (Remember that most text-retrieval systems do not require quotation marks around a string constant, while most database management systems do.)

In the statement SELECT AUTHOR = SMITH, J.C. the usage AUTHOR = SMITH, J.C. is an attribute-value statement, as is just DOG, but in the latter case the attribute name is understood, or reverts to a default value. This is a de facto standard in text-retrieval systems. The default may be called a *basic index* and apply to terms from a title, abstract, or descriptor field. The exact choice of attributes to constitute the default basic index may vary with the database in use.

The usage S1 OR AUTHOR = SMITH, J.C. is a compound attribute-value statement, as is S1 AND (SUBJECT = CAT OR SUBJECT = DOG) AND AUTHOR = SMITH, A.B. The knowledge base must, in some manner, specify all the variations of such usages that are permitted in the language in use. In Dialog, if there has been no set 3 created, the usage SELECT S3 AND DOG will be interpreted as asking for the string S3 and the string DOG, both in the basic index. On occasion this is a source of confusion to the user. In the long run, the omission of quotation marks probably saves more trouble than it creates.

In the Dialog language, both SELECT and EXPAND are valid commands. If the parser receives the statement SELECT EXPAND CAT, it would find a valid command in the first position within the statement and, because the context is now established, will not consider that EXPAND is also the name of a command. It will treat EXPAND as part of the argument of the SELECT command and will not consider the possibility that the user made a mistake but did not know how to correct it, so simply typed a new command following the previous incomplete one. A number of similar statements that appear ambiguous to a human reader are not so to a program because it takes the query statement apart in a prescribed order and never notices any ambiguities:

SSELECT CAT (SELECT misspelled, two leading Ss) is interpreted as SS (abbreviation for the two-word command SELECT SETS) followed by the argument ELECT CAT. There is no legal full command at the start of this statement; hence, an abbreviation is sought and found, and of the two possible abbreviations, SS and S, it selects the longer. What follows is neither a set number nor a parenthetical expression, so it is treated as a search term, even though it was intended as part of the command. Further, since the argument consists of a phrase of two or more words with no attribute designated, Dialog takes it to imply the descriptor attribute.

SELECTION is treated as the command SELECT followed by the argument ION. Nearly all Internet search engines, ORBIT, and the National Library of Medicine's MEDLINE assume that the absence of a command implies the command FIND, that is, that the system is in FIND mode, essentially the same as Dialog's SELECT. MEDLINE would treat FINDER as a term not a command. (ORBIT, like BRS, was founded in the United States, later taken over by a British company.)

S ELECTION is treated by Dialog as the abbreviation S followed by the argument ELECTION.

P 1/TI,AU/1-5 is a complex-looking statement. The argument fits the pattern for a PRINT command and specifies the set (1), the format (attributes TI for title and AU for author, and the record numbers 1-5 of the designated set. The problem, though, is that P is the abbreviation for the PAGE command, which is contextually dependent; i.e., PAGE is only valid if a preceding command had produced a multipage display (or was another PAGE). This is a common and easy mistake for users to make. The left-to-right scanning method will completely misunderstand it: to Dialog this is a PAGE command, to a user it looks like a PRINT command.

In the last example, a right-to-left scan might be able to do better, i.e., one that first recognizes a range of what would be taken to be record numbers, preceded by the /, which separates elements, preceded by a string of attribute names, etc. The parser would scan left from the last character, looking for "/." If this is found, scan back to the right to see if what follows is a set number or series of them. If so, go left again, looking for the next / and verifying that the argument between occurrences of / is a format designation, and so on. Then, if all this is preceded by anything other than DISPLAY, PRINT, TYPE, PR, D, or T there has been an error. Although the format fits three different commands, the presence of P suggests the user probably meant PR. But the extra scan means an expensive computer program and extra time consumed in executing it. The advantage of an interactive IRS is that, using a simple left-to-right scan, as soon as an ambiguity or error is discovered, the user can be told and asked to fix it. There may be no need for overly elaborate error-correction techniques in this situation.

An interpretive issue sometimes found to be vexing is the treatment of missing or extraneous blanks between elements of a query statement. As we noted, Dialog will treat the statement SELECTION as SELECT ION, not as the invalid command SELECTION. Extraneous blanks before the command name or more than one wherever one is called for should always be ignored. ("Should" here is a value judgment by the authors.) The following should all be treated as the same statement:

    SELECT ION
    SELECTION
        SELECT ION (three blanks preceding the command)
    SELECT   ION (four blanks between command and term)

8.1.2 Parsing Natural Language

The parsing of natural language is so complex that we provide only a brief exposure to its methods here. For more information, see Chomsky (1965),

Salton (1989, pp. 377–424), and Tucker (1979). Basically, the same kind of logic is used as for the artificial command language just described. But the difficulty of the problem is much greater. Instead of a list of at most a few dozen valid commands and argument types, we need a sizable dictionary of the language. In English, a 100,000-word dictionary is not unusual, and each word may have various endings and be used as various parts of speech. While the artificial languages are likely to allow only one or two forms of any word, in natural language each word may have many forms, especially irregular verbs. A dictionary would identify the parts of speech that a word could represent, and a separate set of rules (the knowledge base, again) would tell what parts of speech might follow the statement that has been parsed so far. We say "might" because there is no absolute set of such rules. WordNet (Section 4.3.3) is a dictionary of this type.

For example, the word THE would be identified in a dictionary as a form of adjective called an *article*. Its syntactic role is to introduce a *noun phrase*. The noun phrase, in turn, can consist of an almost unlimited string of adjectives followed by a noun. With our modern penchant for treating nouns as adjectives, it can also include a string of nouns used as adjectives. Further, of course, verbs have noun forms. An adjective can be preceded by adverbs, but the occurrence of an adverb is supposed to signal that the next word is either another adverb or an adjective, not a noun. Each entry of the dictionary would list the possible syntactic roles for the entry, and possibly their probabilities. Each step of syntactic analysis tends to narrow the list of probable roles of the next word. Occasionally, as in the *time flies* example, parsing uncovers more possibilities as it moves through the expression.

If a sentence starts with THE, we then expect the next word to be an adjective, adverb, or noun. If the first two words were

THE TREE, then TREE may be the end of the noun phrase, and we might next begin to look for a verb phrase. The sentence might continue as

THE TREE IS (TREE is a noun, IS is a verb.)
THE TREE IN (IN introduces a prepositional phrase.)
THE TREE STRUCTURE (TREE is now acting as an adjective, STRUCTURE as a noun. STRUCTURE could be a verb but then should end in S.)

THE GREEN, then the next word is probably a noun or adjective, although it is possible that GREEN is treated here as a noun (as in golf).

We do not know much more about what is coming next than before having seen GREEN. Possible continuations are

> THE GREEN TREE (GREEN is an adjective, TREE a noun.)
> THE GREEN WAS (GREEN is a noun, WAS a verb.)

THE VERY, then we would use the dictionary to determine that VERY is probably an adverb (although there is an emergency signaling device called a *Very pistol*), and we can expect another adverb or an adjective next, such as
THE VERY GREEN... or THE VERY LOVELY GREEN...
THE BLOSSOMING, then BLOSSOMING is a noun or adjective form of a verb, which can lead to

> THE BLOSSOMING TREE (BLOSSOMING used as an adjective)
> THE BLOSSOMING WAS (BLOSSOMING used as a noun)

There are many possibilities and the program has to work through them, make assumptions, see if the assumptions are consistent with words yet to follow, and backtrack when necessary to start the chain of assumptions over again.

Programs that can do this kind of syntactic analysis are time consuming and expensive, but for users who do not want to take the trouble to learn a new language, the benefits are great. One benefit is that if a user states FIND INFORMATION ON DOGS AND NUTRITION, a good natural-language interpreter would recognize the implied Boolean logic and convert this into a query that searches for records containing both words, DOGS and NUTRITION, but will know not to look for records containing the words FIND or INFORMATION, which contain no subject-defining information in this context. In other words, expressions like FIND..., FIND INFORMATION ON... or GET ME INFORMATION ON... can be defined as inherently meaningless and the IRS instructed to ignore them as initial words of a query.

If the parser attempts to recognize the role of each word in the context only of a query to a given type file, rather than its role and meaning in the natural language, parsing can be much faster (Samstag-Schnook and Meadow, 1993). For example, in a bibliographic context a capitalized word following BY might be taken as an author's name, or a four-digit number following PUBLISHED AFTER as a date.

8.1.3 Processing Menu Choices

Normally, a menu is understood to be an offering to a user of a limited and explicitly stated set of choices. The processing program should have to check only to see which of the offerings was selected. There are, of course, complications in everything (Shneiderman, 1986).

The statement inviting the user to make and indicate a choice must be in some way descriptive of the choices available. Usually, the choices are tagged with numbers or letters. A choice can be indicated (the user indicating which option is wanted) by any of three logically equivalent means: (1) typing the choice number or letter, (2) typing the text of the choice statement or sometimes just the initial letter, or (3) moving a cursor to the choice and pressing the RETURN or ENTER key or a key on a mouse (the "point and shoot" method). The third method has become the most common choice of interface designers with the great expansion of graphic interface operating systems and the growth of the World Wide Web.

While the processing of menu choices is simple, and it is tempting to assume that choices are always clear to users, or that uncertainty can be resolved by a help message, this is not always true.

A user simply may not understand what the consequences of a choice are. A user may not understand why the current menu is being offered and have no idea how to proceed. The user then has the problem not of which choice to make but of how to get back to familiar ground or to understand what brought him or her to this point. Some programs allow a user to back up after a menu choice, in effect saying, "Go back to the previous menu." That requires that the program keep a list of the sequence of choices made by the user. But no commercial program we know of offers an explanation of how the user got to the menu now on view, i.e., not only the sequence of responses, but also an explanation of what actions that sequence produced.

8.2

Executing Retrieval Commands

As we have noted before, the execution of commands does not depend on the type of language used in conveying the commands to the computer. Although commands or menu choices or methods of interpreting natural language may differ widely from IRS to IRS, the *functions* performed are quite similar from system to system. The principal ones, in approximately the order in which they might be used in a search, will be described. The list of commands is similar to the list of functions given in Chapter 7, but here we stress what the IRS must do to interpret or execute the command.

8.2.1 Database Selection

The information conveyed is simple: the command and the name or code for the database to be used. The usual syntax is command followed by database name or number. Note that Web searchers do not usually operate with the concept of a database. Roughly, a site is treated as an equivalent. The actions needed are to prepare various tables for use in parsing records (the list of fields in the record, structure of the record, . . .), computing costs to this point, if there has been a prior database in use, and finding the appropriate inverted file.

8.2.2 Inverted File Search

A search in the inverted file (see Section 7.4.3) is done for the purposes of finding what values are represented there and in what records they occur, and then transferring information from the inverted file to a set. The IRS uses an inverted file search, on its own, to respond to a request to form a set.

Searching can be done on a sequential basis, but some form of indexed or hashed access to values will make a great difference in search time over top-to-bottom sequential searching. The number of entries approximates the number of words or terms that occur in the original records, common words and values of unindexed attributes being omitted. Added to an inverted file entry are record numbers and possibly attribute identifiers (e.g., differentiating between a word's occurrence in a title and an abstract and often the position of the word within the complete value, as the word's position within title. Word numbers are used for *proximity searching*, to be discussed in Chapter 9.

The logic of an inverted file search to create a set is illustrated in Fig. 8.1, where it is assumed that the attribute is named in the query and the symbol for the attribute and its value are stored in the inverted file. Stored with each value are the numbers of all the records having that value. These numbers are extracted and placed in the set.

8.2.3 Set or Subset Creation

Boolean operations are performed on the sets as shown in Fig. 8.2. Unless the sets are very large, these operations go very fast. If a high cost is associated with set creation and set operations, it is in creating, maintaining, and searching the inverted file in the first place, not so much in performing the Boolean operations, again unless the sets are excessively large.

If a set number is used in a Boolean expression, as S1 AND DOG, execution of the AND operation creates a set for DOG, then a set for the combined S1 AND DOG. The set for DOG will be discarded unless the user has specifically

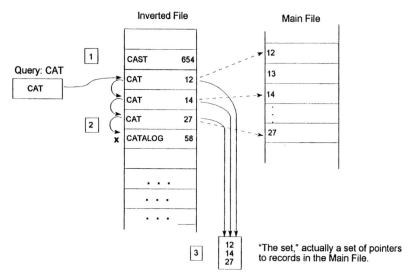

Figure 8.1
Basic logic of an inverted file search: an algorithm (1) operates on the search term to determine a starting point for the search, which proceeds sequentially until a matching term is found. Then it continues until a nonmatching term is found (2). When matches are found, the corresponding main file record number is moved into the set (3).

requested its retention by using a variation of the basic command (SS instead of S in Dialog).

Other commands are used only to limit an existing set. They deal with additional requirements being placed on members of the set. A common example is a command to limit membership in set n to records having DATE < 1976. Such a command may not require recourse to the inverted file, but can be executed by directly performing a sequential search of the records in the set. The BASIS SCAN command or ORBIT's SEARCH command both operate by looking in records of an existing set for a particular string of characters occurring anywhere in a given attribute, essentially the *contains* relationship described in Section 7.3.2. Such a function would be prohibitively expensive if it had to test *every* record of a database.

8.2.4 Truncation and Universal Characters

Execution of a set-forming command using a truncation (see Section 7.4.5) or universal matching symbol is not logically difficult but may be

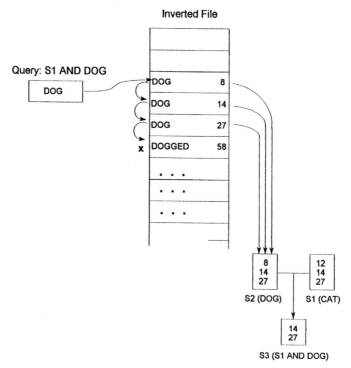

Figure 8.2

Basic Boolean operations: set S1 (CAT) exists. A new query asks for a new set, for DOG, and that the two sets be intersected. Records 14 and 27 are in both sets.

time consuming (see Fig. 8.3). The search program would scan the inverted file, from the beginning or from whatever starting point its logic uses, until an entry is found that is greater than the root but does not contain it. For example, if the search term is ELECTRI*, the search program would start by using whatever method it would normally use if the term were a full word. It finds the first entry beginning with ELECTRI, then searches sequentially until it finds the first term not beginning with that root.

We are supposing that not too many words will match a given root. Searching for A* is not a good idea because it will retrieve so many words of diverse meanings. Use of a universal match symbol near the beginning of a word W*MAN will cost more search time than if used near the end, as WOM*N. The former requires a sequential search of all words beginning with W.

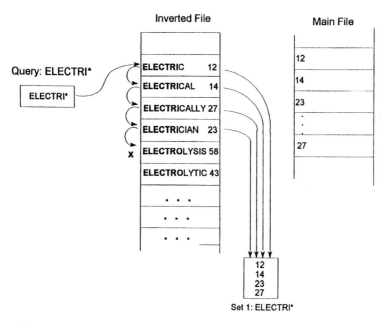

Figure 8.3
Inverted file search on truncated term: the logic is the same as for a full-term search, but only a portion of the inverted file term is used to compare with the search term root.

8.2.5 Left-Hand Truncation

Left-hand truncation is the use of a truncation or universal matching character on the left side of the search term. Left-hand truncation alone is not particularly useful. The assumption is made here that *both* left- and right-hand truncation are possible, possibly on the same term. This gives the equivalent of the *contains* relation, but may be used in a query directed to the entire database, not just an existing set. It would not matter what a term in a record starts with, so long as it contains the given character string. By contrast with right-hand truncation, this is a usage with great implications for execution time and cost. For a search for words that *end* in SULPHATE the fact that the file is in alphabetical order on the complete word is of no help, but left-hand truncation alone can be accommodated by creating a reverse inverted file, in which terms are entered backwards. To find a word ending in SULPHATE, look up ETAHPLUS* in this reverse file. A further and more useful variation is to allow truncation symbols at either end of a search string. Thus, *ETHYL* would retrieve TETRAETHYL LEAD, but *ETHYL or ETHYL* would not.

There are several methods of handling the increasing desire for the availability of this kind of logic. We shall discuss two. The first, as noted in Section 7.4.5, is the use of a string search or CONTAINS by which a search can be conducted for *any* string embedded in any attribute value, and the truncation symbol is not really necessary. The second involves a change in the inverted file.

To look up any term in an inverted file, the data manager finds a starting location and then searches sequentially, looking for an exact match or for verification that no match will be found. How close the starting location is to the stored version of the search term, and how many terms have to be examined sequentially are major factors in determining the speed, and thus cost, of a search. With a hashing system, it is possible to go almost immediately to the individual term sought, but then it may not be possible to find the next record in alphabetical order (Section 6.4.5). Nested indexes or binary search offer somewhat slower starting, because it is unlikely the term will be hit with the first disk accession, but they allow retaining a record sequence based on search key. Since users often browse in the inverted file, ability to retrieve its records in alphanumeric order is important.

If a search term contains a right-hand truncation symbol, little is added to inverted file search time *assuming* that the root is long enough that only a small percentage of the total number of entries can match the search term. As noted above, this would hardly be the case if the search term were A∗. If a left-hand truncation symbol is permitted, then *every* entry in the inverted file must be examined, because a term beginning with any string of symbols could match the root. That would require an exhaustive search of the entire inverted file. For a database of one million records, which could lead to an inverted file of, easily, 100 entries per record or 100 million total entries, an exhaustive sequential search is almost out of the question economically.

For left-hand truncation it is necessary for the inverted file to contain more information about the possible location of the root string within terms of the file, always with the understanding that there is a trade-off involved: more information means more memory devoted to storing it and more time to interpret it. These two can be traded for reduced time in searching the inverted file.

First, let us review the content of an inverted-file entry. It contains a term that may consist of an average of about 10 characters. It must specify the attribute in which the value occurred, typically abbreviated to two or three characters. Often a separator character divides the attribute code from its value. The entry contains the sequential position of the term within the field, if proximity searching is to be allowed, as it commonly is with text records, again requiring two or three characters. And, of course, it must specify the number of the record in which the value occurred, say eight characters. If locations or sequence numbers are used with a main file of a million records, then the record number requires only six bytes. An accession number used by the database producer may run to 12 digits—the difference is 6 megabytes. If the value occurs more than once in the database, there is an entry for each occurrence. There are many ways to reduce the total (here $10 + 3 + 3 + 8 = 24$ characters), involving data compression, binary numbers, or variable-length records to avoid having to repeat values. But, for illustration, we use this almost worst-case estimate.

One possibility, noted previously, is to duplicate the file, each entry being listed both forward and backward in spelling. Another, illustrated in Fig. 8.4, is to create another entry for each character in the term value, basically a permutation of the characters of the string. If the term were CAP, we would have entries for CAP/, AP/C, and P/CA, each showing the complete term, but in different order of character occurrence. The sign / in this case indicates the end of the word. Done this way, left-hand truncation would be done the same way as right-hand, but the inverted file would be, by our estimate, up to 10 (average term length) times as long, and that would increase search time using virtually any file organization.

CAT ——————
CATALOG ——————
CATAPULT ——————
CATO ——————
•
•
•

Conventional inverted file, with term, record number, *etc.* (indicated by ---). There is only one entry for each term.

ALOG/CAT ——————
AT/C ——————
ATALOG/C ——————
ATAPULT/C ——————
APULT/CAT ——————
ATO/C ——————
CAT/ ——————
CATALOG/ ——————
CATAPULT/ ——————
CATO ——————
G/CATALO ——————
LOG/CATA ——————
LT/CATAPU ——————
O/CAT ——————
OG/CATAL ——————
PULT/CATA ——————
T/CA ——————
T/CATAPUL ——————
TALOG/CA ——————
TAPULT/CA ——————
TO/CA ——————
ULT/CATAP ——————
•
•
•

Inverted file with an entry beginning with each letter of each term, hence one entry for each letter.

Figure 8.4
A method for left-hand truncation: there is now an entry for each letter of each word, consisting of the term and occurrence and location, represented by the dashed line. The symbol / indicates the end of a word. This method increases the size of the file, but enables a search on any string within a word.

Another possibility, shown in Fig. 8.5, would be to use a variable-length structure for the records in the inverted file. This would save space if the term were less than the maximal length. Only a segment of the term is needed in the extra entries for left-hand truncation, e.g., AP/C and P/CA as extras for the CAP entry. These strings, or partial entries, would require only a pointer to the full entry, and there would have to be a symbol showing that it was an abbreviated entry. Or, both the full and partial entries might point to a separate file containing the detail about the occurrence of the word containing the string. This method is fairly conservative of space but increases search time.

However it is done, left-hand truncation comes only at a cost. Many users are willing to pay it, especially those who must search chemical and trademark files. The challenge for database search services is to find a method of accomplishing it that does not add to the cost for all searchers, as would, for example, simply extending the size of the inverted file, making every search more expensive. Very likely, the CONTAINS or substring search approach is more economical, especially with an IRS that charges for the time it is connected to the user.

Inverted File   Location File

```
ALOG/CAT        ----------          CAT         ----------------
AT/C            ----------          CATALOG     ----------------
ATALOG/C        ----------          CATAPULT    ----------------
ATAPULT/C       ----------          CATO        ----------------
APULT/CAT       ----------            •
ATO/C           ----------            •
CAT/            ----------            •
CATALOG/        ----------
CATAPULT/       ----------
CATO            ----------
G/CATALO        ----------
LOG/CATA        ----------
LT/CATAPU       ----------
O/CAT           ----------
OG/CATAL        ----------
PULT/CATA       ----------
T/CA            ----------
T/CATAPUL       ----------
TALOG/CA        ----------
TAPULT/CA       ----------
TO/CA           ----------
ULT/CATAP       ----------
  •
  •
  •
```

Figure 8.5
Alternative method for left-hand truncation: there is an entry for each permutation of each word, but these entries have only a pointer to another file. In the second file there is only one entry per term, with all the relevant information as to location in the Main File.

But this approach requires that users learn to use these commands and perhaps even to insist that they be made available.

8.3
Executing Record Analysis and Presentation Commands

Often the functions listed below are either not available or only in relatively primitive form compared with what can be done if users were well trained, demanding, and supplied with a powerful system.

8.3.1 Set Analysis Functions

Since set analysis, as we have defined it (see Section 7.4.6), calls for analysis of the frequency of occurrence of values of attributes or combinations of them, the basic steps are: (1) for each record in a set, extract the value or values of the attribute on which analysis is to be done and append the record number; (2) when the complete set of values has been assembled, sort by attribute value, count the number of occurrences of each value, or number falling in a range, and then sort in descending order of frequency. The result gives the list of attribute values, most frequent first. In order to do this, the programming logic is much like that for formatting a display; i.e., the IRS must be able to parse the record to find the attribute values within it. Sorting is a standard function. An example of a table of attribute frequencies is shown in Fig. 8.6, using author name as the attribute. The data are hypothetical.

Set number: 4
Number of records: 5
Attribute analyzed: author name

Value	Frequency
BOOKSTEIN	12
KRAFT	8
MCGILL	6
SALTON	5
VAN RIJSBERGEN	3

Figure 8.6
Values and frequencies of occurrence: frequencies add to more than the number of records, indicating co-authorship among this group of authors (hypothetical data).

```
Set number: 5
Number of records: 27
Attributes analyzed: subject heading, date
```

Subject		Date	
Value	Frequency	Value	Frequency
ARTIFICIAL INTELLIGENCE	57	1995	26
		1996	18
		1997	9
		1998	4
EXPERT SYSTEMS	32	1995	15
		1997	12
		1998	5
HYPERTEXT	63	1995	2
		1996	8
		1997	19
		1999	34

Figure 8.7

Co-occurrence tables for values of two attributes: such a display can give a quick indication of increasing or waning interest in a certain subject or productivity of an author. The author's name would have been used to define the set, but the analysis is based on subject matter and date (hypothetical data).

A second form of analysis is co-occurrence analysis, for example, compiling a table of the frequencies with which values of attributes SUBJECT and DATE occur together. This can be done in at least two ways. In one, form a list of values of both attributes and the record numbers, and then sort by subject with date as a secondary sort key, with result as shown in Fig. 8.7. Again, data shown are hypothetical.

8.3.2 Display, Format, and Sort

For the IRS to display a set of records (see Section 7.4.7), it must know what portion of each to display, how those portions are to be laid out on the page (whether paper or electronic), in what order the records are to be presented, and whether they are to be output continuously or one at a time, under user control.

Format Control

Either the system must assume default values or the user must provide instructions for setting such variables as the length of each line sent out by the

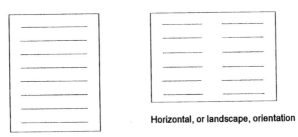

Horizontal, or landscape, orientation

Vertical, or portrait, orientation

Figure 8.8
Orientation of images or text on a page: while it may appear a minor variation, changing orientation could require considerable reorganization of the information contained on a page and this may entail considerable user knowledge and skill.

computer and the number of lines that can be viewed on a video display screen. Formatting is concerned with such details as:

Page or image size
Orientation of the page (Fig. 8.8)
Selection of attributes or fields to be displayed
Placement of fields and labels within a page
Whether to display records without a stop after each until the user signals
  to continue

To avoid excessive demand on users, many retrieval services limit user choice of format, sometimes by offering a set of predetermined formats or by offering user control of *what* attributes may be included, but not necessarily how the page is to be laid out. Documents found on the World Wide Web will be displayed as structured by those that posted them. Most browsers will format such documents for printing exactly as displayed and may allow the use of attachment software such as Adobe Acrobat to display more highly formatted documents not coded in HTML when they are available from the Web site.

Display Mode

The IRS can send output in scrolling mode, in which lines are displayed one after the other until the entire message has been sent. If the user has a printer in use, scrolling may be the preferred method. For a video display, the method often preferred is to transmit one screenful, then stop until the user signals that another line or screen is wanted. *Downloading* is an extension of display. It is an activity at the local level. Records are sent out by a remote system for display or storage locally. Telecommunications software usually has a logging capability, controlled by a toggle switch, that permits storing incoming messages in a file. A local IRS might need a similar function to enable users to copy records from the database into a separate, user-accessible file. Browser software normally will allow the saving of any retrieved Web page in HTML format, or the cutting of selected portions of the text of such pages and their pasting into local documents.

Sorting

The order of listing of records in a database is determined by the search service. Bibliographic and newspaper files are almost always ordered by accession number, which is assigned sequentially as records are added to the file. This means that the records are also roughly in descending order by date (latest date first). Display in the default order is apparently acceptable to most users. This choice of default, however, may not be too meaningful for a directory of businesses or of chemical formulations.

The modern approach is to offer the user control of the sequence of output of records. Thus, they must be sorted on a key or keys specified by the user. Just as a user is given a choice of searchable fields, which does not include all fields, there will be a number of possible sort keys, but they are not likely to include all attributes of the record. Attributes that may have more than one value are likely to be excluded. If a set were to be sorted on subject heading, which one would determine order if there were more than one (the usual case)? It is conceivable that a searcher would like a set sorted on a field such as second author, but it is unlikely that such a request would be acceptable to most IR systems, or even that there is any way to express the concept in the command language.

The process of putting records in order is covered in so many computer-programming books (Knuth, 1973) that we shall not cover it here. It can be a time-consuming process, depending largely on the size of the file or set involved. Sorting 50 or 100 records, for a modern computer with a large memory, is not much of a challenge. But, IRSs do *not* offer to sort an entire database of a million or more records.

If records are to be ranked by any procedure, users will expect them to be displayed in rank order. The results of set analysis can be used for this purpose, as well. The frequency of an attribute value can be added to the record and used as a sort key.

8.3.3 Offline Printing

For just a few records, it is probably as economical and certainly faster to print online. The cost of printing is directly important to the user only when the user pays for connect time. Offline printing may appear less complex than online, but actually opens a number of special control problems. Formatting is the same, but offline printing usually involves a relatively large number of records, which is why it is used. Offline printing is usually done later in the day, probably after normal business hours, when the load on the computer is less. Users like to be able to confirm that a command to print offline is in the print queue and may ask to review it at any time before the command is executed. A later search may obviate the need for printing the earlier results; hence, the command should be cancellable at any time before execution.

Users may ask for an estimate of the cost of printing and transmitting the set they designated. They like to have some say in the mode of transmittal: regular mail, express mail, or electronic mail, all of which require that the IRS keep minute-by-minute records of the status of print jobs and be able to cancel if so ordered. All these options can easily be expressed but call for more optional attributes in a print command compared with an online display command. Modern high-speed modems make this function relatively unimportant, but when we had to deal with speeds as slow as 10 characters per second, it mattered a great deal.

8.4

Executing Other Commands

These functions generally are for the more traditional systems, not most of those on the Web or even local, free systems.

8.4.1 Ordering

The final step in an online retrieval process may be the placing of orders (see Section 7.4.10) for copies of documents referred to in the retrieved records. Of course, this is needed only when the file records are surrogates for or pointers to other documents, or contain the complete text but lack illustrations, or lack good-quality printing. Web documents can be directly downloaded but slow modems or Internet service can make this a time-consuming process for which an alternative to print and mail might be welcome.

Like offline printing, this seemingly straightforward function entails a number of nagging details. More often than not, there is a choice of suppliers and the search services, themselves, are not usually among them. The search service is merely an intermediary and will typically want to remain impartial in selection of a vendor to sell and deliver the documents to the user. The search service must maintain files of approved vendors, present the options to the user, note what records the user has identified, extract from these the information needed to fill an order, and pass the order on to the vendor with a copy to the user. Once again, the user may wish to cancel an order after placing it, and once again the search service has to keep track of the status of the transaction, because cancellation after the order has been passed to a vendor is a different matter from merely dropping a record from an order file. Who is responsible for paying for an order filled after the user thought it had been canceled?

8.4.2 Save, Recall, and Edit Searches

If a query takes a long time to formulate and if there is a likelihood that it may be used again, even in modified form, users will want to be able to store it (see Section 7.4.11) so it can be recalled later and edited, if necessary, before use. Most non-Web search services offer a *search save* function. At minimum, it allows the list of commands used in a search to be saved as a computer file. The user is given a name for the file or may supply the name. Because the file is taking up space in the search service's computer, the service will make some charge for this, but usually not much. Then, there must be a *recall* command and, although all services do not offer it, there should be a chance for the user to modify some of the commands. Perhaps it is only a date range or the name of a person that is changed, but a considerable amount of users' time can be saved this way.

A more modern way to save searches is to do so in the user's personal computer. Retrieval services may even offer software to help do this. That way, the user saves on storage and connect charges, maintains more control over privacy, and can use a familiar word processor to do the editing.

8.4.3 Current Awareness

The logic used in current awareness searches (see Section 7.4.12) does not differ from that for retrospective searches. The current awareness or selective dissemination of information (SDI) query is usually run only against the latest batch of new records about to be added to a database. This will require creating an inverted index for the new records, then searching with the same logic as for a full-scale database search. At the conclusion of the SDI processing, the new inverted file can be merged with the full-scale one.

An SDI search can also be run against the full file, in retrospective mode, using a date or update number selection criterion. The latter implies that one of the attributes of each record must be an identification of the batch of records used to update the file. Typically, this might be a date or a month-year, week-year, or day-year combination, as 9804 might identify records added to a database in month 4 of 1998.

The queries for a batched SDI search must have been stored in the search service's computer, to be available when needed. As we have pointed out, this mode of operation tends to be much less expensive than online searching, so there is a positive incentive to store the searches. In batch mode there is no need to keep the user informed of the status of the search, to tie up communication lines during a search, or to assure that no user waits more than a few seconds for the computer's attention. On the other hand, SDI searches tend to have more terms and more complex logic which, under newly emerging pricing systems, could jeopardize some of the cost advantage.

8.4.4 Cost Summation and Billing

Computation of costs (see Section 7.4.13) requires that the IRS keep track of the kinds of factors listed below. People view searches differently, and these viewpoints can affect the kinds of cost information wanted. In particular, we must distinguish among *connect time*, a *session*, and a *search*. Connect time can refer to total time a user's local computer is connected to a search service or to a telecommunications network. It is possible to connect to a computer without use of a data communications network that charges for time used, excluding therefore, local calls or use of the Web. Hence, the search service must know which network or type of line is in use in order to compute charges. A *session* can be the set of activities performed during a contiguous period of connectedness, or a series of activities, with some aspects in common, that may extend over more than one connect period.

A *search* is usually seen as the activities or commands used to solve one problem, or a set of activities for a particular user or purpose. It, too, may take more than one connect period. A search may also be considered to be all activities between one command that opens a file or begins a search and the next file opening. A session may consist of more than one search, and a search may extend over more than one session. For those users who must charge others for online searches, these differences are important to resolve.

The kinds of information from which charges are computed are the following:

1. Start time of the telecommunication network connection and of the search session
2. Start time "in" the current database
3. End time of connection with a database
4. End time of the search session and of the network connection
5. Number of records displayed or printed (or ordered to be printed), and the formats involved
6. Possibly a count of the number of search terms in use, and perhaps also a count of the number of terms searched through (i.e., the number of entries in the inverted file or the number of records in the database)
7. The amount of space devoted to storage of queries or data and possibly the amount of time devoted to sorting records (either a charge for sorting or a limit on the number of records sorted may be the only defense against an excessive request by a user)

Times must be stored for the start and end of an entire session in order to charge for telecommunications time, and for the time of starting and ending use of each database in order to charge for connect time to each database, since normally different rates are charged for each. In most retrieval systems, a user is always in some database. Upon logging into a system, the user is considered to have selected a default database. It may be an empty one, used solely for bookkeeping purposes, a training database charged at a low rate, a real database of the user's choosing, or a system-assigned default.

The actual formulas for computing costs tend not to be complex, if the data are available. A difficult part of cost computation is acquiring the data when a change is made in the basis for pricing. When Chemical Abstracts Service wanted to begin charging for each search term used (O'Leary, 1988), search services had to revise their programs to acquire this data. Were the data already available, the change might have been trivial, but changing a large and complex computer program, without disrupting its service, is a daunting task.

8.4.5 Terminating a Session

Terminating a session (see Section 7.4.14) is largely a matter of computing the total cost of the search session, returning to the system any storage space devoted exclusively to the searcher who has just logged off, and disconnecting the telecommunications connection. Time of termination must be passed to the billing program.

8.5

Feedback to Users and Error Messages

Section 11.3 covers the subject of feedback from the point of view of information content. Here, we continue our discussion of how an IRS functions.

8.5.1 Response to Command Errors

It has always seemed to us that a minimal response in case of error in an input command should be an explanation of how the program interpreted the command, at what point it discovered a conflict or error, and why it appears to be an error. A computer (or, for that matter, a human) cannot always tell exactly what the error was. Here are a few examples:

FILE 123—the command FILE is used to select a database, and 123 is the user's stated choice. But suppose there is no file 123. Then this was an error. The program should tell the user it assumed the command was FILE, then that it assumed the file was number 123, but that that number does not exist as a file code. It is possible that even the command was wrong, the user absent-mindedly intending to say FIND. If so, simply being told there is no such file would be more confusing than helpful.

SELECT AUT = HOREAU, H.D. (a character transposition in typing AU = THOREAU, H.D.)—the command is SELECT, the attribute specified is aut, but no such attribute abbreviation is in use. The response might be that the command was interpreted as SELECT, the attribute was aut, which is not recognized, and the value HOREAU, H.D. It is very easy for a user not to notice anything wrong with AUT. Henry David Thoreau was a noted American author, and it is relatively easy for an American to spot the error in spelling the name. But it is less so for an English-speaking person of another culture, and very difficult for the IRS—the program—to work out what was intended.

EXXPAND THOREAU (a typing error is made—two Xs in EX-PAND)—this is an inverted-file search command. The result is a display from the inverted file of a series of "words" all beginning with X, mostly Roman numerals. From the IRS's point of view, there is no error. While no full command was found, a valid abbreviation (E, using the Dialog language) was found, and the Dialog rule is that everything following EXPAND or E is treated as the argument or value of the search term. To the user, who is still unaware of the typing error, this outcome is startling. It would be helpful if the user could ask for an interpretation of the command at this point, and be told, as above, what command and argument were assumed.

8.5.2 Set–Size Indication

It has been suggested (Blair, 1980) that set size is an important factor in a searcher's decision of whether to continue modifying set definitions or to end the search. This is a useful statistic for searchers and easy for the computer to compile. It is normally automatically available at the end of any Boolean set operation. This is a function usually provided by Web search engines.

8.5.3 Record Display

We described the function of display of records earlier. This is probably the single most important type of feedback from IRS to user. The user, again especially when searching text, cannot be certain that an apparently reasonable query formulation is necessarily going to retrieve what the user really wanted. Every retrieval system has some kind of browsing capability that, usually (not usually on the Web), offers a variety of formats in which to view the retrieved records. Since the user must explicitly identify the records of a set to be displayed, finding the records is quite simple.

8.5.4 Set Analysis

The mechanics of set analysis were described in Section 8.3.1. Such feedback is probably best left for the user to request, lest the volume of data become overwhelming.

8.5.5 Cost

During a long search, knowing what charges, if any, are accumulating can help a searcher's decision making. While many users would like a cost summary on demand, excessive detail might be self-defeating, discouraging searchers from using it. A brief summary of accumulated costs can be unobtrusively displayed following any set-forming or display command, always with the option for the user to see a full explanation on demand. Even on the Web, where searching seems free, the connect time to an Internet service provider may not be.

8.5.6 Help

One of the enigmas of software design is that help systems are so seldom used. One reason is that they are so often badly designed (Kearsley, 1988). Their potential for helping users, and thereby selling products, is immense. It is point-less to review how they are usually done but may be worth reviewing how they *might* be done.

Perhaps the most common use for help is to explain the current or most recent message from computer to user. The message may have been something like the one we used to get from MS-DOS, the operating system once used in most IBM-like personal computers, after a command calling for erasure of a complete disk or subdirectory, "This will erase your directory. Are you sure? (y/n)." A first-time user might not know why this is being asked and would welcome a short explanation. A more experienced computer user, one who has inadvertently erased a good many files that had no back-up, knows that it intends to advise the user that there may not be any recovery from an error here, and invites the user to think carefully before going ahead. All that is required to implement help here is to allow the use of a special key following any computer output message, and to have a prepared explanation for each. The program is not required to exercise any significant logic, although the producers of the software are required to invest a considerable effort in preparing the texts of help messages and to try to anticipate the state of mind of users. The memory required used to be significant for a PC but in these days of gigabyte memories, it now seems insignificant.

In general, providing help means to provide a message as specific as pos-sible, explaining what may currently be perplexing the user. Retrieving the message is no problem—the problem is determining what the user wants or needs to know, which may be anything from an explanation of a command syntax to an analysis of how a search has progressed thus far, together with a suggestion of what to do next.

Since many error messages have to do with some form of user error, e.g., rejecting a command because it was syntactically invalid or included unknown vocabulary, it is also useful for the searcher to get an explanation of the theory or syntax or rules governing the use of the command in question. Such help goes considerably beyond informing the user that a mistake has been made. It might require programmed logic in order to limit the amount of explanatory material. (Is the error one of syntax, of vocabulary, or of using a set number that has not been defined?)

Picture a user who is doing his or her first database search. The search has progressed to the point where some sets have been created and modified and there are a modest number of records in the last set. The experienced user knows what to do next; the inexperienced user might not. Should the search be terminated? Revised again? Should all records of the final set be printed offline? It would be helpful for the user to be able to ask the question, "What can I do next?" Like the explanations described previously, standard answers to such a question might simply be stored in such a way as to be associated with each computer output. The program, "knowing" what message it sent last, retrieves the explanation for it on request. The user would be told what *can* be done or what typically is done at this point. No suggestion would be made as to what *should* be done. If the goal is limited this way then, again, the logic of help is simple, but requires a great deal of message writing and storing.

The ultimate form of help as we see it today is for the computer to analyze both what the user has done (series of commands issued) and what the results have been. Then, based on this information, the computer makes a suggestion as to what *should* be done next. A few research systems provide some form of this service (Marcus, 1982; Marcus and the CONIT Project Staff, 1987a, 1987b; Meadow, 1988), and indications are that users like it, but there have been no large-scale tests to prove that it is worth the effort on a commercial scale. The program logic required is formidable. We want the advice to be good, yet must avoid a computer–user conversation that appears inane to the user or that gives the impression of far more understanding and wisdom on the part of the computer than is really the case. Since only the user really understands what information is wanted and what is useful, a program can offer help but cannot take over the decision making in a search. The goals of help must be limited.

9

Text Searching

The Special Problems of Text Searching

It has been stated several times previously that there is ambiguity in the mere presence of a word in a natural-language text. The occurrence of a single word in a text cannot be taken as proof positive that the text is "about" the subject usually associated with that word. Throughout this book are occurrences of words such as CAT, DOG, or FOOD, but this book is clearly not about animals or nutrition. Syntax contributes to the problem. A person can understand the meaning of "This book is not about animals," but most retrieval systems today cannot perform the semantic and syntactic analysis needed to comprehend the meaning of that sentence. If they can deal with natural language at all, they are likely to treat the negative sentence as being, itself, about animals. Indeed, it is something of a conundrum whether the text "This book is not about animals" is, itself, about animals. If it poses any serious degree of difficulty for a human, what can we expect of a computer's interpretation?

The length of a text contributes to the difficulty. In nontext files, a typical attribute value consists of a word or a number, or perhaps a short phrase. Further, the syntax and vocabulary are usually controlled. Text usually has none of these restrictions. An author has great freedom in the choice of words and can make up new words or change the meaning of familiar ones. Relatively little is done in most forms of writing to control this problem. The AECMA guide to simplified English (Section 3.2.2) is a rare but limited example of an attempt at natural-language control.

A user of an IRS must be aware of this potential for ambiguity, of the pitfalls of text searching, and of the possible means of getting around them. When searching very short texts it may be sufficient to specify a few words that *should* appear in a text on the desired subject. With longer texts, which are becoming increasingly common, it is necessary to specify *patterns of word occurrence* rather than individual occurrences. That may mean a set of individual words occurring with high frequency, two or more words co-occurring often, or a set of words occurring in a particular pattern or sequence. In our attempts to describe our information needs, we often use the very patterns of word usage we are looking for in texts to be retrieved. One of the tasks, either for the retrieval system or the search intermediary, is to examine the language used to describe needs, looking for the words and patterns that should appear in records. One of the great difficulties is that the information need can be expressed in words in so many different ways. It helps a great deal if either the human intermediary or an interpretive program is able to make the association among the words used and the others implicated.

There has been and continues to be a great deal of work and innovation on the subject of text searching. Salton (1989) remains a seminal work, and a more recent review of progress is found in Sievert (1996).

9.2
Some Characteristics of Text and Their Applications

H. P. Luhn (1958) was among the first to recognize the role that patterns of word usage could play in finding the words that best characterize the subject of a text, in order to index or compile an abstract for it automatically. Once terms are found that can be used for an index, because they represent a subject of the text for search purposes, they could also be used to find the sentences of a text with the highest concentrations of key words, which might constitute a passable abstract (Edmundson and Wyllys, 1961; Luhn, 1958; Salton, 1989, p. 439).

Text can be treated as a set of words connected only by their joint membership in the text. The same words can be analyzed in terms of various patterns of occurrence, including the syntax of natural language. Finally, text can be analyzed and characterized as a whole, rather than as individual terms.

9.2.1 Components of Text

A text has *vocabulary*, but it is not tightly controlled, except by custom. Different words may have common or similar meanings. A dictionary or thesaurus may be needed to help establish meaning in context. These tools are often *domain specific*, such as a thesaurus containing only medical terms or a dictionary of only mathematical terms.

A text has *patterns of vocabulary*. The patterns range from simple co-occurrence of words adjacent to one another (FREEDOM OF CHOICE) to more complex co-occurrence patterns (TREE and KEY are likely to co-occur often in some computer science texts, but not in forestry texts). There are also frequency-of-occurrence and co-occurrence distributions. These patterns can be used to rank texts according to their similarity to a query or to each other. They can also identify words or phrases that can, when separated from the text itself, serve as an index. Until about 10–20 years ago, the only way to search large files of text was to use surrogate records consisting of index terms that were descriptions of content as well as of the document itself—its author, publisher, date of publication, etc. Surrogates have not disappeared from the scene but are decreasing in importance as full-text databases become more common and as text-searching systems, rather than surrogate-searching systems, come into common use. Full-text databases are seen commercially in ever-increasing numbers. Unfortunately, this increase in use of full text often means that the attributes that once collectively constituted a surrogate are now not explicitly identified in the record. Hence, a search, even for something as "obvious" as author, may be unable to find any authors' names.

Finally, a text has *syntax*, the rules of usage for combining individual words into meaningful phrases and sentences. There are also stylistic rules for combining sentences into paragraphs, and so on to multivolume books. Syntax helps to clarify individual word meanings and significance, and the converse is also true. The interdependence of syntax and word meanings can put a high premium on sophisticated analysis, not at all easy for a computer. Words are often defined in terms of a context or domain, and the interpreter may have to learn the context from the text, itself. In recent years teachers and editors have tended to relax enforcement of English syntactic rules, making it ever more difficult for a computer to determine the meaning of words.

9.2.2 Significant Words—Indexing

Luhn (1958) recognized that high-frequency words tended to be the common or non-information-bearing ones. He also felt that one or two occurrences of a word in a large text could not be taken to be significant in defining the subject matter. Therefore, he suggested using the words in the middle of the frequency range. Common words would best be eliminated by using a list of stop words, and low-frequency words, by simply discarding those of frequency 1, 2, or more, depending on size of the text.

Can word frequency alone be used to find the most significant subject-indicating words? If a knowledgable person is going to write a text for publication, of say 2000 words, on a technical subject, a certain vocabulary must be used, and it has to be the vocabulary conventionally used in that subject field. Editors or reviewers will generally insist on this, so while the author has a high degree of freedom, it is not complete freedom of choice. The author may vary the use of individual words but, in the aggregate, the vocabulary must

Table 9.1

Word Frequency Tabulation[a]

58	the	6	one	3	natural	2	complete	2	pipe
48	of	6	s	3	often	2	considered	2	primarily
40	a	5	an	3	other	2	consisting	2	problem
39	is	5	computer	3	p	2	content	2	process
25	in	5	database	3	point	2	created	2	question
25	to	5	databases	3	read	2	day	2	relatively
21	and	5	text	3	searching	2	do	2	remote
18	or	5	they	3	service	2	document	2	represent
17	retrieval	5	user	3	single	2	entire	2	search
14	as	4	being	3	software	2	example	2	searches
13	information	4	between	3	stored	2	files	2	selection
13	it	4	documents	3	term	2	finding	2	selectivity
12	be	4	may	3	terms	2	finds	2	sense
12	not	4	more	3	them	2	first	2	so
12	that	4	query	3	users	2	has	2	some
10	what	4	such	3	view	2	have	2	something
9	are	4	used	3	will	2	henry	2	systems
9	for	4	usually	2	1	2	if	2	think
9	on	3	both	2	2	2	indexes	2	three
9	system	3	by	2	about	2	interactive	2	time
8	ir	3	central	2	activity	2	irs	2	today
7	but	3	communication	2	all	2	king	2	was
7	from	3	difference	2	any	2	languages	2	well
7	how	3	does	2	becoming	2	local	2	when
7	records	3	file	2	best	2	long	2	whether
7	there	3	its	2	blair	2	means	2	while
7	this	3	language	2	called	2	number	2	written
7	we	3	library	2	can	2	only	2	www
7	which	3	mechanical	2	carried	2	operated	590	*words*
7	with	3	much	2	collection	2	palace		*occurring once each*

[a]This list contains the words of Section 1.2 of this book in rank order.

reasonably conform to what the readers understand and expect. The relative frequencies of occurrence of subject-indicative words may not vary much from author to author within a discipline. This condition does not hold for all forms of writing, such as law court testimony.

The most frequently occurring words in English are the very common ones such as *the, of, and* (Dewey, 1923; Zipf, 1949). As we have said, in a 2000-word text almost any word can occur once; hence is not necessarily indicative of the subject. Somewhere between the extremes will lie the words that do indicate subject matter. "Somewhere" is a vague term. The set of *significant*

Table 9.2
Significant Words[a]

Freq.	Term	Freq.	Term
17	retrieval	5	database
13	information	5	databases
9	system	5	text
8	ir	5	user
7	records	4	documents
5	computer	4	query
		4	usually

[a]These are words from Table 9.1 with frequency great than 3 that are not on Fox's list (Fox, 1990) of frequently occurring words. They define the subject matter of the section and, in fact, the entire book. Note that *ir* is an abbreviation for *information retrieval*. Only the word *usually* is of no consequence for subject description.

words in a text is a fuzzy set. We can have high confidence that the important words are in it, but not that we can identify the one or two most important ones.

Table 9.1 shows the frequency distribution of words of Section 1.2 of this book, in descending order of frequency. Table 9.2 shows words from that list after discarding common words and those of frequency less than 4 and then conflating those remaining. Common words were those appearing in the list compiled by Fox (1990).

Figure 9.1 shows a plot of word *frequency* against *rank* (highest frequency term has rank 1, etc., of the text of the paragraph using the logarithm of frequency and rank, rather than their raw values. This curve represents the distribution variously attributed to Condon (1928), Zipf (1949), and Mandelbrot (1953). For larger samples of "well-written" English the curve is usually nearly a straight line. Other languages or other writing styles may produce different shapes (Whitehorn and Zipf, 1943; Meadow, Wang, and Stamboulie, 1993). Superimposed on the figure is a representation of Luhn's concept of where the significant words are. The curve of significance is not exact; it is simply intended to show low significance at both tails of the distribution, and high in the middle.

9.2.3 Significant Sentences—Abstracting

Again historically, the preparation of abstracts, especially of scientific articles and reports, was deemed to be critical to the success of IRSs. These were usually prepared by professional abstractors, after publication, an expensive pro-

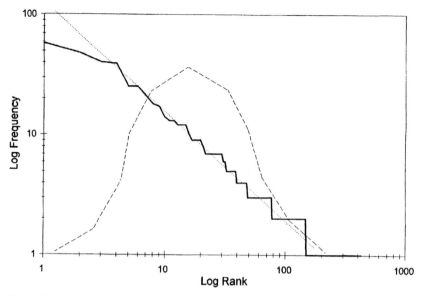

Figure 9.1
Word frequency distribution: the heavy line shows a plot of log frequency vs log rank for the words
of the text in a sample paragraph. A straight line of slope approximately −1.0, shown as a dotted
line, would fit this data well. The dashed line shows a theoretical curve of significance as a function
of rank.

cess; hence, the interest increased in automatically prepared abstracts. Figure 9.2
(at the end of this chapter) shows the 46 sentences of the sample text used for
Table 9.1. Table 9.3 shows, for each sentence: (1) the sentence number; (2) n,
the number of words in the sentence; (3) k, the number of key word tokens,
where a key word is one that appears in Table 9.2; (4) kq, the number of unique
key words or word types, i.e., counting each word only once, regardless of
number of occurrences; (5) k/n, the ratio of key words to the total number of
words; (6) kq/n, the ratio of unique key words to total words; and (7) $\overline{d}$, the
mean distance between key words, if more than one in a sentence.

   One method of abstracting would be to extract the s sentences with the
highest count of key words, s depending on the length of the document and the
desired length of the abstract. But highest count, alone, is not always satisfactory.
Sentence 1 gives a good summary of the text. Sentence 2 adds to this but would
not be too meaningful alone. Sentences 25, 36, and 41 which have 6, 6, and 4
key words, respectively, are not highly informative. These three sentences also
have many more total words. Using the ratio of key words to total words, we
would select sentences 13 and 1. Number 13 suffers from being a question, but

Table 9.3
Numeric Measures for Sentences of the Text of Figure 9.2[a]

Sentence	N	n	k	kq	k/n	kq/n	$\bar{d}$
1	16	4	3	0.25	0.188	3.30
2	26	0	0	0	0	0.00
3	17	2	2	0.12	0.12	6.00
4	11	1	1	0.09	0.09	0.00
5	23	1	1	0.04	0.04	0.00
6	13	1	1	0.08	0.08	0.00
7	10	0	0	0.00	0.00	0.00
8	19	1	1	0.05	0.05	0.00
9	5	1	1	0.20	0.20	0.00
10	41	3	3	0.07	0.07	11.50
11	21	0	0	0.00	0.00	0.00
12	25	1	1	0.04	0.04	0.00
13	6	2	2	0.33	0.33	0.00
14	31	0	0	0.00	0.00	0.00
15	18	4	3	0.22	0.17	3.70
16	24	1	1	0.04	0.04	0.00
17	15	3	3	0.20	0.20	2.00
18	26	3	2	0.12	0.08	7.50
19	18	0	0	0.00	0.00	0.00
20	7	1	1	0.14	0.14	0.00
21	24	1	1	0.04	0.04	0.00
22	13	0	0	0.00	0.00	0.00
23	12	0	0	0.00	0.00	0.00
24	7	1	1	0.14	0.14	0.00
25	87	6	3	0.07	0.03	11.60
26	41	3	3	0.07	0.07	13.00
27	20	1	1	0.05	0.05	0.00
28	17	1	1	0.06	0.06	0.00
29	7	0	0	0.00	0.00	0.00
30	28	3	3	0.11	0.11	2.50
31	11	0	0	0.00	0.00	0.00
32	39	2	2	0.05	0.05	0.00
33	20	1	1	0.05	0.05	0.00
34	18	0	0	0.00	0.00	0.00
35	28	0	0	0.00	0.00	0.00
36	42	6	3	0.14	0.07	5.60
37	16	1	1	0.06	0.06	0.00
38	22	1	1	0.05	0.05	0.00
39	17	3	2	0.18	0.12	3.00
40	37	2	2	0.05	0.05	4.00
41	35	4	4	0.11	0.11	6.30
42	33	1	1	0.03	0.03	0.00
43	23	2	2	0.09	0.09	2.00
44	27	4	3	0.15	0.11	3.70
45	24	2	2	0.08	0.08	17.00
46	32	1	1	0.03	0.03	0.00

[a]Shown are n (number of words, citations not included), k (number of key words), kq (number of unique key words—duplicates not counted), k/n (number of words divided by number of key words—key word density), kq/n (number of word types), and $\bar{d}$ (average distance between key words).

these two alone provide a decent abstract. Using the ratio of unique key words to total would give us sentences 13, 9, 17, and 1.

The rightmost column in Table 9.3 can give us sentences with the important words close together. The highest ranking sentences, by this method, are 1, 15, 39, and 43, which we feel is a fairly good representation of the sense of the original text. A practical system should consider yet more factors, such as inverse term frequency, but we can see the concepts from these examples.

One problem with automatic abstracts, related to one of the authors by a member of an IBM team that originally tested the concept, was that the abstracts were the same for everyone. IBM is, of course, a computer company. It would be no surprise that its library had acquired documents about computers. People in different parts of the company would have wanted information about different aspects of computers, and this method could not provide that. A good modern review of abstracting techniques is found in Paice (1991).

9.2.4 Measures of Complete Texts

Statistical measures of text (Yule, 1944) generally characterize a complete text, on the basis of style rather than subject, and are used for comparing one text with another, one author's work with that of another or earlier works of the same author, or texts in one natural language with those in another. They are not used for selecting words or sentences within a text. Some examples are:

Type–token ratio is the ratio of the number of different words in a text to the total number of words.

Mean frequency is the inverse of the type–token ratio, showing the average number of occurrences of word types in a text.

Yule characteristic—G. U. Yule (1944, pp. 9–82) was concerned with such issues as determining authorship or sequence of production of manuscripts. He worked at a time when computers were not yet available for such applications, and since full-text statistics were therefore very costly, sampling procedures were critical. He found that measures such as mean frequency varied with sample size and statistical procedure; hence, he developed a measure that was characteristic of a text, but independent of sample size, which he simply called the *characteristic*. One definition is

$$K = \frac{\sigma^2 - \overline{f}}{\overline{f}^2}, \tag{9.1}$$

where σ^2 is the variance of the number of occurrences of words with a given frequency (the number of words occurring once, twice, . . .) and $\bar{f}$ is the mean frequency of occurrence of words in the sample text.

These measures have not found application in information retrieval but might conceivably be used to modify word or sentence weights to account for writing style. If the words selected and their relative frequencies are very different between two documents, it is unlikely they were written by the same person at about the same time. These measures also have some potential for characterizing the behavior of language users, if applied to command language (Meadow *et al.*, 1993).

9.3
Command Language for Text Searching

Most current command languages are intended to express binary attribute–value statements linked by Boolean logic, which we shall henceforth call *Boolean statements*. The query statements include words or strings whose presence in a record are criteria or conditions for selection, or that use membership in a previously defined set as criteria. Command languages such as these were once the only means for searching text, but are increasingly being replaced by natural language query systems or hybrids.

9.3.1 Set Membership Statements

Not unique to text searching, but desirable in this and other forms of searching, is the ability to state that a record to be selected must already be a member of an existing set. Not available in all languages.

9.3.2 Word or String Occurrence Statements

The original and most straightforward type of statement is generically an attribute-value expression of the form attribute *relation* value, such as AUTHOR = THOREAU, H.D. As noted in Sections 7.3.5 and 8.2.4, other variations involve truncation or universal match or "wild-card" symbols. Different retrieval systems offer different combinations of these techniques, possibly with still other variations, although the amount of variation is normally slight. Some systems will use more elaborate methods of word conflation, such as automatic removal of stems.

9.3.3 Proximity Statements

A proximity expression involves two or more words or strings and an operator indicating that they must occur within a specified distance of each other. Distance can be expressed as a maximal number of intervening words between two given words or a requirement that the query words be in the same unit of text, such as a sentence, paragraph, or field of a record.

The usages illustrated next are from Dialog and are representative of the many variations of proximity statements:

> ELECTRIC (1W) VEHICLE means that ELECTRIC must precede VEHICLE with at most one intervening word, therefore permitting ELECTRIC VEHICLE and ELECTRIC PASSENGER VEHICLE but not ELECTRIC BATTERY POWERED VEHICLE.
>
> FOOD (N) FISH would retrieve either FOOD FISH or FISH FOOD. The letter N here stands for *near* and specifies distance irrespective of direction. The lack of a digit before the N means no intervening words are permitted. FOOD (1N) FISH would retrieve FOOD FOR FISH or FISH FOR FOOD.
>
> CAT (S) DOG calls for the two words to be present in the same sentence or subfield, regardless of distance apart or relative order. What constitutes a sentence or subfield may vary among databases or search services.
>
> CAT (P) DOG calls for co-occurrence, using the paragraph as a limit.
>
> CAT (F) DOG calls for co-occurrence in the same field or attribute. The particular field may optionally be indicated, as CAT (F) DOG/TI. If not specified, then co-occurrence will be sought in *any* field. If an attribute were **state of prior residence** and a particular record contained two values, SOUTH DAKOTA and NORTH CAROLINA, then SOUTH (F) CAROLINA retrieves the record, but SOUTH (S) CAROLINA does not, because the two words occur in the same field but not the same subfield.

Any of these usages might be combined with truncation or universal or wild-card symbols, and more than two words might be used in an expression, for example:

> CAT? (1N) DOG will retrieve DOG-EARED CATALOG. (The hyphen in a text is usually treated as a space.)
>
> AIR (1N) GROUND (W) MISSILE involves three substantive words and will retrieve both AIR TO GROUND MISSILE and GROUND TO AIR MISSILE.

The use of such relationship expressions allows a great deal more precision in searching than merely specifying co-occurrence of words within a record or attribute, especially when the "attribute" might be a text constituting 90% of the record. Sometimes the relative placement of even very common words can be highly significant and create distinct meanings, as "right to life" or "pro-choice," which have very different implications than do the mere co-occurrence, in one paragraph, of RIGHT and LIFE or PRO and CHOICE.

Proximity searching has a major impact on the composition of an inverted file. In addition to attribute value and record number, and depending on which operators are allowed in any given system, the inverted file will have to identify the attribute in which the value occurs; the paragraph and sentence, or other similar subdivision, of the attribute; and the word number or position within the attribute.

Using the assumptions of Section 8.2.5, an average inverted-file entry contains 24 bytes, about 10 of which are the word or term. Roughly, we see that the inverted file may require two to three times as many bytes as a simple list of the words occurring. Proximity searching is expensive, but users like it, especially as file sizes continue to grow, creating the demand for techniques giving finer resolution of retrieved sets. The inverted-file entry can be compacted, i.e., encoded in such a way as to reduce the memory space needed. There are many ways of doing so (Salton, 1989, pp. 114–129), including such simple ones as representing all numbers as binary numbers or even representing nonnumeric symbols as binary numbers, with a start and end marker to denote strings of such codes. While compaction reduces storage requirements, it adds to the time it takes to enter a new record into storage and to interpret a query. Text compaction is not commonly used in commercial IRSs.

The conditional expressions for set membership, string containment, or word proximity are not commands. They are elements of commands, means of stating the conditions under which a command is to be executed. A typical command actually states the following:

SELECT <selection conditions> states that a subset of records is to be formed, which have the characteristics or meet the conditions given in the conditional expression. A number is assigned to the set.

The conditional part of the expression could be one such as this multi-part statement: (TITLE CONTAINS 'BIRD') AND S3 AND (RED (W) WING?). The complete command states that: (1) a set of records is to be formed (complete records, not just a set of tuples, are implicitly requested because most text-retrieval systems deal only with retrieval of full records); (2) selected records must meet the conditions that the string (not word) BIRD be present in the title attribute, (3) that any records selected must already be members of set number 3, and (4) that the default attribute or attributes must contain the word RED followed by any word beginning with the string WING.

The various forms of non-Boolean statements, or graphic query representation in lieu of statements, can be thought of as shorthand notations for highly complex statements in the traditional Boolean form. For example, the use of a paragraph of text to describe subject matter can be treated by the IRS as simply a statement of the form SELECT WORD1 OR WORD2 OR WORD3. . . . If words are weighted, or if weights are computed based on word-occurrence frequencies in the query, these could be used to define a set, just as if there were no weights, and then to provide a basis for ranking within the set.

The basic set-forming command, whether it is called SELECT, FIND, or SEARCH performs virtually the same function in all text-searching systems. In addition, other commands may operate on existing sets to form subsets of existing ones. A common command is LIMIT, which creates a subset based on a single new criterion, such as LIMIT S3 DATE = 1996:1999, which might mean that records of set 3 are to be included in a new subset only if the date is in the range 1996–1999. The various IRSs have different syntaxes for this command. LIMIT applies to an existing set; hence it does not require recourse to the inverted file. It could be executed by sequentially searching the records of the indicated set. If the set is small and the database large this is a significant time saver.

The *contain* relationship (Section 7.3.2) can be made into a separate command, requiring fewer words. For example, in BASIS, SCAN S2 ' RED WING'/AB means select a record if it is in s2 and its abstract contains ' RED WING'. No truncation symbol is needed because the characters within the quotation marks delimit a string, not a pair of words. Here, the space before RED indicates that that string starts a word, hence that TAPERED WING would not be retrieved. The absence of a space after WING indicates that RED WINGED would be acceptable.

The set-forming commands tend to be few in number and simple in concept. Any complexity tends to occur in the relational expressions that make up the conditional part of the commands. In general, these simple, individual text-searching methods can work well, but the larger and more diverse the text or the greater the number of texts to be searched, the less well do they work in the sense of finding exactly what the user wants. This is because these commands are based upon exactitude of statements, and generally are not able to expand on what the user has said.

9.4

Term Weighting

The general idea of term weighting in text searching is to improve the discriminating power of a search term by indicating its relative importance in a query. Such weights may also be used to rank documents as to their similarity with a query or another document.

Some IRSs that make use of weighting techniques, also assign weights to index terms for documents, to be stored in the inverted file, or to indicate the strength of the term's application to a document in a term-document matrix. It is, however, possible to create a query which consists of a string of weighted terms, and a relevance threshold for use with a file where index terms are not weighted. The presence of such a term in a document adds the term's weight to an accumulator for that document, and if enough terms are present that the sum of their weights exceeds the threshold, the document is moved to the answer set. The set can be ranked by the value of the amount by which each document exceeds the stated threshold. See more on ranking in Chapter 10.

A series of weighted terms allows the formation of a set or *polythetic* class. Such a class is one whose members qualify for membership by any of several sets of criteria. If there is only a single criterion, the class is called *monothetic*. In this case, we have documents that may have any number of any of the terms in a query and whose weights, when summed, exceed the threshold. Assume the query (A2, B1, C1, D1, E5, F3)(T4), where A, . . . , F indicate query terms whose weights are given by the integers immediately following and T indicates that the following integer is the threshold value, here a 4. Any document containing term E is always in the class because of its high weight, whatever other terms may be present. Assuming E is not present, a document with term A is in only if F is also present, or B, C, and D are also present. A record containing F is also in the retrieval set if any two of B, C, or D are also present. Angione (1975) has shown that Boolean expressions may be converted to equivalent weighted expressions of this nature.

Query terms may also, at least in theory, be weighted as to their probability of relevance. If we know the number r_j, of relevant documents in which term j occurs; the total number of records in, or magnitude of, the database, MD; the number of records, R, relevant to a query; and the total number of records in which the term is present, n_j; then the *term relevance* of term j in a document (Salton and McGill, 1983, p. 98) can be computed as

$$\text{TermRel}_j = \frac{r_j/(R-r_j)}{(n_j-r_j)/(MD-n_j-(R-r_j))} \qquad (9.2)$$

$$= \frac{r \cdot (MD-n_j-(R-r_j))}{(n_j-r_j) \cdot (R-r_j)}. \qquad (9.3)$$

If, in the course of a retrieval process, additional information on the likelihood of relevance is ascertained, these weights can be recomputed.

If term occurrences are assumed to be independent of each other (a major and not fully warranted assumption), it is not difficult to determine good decision rules for selecting relevant documents. This requires *a priori* knowledge of the probability of a document being retrieved given its relevance or non-relevance. We may use the probabilities that terms are assigned to relevant or nonrelevant documents to find these values. In general, it is not easy to generate the underlying values of TermRel. It would have to be done when the database is compiled or whenever any major changes are made.

The assignment of weights in a Boolean query allows the searcher to indicate the importance of one term over another, and provides a means of ranking the output of a Boolean search. Consider a database describing available houses in a real estate office. A user seeking to buy a house may wish to search the database looking for an ideal match with his or her requirements. Factors such as location and cost may be more important than other factors such as color or the existence of a garage or fireplace. Such preferences will likely be expressed in a subjective manner (i.e., "important," "very important," "not important," "would be nice but not essential") that would require conversion into numerical weights.

9.4.1 Indexing with Weights

The simplest application of weights to document indexing is the assignment of binary weights. A term is either assigned to a document (a weight of 1) or it is not (a weight of 0).

Some database suppliers assign more terms to the documents than can fit in their printed publications. The terms to be printed are flagged as print terms in the database. Then we have three weights for a term: printed (important), not printed (not so important, but still an index term), and not selected. These are ternary-valued weights. Searchers may specify that terms must be tagged or not. A query that includes the flagged term will have fewer hits, but presumably more relevant ones.

The indexer might also subjectively apply a nonbinary weight to a term assigned to a document, perhaps a value anywhere in the range 0 to 1. If the query then contains a threshold value for each term the IRS will only send documents to the answer set where the matched term has a weight equal to or higher than that specified in the query. Most indexers and most searchers find the assignment of weights to terms to be onerous, subjective, and imprecise. Therefore, weighted indexing tends to be limited to use in conjunction with automated indexing.

9.4.2 Automated Assignment of Weights

How are weights automatically assigned? A common method is to make use of ~~inverse document frequency~~ (Salton and McGill, 1983, p. 63). Although called *document frequency*, the measure is of term or word frequency, and might also be called *inverse term frequency*:

$$\text{Weight}_{ij} = \text{Freq}_{ij} \cdot \log_2 \left(\frac{n}{\text{DocFreq}_j} \right) \tag{9.4}$$

where Weigt_{ij} is the weight term j in document i; Freq_{ij} is the frequency of occurrence of term j in document i; n is the number of documents in the database; and DocFreq_j is the number of documents in which term j occurs. A term that occurs with high frequency in a small number of documents is highly significant to those documents. If it occurred with high frequency in all documents, as does the word *the*, it is of no significance.

It is also possible to compute the discrimination value of a term by computing a document similarity measure for all documents in which both terms occur, then finding the average similarity for the collection. Then remove a term and recompute the average to show how much that term contributes to the average similarity. The difference between the average without the term and original average will indicate the discrimination power of the term and can be used as its weight (Salton and McGill, 1983, pp. 66–71). This process requires a great deal of computation when the database is compiled or modified, prior to retrieval.

Weights are best used with the vector-space model of an IRS where a measure of similarity between a vector of term weights representing a document can be compared with a similar vector representing a query. The cosine measure of the angle between document and query vectors, to be described in Section 9.6.1, is the most likely choice for similarity.

However, it has also been suggested that these weights can be viewed as membership functions in fuzzy sets. A fuzzy set is a set whose elements are usually neither totally in the set nor out of the set. (See Section 7.3.4.) This interpretation allows the weights to indicate how much a given document belongs in the set of documents about a concept represented by a given term.

9.4.3 Improving Weights

Relevance feedback may be used to automatically modify weights. Once the IRS has a relatively small retrieved set whose members have been evaluated for relevance by the user, this information can be used to recompute the weights. The weights of terms present in relevant documents can be increased, while those in nonrelevant documents can be decreased. After the query's weights have been modified, the query could be rerun in hopes of improving retrieval performance. This method is examined in more detail in Section 11.5.

9.5
Word Association Techniques

One of the most difficult tasks for the searcher is to think of all the words that an author might have used in a text when writing on a particular subject. It is, again, compounded by the large number of words in the text, the lack of standardized meanings, and the authors' practice of using synonyms and pronouns to avoid excessive repetition. Words that are used to refer to other words are called *anaphora*. These are a great burden for information retrieval because it is so difficult for a program to determine what word is referred to (Liddy, 1990).

Information retrieval systems are able to assist searchers to find words associated with the words the searcher provides. *Association* may have different meanings in different IRSs and sometimes considerably different costs are involved. Assistance may be provided in the form of documents or databases showing term relationships (*lexicons*) or automatically by having a program compute relationships or strength of relationships among words. Automatic term association techniques are particularly important in processing natural language queries wherein a searcher usually cannot use such techniques as truncation or demarcation of words that must be found together. Here are some common methods of word association.

9.5.1 Dictionaries and Thesauri

While a conventional dictionary primarily provides definitions of words, it may also provide synonyms and antonyms and amplifying examples of use. The texts of both the definitions and the examples include words that, while not synonyms, frequently co-occur with the word being defined. A thesaurus usually provides lists of words that are related to the entry word and the nature of the relationship, but no definition of meaning. The nature of the relationship may vary, although synonyms and antonyms are usually included.

A thesaurus for a controlled language will have a specified set of relationships. The online version of the *ERIC Thesaurus of Descriptors* was illustrated in Fig. 7.3. Database-specific thesauri generally use the following relationships in an entry to describe the *entry term*:

BT for *broader term*, one whose meaning *contains* that of the entry term

NT for *narrower term*, one *contained in* the meaning of the entry term

RT for *related term*, but where the relationship is not exactly defined (Usually it identifies conditional synonyms, i.e., terms that may be synonyms, depending on context.)

UF for *used for*, which does identify a synonym *not used* or *no longer used* in the controlled language (A controlled language does not (normally) have exact synonyms.)

U for *use*, the converse of UF, indicating that the entry term is not now used, but the referred term is to be used instead

Such a thesaurus can be searched with ease, and it is relatively easy to program a computer to augment a query word by copying words related to query words from the thesaurus. For example, if a query calls for descriptors A and B and does not yield as many records as the user expects, one step that might be taken to improve the query is to replace each term with the union of all its broader and narrower terms in the thesaurus. Recall that thesaurus terms are descriptors or subject headings, not words in a natural-language text. The thesaurus relationships may be valid only in a limited context or domain.

Another form of automatic expansion of a query term that has been successful is that of *exploding* a query term that is part of a highly controlled, hierarchical language or set of codes for subject headings. In MEDLINE, the phrase EXPLODE ANALGESICS means to also include in the query all records containing the term ANALGESICS as well as all narrower terms in the thesaurus.

9.5.2 Minithesauri

In some organizations there are complex concepts that are going to be used again and again as part of a search. Terms reflecting the concept of a chemical hazard in a factory safety office are an example. Blair and Maron (1985) studied the use of an IRS in a law firm that maintained the full text of depositions and transcripts of meetings, among other records. These were not indexed in the usual way; great reliance was placed on searching the full text. The lack of indexing often led to an electronic document's not having the words in it that were needed for retrieval. A librarian or professional searcher could have made up a minithesaurus of terms likely to be of importance to lawyers working on a particular case, representing common usage, technical terminology, and slang, and not leaving it to each searcher to think of all the synonyms and variations for each term. In general, the equivalent of query subroutines can be used. These would be portions of queries that define certain difficult concepts likely to be used often by searchers in an organization and that can be included as part of any query. Professional searchers are more likely than are end users to want to and know how to make these up.

Such a word list (the minithesaurus) may be used as a key word selection tool, the opposite of a stop list. Any word in the *select list* may be used as an index term or assigned a high weight for any document in which it occurs. There is, of course, a limit to the extent to which slang or generalizations can be anticipated and assigned a specific meaning.

9.5.3 Word Co-occurrence Statistics

A promising technique is to compute the frequency of co-occurrence of every word in every record of the database with every other word. This procedure does not tell the nature of or meaning of co-occurrence, i.e., whether frequently co-occurring words are synonyms, words that together define a term (as in FREEDOM OF CHOICE) or redundancies in common use (as in CONSENSUS OF OPINION). If SERVICE occurs often (but not always) with FAULT in the context of TENNIS in a sports database, then a search for specific information about a particular player's performance in serving might do well to search for either word, rather than just one of them. Or, co-occurring words could be added to a query to improve outcome.

The strength of association can be weighted, if weights are used, by also measuring the distance apart of the two terms at each instance of co-occurrence. If INDEX and TERM often occur near each other in some document collection, that indicates a far more likely relationship than if they co-occur but not in close proximity.

Clearly, maintaining such a table or matrix of co-occurrences uses a good deal of computer time when adding records to a database, and memory space for storing the matrix. The same kind of table can be used in set analysis, to show co-occurrences only within a set and only on request by the user. This does not bring out words in records not retrieved, but may still suggest words that could be used in a query to improve the retrieval set.

Some measures related to co-occurrence are:

Frequency of occurrence—the number of times a term occurs in a text

Probability of occurrence—the relative frequency or raw frequency divided by total number of terms

Comparative occurrence rate—the ratio of a term's occurrence rate in one document or set of documents to that in another

Word pair co-occurrence rate—the frequency or probability of word A occurring in the same document as word B (or in a specified subset of either)

9.5.4 Stemming and Conflation

Truncation is a useful and economical way to add words to a query that represent only spelling and form variations. Ideally, a searcher might like those variations in which the basic *meaning* is retained, regardless of how much the *form* is changed. As a simple example, HALF, HALVE, HALVED, HALVES, and HALVING all convey a commonality of meaning. Taking only the common stem, HAL, if used with a truncation symbol, would admit too many unrelated words, such as HALBRED, HALCYON, HALE, and HALL. It would have been better to use a combination of roots: HALF OR HALV. *Conflation* is the term meaning to combine different forms into a single form, here probably HALF. Perhaps the ideal solution for this would be to command the IRS to CONFLATE HALF or to be assured it will be done automatically, but not all systems will do this.

Even better would be to have the IRS find the true semantic root of a term and match it against the semantic root of words in the database. While it can be done, the process of computing or determining the semantic root, or stem, of a word, or a standardized form of a word, is not based on any single theory or rule, as shown in Section 4.3.1. It involves applying a series of rules, recording exceptions, and accepting that very few of the rules will never result in an error. Stemming can be applied in several ways. One involves stemming each word on its entry into the database, with both the original form and the stem entered into the inverted file. A second is to store only the stem or conflated term in the inverted file, at a considerable space saving. This method loses the original term, so it is not possible to search for, say, HALVING only. In a third case, stemming could be applied to each query term and then to each word in the inverted index only at the time that file is searched. The first method saves time; the second saves space. The third leaves the inverted file the length it would ordinarily be, but allows the advantages of stemming, at a possibly high execution cost. Yet a fourth approach is to keep the original, for display purposes, as well as the conflated form, for matching.

9.6
Text or Record Association Techniques

Term–association techniques deal with individual words or phrases used in a query, whether of the command-language type or not, and help find other words that might usefully be included in the query. Now we turn our attention to methods of relating one complete text with another, rather than individual words. Command languages tend to use sets of words, perhaps with weights, to represent the records the query was written to find. They ask for retrieval of records that have explicitly stated characteristics. Another form of query presents a natural-language text and asks for retrieval of records whose text resembles the query without an explicit definition of *resemble*. Yet another uses a record that has been retrieved and asks for others that resemble it, again only implicitly defined. All have in common that the IRS is required in some way to measure the extent to which one record is like another.

There are many methods of determining the similarity of one text to another (Losee, 1990), but in text searching they are all based on the number of words co-occurring in the two texts and their respective frequencies of occurrence. If text *a* has 10 words that also occur in text *b* then the number 10, itself, is one measure of the strength of association between them. If, additionally, the frequencies or probabilities of occurrence of the 10 words are similar in value, then the strength of the relationship may be even stronger, that is, if they were both equal and higher than average.

Basically, text or document association measures use word occurrence, not meaning, to measure the strength of association. Of course, the subject matter of a text might be represented as a subject classification code and that, in one sense, conveys meaning. But in the text itself, the occurrence of a word is the basic event being observed, not the conveyance of meaning.

We shall review four methods of determining document-to-document relationships. The first is a group of methods that involve computing a *similarity measure*. They are applied to two records at a time and are based on frequencies of word occurrence. Traditionally, similarity measures are based only upon words in a text, not upon other attributes of the text as its author, subject heading, or cited works which, of course, could well be the basis for similarity in the user's mind.

The second method, called *clustering*, works on a set of records and puts groups of like records together. The third is called *fingerprinting* or *signature analysis* and, like the similarity measure, is a way of comparing a query, or a text in the database, with representations of stored documents on the basis of co-occurrence of sets of words, not discrete, individual words. The fourth is a *discriminant method* in which a relatively small number of terms are found in groups of preclassified texts, and these are used to determine into which group a new text should be classed.

9.6.1 Similarity Measures

In a brief example, we showed that the number of co-occurring words could serve as a measure of similarity between two texts and that percentage of co-occurring words would probably better serve the purpose. More precision can be gained by considering the number in common and the number not in common. There are several ways to measure how similar two texts are. They all make use of the number of terms in common to the two texts and some then go on to also make use of the sizes of the texts and the number of words not in common. Several are presented next and are discussed at greater length in Boyce, Meadow, and Kraft (1994, pp. 86–88), van Rijsbergen (1979, pp. 38–42), and Salton and McGill (1983, pp. 201–204).

1. *Count of terms in common—*

$$\text{DocSim1}(D1, D2) = \sum_{i=1}^{T} (t_{D1j} \cdot t_{D2j}),\qquad (9.5)$$

where t_{Dij} represents the weight of an occurrence of term j in document i, T is the number of terms in a vocabulary, therefore the maximum number of terms in the two documents combined, and summation is over all terms in the two texts. If we are using binary weights, then the t's have the value 1 and the symbol between them is ordinary multiplication. If some other weighting range is used, an operation appropriate to the values must be used. This simple formula is not much used because it does not consider how many terms were involved.

2. *Dice's coefficient*—this measure takes the sizes of the documents into consideration:

$$\text{DocSim2}(D1, D2) = \frac{2 \sum (t_{D1j} \cdot t_{D2j})}{\sum t_{D1j} + \sum t_{D2j}}.\qquad (9.6)$$

Here, we divide the first measure by the mean number of terms in the two sets, $(\sum t_{1j} + \sum t_{2j})/2$. Summation is over the number of terms in a document.

3. *Jaccard's coefficient*—this is similar to Dice's coefficient but divides not by the mean of the two sets, but by the number of terms *not* in common to them:

$$\text{DocSim3}(D1, D2) = \frac{\sum (t_{D1j} \cdot t_{D2j})}{\sum t_{D1j} + \sum t_{D2j} - \sum t_{D1j} \cdot t_{D2j}}.\qquad (9.7)$$

This is the ratio of term co-occurrences to non-co-occurrences.

4. *The cosine coefficient*—this is a frequently used measure. Recalling the vector model of text representation (Section 3.2.5) this computes the cosine of the angle between two vectors. The closer the documents are in the sense of containing a similar set of terms, the larger the cosine (remember that the cosine of an angle of zero degrees is 1 and it then decreases as the angle widens to its maximum):

$$\text{DocSim4}(D1, D2) = \frac{\sum (t_{D1j} \cdot t_{D2j})}{(\sum (t_{D1j}^2 + \sum t_{D2j}^2))^{1/2}}.\qquad (9.8)$$

In practice, the cosine coefficient can be used to compute similarity between a query, treated as a document, and a stored document. Or, as each record is added to a database, its coefficient relative to each other record can be computed and stored, although at high cost. The coefficient could then be used either to find other texts that are similar but did not formally meet some query condition, or to rank the records of a retrieved set by closeness to the query.

Note, in all these measures, that $t_{i,j}$ is 0 if term j is not in document i and, of course, $t_{1,j} \cdot t_{2,j}$ is 0 if term j is absent from either document 1 or 2.

9.6.2 Clustering

Clustering in IR means the grouping together of records that have similar attribute values or word frequency distributions. It is not a method of computing the degree of closeness between two specific records. Once clusters are formed, it would be possible to do a test to see in which cluster a new document would fall, and in that way to find which cluster of records a query best fits. As with the similarity measures, there are many ways to compute cluster membership, but the essence is common to most. It is important to recognize that clustering is used to group records according to their attributes—it does not put them into groups according to any predetermined or *a priori* criteria. Thus, a cluster in this sense is a polythetic set.

Here is one simple method of clustering, reported by Bonner (1964). It involves creating a matrix of attributes of the individual records, then a matrix showing the similarity of records represented in the first matrix. Next, a second similarity matrix is computed, and in this, a number of clusters can be detected. Finally, from the list of candidate clusters, the subset is selected that best fits the needs of the application. We stress that clustering is a *kind of process*, not a specific mathematical technique. There are, again, many different algorithms (Miyamoto, 1990; Salton and McGill, 1983, pp. 137–140) for producing clusters, varying on characteristics of the clusters produced and computational resource requirements.

Bonner proposed a measure of similarity between records using SetSim3, or Jaccard's coefficient (Eq. 9.7)).

The first step in cluster formation is to form an *attribute matrix* showing which terms or attribute values are present for each record. Each term or attribute value is represented by a column and each document, by a row. In any cell, enter a 1 for presence of the value, 0 for its absence. An example for a small number of documents is shown in Fig. 9.3. The first similarity matrix, SM1, is formed by computing the value of SetSim3 for each record pair as shown in

Fig. 9.4. As an example, record 1 has attributes 1 and 4, and record 2 has 1, 2, and 4, giving two in common. The SetSim3 value for records 1 and 2 is then $2/(2 + 3 - 2)$ or $2/3$.

We now compute SM2 simply by converting to 0 all values in SM1 that are below some threshold, and those above 0 to 1. The threshold used in this example is 0.45. In practice, this must be determined experimentally, by trying various values to see which produces the best results. SM2, using a threshold of 0.45 is shown in Fig. 9.5.

Now, a candidate cluster consists of all records on any row for which there is a 1 in any column. The possible clusters for SM2 are listed in Table 9.4, each set of record numbers being in numeric order.

From this list select the final clusters by applying the following rules, in order:

1. Eliminate any duplicate clusters. (Cluster 5 duplicates 1; 6 duplicates 3. The list now contains 1, 2, 3, 4, 7, 8.)
2. Eliminate any clusters wholly containing any remaining clusters. (Cluster 2 contains 1. This leaves 1, 3, 4, 7, 8.)
3. Eliminate any remaining clusters all of whose members are individually contained in some other cluster. (Cluster 4's records are all in clusters 7 and 8. On the other hand, clusters 7 and 8 have all their records in 1 and 4. Eliminating 7 and 8 reduces the overlap among clusters more than does eliminating cluster 4.)

Record No.	Attribute Value No.					
	1	2	3	4	5	6
1	1	0	0	1	0	0
2	1	1	0	1	0	0
3	0	0	1	1	1	1
4	0	1	1	0	0	1
5	1	0	0	1	1	0
6	0	0	1	0	1	0
7	0	1	0	1	0	1
8	1	1	1	0	0	0

Figure 9.3
An attribute matrix for use in clustering: the first step is to form an attribute matrix showing, for each record, which terms or values are present. Each term or attribute value is represented by a column and each document, by a row. In any cell, enter a 1 for presence of the value, 0 for absence.

Record	Record No.							
No.	1	2	3	4	5	6	7	8
1	1	$2/3$	$1/5$	0	$2/3$	0	$1/4$	$1/4$
2		1	$1/6$	$1/5$	$2/4$	0	$2/4$	$2/4$
3			1	$2/5$	$2/5$	$2/4$	$2/5$	$1/6$
4				1	0	$1/4$	$2/4$	$2/4$
5					1	$1/4$	$1/6$	$1/5$
6						1	0	$1/4$
7							1	$1/5$
8								1

Figure 9.4

First similarity matrix: the matrix SM1 is formed by computing the value of SetSim3 for each record pair. The similarity of any record with itself is always 1. Records 1 and 2 have two attribute values in common, but 2 has one that is not in record 1, hence SetSim3 = 2/3.

This leaves us with clusters 1, 3, and 4 containing records 1, 2, 5; 3, 6; and 4, 7, 8. Conveniently, all members are in only one cluster, and all records are in a cluster. It will not always work out so conveniently. A threshold value of 0.6 would have yielded only candidate clusters 1, 2, 5 and 1, 2. The first would have been eliminated by rule 2. On the other hand, a much larger number of attributes would make the process less sensitive to the threshold value. The presumption is that the records within each cluster formed this way are closely related to each other.

Record	Record No.							
No.	1	2	3	4	5	6	7	8
1	1	1	0	0	1	0	0	0
2	1	1	0	0	1	0	1	1
3	0	0	1	0	0	1	0	0
4	0	0	0	1	0	0	1	1
5	1	1	0	0	1	0	0	0
6	0	0	1	0	0	1	0	0
7	0	1	0	1	0	0	1	0
8	0	1	0	1	0	0	1	0

Figure 9.5

Second similarity matrix: elements of this matrix, SM2, show a 1 if the corresponding value in SM1 was at or above the threshold value of 0.45. In practice, the threshold must be determined experimentally, by trying various values to see which produces the best results.

Table 9.4
Initial Clusters Formed by Bonner's Method[a]

Cluster based on record no.	Records contained
1	1, 2, 5
2	1, 2, 5, 7, 8
3	3, 6
4	4, 7, 8
5	1, 2, 5
6	3, 6
7	2, 4, 7
8	2, 4, 8

[a]This is the first set of clusters formed. Note that number 2 contains numbers 1 and 5, which are identical. Also, numbers 3 and 6 are identical. All members of clusters 7 and 8 contained in 1 or 4.

A variant of clustering permits starting with an initial set of records, computing the cluster matrices and then, as new records are added, their relationships to the existing clusters are computed on arrival. This would reduce the computational load over recomputing all the matrices each time. However, after a sufficient number of new records, the clusters originally formed might no longer best represent the grouping of the now enlarged file.

Clustering offers a way to classify documents according to their actual content and to the actual distribution of contents, rather than according to a predetermined classification scheme. If a query matches one particular cluster well, then all records in that cluster could be retrieved. This might yield better results than would manually classifying the query and then retrieving those records that had been manually classified into the same category. This is because human classification is actually a fuzzy operation—documents are in classes with certain probabilities and from certain points of view. But if a query matches a cluster based on actual word occurrences, we are sure that it is reasonably close to the word occurrence patterns of all of the records. This does not, however, mean that this form of clustering should completely replace traditional classification systems. The latter are fairly well known (or are they?), fairly well documented, and represent a means of communication between people about documents. Automatically generated clusters may be different in each library or collection, will have no familiar names or connotations, and may not serve well for communication between people. Human classification also permits classification according to meaning or implication, even if the "right" specific words have not been used.

9.6.3 Signature Matching

A basic dilemma of IR is that a complete text can be lengthy, and if every word in it is stored in an index, a great deal of memory and search time are required. If *every word* is not in the index, then there must be a possibly expensive selection process, called indexing, which runs the risk of omitting important terms and including unimportant ones. Reducing the document to a few attributes and index terms is far more economical initially, but may simply fail to meet the objectives of the IRS. One compromise is a family of methods that vastly simplify the manner of representing words in the index which, in its traditional form, can be several times larger than the original text.

Instead of storing the complete word in an index, first convert it to a number. This is done by a process equivalent to hashing (Section 6.4.5). Then, rather than storing the record number or address, store only a 0 or 1 in a *bit map*, which must have one bit for each word-equivalent that might be stored; hence, it would have one bit for each unique hashed outcome. This bit map becomes the *signature* of the document, a symbol or attribute characteristic of the individual record. If there were only, say, 1000 possible words then the signature would be 1000 bits long and represents every word type of the text. This is illustrated in part *a* of Fig. 9.6, with a map of 100 bits. Clearly, the technique is limited if the vocabulary is large and the map small. As with hashing, more than one word could be encoded with the same value. For natural language we could have maps of tens of thousands of bits—not too conservative of space. Remember that news or journal articles, patents, and the like make use of many proper names, abbreviations, product names, numerals, etc., so that their number of different symbols may be much greater than a typical vocabulary.

A variation is to use a binary hashed value to represent each word, then to OR these values together, as illustrated in part *b* of Fig. 9.6, from which it can be seen that the coding method must not produce too many 1's in a code, as we have done in the figure. This method produces a very compact document representation, but with the drawback that representations are not unique. Similar records will have similar representations, but non-similar documents may also result in the same representations. The signature method is very fast but has other drawbacks, which we shall shortly consider (Faloutsos and Christodoulakis, 1984). Note that frequency of occurrence is not represented. Spelling variations may be handled by use of a stemmer or dictionary.

If each word is converted by hashing into a number, just as a record key was in Chapter 6, we have the same need to define precise parameters for hashing and to deal with collisions. In using hashing as a file-organization technique, a chain of pointers was set up from one synonym or colliding record to another. In a document signature application, this is not done. We simply

Document text: THE QUICK BROWN FOX.

a. Convert each word to a number, by assigning a value letter corresponding to its position in the alphabet (T=20, H=11, E=5) Hence THE = 36, QUICK = 61, BROWN = 72, and FOX=45. A bit map of 100 elements can then be as follows (spaces are for legibility only):

```
      1          2          3          4          5
1234567890 1234567890 12344567890 1234567890 1234567890
0000000000 0000000000 00000000000 0000010000 0000100000


      6          7          8          9         10
1234567890 1234567890 12344567890 1234567890 1234567890
0000000000 1000000000 01000000000 0000000000 0000000000
```

b. Convert each word number to binary, whereupon THE=36_{10} = 0100100_2. The complete document becomes:

```
          0100100        (THE)
          0111101        (QUICK)
          1001000        (BROWN)
          0101101        (FOX)
```

Form the signature by ORing each column separately, *i.e.* if a 1 appears anywhere in the column the resultant value is 1, otherwise 0. The outcome is
          1111101

Figure 9.6
Signature map: two methods of compiling signatures of a text. The first (a) assigns one bit for each word present, using a numeric value of each letter to represent the word. This produces a very sparse map. The second (b) starts the same way, but combines all the word maps into a single map which is economical of storage but may lose to much information.

accept that more than one word could have produced the same coded value. Here, of course, the fingerprint is the transformed version of the text, making the analogy to human fingerprints something less than precise. It is actually closer in concept to the set of minutiae extracted from a fingerprint. However, the likelihood of exact duplication of the entire bit map is low, and that is probably what leads to adoption of this usage.

The strength of the signature method is that the bit map, whichever method is used to produce it, is compact. The document's map can be compared with the query's map, and the extent of the similarity quickly determined. The weakness is that what is being compared is a set of surrogates for the original words, and we do not know for sure that the words used in the query were the same words that produced the matching codes in the document. The more words in the query, the lower the probability of false drops due to encoding. The encoding process can vary, producing more or fewer possible word-representation numbers. That is one way to control the formation of signatures. The matching of two signatures produces a single number, the count of codes in common. The threshold to determine what constitutes a match can be varied. As an alternative, the count can be used to rank the documents according to apparent closeness to the query, thus forming a fuzzy set of matched records.

Regardless of application or precise method of use, the signature-matching method produces a number of false drops. Any retrieval method can retrieve a record that has the requested attributes but is not really on the subject the user wanted. Here, both the requested attributes and the stored attributes have been encoded nonuniquely so that a match may be made between dissimilar term surrogates. Financially, the method makes sense, because it can be fast and inexpensive. Behaviorally, it is labor intensive because it requires training or assistance to inure users to false drops and teach them how to respond. This may explain the lack of commercial acceptance of the technique. While it has not been used in commercial public-access retrieval systems, it has been proposed for use in office automation systems for filing and retrieving office documents. These pose the same problem of storage and retrieval as do any other text documents.

False drops could be reduced by a two-pass system in which records selected by signature matching are then subjected to another match process based upon the actual words of the query. The computer time required for this should not be excessive unless the average size of sets selected by the first process is very large.

9.6.4 Discriminant Methods

The basic concept is to choose a limited set of words on which to base the decision of what other documents or clusters a given document best matches. The concept was first used with text in conjunction with authorship studies (Mosteller and Wallace, 1963), in particular one study involving a set of essays, the *Federalist Papers*, debating the adoption of the Constitution of the United States in the late 18th century. Some of the essays were signed and some published anonymously. Word frequency studies were used to determine who wrote the unsigned papers. The first step was to find a set of *discriminator words*, those used with a markedly different frequency in documents by different authors in documents of known authorship. Again, there was little point in considering words that tend to occur uniformly across all documents. Since the subject matter was generally the same, subject words were not necessarily the best discriminator words. Many of those that were good discriminators were

Doc. 1	Doc. 2	Doc. 3	Doc. 4	Doc. 5
term	term	term	term	term
term	**term**	**term**	**term**	**term**
term	term	term	term	term
term	**term**	**term**	**term**	term
term	**term**	**term**		**term**
term		term		term

Figure 9.7
Finding discriminating words: words of near-uniform frequency across a collection of documents deemed to be on the same subject can play a discriminating role in classifying new documents. Different words would play this role at different levels or branches of a hierarchy.

non-subject-bearing words, such as *while* and *whilst*. The semantic difference between these two is essentially nil; their use is largely a matter of personal style.

The method was used by J. H. Williams (1963), to perform subject classification of documents. The first step is to manually classify a body of texts, organizing them into classes according to subject matter as determined by the human classifier. Then, for each term occurring in any of the initially formed classes, compute a *discriminant coefficient*, D_i:

$$D_j = \frac{(p_{cj} - \bar{p}_{cj})^2}{p_{cj}}, \qquad (9.9)$$

where p_{cj} is the probability of occurrence of word j in class c, $\bar{p}_{cj}$ is the mean probability of term j across all classes, $c = 1, \ldots, n$, and and n is the number of classes.

This measure has a high value for words that occur with probability much different from the mean. The "common" words should have fairly uniform probabilities across classes, fall close to the overall mean, and consequently have low values of D_j. Compare the inverse document frequency concept in Eq. (9.2). An example of its use is shown in Fig. 9.7. Here, we show schematically a set of documents that are assumed to have been manually classified. Across this set some words (indicated by bold face) would have fairly uniformly high frequency. These would serve as the discriminators.

Select the set of terms with the highest values of D_j. The number to be selected would have to be empirically determined. Williams used as few as four terms per class. Since the high-value terms are selected, common words would drop out in this step. Then compare the probability of occurrence of discriminator words, in a new text to be classified, with the discriminator words and probabilities for each class. The class that comes closest receives the text, which could be measured by computing the sums of the deviations of document p's from the class p's or the sums of squares of the deviations.

To group into subclasses, repeat the process within the class selected in the first iteration. That is, the discriminator words for each subclass within a class will be different at each hierarchical level. When used for subject classification, the discriminator words for any subclass, at any level, together with the words for superior classes, should have semantic significance to a human reader. This changing of discrimnator words at different levels might be used to make automatic abstracts that are more tailored to individual reader interests, if each potential reader could identify the node in the hierarchy of interest.

9.7

Other Processes with Words of a Text

In this final section we discuss some processes that could be used in combination with any of the methods of Section 9.5 or 9.6. They are (1) use a dictionary to omit *stop words*, (2) replace words with their roots or with related words, or (3) vary the weight or significance of co-occurring words as a function of their frequency of occurrence.

9.7.1 Stop Words

Since words like *the*, *of*, and *an* are so common in English, it cannot be considered significant that they occur in any text of more than a few sentences. These words are frequently consciously omitted from newspaper headlines, but lengthy texts without them might be ambiguous and difficult to read. Dropping common words before computing record association measures would reduce the cost of almost any of the processes. But what *are* common words? How is a list of them compiled?

One answer is that common words are those without inherent meaning or news value, or without an indication of subject content. The words *the*, *of*, *an*, taken out of context, tell nothing whatever about the subject of the text in which they occurred. Words such as *whereas* and *thereunto* also carry no subject information, but they are more likely to occur in the context of a formal legal document, contract, proclamation, or statute than in a news article or scientific research report; hence, they may carry *some* useful information. The word A, without meaning in general, can be the name of a vitamin. In the health sciences, eliminating A could mean loss of an important word. Dialog, attempting uniformity across its many and diverse databases, uses only nine stop words (Section 9.5), and these are the same for all its text databases. Fox (1990), by contrast, compiled a list of the most frequently occurring English words, added others, and came up with a list of 278 words.

Another view of what a common word is is that it is one that occurs often or, more precisely, occurs frequently in all or nearly all documents at any given level of hierarchy. This is the definition that fits the discriminant method. It inverts the definition of common as non-information-bearing. Conventionally, a word is not common because it carries no information; now, it carries no information because it is common. This is in keeping with Shannon and Weaver (1959). Common words have a probability nearly 1 of occurring in a document and a very high probability that they will occur with a fairly uniform high frequency. Therefore, their occurrence at all, or at approximately the expected frequency, conveys little or no information. On the other hand, the words we would use to indicate subject content *have* to vary from document to document, or else all subjects would use the same words.

9.7.2 Replacement of Words with Roots or Associated Words

Instead of using the set of words that actually occur in the documents, it would be possible to precede the similarity or matching computation with one or more conflation transformations of the vocabulary, such as the stemming techniques of Chapter 4. One possibility is to replace words with their stems, so as to reduce the number of different words and raise the number of frequently occurring concepts or, in a sense, raise the signal-to-noise ratio. A second possibility, which can be used instead of the first or in addition to it, is to add to the list of words in any document other words that word-association methods find to be highly associated. Adding additional terms related to term *t* of document *d* would increase the probability of matching *d* with another document that contained words related to *t*, but did not contain *t* itself, or contained it only with a low frequency. These word-replacement techniques are not commonly used with commercial database systems but are beginning to gain favor.

9.7.3 Varying Significance as a Function of Frequency

We have actually described several variations of this concept, from Luhn's use of a dictionary at one end and a low-frequency cutoff at the other, to Williams' different evaluation of word significance at different hierarchic levels. Probably most word- or record-association techniques that use frequency or probability could use significance instead. What the methods of Williams,

Mosteller and Wallace, and Salton suggest is that word significance, in the statistical sense, is unexpected high frequency. *Predictable* high frequency is not significant. Discriminator words are those with highest frequency *after* words with uniform or predictably higher frequency in a domain have been eliminated. This is consistent with all information theoretic principles.

9.7.4 Comments on the Computation of the Strength of Document Association

The methods of Section 9.6, in one way or another, compute a measure of association between a query and a text or between two texts, based entirely on the set of words in each. If the cosine coefficient, for example, represents the "true" strength of the association at the time a query is presented to the IRS, is the strength of association the same on the next day? A year later? The answer, in terms of a computational technique, would have to be *yes*. If two persons, with similar but not identical information needs, were to formulate queries with the same terms represented, would a given document bear the same relationship to both queries? Would it be equally useful to both persons? Would one person value a set of records the same today as a year later? The answers, now, seem intuitively to be *no*.

There are no formal, proven answers to these questions, but when we consider the human user and his or her information need, the answer seems to be that all formal measures of association are only approximations, albeit some may be good ones. They should not be mistakenly taken to *be* the relationship approximated. These measures are based on the occurrence of words as tokens, not on their meaning, intent, truth, or value. Their value lies in enabling an IRS to bring before a user a likely set of records from which to select those that answer the need or from which the user can determine how to modify a query to better answer the need.

We shall reintroduce this matter in Chapter 16, when we discuss measurement and evaluation of information retrieval in a larger context.

1. In brief, **IR** involves finding some desired **information** in a *store* of **information** or a **database**.

2. Implicit in this view is the concept of *selectivity*; to exercise selectivity usually requires that a price be paid in effort, time, money, or all three.

3. **Information** recovery is not the same as **IR** unless there has been a search and selection process.

4. Copying a complete disk file is not **retrieval** in our sense.

5. Watching an entire news program on television, during which the viewer exercises no control over what is being shown, is not **retrieval**, either.

6. A library is the best example of an institution devoted to selective **retrieval**.

7. One does not go there to read the entire collection.

8. One goes to look for something selectively, often something that will satisfy a set of highly individualized **information** needs.

9. **IR** is a communication process.

10. In one sense it is a means by which authors or creators of **records** communicate with readers, but indirectly and with a possibly long time lag between creation of a message or **text** and its delivery to the **IR** system user.

11. The records of a database are created and assembled without knowledge of exactly who will read them, or under what circumstances.

12. The languages and channels of such a communication **system** are quite different from other well-known models, such as broadcasting or point-to-point communication.

13. Is **information retrieval** a computer activity?

14. It is not strictly necessary that it be, but as a practical matter, that is what we usually imply by the term, and that is what this book is primarily about.

15. The computer **system**, consisting of both hardware and software, is what we call the **information retrieval system** (IRS).

16. The term IRS may include the **database**, but whether or not it does may depend on the context in which the expression is used.

17. However, all the important principles of **information retrieval** apply to purely nonmechanical **IR** as well.

18. For example, a nonmechanized library functions as a **retrieval system**, in this case the staff or patrons being the instruments of search, decision-making, and **retrieval**.

19. King Henry II of England, in 1160, rode with is entourage from palace to palace, permanently on tour.

20. Written **records** had to be carried along.

21. **Records**, such as memos or letters, were stitched one to the previous one, creating an ever-growing scroll carried on the backs of mules.

22. It grew so large it was called the Great Roll of the Pipe.

23. A new one was started on the first day of each year.

Figure 9.2

Ranked sentences from text: here are the 46 sentences of the text, in order of occurrence. Numeric measures of these sentences are found in Table 9.3.

24. We will primarily be discussing *interactive* **IR**.

25. Today, this is found in three primary modes: (1) a central service, consisting of a number of **databases** with usually a single **system** for searching them, operated remotely from most users and requiring a telecommunications network for access, (2) a browsing service on the World Wide Web (WWW), which does not have its own **databases** but finds and searches "sites" owned by others, and (3) a local **system** operating in a single computer, in which are stored both **retrieval** software and a **database**, often on CD-ROMs.

26. A remote **retrieval** service is operated through the medium of a computer in which the data are stored in files or **databases** and in which software -interprets users' requests for **information**, finds it, and controls its transmission it to the requester.

27. There is relatively little difference between local and remote **systems** in terms of operation from the user's point of view.

28. Both are interactive in that there is almost continuous conversation between the user and the **database** computer.

29. There is considerable difference in the cost.

30. There tends to be a big difference between WWW browsers and other **retrieval systems** in terms of how deeply **records** are indexed and how specific searches may be.

31. Any of them is a long way from King Henry's pipe.

32. Yet another view of the question of the mechanical nature of **information retrieval** is that we do not usually think of library catalogs, printed indexes, or encyclopedias as mechanical aids, but they are, even if they are older technologies.

33. When first created, they may have seemed as strangely mechanical as today's computers do to some present-day **information** users.

34. An encyclopedia is a collection of relatively small works bundled together with extensive indexes, citations, and cross references.

35. It is not designed to be read from beginning to end, but to be used as a mechanism for finding articles of interest, often only after much searching.

36. While the selection of a **record** from an inventory file or a file of bank depositor accounts can be considered **IR**, the term is more commonly applied to the searching of files of **text records** or **records** descriptive of **text** or graphics.

37. The uncertainty about how the content should be queried underlies much of the activity of **IR**.

38. When **querying** is restricted to use of a single key, such as a part or account number, there is not much challenge.

39. Blair has stated that the "central problem of **Information Retrieval** is how to represent documents for **retrieval**."

40. We are inclined to think that this is becoming less true as more and more **databases** consist of the complete **text** of documents, while previously they consisted of index or classification terms that represented the document's content.

41. Not only is the original, natural language of the **text** being used in the **databases**, but natural language is being used, increasingly, as the means of a user's telling the **retrieval system** what is wanted.

42. This is called the *query*; whether it is written in natural language or any of the many artificial languages developed for the purpose, the trend is certainly toward more complex and expressive statements.

43. The central problem is becoming how to match, compare, or relate the user's request for

Figure 9.2   (*Continued*)

information with the **texts** stored in the database.

44. As Liddy *et al.* put it, "[A] successful **retrieval system** must **retrieve** on the basis of what people mean in their **query**, not just what they say."

45. On the other hand, the **query** might be considered a form of document representation, in that it represents characteristics of documents to be **retrieved**.

46. If so, we can agree with Blair that it is a question of major importance how best to phrase this **query**, *i.e.*, how to represent what we want to find in documents.

Figure 9.2 (*Continued*)

10

System-Computed Relevance and Ranking

10.1

The Retrieval Status Value (rsv)

An information retrieval system needs a mechanism for calculating the closeness of a match between a user query and a document. The result of this calculation can then be used to determine whether or not the system should retrieve the document, and perhaps how to rank it among all others that are retrieved. That is to say, this calculation provides the *system's estimate* of the relevance of the document, and the goal is that this estimate should be strongly correlated to the *user's judgment* of the relevance of the document. The result of this calculation, the value given to the closeness of the match between the query and the document, has been called the *retrieval status value* (rsv). We use this term for all its many applications, but it is not universally used in publications. The system's estimate of relevance, or rsv, can be used to decide which retrieved records to present to a user as representing likely documents of value. It can also be used to rank all retrieved records in descending order of probable relevance from the system's point of view. Ranking, relatively new in applied systems, has been under consideration for some time (W. S. Cooper, 1970; Robertson, 1977).

In a strict Boolean query system, one that specifies attribute values that must be present if a record is to be selected, each term present in the query or document could only have a weight of 0 or 1 and the resulting rsv of a document could only have a value of 1 (accept) or 0 (reject). If weighted Boolean or natural language queries are used, the rsv can range anywhere from 0 to 1 and is therefore potentially much more useful.

238

10.2

Ranking

Since the purpose of the rsv is to provide a mechanism for evaluating the match between a document and a query, it allows the system to rank documents in descending order on the basis of their rsv. This means that the system can go down the ranked list and present the user with a complete, ordered list of all documents that have a positive value of rsv or the top-ranking *l* documents of the list, where *l* is set by the user. These would be those the system judges most likely to be deemed relevant by the user. Of course, this is what is called mathematically a weak ordering, meaning that ties are allowed. If the rsv is binary there is no choice but to present all documents that meet the formal requirements of the query, an option often frustrating to users. Increasingly, IR systems are ranking output, especially on the World Wide Web where precise queries may not be possible and document attributes not explicit.

A difficulty with ranking is that users are not usually told what the system's basis for ranking is. Where users have been polled for their reactions, they seem to like it. Would it make any significant difference if they were told the basis or given an opportunity to make a contribution to the method, perhaps to emphasize words occurring in the text, name of the author, or source? There is no research on this question to date. Asking users to make such choices calls for more involvement on their part, necessitating more knowledge of the system, something not all users want to invest in. But, it could lead to better retrieval outcomes.

10.3

Methods of Evaluating the rsv

The specific method of evaluating the rsv depends on the document representation model being used. We focus on a few of the common, proven ones. For many years only binary-valued relevance measures were used in information retrieval, apparently because they are simpler to deal with mathematically. The case simply cannot be made that they are representative of the way people perceive relevance. We show both binary- and multiple-valued evaluation forms.

10.3.1 The Vector Space Model

The vector space model, recall, deals with the positive quadrant of a Cartesian coordinate system as a space. (See Section 3.2.5.) The axes represent the terms of the indexing vocabulary. Each text is represented as a vector of MD_i terms (where MD_i is the cardinality of, or the number of terms used in, the document. The number of terms in the entire database vocabulary is MT. Each element of the vector representing a text is a numerical weight in the interval $[0, 1]$ or, if only binary weights are used, 0 or 1.

A query can also be represented as a vector in that hypercube. The rsv for a document is calculated as the similarity of the query and document, that is to say, as the closeness of the query and the document vectors. This is calculated as the inverse, in a sense, of the distance between the document and the query in this space. There are several related means of calculating the inverse of this distance. The first, the vector product, is a generalization of the count of the terms in common calculated as we did in Eq. (9.5), Section 9.6.1. It gives the rsv for document i relative to query k as

$$\text{rsv}_{i,k} = \frac{\sum_{j=1}^{MT} dtw_{i,j} \cdot qtw_{j,k}}{NF}, \tag{10.1}$$

where $dtw_{i,j}$ is the weight of the term j in document i, $qtw_{j,k}$ is the weight of term j in query k, MT is the magnitude of the set of terms, T_j, and NF is a normalization factor to locate the rsv in the interval $[0, 1]$. If all values are either zero or one, this is a count of the number of terms that are in both the query and the document in question. Of course, this is problematic in that we must normalize this expression to take into account the lengths of the document and the query. This leads directly to the several other possible similarity measures, some of which we discussed in Section 9.6.1. Any of these—Dice, Jaccard, or cosine, or possibly some other formulation—might be used to normalize for document and query length. All will yield a useable rsv for the vector-space model. However, retrieval experiments have led to quite general use of the cosine version of the rsv.

Some researchers have questioned the desirability of treating the query in the space of documents (Bollmann-Sdora and Raghavan, 1993). Other researchers have fretted over the idea of treating the terms as orthogonal, i.e., independent of each other (Salton and McGill, 1983, p. 423). Still others have been concerned, in this model, with the lack of a means of taking into account the Boolean operators used in a query (Salton, 1989, pp. 353–361). For example, if a document contains terms A and B, should there be a measurable difference in the similarity of that document to queries calling for A OR B, A AND B, or A NOT B?

10.3.2 The Probabilistic Model

The probabilistic model is based on a different treatment of term weights (Bookstein, 1983). This model views weights as probability statements, enabling us to rank documents in descending order of the likelihood of relevance, the *probability ranking principle* (Robertson, 1977; van Rijsbergen, 1979, p. 113).

The main thrust is to consider a weight, i.e., a value for each term in the query, based on the likelihood of the document being relevant given that the term is present in the document. This is denoted as $qtw_{j,k}$. These weights are then aggregated, usually by adding them together for all query terms found in a given document. The documents with the highest aggregated weights are then presented in descending order until some threshold is reached. We thus need to collect all documents which contain any of the query terms (in effect, an OR search), then assign each a weight which becomes the initial rsv, sort on this value, and present the list.

Based on statistical decision theory, the following probability statement has been found to be useful as a probability weight, or term weight, for term j in query k:

$$qtw_{j,k} = \frac{r_j \cdot (MD - n_j - R_k + r_j)}{(n_j - r_j) \cdot (R_k - r_j)}, \qquad (10.2)$$

where r_j is the number of relevant documents in which the term in question occurs, n_j is the total number of documents in which the term occurs, R_k is the total number of relevant documents for query k, and MD is the total number of documents in, or magnitude of, the database. This is a generalization of Eq. (9.3). Note that this computation requires that we know the number of documents relevant to a given query, not readily available information. The rsv for document i relative to query k is then the sum of these weights, $qtw_{i,k}$ for terms in document i, or

$$rsv_{i,k} = \sum_{Q_k \cap D_i} qtw_{j,k}, \qquad (10.3)$$

where summation is over all terms contained in both document i and query j. As should be obvious, this is a feedback model. R and r will be known only after an initial set of documents has been evaluated for relevance by the user. We can assume all terms have equal probability of relevance on the initial pass, which means the disjunction of the query terms.

There are variants of this formula found in the literature. That it assumes statistical independence for the terms remains a major concern. As a practical matter, the appearance of one term *is* likely to affect the probability of appearance of others. This assumption can be avoided, but at the cost of assuming a given form for the term relationships with regard to the joint probabilities, which is usually quite complicated mathematically. Another concern is again the lack of any consideration of the effect of Boolean operators for the query.

10.3.3 The Extended Boolean Model

The extension of the previous models to incorporate Boolean operators has added value to those models. The use of fuzzy sets, where a membership function determines for each document D_i of the file D the strength of its association with a given subset of that file, can illustrate how this can be done. Such sets are termed fuzzy since all documents with a positive weight are in the retrieved set for each term, but to differing degrees, depending upon the assigned weight.

Fuzzy Sets

The first goal is to establish an rsv for each document relative to one term in the query. In a simple case, if we stipulate that document D_i is related to the concept represented by term A at some level between 0 and 1, say 0.4, which we will call the document weight for that term, and query Q_1 requires the concept represented by term A to be present at some level between 0 and 1, say 0.3, we would then consider that document D_i was a member of an answer set QR_1 for query Q_1, since its rsv for the single term search was 0.4, which is greater than the required 0.3.

We might define the relationship between the query term threshold and the document term weight in many ways. We might (1) assign the document term weight as the rsv (as in the example in the previous paragraph), (2) assign the query term weight as the rsv, (3) assign their mean or product as the rsv, or (4) devise a scheme where a new value was generated based upon the amount by which the document term weight exceeded the query threshold for that term, and (5) we might also give a "partial credit" for document term weights below the threshold based upon the difference between the two values. Whatever the scheme, the result of this operation will be a set of documents for each term in the query, where the documents in the set will be ranked by an rsv based on some operation on the query and document weights for that term. Since all documents in D will be in each set QR_k at some level, these sets collectively could be viewed as a document–term matrix for the query, incorporating all documents in the file and all terms in the query. To aggregate the multiple query terms we would need to take into consideration the Boolean operations in the query. We could simply perform normal Boolean operations on the sets formed by the previous process, but this would lose the rankings available in the sets.

Suppose we have the situation illustrated in Table 10.1 which shows two queries, each calling for a single term, A in Q_1 and B in Q_2. The weights assigned to these terms in the queries are 0.3 and 0.2, respectively. The retrieval set for each query consists of a single document. In one, QR_1, A occurs with weight 0.4 and in QR_2 term B occurs with weight 0.5. Then the result of

Table 10.1
Parameters of Queries[a]

Query	Set	Term	Query weight	Document weight
Q_1	QR_1	A	0.3	0.4
Q_2	QR_2	B	0.2	0.5

[a]Queries Q_1 and Q_2 result in retrieval sets QR_1 and QR_2. Each query designates only one term, A or B, and the weights assigned in the query are 0.3 and 0.2, respectively. The weights assigned to these terms as they appear in documents are 0.4 and 0.5.

forming the intersection of the two sets is

$$QR_3 = QR_1 \text{ AND } R_2,$$
$$\text{rsv}_{i,3} = \min(\text{rsv}_{i,1}, \text{rsv}_{i,2}).$$
(10.4)

Equation (10.4) holds for each D_i. In the illustrated case, $\min(\text{rsv}_{i,1}, \text{rsv}_{i,2} = \min(0.4, 0.5) = 0.4$. If we were to form the union of the two retrieval sets we would have

$$QR_3 = QR_1 \text{ OR } QR_2,$$
$$\text{rsv}_{i,3} = \max(\text{rsv}_{i,1}, \text{rsv}_{i,2}),$$
(10.5)

and $\text{rsv}_{i,3} = \max(0.4, 0.5) = 0.5$. All documents in the set D_i would be rated in a similar fashion. For the complement, QR_3 of QR_1, $1\text{-rsv}_{i,1}$ would be utilized, so that for

$$QR_3 = \text{NOT } QR_1,$$
$$\text{rsv}_{i,3} = 1 - \text{rsv}_{i,1},$$
(10.6)

for each D_i in QR_1, where $\text{rsv}_{i,1}$ is the rsv of document D_i in QR_1. Since the rsv of D_i in our example was 0.4, $1 - 0.4 = 0.6$ constitutes a ranking value for document D_i for QR_3, the complement of QR_1.

Using these definitions we can create a ranked set of documents for any Boolean query (Buell, 1985; Bookstein, 1985; Buell, 1983; Kraft and Buell, 1992).

P-Norm

In the vector-space model we can simulate Boolean operations by the use of a similarity measure between a document and query that incorporates a parameter P which is used as an exponent on each document's weight for a term and the query's weight for the same term. For an OR operation, the product of these weights is then added to a similar formulation for another document term weight–query term weight pair, this sum divided by the sum of the query term weights each to the power P, and the whole value taken to the power $1/P$. For an AND operation one minus the document term weight is used. The term and document weights of single-term queries whose products would provide their individual rsv, are thus combined to produce a single similarity measure, used as an rsv for the resulting set (a reminder—the assumption here is that the queries each consist of a single term):

$$QR_3 = QR_1 \text{ OR } QR_2,$$

$$rsv_{i,3} = \frac{(dtw_{i,1}^P \cdot qtw_{1,1}^P + dtw_{i,2}^P \cdot qtw_{1,2}^P)^{1/P}}{(qtw_{1,1}^P + qtw_{2,2}^P)^{1/P}}; \qquad (10.7)$$

$$QR_3 = QR_1 \text{ AND } QR_2,$$

$$rsv_{i,3} = \frac{((1 - dtw_{i,1}^P \cdot qtw_{1,1}^P) + (1 - dtw_{i,2}^P \cdot qtw_{2,2}^P))^{1/P}}{(qtw_{1,1}^P + qtw_{2,2}^P)^{1/P}}, \qquad (10.8)$$

where $dtw_{i,j}$ is the weight of term j in document i, and $qtw_{j,k}$ is the weight of term j in query k. When the parameter $P = 1$ the rsv's are identical whatever the Boolean operator may be. This is analogous to the cosine measure. When P approaches infinity the query is not weighted and we get the max and min definitions of the Boolean AND and OR (Salton, 1989, pp. 353–361). The P-norm thus controls by parameter the strictness of each AND or OR operator, and provides a general model that has as special cases the standard Boolean model with a fuzzy set interpretation when p is infinity and the vector-space model with inner-product similarity when P is one.

Inference Networks

In the probabilistic model we aggregated the document term weights by summing them in formula (10.3) to produce an rsv for a document. If we wish to use Boolean operations to combine individual term searches rather than aggregation by summation, we may generate values for terms using Eq. (10.2) as before. Then the document term weight $dtw_{1,1}$ for QR_1 (which is also the rsv because this is a single-term search) could be combined with the document term weight $dtw_{1,2}$ for QR_2 to aggregate the sets by using the product of the weights for an AND operation and one minus the product of the reciprocals of the weights for an OR operation (Turtle and Croft, 1990):

$$QR_3 = QR_1 \text{ AND } QR_2,$$

$$rsv_{i,3} = dtw_{i,1} \cdot dtw_{i,2}; \qquad (10.9)$$

$$QR_3 = QR_1 \text{ OR } QR_2,$$

$$\text{rsv}_{i,3} = 1 - (1 - dtw_{i,1}) \cdot (1 - dtw_{i,2}). \tag{10.10}$$

These methods allow us to maintain a list of documents ranked by rsv while performing Boolean operations on any of the standard non-Boolean information retrieval models.

11

Search Feedback and Iteration

Basic Concepts of Feedback and Iteration

Feedback is an engineering term denoting information that is derived from the output of a process and then used to control the process in the future. A more formal definition is that feedback returns a portion of some output quantity and uses it to manipulate an input quantity (*McGraw-Hill*, 1971). An example is the use of a pressure gauge to feed information to a control that regulates the amount of heat applied to a water boiler. As the pressure rises above a safety threshold, the heat level can be decreased by reducing the input rate of fuel, thereby decreasing subsequent pressure. Should the pressure fall below a preset level, the heat could be increased to raise the pressure. Although fairly primitive, this is a fully automatic use of feedback.

If a machine in a factory were grinding ball bearings and these were manually sampled following production, the inspector could suggest adjustments to the grinding process depending on the average diameter of the bearings relative to the established standard. While this example is also fairly primitive, it shows that feedback may be based on decisions made by a human observer and is not necessarily automatic. It depends on the judgment of the observer as to what to measure and what to do with the information.

Iteration means to repeat or do again. In mathematics it refers to a procedure in which a process is repeated with varying input until some basis for stopping is reached, typically that the current result differs by a negligible amount from the previous result. Long division is the first example many of us encounter. The divisor is divided into a portion of the dividend repeatedly, each time changing the portion used, until digits in the quotient are seen to repeat endlessly (as in dividing 16 by 3), or reach a zero remainder, or until no more accuracy is needed (the remainder of the most recent iteration is only negligibly different from the previous one). In searching, iteration means to repeat the query–retrieve–browse process, modifying the query each time, until some identifiable goal is reached. The goal might be a set of a given size, a certain number or proportion of highly valued records retrieved, or some specific information found. The information used to make the decision whether to iterate again and, if so, what adjustments to make, comes from feedback. There are some conventions in searching, but few well-established forms of feedback.

While thoughtful people might prefer that the decision be made on the *content* of records, not their number, the temptation to decide on set size, alone, is there and can be hard to resist. The typical sequence might be that the user defines a set, checks the number of records, and, if too large, immediately revises the definition to create another set. If the number retrieved is, say, 35,000, this seems a reasonable basis for decision making. In World Wide Web searching, sets numbering more than a million records are not uncommon. Even if such a set were to contain all the records the user wanted, finding them among thousands of unwanted ones could be a formidable job, so why not set about reducing the set immediately?

On the other hand, suppose after creating a subsequent set or two, the number is reduced to 23. There is the temptation to quit, feeling that this is a good number, even if only a few of them are ultimately useful. The point now is that this set is small enough to permit the user to browse through a reasonable number of its records and to make the continuation decision on the basis of content. The decision on whether or not to perform another iteration seems to be based on an assessment of how much work remains to be done by the searcher to reach a satisfactory result. Feedback can help in such situations by pointing out terms that caused excessively large or small sets, and by noting the absence of browsing if users show a tendency to make decisions without looking at a "reasonable" number (obviously a subjective value) of retrieved records, probably therefore basing the decision on set size, alone.

Experienced searchers or teachers of searching usually assume that a database search involving text is going to be repeated with modifications until some desired and recognizable outcome is achieved or a threshold, perhaps of elapsed time or cost, is crossed. Some patterns of command usage or of retrieved set sizes occur frequently in the performance of searches, and these can be used as the basis for both planning and feedback.

11.2

Command Sequences

Several research studies have shown (Chapman, 1981; Meadow, Loranger, and Olander, 1985; Penniman, 1975a, 1975b) that searchers of bibliographic text databases tend to employ a sequence of *cycles*, each of which in turn consists of a sequence of commands or menu choices. More is known about the commands that make up a cycle than about the sequence of cycles. Because commands are so specific, it is usually clear what a command was intended to accomplish, but a cycle is more at the strategic level and its exact objective is rarely clear.

The typical cycle begins with the selection of a database. This is followed by exploration of individual terms—looking them up in the inverted file or thesaurus with the objective of deciding which terms to use in a query. Once terms are chosen, sets are formed, using attribute–value expressions. This may also be thought of as probing the database for combinations of terms. Only after sets are formed can browsing of records be done to evaluate the records and look for new terms or logical combinations to try in a revised query. Sometime during browsing a decision is made whether to stop the search or to revise the query and try again. Finally, when the results seem satisfactory, some or all of the retrieved records are printed, otherwise displayed, or set aside, and any placing of orders for or printing of documents is done.

Each major function may have more than one command as a part of it. For example, there may be several different set-forming commands or different modes of displaying records for browsing. Penniman and Dominick (1980) investigated the sequence of commands, grouped these by function, and suggested that a searcher is in a particular *state* when using any of the commands that are associated with a given function. Chapman (1981) investigated the sequence of states. Both found repeated patterns and were able to distinguish between groups of searchers with different characteristics on the basis of the patterns of command or state sequences they used. The following is a typical list of functions by state:

1. *File or database selection*—opening or designating the databases to be searched
2. *Term search or browsing in dictionary, thesaurus, or inverted file*—looking up individual terms to see how often they occur and what related terms may be found
3. *Record search or set formation*—selecting records that exist in the main file by storing their access numbers in a set
4. *Record display and browsing*—calling up records of the set for perusal by the searcher
5. *Document acquisition*—Ordering the printing of records or ordering hard-copy documents
6. *Requests for information about the retrieval system*—requesting information on commands, database contents, or prices
7. *Establishing display or communications parameters*—setting page or display line widths, page lengths, telephone numbers of networks, etc.

Other functions, such as reading news from the search service, asking about accumulated costs, or asking for help in understanding the use of a command, do not necessarily occur in any established order and often are not used at all. They do not seem to play a role in the logical structure of a search.

If certain patterns occur regularly, this information can be used in the design of systems and in the training of searchers. Of particular importance in this chapter is that the regularity of these patterns allows designers to plan the feedback that users need in their progression through a series of states.

11.3
Information Available as Feedback

Listed here are the kinds of information available, classified by state, as listed in Section 11.2. Some types of information are a direct outcome of a specific command, while others result from a cumulation of command results.

11.3.1 File or Database Selection

From this state the searcher can receive confirmation of the database selected and summary information about it, such as the date range of its records or number of records contained, or the price. The pricing methods used might be provided to the user but rarely are. It may seem that feeding back the name of the database in use should not be necessary, but as a user moves from one to another, it is possible to forget and to use attribute names and values pertaining to the wrong database. This form of feedback, then, is not so much for positive control as for avoidance of error.

11.3.2 Term Search or Browsing

A wealth of information is potentially available from commands or actions in this category. At minimum, the user can see a list of attribute values close to the value keyed in, based on alphanumeric sequence. An example is shown in Fig. 11.1. Commonly, such a display will also show the number of records containing each value, and there may be an option to show the attributes in which the value occurs. In a large database, a value of zero for number of occurrences often means that the word was mistyped. Users, especially beginners, often miss this message and may attempt to form sets using nonexistent term values. The second part of the illustration shows the result of asking for a search for RELEVANCE as a tagged attribute, which does not exist in the database being searched. The result is a confusing message.

If there is a thesaurus, its contents are usually displayed in addition to the information listed above. General purpose thesauri are rarely found in an IRS. Thesauri tend to show the relationships only among terms of a controlled language which, in turn, is likely to be specific to a database or industry. If, for example, one is interested in the effect on family life of an influenza epidemic, it is unlikely that a sociological database will show the various types of influenza

```
1 /
expand relevance/8
        ITEMS              TERMS
A           1      BI=RELEFU
B           1      BI=RELEIVING
C           1      BI=RELEMAKING
D           1      BI=RELENTLESS
E         447    **BI=RELEVANCE
F           1      BI=RELEVANCES
G           8      BI=RELEVANCY
H         575    BI=RELEVANT
Enter MORE to see additional terms
Enter letters (e.g. a,f-h) to search and
combine terms
        1/

expand ti=relevance/5
        ITEMS              TERMS
A           1      SP=96503
B          25      SP=96555
*****  YOUR TERM  *****
C       57886      UD=1:6712
D       21881      UD=6801:6812
E       26524      UD=6901:6912
Enter MORE to see additional terms
Enter letters (e.g. a,f-h) to search and
combine terms
```

Figure 11.1
Feedback from a term search: the first command shows what happened when the word RELE-VANCE was searched in the index. Since no attribute was identified, the basic index was assumed, and a listing of eight terms was requested. We see that RELEVANCE occurred 447 times, and we can see several words that are close in spelling and probably also in meaning, with their occurrence rates. We can also see at least one clear misspelling (RELEIVING). The second command asked for RELEVANCE as a term in a title, but title does not have a separate index associated with it. Hence, the display seems meaningless. Actually, it shows the end of the list of terms in the SP attribute and the beginning of those for UP. It would have been better if the system fed back a message like, "There is no such term," or "There is no such index." (Reproduced by courtesy of Dialog Corporation.)

as part of its controlled language. But, in a medical thesaurus, the searcher could learn that there are many types of influenza and that it is appropriate to identify which one is being searched for. Much valuable information can be gained from inspecting the terms, related to the original query terms used by the database producer.

11.3.3 Record Search or Set Formation

What cannot be learned from term browsing is how two or more terms may co-occur in records. To find this information, it is necessary to form sets. The feedback from a set-forming command includes a set number and size. Figure 11.2 shows the results of a set-forming command in Dialog. Not only is the size of the final set displayed, but the occurrence frequencies for each term are displayed. This gives users a sense of which term might be causing trouble due to excessive or minimal numbers of occurrences. Users should be aware of the danger of forming combinations of terms with excessively small or large numbers of associated records. The former, in combination, are likely to yield null sets. The latter may contribute little to the final set, and serve only to obscure the picture. For example, suppose a search is to be conducted on hashing functions and signature analysis and their effect on IRS performance. This could be expressed as HASHING (W) FUNCTIONS AND SIGNATURE (W) ANALYSIS AND INFORMATION (W) RETRIEVAL (W) SYSTEMS, but these are three very specific, limiting facets. Minor variations in wording could lead to missing useful records. Alternatively, (EFFECT? OR PERFORMANCE) AND (HASHING OR SIGNATURE) AND RETRIEVAL uses terms so broad the searcher could be deluged. A middle approach as simple as HASH? AND SIGNATURE? could be highly effective, or at least a good starting point. If the feedback includes the

```
    1/
search online and (database or file)
       856 online
      8028 database
      4961 file
   SET   1: 72 (online AND (database or file))
```

Figure 11.2
The SELECT command: feedback from this command for information about ONLINE AND (DATABASE OR FILE) gives the number of records containing each of the three individual search terms and the number containing the Boolean combination specified. These data can be used to decide upon subsequent version of query. (Reproduced by courtesy of Dialog Corporation.)

number of hits for each constituent term of a command or query, it might be possible to see what led to a null or overly large result.

There is a common tendency among users to assume that a number of hits in the range of about 10 to 50 is "right," without considering what is *in* the set (Bates, 1984). A searcher might be discouraged by finding several thousand hits, but this might only imply that another facet should be added to the query, perhaps merely a date restriction. Similarly, a null set may result from one too many required conditions, easily removed once the circumstance is recognized. Set size is a useful number, but it does not equate to set quality. Set analysis, giving the searcher a statistical picture of what was retrieved, might be of great value at this point.

11.3.4 Record Display and Browsing

The real meat of search feedback comes here. The user sees the content of retrieved records, as in Fig. 11.3, and should be able to answer some of these questions:

Does the record satisfy the need for information?
Does the set of records, collectively, satisfy the need?
Is there information in the records that suggests query values that might better *not* be used, for example, a synonym that has too broad a meaning or too many meanings?
Does information in the records suggest values that were not used, but might have been, such as a subject heading that occurs in most highly valued records, but was not part of the query?
Is there information that suggests changes in query values or logic, such as over-restrictive dates or author logic (requiring, say, two names to be co-authors, rather than accepting either one of them), use of AND instead of OR (or vice versa), or improper use of NOT?

Such information, in a sense, is always there if the searcher knows how to look for and use it. Relatively rarely do IRSs explicitly bring it to the attention of the searcher.

11.3.5 Record Acquisition

We could look at three types of retrieval and browsing as an ordered sequence: term search and browsing, set search and browsing, and document search and browsing. The first gives preliminary information, used to decide

```
type s1/full/3 tag
```

```
        5 / 3
AN  -   2852877
VN  -   D8918
RE  -   ED-303 163
TI  -   ANNUAL REVIEW OF OCLC (ONLINE COMPUTER LIBRARY
        CENTER) RESEARCH, JUNE 1987-JUNE 1988.
CS  -   OCLC ONLINE COMPUTER LIBRARY CENTER, INC.,
        DUBLIN, OH.; 076139000PU - 1988; 89P; AVAILABLE
        FROM ERIC DOCUMENT REPRODUCTION SERVICE
        (COMPUTER MICROFILM INTERNATIONAL CORPORATION),
        3900 WHEELER AVE., ALEXANDRIA, VA 22304-5110;
        FOR THE 1985-86 REVIEW, SEE ED 278 397; NOT
        AVAILABLE NTIS
LA  -   English
CC  -   88A
DE  -   *BIBLIOGRAPHIC UTILITIES; *INFORMATION
        RETRIEVAL; *MANAGEMENT INFORMATION SYSTEMS; *MAN
        MACHINE SYSTEMS; *RESEARCH AND DEVELOPMENT
        CENTERS; *RESEARCH PROJECTS; ADVISORY
        COMMITTEES; ANNUAL REPORTS; DATABASE MANAGEMENT
        SYSTEMS; INFORMATION SCIENCE; LIBRARY
        STATISTICS; PROGRAM DESCRIPTIONS; UNION
        CATALOGS; USER NEEDS(INFORMATION);
        BIBLIOGRAPHIES; FULL TEXT SEARCHING; *OCLC;
        NTISHEWERI
AB  -   THE PROJECTS REVIEWED IN THIS ANNUAL REPORT OF
        THE ONLINE COMPUTER LIBRARY CENTER, INC. (OCLC)
        FOCUS ON FOUR STRATEGIC AREAS: (1) ENHANCING THE
        USE OF THE OCLC ONLINE UNION CATALOG; (2)
        INVESTIGATING FULL DOCUMENT STORAGE, RETRIEVAL,
        AND PRESENTATION; (3) STRENGTHENING THE
        INTERFACE BETWEEN PATRON AND SYSTEM; AND (4)
        PROVIDING STATISTICAL INFORMATION FOR IMPROVED
        DATABASE MANAGEMENT. INTRODUCTORY MATERIALS
        INCLUDE BRIEF STATEMENTS BY INDIVIDUAL MEMBERS
        OF THE RESEARCH ADVISORY COMMITTEE AND AN
        OVERVIEW OF THE OCLC RESEARCH PROGRAM.
```

Figure 11.3
A portion of a record printed out while browsing: this is a record that resulted from the command of Fig. 11.2. The user can see the formal subject headings (here called **descriptors**) and can select those that might lead to other, related records. The user may also see very specific phrases or sets of words, such as "interface between patron and system," that can be a clue to better retrieval on the next try. The use of TAG in the command is what results in this form of display, with each attribute identified. (Reproduced by courtesy of Dialog Corporation.)

how to express an information need as a query. Following the creation of the first of a series of sets, the set size provides some useful information, but examining the content provides even more. Document browsing differs from set browsing only when the database consists of surrogates, rather than the original texts. In a nonbibliographic system, this middle level might not exist; the search would go from a term index directly to the ultimate information-bearing records. In using a bibliographic system, obtaining the ultimate information bearing terms—the articles or books—might take days because it normally means going outside the IRS to a library or other document source. Procuring the documents, reading them, and *then* deciding whether the query results satisfied the information need is an extension of the concept of browsing and may be a necessary part of the process.

11.3.6 Requests for Information about the Retrieval System

The most obvious form of feedback is that given in response to a direct question. Almost all retrieval systems have some form of help, typically providing specifics on the use of commands or other system features, upon a user request for that information. More modern systems attempt to answer what are probably the ultimate user questions: What is happening here? How did I get here? What should I do now? To answer the last question would require that the system understand the user's objectives and basis for evaluation and be able to make its own evaluations accordingly. The first two questions, however, can be answered by a computer by interpreting the sequence of commands and their results. Ability to do so is included in some definitions of a modern *expert system*, one that can explain its own actions (Forsyth, 1984).

At this point, it is important to note that information about how a user reached a given point in a search can be of great value in planning future actions and also to note that users do not always understand the situation they are in. For example, a user may have a well-formed information need but be unclear in what form the information retrieved will be, and possibly be surprised if it is text rather than numbers, or references rather than the entities referred to. Confusion at this level would hardly be expected of a professional searcher, but is possible when the searcher is inexperienced and using a database for the first time.

11.3.7 Establishing Communication Parameters

Perhaps the most frustrating of all outcomes of a search is total failure even to reach the search service or appropriate local software because of a defect in password, Web URL, telephone, or setup of the operating system. There is not normally any way for the computer system to know what was attempted, especially if the IRS (or other applications software) has not yet been reached. Hence, there is little if any feedback related to this problem, because the system has so little information to go on.

11.3.8 Trends over Sequences and Cycles

Most of the feedback variables discussed so far have been individual or pertaining to the status of the search at a particular time. Another class of feedback variables provides summary data as to what has transpired over a series of search cycles, which can give the searcher clues as to not only what to do next in a search but also how to improve the entire approach to searching. Here are some examples of variables that are possible for a system to provide:

1. *Frequencies*—the number or percentage of terms with very low or very high numbers of hits, per cycle, showing any *tendency* to use overly general, overly specific, or nonexistent terms in a search. Single instances are not critical, but repeated use of unsuccessful terms can be.

2. *Number of records examined per cycle*—when browsing there may be a tendency to look at too few or too many. Does the searcher make hasty decisions or spend too much time on overly large samples?

3. *Evaluation of records viewed*—sometimes searchers, especially novices, are unsure when to quit a search. Because the usual result is neither perfection nor nothing, it is a matter of judgment when a *good enough* result is obtained. Being reminded of results of previous cycles can help decide whether more cycles are likely to be useful.

4. *Query complexity*—this can be measured by the number of facets (individual terms or combinations) or number of Boolean operations or of equivalence statements. While there are no established values, very small sets will result from too few or too many terms or combinations of terms intersected, and very large sets, from too few facets. If either of these occurs with any regularity, it is likely to lead to user frustration. A related measure is that of the sequence of set sizes that result from each cycle—are they consistently too large or too small?

11.4

Adjustments in the Search

The general approach to online searching by experienced searchers or instructors is to use a series of cycles: probes for terms, set formations, browsing, and revision, and then repetition of these steps. During each cycle there should be enough feedback to give the searcher a basis for undertaking the next cycle and, ideally, the searcher should have some concept of what would end the process. In one particular situation, the single cycle is standard. In a library that pays for its patrons' searches, it is often deemed too expensive to undertake multiple cycles on their behalf. Particularly if the patrons are inexperienced, it may not be necessary to provide the advantages of feedback to satisfy them.

The kinds of adjustments that can be made, based on information received from an earlier cycle, are discussed next. Changes are always made subject to some constraints, most commonly time or cost or final set size (if, for example, an end user wanted only three items, or insisted on *everything*).

Here, we review the specific kinds of steps or actions that can be taken in terms of immediate goals. In Chapter 13 we shall consider the broader subject of overall strategy used in planning and executing a search.

11.4.1 Improve Term Selection

When records are retrieved, a searcher can notice the attribute values that occur in relevant records as well as values that *do not* occur in irrelevant records. This information could be, but rarely is, provided by the IRS; the user must usually find it unaided. Encyclopedia search software, some of which is described in Chapter 15, may provide such help. Look for variations in spelling and usage. Look for synonyms not previously used. Avoid use of values that occur in most records (e.g., ENERGY in an energy database, STUDENT in an educational database, HYPOTHESIS or RESULT in a database concerned with any statistically based science).

11.4.2 Improve Set Formation Logic

Inexperienced searchers sometimes make errors in the use of Boolean operators, such as using AND when OR is more appropriate, which makes the search needlessly restrictive. Another is a tendency to write into a query expression everything that is wanted in retrieved records, rather than only enough information to retrieve a reasonable-size set containing the information wanted. An ill-conceived query makes it difficult for a computer to provide meaningful feedback, but users should always be aware of the possible need to restructure the query.

11.4.3 Improve Final Set Size

This objective is meaningful to most searchers, especially since it has a direct bearing on time and cost. While they may not start with a realistic goal, it becomes quickly apparent that something must be done if 3000 records are retrieved. Similarly, if the search is for an extensive bibliography, and only three items are retrieved, revision is clearly indicated. Good instruction should convince users that size and content must be balanced. Set size should become the primary concern only *after* reasonable content goals are achieved.

11.4.4 Improve Precision, Recall, or Total Utility

Precision and recall measure, respectively, the proportion of relevant records among all those retrieved and the proportion retrieved of all those in the database. These will be discussed in more detail in Section 16.3. It is our belief that few searchers set out with an explicit goal for a certain level of precision. They *may* do so with respect to recall if working in a field in which a truly exhaustive search is necessary, patent searching being the usual example here. An intermediary is more likely than an end user to be concerned if the precision is low, because lack of precision may appear to reflect on the performance of the intermediary, irrespective of the user's own satisfaction with the information retrieved. We have no measure of total utility, about which more will be said in Chapter 16. Unless the number of records is large, end users probably only care about the *value* of the "good" records, not the *number* of "bad" ones. An intermediary may feel that high precision should be delivered as a matter of professional pride.

11.5 ──

Feedback from User to System

As IRSs become more intelligent, it becomes as meaningful for a user to provide feedback to the system, which can use this information to control its own actions, as for the system to provide feedback to the user. We are approaching a condition anticipated many years ago by J. C. R. Licklider (1960), which he called *man–machine symbiosis*, indicating two organisms working together in mutual dependency, to solve a problem, each contributing what it does best.

In a sense, after the search has started, any command given by a user to a computer can be considered feedback. But unless the computer controls the process or a major part of it, using the commands only for adjustment, the point is moot. Early retrieval systems were designed so that the user was in complete control, and feedback went to him or her. More modern systems have the system take an ever greater degree of control and, in doing so, become more dependent on receiving feedback from the user.

Salton and McGill (1983, pp. 236–240) proposed the concept of *relevance feedback*. After a user has retrieved a set of records, some subset of them is evaluated by the user. The subject terms in highly rated records can be extracted, assigned a high weight, and used in an automatically revised query for the next iteration. Conversely, query terms that appear often in low-rated records might be reduced in weight for the next iteration.

Salton and McGill described how a query can be modified. The query is a vector of weights for each term in the vocabulary. Once an initial query has been tried, it can be revised based on the contents of those retrieved documents deemed relevant by the user who submitted the original query. The modified query can then be used to search for additional or different relevant documents.

The formula used can also be seen in some of the pattern recognition algorithms now available. In effect, it moves the query in the vector space closer to the relevant documents and further away from the nonrelevant ones. "Closer" is used here in the sense of the angle between vectors. Thus, the new query will tend to retrieve the relevant documents and those documents that are similar to them while tending not to retrieve the nonrelevant documents and those similar to them.

We can represent the weights of the original query trems as $QW = w_1, \ldots, w_n$ where w_j is the weight of term j. Initially, the weights might be binary, zero or one. We want to transform this vector into a new one where the weights are based upon weights of words that occurred in documents deemed relevant or non-relevant after the initial query. A document or text is also represented as a set of weights applied to each possible term. Hence, weights of document D_i of m terms are $DW_i = w_1, \ldots, w_m$. These weights might have been assigned by an indexer or computed based upon frequency of occurrence or related variables. Those documents in the retrieval set that were evaluated by the user are assigned either to a relevant set or a non-relevant set.

Where R is the number of documents found relevant in the first retrieval set, N is the number found not relevant, the new vector, QW', will be:

$$QW' = QW + \alpha \left(\frac{1}{R} \sum_{D_i \in D_R} DW_i \right) - \beta \left(\frac{1}{N} \sum_{D_i \in D_N} DW_i \right). \qquad (11.1)$$

Here, start with the original weights (QW), then add to each a multiple of the average weights in relevant documents, and subtract a multiple of the weights given to non-relevant ones. As so often happens with such empirically based formulae, the values α and β must be determined experimentally. It was intended that α and β would be chosen so as to control the movement of the query, avoiding too drastic a move in either direction. This is a slight modification to the Salton–McGill formula.

There are many different ways this basic concept can be implemented. If the query is in the form of conventional Boolean commands, then there will be no weights assigned to terms. In order to modify a query automatically, it is necessary for the IRS to know which terms from retrieved records should be used in revision and how they relate to terms in the original query. We might use word-association techniques (Section 9.5) to find which of the new terms are associated with which query terms; then closely associated terms can be linked by or to the original terms. For example, suppose a query statement is SELECT EARTHQUAKE AND CONSTRUCTION, the user being interested in construction techniques in earthquake-prone areas. Suppose further that this query retrieves 100 records, and the user reviews six of them, giving four of the six a high rating, and two, a low rating. Within the high-rated subset the words TREMOR, SHOCK, BUILDING, and STEEL are the highest frequency, noncommon terms. A word-association matrix would probably show TREMOR and SHOCK closely related to EARTHQUAKE and BUILDING, and STEEL close to CONSTRUCTION. Then the query could be reformulated as SELECT (EARTHQUAKE OR TREMOR OR SHOCK) AND (CONSTRUCTION OR BUILDING OR STEEL).

The kinds of word associations just illustrated were incorporated, along with a number of other user-assistance and feedback features, in the CITE system at the National Library of Medicine (Doszkocs, 1983a, 1983b) and in *The 1998 Canadian & World Encyclopedia* (1998). There is a high cost of such processing and no guarantee it will work out so neatly. These are probabilistic techniques, but it can be expected that the query can be improved most of the time. If the user were shown the revised query and given the opportunity to check and edit it, the results might be still more improved. The method is also dependent on the user's choice of a sample and judgment in evaluating the records.

The more conventional form of relevance feedback would involve a natural-language query or a word list with weights assigned to the individual terms. If the natural-language query is long enough, the frequency of words in it can be used to establish weights, but often such queries consist of so few words that frequency statistics are not of much value. In any case, the query would be run, and a subset of the retrieved records, examined by the user. In this case, the terms from highly rated records can be directly added to the query, since syntax is not considered. Term weights can be addded if they were used in the original. If not, their relative frequency in the records might be preserved, so that in the revised query relative frequency can be used. Terms that have high frequency in low-rated records, but that occurred in the original query, might be deleted from the query. Again, there can be no guarantee that each term added or deleted is formulated correctly, but Salton and others report success with the method (Salton and McGill, 1983) in general.

12

Multidatabase Searching and Mapping

12.1

Basic Concepts

In all the examples of searches given so far, a query has been directed to a single database. But there are several reasons for searching more than one database at a time, or more than one in sequence.

In the most obvious case, the user knows several databases are relevant, wants to search them all using a single query, and knows of no reason that this cannot be done at the same time. Although there are some technical reasons why simultaneous searching is not common, a more important factor may be that databases are almost always to some extent different from each other, even if basically similar in content. If a query were not completely successful, the user's next action might have to be different for each individual database, but can be a single action only if all can be searched at once from a single query and all attribute names and value restrictions are the same.

The less obvious type of multidatabase search involves searching one database, retrieving from it some data, and then using those data as part of a query to another. Mathematically, and in some retrieval services, this process is called *mapping*. It means transforming a set of input values into a different set of output values. Cartographers map points on the earth's nearly spherical surface onto points on a flat plane. Where, exactly, the mapped points are to lie depends on the mapping algorithm or projection used. Of course, in a sense, the information retrieval system does this with any query—it transforms the attribute values and logic in the query into a set of output records—the word *mapping* is not used in searching unless there is a distinct intermediate step:

$$\text{Query values} \rightarrow \text{Intermediate values} \rightarrow \text{Output values}$$

A query could also be considered the statement of information need, or of the problem to be solved. The user poses the problem; the retrieval system solves it, just as if it were performing a mathematical calculation. Mapping is not a complex concept, but it is relatively seldomly used in information retrieval. It has the potential, however, for permitting much more complex problems to be presented to, and solved by, a retrieval system.

12.2

Multidatabase Search

In the "normal" method of database searching, a query is presented to the IRS, which converts it into a set of search parameters that control a search of an inverted file. Enough information is retrieved from the inverted file search to find complete records in the main file.

When the IRS charges for its service, the allocation of costs among the databases is a complicating problem. Is the query composition time split equally among the databases to be searched? If so, searchers would presumably compose the query while in an inexpensive file, and switch over only when ready for the actual search. Does this reduce the income potential of the more expensive databases? The cost of inverted file searching does not increase linearly with the size of the file. But should the allocation of revenue be equal among databases, weighted according to size of the database, or weighted according to number of hits in each database? The data needed to bill users and the program to prepare invoices may be much more complex than for single-database searches.

When record sets are retrieved, they might include some duplicates. This could happen when more than one database has a record on the same entity, such as reporting on the same book or journal article. A user will probably not want more than one record representing that entity and will not want to pay the price for duplicates and may have preferences as to which database's records are to be retained. We shall discuss the problems and methods of detecting duplicates below. Assuming for the moment that duplicates are retrieved and identified as such, which records should be dropped? To offer multidatabase searching, a search service must not only offer the technological capability but also a pricing plan that can be seen to be equitable for all concerned.

12.2.1 The Nature of Duplicate Records

Whether duplicate records constitute a problem of any importance depends on the design of the databases to be searched. If, for example, a corporation maintained a series of decentralized personnel databases, say one for each major division, it would not expect to find the same record in more than one of them. "The same record" would presumably mean a record for the same employee, found in two or more divisional databases simultaneously. Such a situation could happen through an error in keystroking while entering data. Suppose an employee were transferred from one division to another, but the respective data systems did not communicate properly, or the employee quit one division and was hired by another, but the first division did not drop the record immediately. The error could have happened when any new employee's data was being typed into the information system; inadvertently, one employee or social security number could be changed into another, thereby seemingly, but not actually, duplicating an existing entry. However it happened, if detected, the condition would probably be considered an error by a database administrator, and any of a number of steps could be taken to clean up the file, where "cleaning up" means assuring the presence of one and only one record for each employee in the company, or dates clearly showing no overlapping periods of employment in separate divisions.

Certain kinds of information, say about the behavior of school children from a certain ethnic group, might be found in bibliographic databases concerned with education, psychology, sociology, or medicine. It is not unusual for a record of the same research article to appear in several of them.

Yet another situation is typified by a search of several newspaper databases, in full text. If the search is for information about an important event, it is likely that several papers have covered it, but, newspapers being what they are, the content of articles is almost certain to differ among them. Newspaper searchers would understand this and might want all the articles. This is said in full recognition of the hazard of generalizing about what users want. But, if only one article per event is wanted, we would face a difficult problem in recognizing and eliminating others that reported on the event because they are not exact duplicates. They are different articles reporting on the same event.

We have presented three cases involving duplicates:

1. Duplicate records may exist, and this is normally considered to imply error.
2. Duplicates exist and are expected, but are considered redundant and undesirable.
3. Duplicates are considered interesting and wanted, although they may be duplicates only in terms of subject or other attribute.

For fully effective multidatabase searching, the user has to be aware of the problem and to have some facility for instructing the retrieval system what to do with the duplicates. This can be done with a command or command argument as simple as that used to specify a display format, although such commands are not available from all search services.

12.2.2 Detection of Duplicates

If there is a unique key for each record, detecting duplicate records in a set is a trivial function. Bibliographic and text records tend not to have this convenience, except for an acquisition number which, unlike a social security number, is not a particularly helpful search term. Each database is likely to use a different access number for its version of a commonly held record. Bibliographic records reporting on the same entity may have different attribute values because of differences among database producers in rules for entering authors' names or journal titles. There is also the possibility of keying error in entering, say, a lengthy article title using words not familiar to the data entry operator.

Different newspaper stories on the same event may have little in common except the high-frequency words used to describe the event, and they will certainly not occur in the same order. The date may differ, although only by a day or two if reports are on the same event. The by-line will certainly differ, as may the place of origin of the story, depending on where the report was written as much as on where the event occurred.

We present here some typical methods used to detect duplicates, based on the type of records involved. None is definitive, and none is guaranteed to work in all cases.

1. *Records with unique keys*—the employee personnel record or bank account are the common examples of this type of record. The intent of the database administrators is to have no duplicates. *Duplicate* here means two or more records with the same key—not necessarily other duplicated content. On creation of a new record, a check should be made that none already exists with the given key, but that is done by a program and such programs are not guaranteed error-free. It may be left to users of the database to detect any error. Removing or revising duplicate records would be handled as individual cases, and removal would presumably mean expunging them from the database, not merely from a retrieved set.

2. *Records with common attributes but different representations*—bibliographic records are the best example. Here we would expect that the entity represented by duplicate records is the same, and any differences in value have to do with *how* the information is represented, rather than *what entity* is represented. We have previously discussed minor variations in the style of recording an author's name. There are far greater variations in how journal names are abbreviated and volume, issue, date, and page are recorded. The best approach is to try to measure the degree of similarity between attribute values in two records being tested, and to establish a threshold for decision making.

Hickey and Rypka, of the Online Computer Library Center (OCLC), proposed a procedure for detecting duplicates among library catalog records for monographs in a large, shared catalog file. Intuitively, we might expect little need for a procedure to tell whether the descriptions of a book by two different professional library catalogers is the same, but the authors state "With many records, it is impossible to tell whether two... are duplicates... because of missing, incomplete, or conflicting information" (Hickey and Rypka, 1979, p. 125).

The Online Computer Library Center maintains a large database of catalog records, shared among many libraries. The file, in 1979 when the paper was published, stood at 5 million records and was growing at the rate of 20,000 per week. Librarian users were doing 300,000 searches per week seeking to find whether new (to them) books were already in the database. Since only 20,000 of these searches resulted in new entries, we may assume a high percentage were found to be already present, libraries with the new copies of the book saved the time and cost of data entry, and OCLC saved the cost of maintaining duplicate items in the file.

The Hickey–Rypka system involves encoding the value of up to 14 attributes, not all of which (illustrator, for example) are present for all books. Here are a few examples of the coding used:

place (of publication) is coded by taking the first six nonblank characters. Thus, NEW YORK becomes NEWYOR and TROY remains TROY.

publisher is hashed into a 61-bit key.

title is mapped into a string consisting of characters 1, 2, 3, 5, 8, 13, 21, and 34 extracted from the actual title, after deletion of leading articles. This series, called a *Fibonacci series*, places relatively greater emphasis on letters occurring early in the title string. GONE WITH THE WIND becomes GONWHI.

Once all the test attributes are encoded for a search, matching is determined by a series of rules. For each individual attribute, a program decides whether the degree of match is exact, partial, or nonexistent, and then records are deemed to match, depending on the matching of other attribute values. Since a test record has to be compared with 5 million stored records, execution time was a severe factor in the design of this algorithm because there would be 1.5 trillion comparisons per week.

3. *Records with a common entity but no common attributes*—when dealing with records such as news articles, which give very few attributes on which a match might be based, it is probable that we would need some of the record-association procedures introduced in Section 9.6. Exact duplicates are unlikely because databases are usually created by publishers of the newspapers, not according to any general standard, but searchers might want to find similar articles on the same topic. The matching procedures can be augmented with date and

location attributes, which would have to be given some leeway, e.g., two dates might be taken to match if they were within one or two days of each other.

Another algorithm, used for journal article citations (Giles, Brooks, Doszkocs, and Hummel, 1976) encodes the author's name using Soundex (Section 4.3.2), condenses publication date to the last two digits of the year, uses coden (a standardized code designating the journal, but not universally used), encodes the journal name as a series of the first two letters of the words in its name, the volume number, and a condensation of the title, also using the first two letters of each word. In other applications condensation of the date field, to save space, resulted in the infamous Year 2000 problem, whereby the abbreviated form of 1900 was the same as that of 2000. In this case, it does not matter. The two date digits are merely a way of telling one record from another, not necessarily to provide the actual date.

Bear in mind that any of these detection approaches requires computer time, possibly a considerable amount. But, depending on exactly what charging algorithm is in use, this extra processing might cost less than the per-record charges for receiving the duplicate records.

12.2.3 Scanning Multiple Databases

In a normal database search, search parameters are used to look up information in an inverted file. The data retrieved from this file can be used for set formation and Boolean operations on these sets. (Remember, Boolean operations are performed even when the query manager is used to interpret natural language rather than explicit Boolean operation commands.) It is not necessary to have access to the main file containing the primary records, unless the user wants to view them or, in some systems, to process a string search command. Going into the main file is a second-step operation after use of the inverted file. Inexperienced users who may be familiar and comfortable with this two-step process in a library (first consult the catalog, second the book stacks) may not realize it is happening also in an online search. Hence, they normally do not address queries to a *file*, but to a *database*, which they may not realize consists of two files. The fact that this is a two-stage, mapping operation is lost on them.

Dialog has a database called *Dialindex*, numbered 411, by intent matching the number of telephone directory service. File 411 is a combined multidatabase inverted file, or functions as such. It cannot be used to create sets, but can be used to find out how many records in any other Dialog database would be retrieved by a given query. It is then necessary to run the query again in the selected database, to create a set and be able to view retrieved records.

Figure 12.1 shows a use of *Dialindex*. The information need is for published material on various Spanish dialects used in the Americas. The query uses CASTILIAN as a possible synonym for SPANISH, and incorporates the additional terms DIALECT? and AMERICA?. The search in *Dialindex* will

```
File 411: DIALINDEX (tm)
(Copr. DIALOG Inf. Ser. Inc.)

? select files 1,36, 71
File   1: ERIC - 66-87/JUNE
File  36: LANGUAGE ABSTRACTS - 1973 THRU Dec 1986
File  71: MLA BIBLIOGRAPHY 1965-1986/MAY

File          Items Description
? select (castilian or spanish) and dialect? and
america?

       1: ERIC 66-87/JUNE
              16   CASTILIAN
            9273   SPANISH
            4133   DIALECT?
           52618   AMERICA?
             187   (CASTILIAN OR SPANISH) AND
                   DIALECT? AND AMERICA?

      36: LANGUAGE ABSTRACTS - 1973 THRU Dec 1986
             117   CASTILIAN
            5405   SPANISH
            6282   DIALECT?
            3939   AMERICA?
             114   (CASTILIAN OR SPANISH) AND
                   DIALECT? AND AMERICA?

      71: MLA BIBLIOGRAPHY 1965-1986
              68   CASTILIAN
           43125   SPANISH
           15802   DIALECT?
           55279   AMERICA?
             197   (CASTILIAN OR SPANISH) AND
                   DIALECT? AND AMERICA?
?save temp
```

Figure 12.1

Dialindex search: the *Dialindex* file is used to determine the best database in which to do a search, in this case on the use of Spanish in America. These results (the search was run in 1991) show how many records would be recovered, but no sets were actually formed. To do so, the user must repeat the commands in another database (any or all of 1, 36, 71). In this case, the number of records that would be retrieved is roughly equal across the three database probed. (Reproduced by courtesy of Dialog Corporation.)

investigate three databases: *ERIC, Language Abstracts*, and *MLA* (Modern Language Association) *Abstracts*. The user would then obtain record counts and decide in which databases to conduct the real search.

The results of the SELECT command, for each database, are shown in the figure, term by term, and the result for the Boolean expression combining them is also shown. No sets are created. The user is told what the set sizes *would be* if created in each database. By saving the search (the SAVE TEMP command), the user avoids having to reenter it later, after moving to the database of choice.

12.3

Mapping

True mapping is at least a two-step operation, but the information retrieved from step 1 is used in a different query in step 2. It is not necessary that the two files be different. A search might have the purpose of retrieving a sample of the range of published opinions on general economic issues of the news reporters and columnists who at least some of the time write on issues related to the petroleum industry and environmental protection. In other words, what more can we find out about the opinions of the writers who cover the petroleum industry? This would entail one query based on subject (petroleum and environmental protection) plus economic subject terms, whose goal is to retrieve the names of authors, and then another based on the authors (retrieved in step 1) and economic search terms, to find texts giving their opinions on other topics.

Today, mapping is probably most commonly applied in chemical information searching. Many chemical substances have a large number of names: common names, chemical names, trade names, or, in lieu of a name, a structural description of the substance. Common salt may be known as SALT, SODIUM CHLORIDE, NACL, or a trade name such as FASTMELT (fictitious) for a salt product used for ice removal. Drug names may have more synonyms in every category. Fortunately, Chemical Abstracts Service produces a database called *Chemname* that can convert any of these names into a common key value, the Chemical Abstracts Service (CAS) registry number. Since this attribute will be part of every CAS bibliographic record, it can in turn be used to retrieve information about a substance, no matter what name was used in the original publication.

Figure 12.2 shows an example of mapping in a Dialog chemical search. The user begins with a query to the file *Chemname*. Among its attributes is one called synonyms, abbreviated sy, whose values are all the various names by which a substance is known. Here, the initial command is simply SELECT SY = ALUMINA. The user knows this name and knows that there are other names

```
1     ? b 301

2     ? select sy=alumina
           S1        1   SY=ALUMINA

3     map rn

4     3 Select Statements, 28 search terms
      Serial# TD184

5     begin 399
      exs TD184

6     S3: 136,801
```

Figure 12.2

A mapped search for a chemical substance: the search begins (1) by opening a file that contains the names of known chemical substances, a registry number for each, and all the 434 other names by which this substance is known. The command MAP RN (3) retrieves all the registry numbers for these substances. The retrieval system tells us that it has composed select commands combining searches for 28 rns. (Not every synonym has a separate rn.) We are also given (4) a number (TD184) under which these commands are saved. We then switch (5) to the main bibliographic file (399) for chemical information and ask that the saved commands be executed, using the command EXS TD184. This results in a set containing the 136,801 bibliographic records for any of the various names by which alumina is known. The searcher has not needed to know all these synonyms.

as well but does not know what they are. Regardless of any other name by which the substance may be known, at least one record will contain ALUMINA in its SY attribute and will also contain the CAS registry number. Following the SELECT, the user enters the command MAP RN, which retrieves the rn from every record containing ALUMINA and stores the rns as part of a new SELECT command. There may be more than one substance involved. Alumina is a name for aluminum oxide, Al_2O_3, also known by a large number of other names, mostly trade names, such as Baikalox, Membralox, alumite, and white morundum.

The retrieved data (SELECT command with the rns) is automatically saved by Dialog and the user is given a serial number for this search. The user then switches to the *CA Search* database, which contains conventional bibliographic information and asks for execution of the saved search. The resulting message shows individual results for each rn and for the combination of all of them.

Another example of a mapping-type search cannot at present be solved automatically by a mapping command. In well-established fields of science, research people tend to know who the principal researchers are in their field. A quick way for them to scan the literature for news of new developments in the field is to search by author to see what these key people have been publishing. They may also want to know who has done recent work based on prior works of the key researchers, i.e., who are the likely new research stars. It is not conventional for bibliographic records to include the names or descriptions of works cited in the article being described. That is, if A writes a paper citing works by B and C, those facts will not appear in the bibliographic record for A's article. There are, however, databases devoted primarily to this very kind of information.

The *Scisearch* (Savage and Pemberton, 1978) database contains records that have only an abbreviated bibliographic description for a published article, but contain the complete list of all citations in the article. This is known as *citation indexing*. When users know enough about a field to associate a person or group of people with a well-defined subject, it can be easier, faster, and more reliable to find information by starting with the well-known names than by using elaborate bibliographic descriptors. To find what works have cited anything by author A or any particular work by A, a search is done on A's articles as cited works; then the retrieved, abbreviated information can be used to retrieve the conventional bibliographic records of the *citing* works from another database. To save time, it might be desirable to write a single query to accomplish both steps.

Designers and builders of information retrieval systems have long wished for a means of what might be called mapping terminology. This means that if a searcher uses a term, perhaps based upon one thesaurus or local usage, the system could find all equivalent or related terms in other vocabularies. A simple-sounding example would be to map Library of Congress classification terms into Dewey Decimal classes—not easily done. The National Library of Medicine has recently produced such a system for use with medical terminology, called the Unified Medical Language System (Humphreys and Lindberg, 1993; National Library, 1998; Squires, 1993). It can map terms used in a user's query into the vocabulary of medical terms based on 71 distinct medical information sources. This can be very helpful when trying to search literature in a speciality with whose terminology the searcher is not fluent.

12.4

Value of Mapping

A mapping search does not provide any capability that was not already available as a sequence of single-cycle retrievals, but it can save the user considerable manual work. If chemical searchers had to copy down lists of registry numbers, the amount of work could be excessive and the probability of error or omission would be fairly high. But the principal value of mapping is that it encourages users to use statements of actual information problems as queries—to tell the IRS what information is at hand (a chemical name) and what is wanted (information about it under any name). Any time or energy spent on composing intermediate searches or copying down intermediate information is diversionary and discourages the user from seeing the retrieval system as a problem-solving aid, not merely a file-search service. This simple step of separating and making explicit what is known and what is sought is *not* the usual way searchers approach the composition of a query. More usual practice is to go only to a description of the *records* wanted, not necessarily the *information* wanted.

13

Search Strategy

13.1

The Nature of Searching Reconsidered

Database searching has been compared (Janes, 1989; Leimkuhler, 1968) with the maritime problem of searching for a ship at sea—a hostile submarine, a friendly ship in distress, or shipwreck survivors. Developing optimum search plans was a major consideration during World War II for the then new science of operations research. Among the questions that must be considered in conducting a search of open sea, say by an airplane, are:

> Is it known in what part of the area to be surveyed the target is most likely to be found?
>
> Are there high priority areas of search for reasons other than probability of finding, such as excessive danger should survivors be found there?
>
> How likely is it that the searcher will recognize the target as such, if it is sighted?
>
> Is there one known, specific target, such as a particular ship in danger; several similar targets, such as a set of lifeboats; or an unknown number (including possibly zero) of enemy craft, as is probably the case when chasing submarines?

If we extend our consideration to include scouting out territory, say to look for a lost hiking party, look for a new campsite, or map previously unknown territory, we might have any of the following types of search missions:

1. *We know who or what we are looking for.* We know where the target *should* be (or that it is more likely to be in some parts of the search area than others) and we have a high expectation of being able to recognize the target if spotted. This may fit the lost-hiker situation.

2. *We know the type of target being sought.* It could be a person, tent, ship, or boat, and we will probably recognize it if we see it, but do not know where, within the broad survey area, to look.

3. *We are not looking for a specific target.* Rather, we search for a generic type of target, of which there may be more than one, such as a camp site, anchorage, or helicopter landing site.

4. *We have no specific target.* Rather, we wish to know what there is of interest in the area, perhaps topography, bodies of water, or unusual flora, fauna, or minerals.

By analogy with these four, we can identify four generic types of database search: the *known item search*, the *specific information search*, the *general information search*, and a *search to explore the database*.

13.1.1 Known Item Search

The searcher knows exactly what records are wanted, as identified by attribute values. The searcher will recognize the desired records if seen. An example is a search to verify or complete a bibliographic citation, where enough information is known to identify the record, but some facts, such as publication date, are not known. Or, the search may be for the inventory status of a product whose unique identifier, part number, is known. While the physical locations of the records are not known, they can be uniquely specified by attribute values. Some exploration is necessary but, because the searcher knows what the final answer or set of information should look like, there must be some known terms or attribute values with which to start. Typically, there will be no need to look for more than one record with the desired information; hence one of the most difficult aspects of some searches is avoided—finding all or enough material without retrieving too much that is unwanted.

13.1.2 Specific Information Search

The searcher is looking for specific information, but not necessarily specific records. The information sought may be found in any of a number of locations, and may occur more than once. On what date was President Kennedy assassinated? What was the gross domestic product of the United Kingdom in 1987? The searcher will probably recognize the answer, although it might be given indirectly (e.g., "President Kennedy was assassinated yesterday"). It is not certain what attributes and values to use for searching, but some starting combinations are readily at hand.

13.1.3 General Information Search

The searcher is looking for information on a subject in general, such as about a company being considered for acquisition or a method for solving a particular differential equation. There is no one way to describe the subject and there is no one way the desired information will be represented. There is no reason to expect that it will all be found in a single record. It is possible that important information may be unrecognized, even if seen. It is essential to probe to find out what information may be available and even what attributes and values should be used to recover it in a revised query.

13.1.4 Exploration of the Database

Here, the object of the search is to find out what kinds of information are in the database, not to answer a specific question. We do this sort of thing when, on first entering another person's home or office, we scan the book shelves, not to see if a particular book is found there, but to see *what kinds of books* are found there. We often do it on entering a new library for the first time and might well do it on first encountering a new database. Even when searching the stacks of a library for a specific book, we might look around to see what else there is of interest, without necessarily restricting our scope to the same subject as the one that brought us there.

Swanson (1979) pointed out that scientific research is usually a specific search, that is, the pursuit of a solution to a specific problem, while a different meaning of *research* is to find out what is known about a subject, more like our third category. Bates (1989) comments on the importance of browsing, our fourth type of search, even outside the context of the current search.

Any information retrieval system design should recognize that users may do any of these types of searches, may not have the categories separated in their own minds, and may switch from one type to another during a search session, just as they might during a search of book stacks.

This is particularly the case in searches of the World Wide Web. Searches of known sites may reveal new links to other sites that will be followed simply to see what is there, to expand on currently known material, or even to find specific information whose availability suddenly is inferred.

Exploration of a database could be based on subject content, but might also be based on metadata: what attributes are available for searching on or for retrieval. A service such as Dialog has a separate file describing the content and structure of each of its databases. A typical Web site has no such aid. Other services will fall between these extremes. As we shall show in Chapter 15, some

Web search engines may allow for searching for particular attributes if these are detectable in the record.

13.2
The Nature of Search Strategy

Strategy is defined by the dictionary as "planning or directing large-scale military operations" (*Webster's*, 1962). It contrasts strategy with *tactics*, pointing out that the former is primarily concerned with maneuvering forces prior to engagement. Tactics, then, is concerned with conducting the operations previously planned. The Prussian strategist Karl von Clausewitz (1943) defined the difference in terms of tactics being "individually arranging and conducting. . . single engagements," while strategy is "combining [these engagements] with one another to attain the object. . . ." A tactical military objective might be to capture a hill or bridge. A strategic objective is more likely to be the destruction or neutralization of an enemy armed force.

In database searching we sometimes find this meaning of the word *strategy* considerably changed, being occasionally used to describe as small an operation as a single search command. The major objection to this usage is that it leaves no word for describing the overall plan of which any one command might be but a tactical component. In both war and searching, the distinction between strategy and tactics can blur. What is important is not under which category an intended action falls, but that there *is* a plan and that actions *are* carried out. Bates (1979) proposed two brief definitions along this line: search strategy as a "plan for the whole search," while a search tactic is "a move made to further a search."

On the assumption that a search has a goal and is constrained by limited resources of time, money, and knowledge of the retrieval system and database, a plan is needed to accomplish the goal within the constraints. A *search strategy* is a plan for conducting a database search and should ideally (although in practice it often does not) include a search objective, a general plan of operation, and a specific plan of operation.

13.2.1 Search Objective

In most human endeavors it is desirable to begin with a clear understanding of the objective. Yet, we often do not. We marry, buy houses, design software, undertake writing assignments, and certainly begin searches for information without necessarily knowing *exactly* what we want to accomplish. The reason these undertakings work most of the time is that we have an idea of what we want, implicit and possibly ill-understood, but not totally lacking. If we do not know what we want, or where we are trying to go, then any road is as likely as any other to take us there.

In the case of a search, the objective can usually be stated in terms of identifying the type of information desired and possibly the quantity desired, the reliability required, the age of the information, and so on.

13.2.2 General Plan of Operation

The general plan should encompass the initial approach, the terms or values to be explored, and a sense of what basis will be used for judging the outcome. Also considered are any constraints on resources: time, money, or tying up of computer or communication resources. Typically, the general plan should include the first approximation to identifying the major facets of a search: the attributes and perhaps values to be used at first and the approximate logic relating them. Some searchers use a concept map for planning the content of the query. There must also be a reconnaissance plan for discovering more about attribute values to be used. Unless the searcher is very familiar with the database and subject of the search, it is usually necessary first to find out what might be available, then to work out a plan accordingly. This means that to accomplish any type 2 or 3 search, as defined in Section 13.1, a type 4 search may be a necessary preliminary.

13.2.3 The Essential Information Elements of a Search

There is certain information that, ideally, anyone ought to know before undertaking a search. It has to be accepted that sometimes, perhaps even most times, the searcher will not know all this information but will proceed anyway. Sometimes, the missing information will become part of what is to be sought and sometimes the searcher proceeds in blissful ignorance that anything might be missing. Listed below is a *guideline*, a set of suggestions not just for the searcher, but for the trainer or database or system designer as well.

1. *Information about the database* (refer to the discussion in Chapter 1):
   Scope of the database, in terms of the entities represented
   Content, in terms of the attributes represented
   Structure, in terms of how the attributes are stored and are related to each
      other

Currency, in terms of the date range of the information contained and the timeliness (delay between existence of information and its entry into the database)

Reliability, or the accuracy or believability of the information

Cost of use of the database

2. *Information about search procedure*:

   Functions or commands available.

3. *Information about what is to be recovered by the search*:

   Type of information sought—is it general or specific or is it exploratory information about the database?

   Definition of information—the traditional description of information sought in terms of attribute values and logic

   Quantity desired—how much is wanted? All on a topic? A single record?

   Recognition and evaluation—how will correct results be recognized? How will retrieved information be evaluated?

4. *Prior knowledge of the searcher*—of the information that is desirable, what is actually known?

   Information about the database—what does the searcher actually know about the database?

   Information about the IRS—what does the user know about the system and its commands or functions?

   Information about the search objective—what does the searcher actually know about what is being sought?

   Information about constraints—are there constraints on this search, in terms of cost, time, amount to be retrieved, or style, timeliness, or reliability of information?

When the searcher is aware that certain information needed to perform the search is not known, then acquiring that information can be included in the plan. Problems arise, during or after the search, when the searcher does not recognize what is missing. For example, if no information is available about reliability or timeliness constraints, then information that is exact as to subject may be useless to the requester.

13.2.4 Specific Plan of Operation

It may not be possible to formulate a detailed search plan until some of the preliminary reconnaissance or browsing has been done. Then we must address the exact attribute values to be used, down to whether or not to truncate, the logic, and the sequence of commands. For example, it can be more economical to ask first for the rarest, or least likely to occur, of the required attribute values.

Any subsequent intersection of this set with another will keep all the sets produced economically small. We must know the basis for ending the search, and details of cost and time constraints. We must know what is to be done with the final results. Rarely can the sequence of iterations be fully planned in advance, because rarely can we anticipate what the outcomes are going to be, and there are many possibilities. But we *can* often see, early on, whether the essential task is to reduce a large set, increase a small one, or redefine the search altogether.

13.3
Types of Strategies

In football and chess, there are certain standard strategies which can be adopted *in toto* or modified for the specific situation at hand. There have been a few attempts to define some standard strategies for database searching (Bates, 1989; Harter, 1986, pp. 170–204; Meadow and Cochrane, 1981, pp. 133–142), although we have no hard evidence that searchers consciously use any of these models as the basis for their own approach to a particular problem. The four aspects of a strategic plan described in Section 13.1 clearly have much overlap. The fact that they are not pure forms for use in precisely defined situations should make searchers aware of the need to carefully consider them in each instance.

This section and the following one on search tactics are brief. It is our intent to discuss types of strategies and tactics and how they affect a search and may be affected by the design of a system. A discussion in the depth necessary to train a searcher is not appropriate for this book.

13.3.1 Categorizing by Objective

The types of search objective listed in Section 13.1 are analogous to types of search in the geographic sense. In the bibliographic world they are *known item, specific information, general information*, and *exploration of the database*. In the known item search, the searcher knows what is wanted, how to specify it in a query, and how to recognize or confirm that the right information was recovered. There is little uncertainty and not much wile or cleverness required to devise a winning strategy.

The *specific information search* is one for which we know the objective clearly, although not necessarily how to achieve it.

The *general information search* is characterized by the searcher knowing the objective in terms of subject matter, but not knowing exactly what aspects he or she is looking for. Such a search is hard to plan in advance because an initial reconnaissance is a necessary part of it, to determine the essential elements of search information. The final plans depend on the outcome of the early probes.

The *exploration* strategy is one that does not aim for recovery of any specific information, but rather for information about the database in general. The very need for exploration indicates a lack of knowledge of specific objectives. It provides information for future searches. Such a search is characterized by some degree of intentional randomness, i.e., exploration of avenues or directions suggested by earlier retrieval, but not intentionally sought from the beginning and not strictly limited in scope. Still, even a casual perusal of a library has to have some objective if it is expected to achieve anything of value. Is the browser looking at the age of books? Their subjects or authors? Evidence of use? The database explorer may be concerned with the breadth of journal coverage in a field, the research productivity of an institution, or the current "hot" research areas in a discipline. The difficulty of such a search is that the plan must assure adequate coverage of the search area, but the exact dimensions of the area are not known in advance.

13.3.2 Categorizing by Plan of Operation

This is the more conventional aspect of strategy—what actions are to be taken, under what circumstances.

Direct attack—however much it may be stressed by instructors, some users will elect to ignore an iterative plan and try to solve the problem in one step. This may seem the most expeditious strategy, an attempt to gain the desired result immediately by a search of a single cycle. Just as in football or war, if it works it is spectacular but if it fails, it may leave the strategist with nothing at all, not even the informational basis for planning and executing the next iteration.

Brief search—a brief search (Meadow and Cochrane, 1981, p. 135; Harter, 1986, pp. 171–172) is a direct attack, intended to be "one shot," and aimed at retrieving only a few relevant records, possibly among a great many not relevant. The intent is to get something of value for a limited investment in searcher time and search cost. This is a common strategy with World Wide Web search engines where iterations normally involve total re-entry of a query, and the links found on one or two good pages may move the search in the right direction.

A different approach to categorizing strategies was suggested by Bourne (described in Meadow and Cochrane, 1981, pp. 133–142) and is presented here in condensed form. He recognizes the following types of search:

Small to Large

Bourne used the expression "pearl growing" for this type plan. It means to start with a precise statement aimed at retrieving some records virtually sure to be relevant and, preferably, little else. Then, starting from this small "pearl," the user can gradually modify the query to expand the output, hoping thereby to find more relevant material. In the extreme, it can be almost guaranteed to work, if a single relevant item—the seed pearl—can be found with which to start. However, if the initial definition is not well done, the seed may be missed. There are no guarantees. Pearl growing is commonly done on the Web by way of hypertext links to other sites, rather than by query modification, although modification remains a possibility. That is, we find one useful site, then follow links to try to expand our catchment of good records.

In a bibliographic search, the starting point might be a record about an article the searcher has recently read. Retrieving it shows the searcher how it is indexed or classified and shows information that may have been unknown at the start, such as the name of the journal, full name of the author, or any co-authors. Index and classification terms, journal names, authors' names, and, if a citation index is used, other articles that cited this one or were cited by this one are other attributes that can be used to find additional, related records. On the Web these attributes may be directly linked to the source document and easily accessible. From those second-round records, more terms and names can be recovered.

Reference librarians, on being asked for help in finding vaguely described material, may ask the client if he or she has an example of a paper or a book that was helpful or considered to be "on target." This is a practical example of the known-item approach to searching.

Large to Small

If the small-to-large approach is called pearl growing, a large-to-small search was likened by Bourne to peeling an onion, i.e., starting with a whole and gradually peeling away unwanted layers until only the part wanted remains. In information terms it means intentionally defining an information need broadly to virtually ensure that the result will include everything the user wants, then gradually working to rid the resultant set of unwanted records. In Web searching, broad definition of a problem is often unwise since the number of retrieved pages will tend to be exceedingly high. In most cases a complete re-entry of the modified query must be carried out.

This is the conventional strategy for those retrieval systems that operate on the assumption that a subsequent command always narrows the set formed by the previous one, that the first set-forming command defines a broad set and succeeding ones shrink the set by adding on new requirements which will result in an intersection with the previous set. If that assumption is valid, then commands are somewhat easier to enter, because it is never necessary to bother to command the intersection of the next with the most recent set. The method, however, can be cumbersome if the user's thought processes do *not* follow this logic.

To make the method work, a serious attempt should be made to define the information wanted, keeping the definition on the general side. It involves some amount of risk that, in spite of efforts to the contrary, the defined set will still be too small and will exclude some useful or desired records. The method, used online, can be expensive in terms of time used and records retrieved for browsing. Used locally, with a compact disk, it would be more economical. But all strategies involve some risk. It cannot be avoided.

Building Block

Some searchers prefer not to be limited to a large-to-small or small-to-large approach, but prefer to define the major logical components of their desired set and then to experiment with combinations of these and possibly other components later to be created as needed. In other words, create a set of basic building blocks, then see how best to combine them into the structure that fits the problem at hand, trying first one, then another combination. This approach lacks the benefits of a well-defined structure in which to work, but gives flexibility, possibly too much, since there is nothing in the plan that suggests what steps to take next. At each step the user must work out the next step to take.

The building block approach is probably more used by professional searchers who can be reasonably sure their blocks are going to be needed and who can experiment with the best way to combine blocks for best results or lowest cost.

13.4

Tactics

Bates (1979) recognized the basic distinction between strategy and tactics and defined a set of tactics. These tactics do not differ to any great extent from what others call strategy, but identifying them helps preserve understanding of the level at which a problem is being addressed. She defined four classes of tactical actions: *monitoring tactics, file structure tactics, search formulation tactics,* and *term tactics.*

13.4.1 Monitoring Tactics

These are steps taken to gain the kinds of information we have called the essential elements and which might be provided by the system as feedback. The searcher may have to take responsibility for asking for the feedback.

13.4.2 File Structure Tactics

These are "techniques for threading one's way through the file structure of the information facility to the desired file, source, or information within source." They basically represent procedures for browsing in inverted files and experimenting with set formations.

13.4.3 Search Formulation Tactics

These "aid in the process of designing or redesigning the search formulation." This is not terribly tactical, since it implies design of the iterative plan. However, its presence in the list does help assure attention to the overall planning activity.

13.4.4 Term Tactics

These "aid in the selection and revision of specific terms within the search formulation." These are truly tactical moves, contributing to the success of an iteration of a search.

13.5
Summary

For some search situations we can clearly define objectives and constraints and devise a plan accordingly. For other situations, objectives or constraints may not be well established or even understood by the searcher and this, of course, limits planning ability and often success of execution. Any user risks frustration who is not trained in planning or in the art of converting results of earlier forays into the database into tactics for the next ones. Much work needs to be done before we fully understand what people really do in a search, and why, and what works well, and why.

14

The Information Retrieval
System Interface

General Model of Message Flow

As pointed out in Chapter 1, an information retrieval system is a communication process. It is the purpose of this chapter to review this process, not in terms of commands issued or feedback received, but in terms of the exchange of messages, their transformations, and the possibilities for both useful information and errors that these exchanges create. It is important to realize that not everyone will use an IRS in the same way, that we all have different degrees of skill or patience. Hence, while some generalizations about how to communicate are possible and they do aid understanding, they must not be taken as rigid rules.

An interface is something that lies between two entities and may be part of either or both. The interface affects passage of anything that flows between the entities. When two optical lenses or prisms share a common face, that interface marks the beginning of a different angle of refraction of a light ray moving from one lens to the other. An international border is an interface and travellers crossing it may find that they are treated differently on one side than on the other.

Every computer system that interacts with people has an interface. This is the combination of hardware and software that enables the user to use the system and it may offer help in doing so. Some interfaces are highly interactive, some make extensive use of graphic images, some simply passively await a valid command from a user. We shall discuss these below, but when considering communications, it is important to recognize that some features are primarily communications-oriented and others are primarily retrieval functions. In this chapter we concentrate on the latter. Extensive coverage of interfaces in general is found in such works as Shneiderman (1987). Using menus instead of commands is an example of the former—this is a communication technique. Having a front-end program alter a query on the basis of the result of an earlier query is an example of retrieval functionality.

We can characterize the flow of information between user and system as cyclic, involving the types of information we have previously identified in Chapter 1. The use of an information system typically begins with recognizing or sensing the existence of an ASK, anomalous state, or lack of knowledge. It can take many forms, from an explicit recognition that a specific fact is needed to a general desire to find out what is new or interesting. The ASK is then converted, successively, into a statement of information need, a query, a set of retrieval parameters, a set of retrieved records or portions thereof, and feedback from the system about the search. Between each of these message types there is some sort of translation or conversion process, such as the translation of the information need into a query or of search parameters into retrieved records. While the retrieval of records is often seen as the very heart of an IRS, the other conversions are no less important.

Feedback from IRS to user, the last of the message types, is used to revise the search and initiate repetition of the sequence, or to decide to stop. Revising the search traditionally means revising the query in accordance with the information need and the results of the previous iteration. But it can also mean recognizing that satisfying the stated information need may not resolve the ASK and that starting all over again is necessary. How a given iteration is handled depends on what the user learns from early tries at the process.

We show this model in Fig. 14.1. Numbered items here are keyed to numbers in the figure.

1. *ASK-to-information-need translation*—this is not a formal translation and may be the weakest link in the entire structure. Since the ASK often cannot be fully identified, even by the user, its translation into an information need statement cannot be verified or evaluated by an external person or device.

2. *Information-need-to-query translation*—if the end user is also the searcher, then there is probably no intermediary and it is likely there will be no explicit information need statement. In this case, the ASK is directly translated into a query, with the same risks of unverifiability as in ASK-to-need translation. If there is an intermediary, then this step is normally done by that person. The intermediary's important function is the subject of Section 14.3.

3. *Query-to-search-parameters translation*—if the query language is a low-level command language, then this translation is largely a matter of parsing well-defined commands. There is little interpretation or decision-making.

If, on the other hand, the query is in natural language or a very high-order command language that does not explicitly identify each attribute–value combination to be used for set definition, then this is a key translation step. It is possible to evaluate the effectiveness of the translation, at least to some extent,

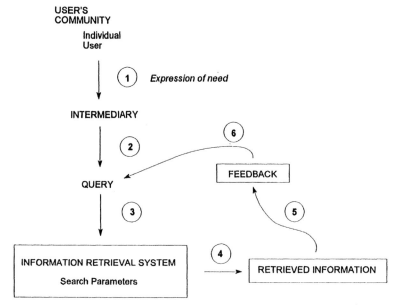

Figure 14.1
Steps in the retrieval process: this simplified sketch of the retrieval process shows points where errors or misunderstandings could occur and where feedback might help. Step 1 is expression of the information need to an intermediary; 2 is conversion of that statement into a formal query, and 3 is interpretation of the query by the system. Step 4 involves selecting useful records from among those retrieved, 5 deciding what feedback to provide the user concerning what was found relevant and what was not, and 6 shows the process being repeated.

because there is a formal input statement (query) and a formal output statement (search results) and it is possible to compare the results of this translation with results of other forms of translation. An example of this sort of translation is the use of any of the word association techniques of Section 9.5.

   4. *Search-parameters-to-retrieved-information translation*—this is a relatively deterministic translation, i.e., not subject to much variation as a result of the translation process, unless the IRS is expected to find records *related* to those retrieved by the query, but which did not themselves satisfy the query. This might involve the use of record association techniques such as those described in Section 9.6.

   5. *Retrieved-information-to-feedback translation*—if performed by an intermediary, this translation is another of that person's major functions. It involves analyzing the pattern of retrieved output or messages from the system (errors, null sets, etc.) and deciding what to recommend to the user.

If performed by a program, the key decisions on what to look for and how to do the analysis are done at the *time of designing the program*. The program may have to decide, at execution time, which of several possible and relevant messages to send. Too much feedback, i.e., telling the user about every conceivable error made, can be as bothersome as not enough.

6. *Feedback-to-reformulation translation*—the nature of the feedback to the user was covered in Chapter 11.

We discuss here the main problems of designing or serving as an interface: ambiguity in statements made to the interface, the role of an intermediary, automated intermediaries, and the general role of intermediaries, particularly noting that all computer programs have some sort of interface, even if not well suited to some particular class of user.

14.2
Sources of Ambiguity

Regretfully, communication between user and intermediary is not always clear. The role of an intermediary or interface is ideally to help—to explain, offer suggestions, or identify the cause and nature of errors. We are at least a decade beyond the time when a computer system might simply have responded "Syntax error" if it got an input it did not recognize. It would then have been left to the user to determine the nature of the error. One step up from such responses would be a primitive attempt to identify the cause of the error which could be confusing if wrong. For example, in some computer programming languages the statement $X = Y = Z$ is acceptable. It is identical to the two consecutive commands $Y = Z$ and $X = Z$. If such a statement is presented to a programming language compiler that does not allow for the usage, it could reply, "This usage not permitted in this language. Make separate statements." or it could say "Syntax error" and place a question mark under the second equal sign. The latter may be helpful to a person who had intended to say $X = Y - Z$ and who would then see a computer response of

$$X = Y = Z$$
$$?$$

The ? points to the character that the query interpreter or compiler did not expect and could not understand. On the other hand, a response about making separate commands could be baffling to a beginning programmer who knows no other languages. What is right? There is no fixed answer.

Similar problems arise with IR systems. Those that allow natural language queries do not always provide meaningful help to users trying to decide how to improve outcome. Such systems *appear* to offer communication in natural language, as would another person, but are unable to deal with answers to such questions as, "What do you mean?" The user who truly believes he or she is communicating in natural language may be quite frustrated that the system seems not to understand but does not explain itself.

We seem to have to settle for a general principle. A system interface should be designed to assume certain user characteristics but should be able to cope when users who do not have these characteristics are using the system. What is meaningful to an experienced person may be baffling to the novice. And *novice* may refer to state of knowledge or experience in using a system, using a database, or communicating in the argot or jargon of a discipline. It may require as much investment in development time to deal with such a range of users as it takes to provide the basic functionality of the system. Some retailers have learned that the service that goes with a product may be valued more highly by customers than the product, itself, especially if the product does not differ much from its competition.

14.3
The Role of a Search Intermediary

When most effective, an intermediary works as a consultant to the end user, usually complementing the user's knowledge of subject matter with knowledge of how to search. The user brings to the interaction with the intermediary an understanding of the problem to be solved and the context of the problem. The intermediary should bring a range of knowledge and skills. These include:

Help with understanding of the range of databases available
Knowledge of database content and structure
Knowledge of search and communications procedure
Postprocessing functions available and how to use them and, of critical importance,
the *human communication skill* to be able to elicit the statement of information need from the user and help the user to realistically interpret and evaluate the output

Usually such a person is a librarian, but the skills may be acquired through other career paths. Sometimes, highly specialized libraries put more emphasis on the intermediary's subject knowledge than on procedural or general library skills. The reason for this is to take advantage of the intermediary's ability to help the user express the information need and interpret the results. There is a large literature on the role of the intermediary, which begins before the user

arrives on the scene, when decisions are made about what information to collect
or what search services to subscribe to. Several works on intermediaries are
Auster (1990), Cochrane (1981), de Stricker and Dysart (1989), Harter (1986),
Meadow (1979), Meadow and Cochrane (1981, pp. 25–38), and Taylor (1968).

There is some evidence (Marchionini, Lin, and Dwiggins, 1990) that professional searchers and end users plan and conduct searches differently. The two
groups' behavioral patterns reflect their different knowledge and objectives: one
knowing the database subject matter and knowing what the objective knowledge is, the other knowing how to plan and conduct an effective search.

The actual tasks performed, which will of course vary from time to time,
are described next.

14.3.1 Establishing the Information Need

Our entire educational system deals only to a limited extent with the
question of how to search for and find information. Most of us are given library tours and lectures but are rarely taught how to define information needs,
evaluate results, or make most effective use of the resources available, especially
not how to enlist the librarian as a resource. In the workplace, potential users
may resist using a library. Reasons for this may include a reluctance to admit
not knowing something, or a perception that those doing the actual search are
of lesser status than the end user, or some unpleasant experience in a library in
the past.

Thus, the intermediary must be a skilled interviewer, able to understand
the user's information needs and patterns of behavior. The intermediary must
proceed from the knowledge that the user often does not know what information is necessary to begin a search or to end it. The intermediary knows it
is pointless to proceed without a meaningful need statement, but may begin a
vaguely defined search to enable the user to browse and thereby to help establish
what aspect of a subject is important. For example, a user in a library asking for
information about automobile tires may be confused or inarticulate about what
aspects of the subject are considered important. One approach is for the intermediary to point out that there is information on how to make tires, their effect
on automobile performance, their role in the national economy, or evaluations
of tire performance for the retail buyer. This gives the user something tangible
to use as the basis for refining the question. In the public library, characterized
by a wide range of users and types of information, the primary intermediary
skill may be human interaction. In the special library, the intermediary's ability
to pose questions in the user's professional terms may be paramount.

14.3.2 Development of a Search Strategy

Chapter 13 covered the premise that the next step for an intermediary, having achieved a statement of information need, is to devise a search strategy.

14.3.3 Translation of the Need Statement into a Query

The query should reflect the strategy—such as an attempt to retrieve a large, all-encompassing set or a minimal information seed pearl—and the need for feedback information. This translation is particularly difficult for end users because knowledge of command languages tends to atrophy if not frequently used. If the language was not learned well in the first place, it may be difficult to frame a complex subject in unfamiliar terms. An intermediary, on the other hand, may be current in several retrieval system languages.

14.3.4 Interpretation and Evaluation of Output

Evaluation will be discussed at length in Chapter 16. For now, let us recognize that this may be a critical function in the joint undertaking of the user and intermediary. The user can probably easily assess the *value* of retrieved records to himself or herself but may not be skilled at articulating the *characteristics* of the highly valued records that distinguish them from others. The intermediary, on the other hand, once shown two sets of records, one highly valued, one not, probably *can* express the differences in terms meaningful to the IRS, i.e., in terms of record attributes and values. This, of course, is a form of nonmechanized relevance feedback.

If the end user is not present during a search, as is often the case, an intermediary is likely to evaluate output on the basis of subject relatedness rather than value, because he or she has to make the judgment based on the stated information need, and cannot know what else, left unstated, was in the mind of the user.

14.3.5 Search Iteration within the Strategic Plan

Generally, understanding the value of iteration, especially *planned* iteration, comes with experience; hence it represents another area in which an intermediary can be of great value. It is as important to know when to stop as when to continue.

14.3.6 Change of Strategy When Necessary

Still another area where an inexperienced user may be stymied is in recognizing that the initial search strategy, and possibly the statement of information need, must be revised. Perhaps there is not enough information in the database, or there is so much that a far more specific need must be established, or simply a recognition that the language of the database is different from the language of the user, and there must be a translation. Such is the case when a lay person uses a highly technical database. Helping an inexperienced searcher who is knowledgeable in the general subject matter of the search but not the database, and who has had an inconclusive search result, may be among the most difficult tasks for an intermediary. What to do next is rarely clear in case of an inconclusive result, and a user who does not appreciate the need for a change in direction, or who cannot point to the new direction, adds to the problem.

14.3.7 Help in Using an IRS

Modern software tends to come with built-in help and tutorial programs. Some even have a form of help entitled something like, "How Do I…?" Unfortunately, a great deal of help is based on the assumption that the user will be able to ask a question phrased in the system's vocabulary. If the problem is that the user does not know either how to perform some task or even what the system's designers called the task, the result can be quite frustrating. Here, again, a professional intermediary can be of great help. If the intermediary is familiar with the software the conversation can take place in a different manner than that between user and system. The intermediary need not understand the content aspects of the problem to render this form of assistance.

14.4

Automated Search Mediation

It has long been a dream of computer aficionados to have a computer that could converse with a human as another human can, providing information on demand, and asking insightful questions when necessary to understand the original question. This, of course, has never happened, but we have made some progress in that direction. Generally, success has been more likely when the scope is limited. Here, we review first some background and then the functions of a computer intermediary for information retrieval.

14.4.1 Early Development

Around 1980 we saw the first of what became a large number of computer programs that performed some part of the intermediary role in a database search (for example, Benson and Weinberg, 1988; Marcus, 1987a, 1987b; Meadow, Cerny, Borgman, and Case, 1989; Williams, 1984). A program playing this role has some advantages over a person: it is always at hand when the user wants to do a search; it does some functions fully automatically, not requiring the kinds of detailed input some users find frustrating or embarrassing to be asked for; and it can be less expensive than a professional intermediary. On the other hand, it is hardly credible that a program can better *understand* the user than can a trained intermediary operating in a known subject domain. When the problem is really difficult, that level of understanding may be necessary; if the search problem is relatively trivial, it may not be. A human intermediary should be far better, for example, at recognizing and correcting an unpromising approach to a problem or recognizing uncertainty and lack of clarity on the part of a client. It is most difficult for a program to recognize that the problem it has been asked to solve may be the wrong one. For a program to do this, it would require, at minimum, that the program know the true search objective—the ASK—as well as the user's state of knowledge and comprehension of the material being retrieved.

When they first appeared on the scene, computer intermediaries were generally programs that helped a person to use a database search system. Today, some form of intermediary function is often built into the retrieval system, especially into Web searchers.

Another form of intermediary was generally called a *gateway*. Such a program would connect a user to any of several remote retrieval systems, possibly also offering help in deciding which one or in formulating a query. After some initial success in the early 1980s, these faded out of use, but have returned with the Web, first as search programs or home pages that will link a user to another site or program, and more recently as, again, programs that take a user's query to one or more other search systems and combine results.

14.4.2 Fully Automatic Intermediary Functions

Intermediaries typically may perform the following functions fully automatically on behalf of the user:

1. *Translation of commands*—most intermediaries simplify target system commands or make use of a single command language for all possible targets of one intermediary.

2. *Displays*—an intermediary program can provide enhanced displays, showing the same information as provided by the target system, but in a more meaningful format or in a manner to make browsing easier.
3. *Cost computation*—some intermediary programs compute the cost of a search session on behalf of the user, a function particularly useful when the searcher is an intermediary who must charge his or her clients for the cost of the search.
4. *Saving and recalling of searches*—an intermediary program may simplify saving, recalling, and editing of searches, or standard search components, whether in the user's personal computer or in the target system's computer. Saving, recalling, and editing in a local computer can save the cost of performing the same functions online, in the target system.
5. *Postprocessing*—this term covers a wide range of functions that may be performed on data retrieved by an IRS. They may range from formatting records for easier reading by the ultimate recipients to performing statistical analyses on the content of records. Moving these functions into an IRS, or enabling an IRS to communicate with other software that performs these functions, enables users or intermediaries to specify, all at one time, what data is to be retrieved and what is to be done with it—how it is to be put into a form that solves the original problem.

14.4.3 Interactive Intermediary Functions

The more advanced automated intermediaries, each in its own way, work with the user to help produce a successful outcome. In this section we describe a number of functions, recognizing that little is standard from one intermediary to another.

Selection of a Database

For the professional searcher, selection of a database is not a highly challenging problem. Knowledge of the various databases is part of the basic stock in trade. For the inexperienced searcher, however, it can be a daunting prospect because there are so many and because documentation of the differences among similar ones is skimpy. Hence, selection of the database is a function performed by some intermediary programs. It might be done by comparing a list of words in a natural-language statement of the information need with a list from a natural-language description of the databases, i.e., computing the degree of record association between the need statement and the database description. If the first selection were not appropriate, the process would have to be repeated. The difficulty, of course, is that determining what is appropriate requires knowledge of the database or outcome of the search or both.

The problem of database selection admits of no easy solution. There are so many factors that bear on it, some being rather subtle, that it is not practical to expect an inexperienced user to have either the patience or knowledge to make the decision. As a practical matter, it makes more sense to limit the choice. This is not entirely satisfactory because failure to retrieve useful information *can* be the fault of the database choice, but also because the user who has not made an informed decision may never know it. For this reason many intermediary programs offer only a limited number of databases, usually restricted to a single domain, such as medicine. A major problem of Web searching is that it is not easy, for example, to limit a search only to the medical or computer science literature.

Formulation and Editing of a Query

This is the heart of most computer intermediaries. A number of methods are possible:

i. The query is written in natural language and the input is converted by the program into another form of query.

ii. The query is written in a simplified or standardized command language which is then translated into the command language of the target system.

iii. An expert system embedded in the intermediary provides a series of prompts, using its own hierarchy, user-provided key words and phrases, and its knowledge of the subject matter, to play a sort of "twenty questions" game with the searcher, as in Vickery and Brooks (1987). Thus, the user need not explicitly write the query as a single statement or series of statements.

iv. The intermediary offers a simplified structure, such as the concept map, and assists in its completion by offering categories of search facets (subject, author, etc.), automated look-up of terms in online indexes, and, while no guarantee against error, a reduction in the probability of the user creating a query that cannot be executed (Meadow *et al.*, 1989).

v. The intermediary offers direct advice to the user on how to modify a previous iteration of a query, based on information it elicits from the user as to the latter's goal: more retrieved records, fewer retrieved records, a higher precision ratio, etc. (Marcus, 1987a, 1987b).

vi. Retrieved records are used to compose the next query formulation. This is a form of relevance feedback. The user identifies complete records or, ideally, portions of records, which the system converts into weighted key words for a query.

Interpretation of Results

The closest we have come to having a program evaluate results, or help a user to do so on the basis of content, is the use of the related techniques of relevance feedback (Section 11.5), set analysis (Section 8.3.1), and the use of retrieved records for reformulating a query (Section 11.3.4). The help is indirect, but it does focus the user's attention on which records are preferred and in some cases why, i.e., what attribute–value combinations may be of use.

It is important and useful for a user to make some kind of statement about the output of a query: what was valued and what was not, and why. A skilled human intermediary can greatly help the process and can probably out-perform a program doing the same task, but it is not always possible for the user to find an intermediary skilled in the user's special field of interest. Hence, work continues on the development of ever more intelligent search assistance systems.

Revision of a Query

In relevance feedback, the user is asked which records are most relevant or valuable. In most implementations reported, the assumption is made that it is subject that is of primary importance; hence subject-defining words and combinations are weighted and used to revise the query.

Set analysis provides users with the raw data to make their own decisions as to what attributes are most important, and provides information about values of those attributes. The user, seeing information about the composition of a retrieved set, then can decide what changes to make in the query, although more detailed effort is required.

Use of a retrieved record for reformulation is much like relevance feedback, but the user does not rate each individual record. Instead, a single model record is selected and possibly only a portion of it. Thereafter, the system's actions are much like those in the relevance feedback method. Terms or values must be extracted from the indicated portion of a record and used as the basis for the new query. The user does not explicitly identify words or individual values of high or low weight.

Help in Understanding the Retrieval System

Only relatively recently in the history of computers has serious attention been paid to the need to inform a user of what is happening with the hardware and software, i.e., how the system is operating. The modern approach (Forsyth, 1984) is to have an expert system explain its actions as it performs them. Thus, if the intermediary is selecting a database or deciding how to revise a query, it would explain its actions, teaching the user as it did so. The intermediary expert system could also be used to diagnose the manner of use of a system and offer help in explaining to the user why certain actions had the results they did.

14.5

The User Interface as a Component of All Systems

In most systems, especially the older ones, there is only one way the user and the IRS communicate with each other. There is one language and one set of feedback messages. A few older systems offered minor variations, such as allowing for shortened versions of commands or abbreviated system response messages, at the user's option. Some offer a choice of a command language or a menu system and at least one offered users the option to rename the commands of one language to make them look like another. The reason why independent front ends exist is the demand by users, or perceived demand by developers, for more options.

Regardless of the degree of user option, however, every IRS has a user interface in that it has an associated language, a language or query interpreter program, and a set of messages providing system responses and feedback. All that is fundamentally new in front-end software is the set of options given to users. Many of the front-end or gateway functions described here could easily be provided by the target systems.

Because online services now offer somewhat more flexibility to users, separate front ends have never become a large-scale commercial success, and CD-ROM software, operating in the user's own computer, and Web searchers are encroaching on both markets. A possible direction for future development is for all information retrieval software to be so designed that an independently developed user interface can be attached easily. In effect, this means designing software that has a standard interface with other software. In that way, a user could buy (or rent by the minute) any retrieval software and also buy or rent any user interface. While such interchangability among software products has never been a characteristic of the computer industry, comparable interchangability is found in other industries, from automobiles (standardized sizes for tires, spark plugs, and the like) to air travel (interline transfers and exchange of tickets).

Many a teacher has tried to explain to technically oriented students who disdain to learn expository composition that it is of little value to have good ideas if you cannot make others understand them. So, we may reach the point where software developers come to the same conclusion: good functionality is not of much benefit to people who cannot understand how to use it.

15

A Sampling of Information Retrieval Systems

15.1

Introduction

There are a great many information retrieval systems in current use. Only relatively recently have significant differences among them begun to appear. The differences tend to be in the language used to query the systems and the functionality permitted by the language and database structure. Specifically, whether or not a system is accessible through the World Wide Web does not directly affect the method of query. The query languages are overwhelmingly based either on Boolean algebra or on so-called natural-language queries. We say "so-called" because they may invite the user to state a question in natural language, but may make no attempt to understand what the question means. One reason for the limitations on Web searches is the lack of well-defined structure of records. As HTML and such efforts as the Dublin Core gain popularity, we may see significant improvement in the identification of specific elements of a Web document.

Overwhelmingly, the systems treat natural language as simply a list of words, but there are differences in how they do it. Information retrieval languages are almost universally descriptive or nonprocedural in that they describe the output desired, not the steps needed to produce it.

The systems reviewed in this chapter represent an attempt to describe the range of systems available, and this review is not proposed as comprehensive.

15.2

Dialog

One of the oldest of the online retrieval systems, Dialog became a public service in 1972. For many years it offered users only one language, Boolean, based on a small number of simple commands. Its primary users were assumed to be librarians and other professional searchers. Over the years, variations have been introduced to meet the needs and skill levels of different classes of users. We review the basic Boolean language, a newer approach using natural language, and Dialog on the Web.

15.2.1 A Command Language Using Boolean Logic

The essence of what Dialog's basic language can do can be shown in six commands: BEGIN, EXPAND, SELECT, DISPLAY, PRINT, and LOGOFF. Our explanations will omit some of the subtlety of the language and concentrate only on the most important usages (*Successful Searching*, 1998). Some of these commands have been illustrated previously (Figs. 7.3, 11.1–11.3, and 12.1).

1. *BEGIN*—this command serves two functions: it signals the beginning of a new search and it conveys to the system the name or number of the file the user wants to search. It has a single argument or a list of similar arguments, the file or database names or numbers; for example, BEGIN 1 designates the ERIC database. BEGIN 1, 11 opens both ERIC and the Psychological Abstracts databases. In general, in Dialog, when members of a list are separated by commas, it has the effect of the Boolean OR, meaning here that we are opening any file having number 1 or 11 or both. If a search was already in progress, BEGIN resets such variables as last set number created, but not the accumulated cost for the session.

2. *EXPAND*—this is the command for displaying part of the inverted file. It, too, has a single argument, although that may consist of a string containing more than one word. Whatever the argument, Dialog looks it up in the inverted file and displays, as a default, 12 terms, in alphabetical order, with the search argument in position 3. This gives the user a look at words or terms whose spelling is near that of the command argument. Indeed, the MEDLINE service calls their version of this command NEIGHBOR. Figure 7.3 showed the result of the command EXPAND TESTING in ERIC. A search for an author, or for certain attributes other than subject-related ones, must be preceded by the abbreviation of the attribute and the symbol =, as to search for Charles Davis as author, enter EXPAND AU = DAVIS, CHARLES. Figure 11.1 showed another example of this command.

3. *SELECT*—this is the set-forming command. Without it the IRS cannot retrieve records from the main file. The command results in the formation of a set and sending the user a message stating how many records were in the

set. The syntax is a bit complex. An example of its use is in Fig. 11.2. Here are some forms:

SELECT TEACHER—single search term as argument. This might create set 1.

SELECT S1 AND PUPIL—Boolean combination of a previously defined set (S1) and a new term. Another new set is generated.

SELECT (PUPIL OR STUDENT) AND TEACH?—this shows the use of parentheses to group terms and of the truncation function. The command calls for records containing either PUPIL or STUDENT and also having a word beginning with the letters TEACH. More exactly, TEACH? defines a set that is the equivalent of one defined as the union of all records having a word beginning with TEACH.

There are two versions of SELECT. One creates a numbered set only for the final result of all the Boolean operations called for by the command, and another creates a set for each term used in a Boolean expression as well as for the final result. For example, in the basic form at the start of a search, SELECT STUDENT OR PUPIL results in creation of set number 1 for the union of the sets for STUDENT and for PUPIL. The second form, called SELECT STEPS (in full, SELECT STEPS STUDENT OR PUPIL), would result in three sets: set 1 for the STUDENT record, 2 for the PUPIL records, and 3 for the union of sets 1 and 2. The latter form saves time and money in revising a set later if, say, the user wanted to use only PUPIL in a revised query. But saving many sets adds to the cost of a search, so a compromise should be reached.

4. *DISPLAY*—once a set has been created, using a SELECT command, its records can be displayed on the user's computer. There are three arguments, specifying the set selected, the format desired, and the particular records within the set. Here are some forms of a display command:

DISPLAY S2/TI/1-5—display records 1–5 of set 2, showing only the attribute title.

DISPLAY S4/5/1,4,8—display records 1, 4, and 8 of set 4, using a format (5) predefined by Dialog, the meaning of which may vary from database to database.

5. *PRINT*—this command asks Dialog either to print records offline, on its own printer, and send them to the user by what was once the more economical post or to send by electronic mail. With modern telecommunications facilities there is less need for such a command but it still has value. The arguments are the same as for DISPLAY.

6. *LOGOFF*—this command ends a search *session*. If the user wanted only to end one search and begin another, the BEGIN command would be

used. (BEGIN denotes the beginning of a new search and the end of the current one, if any.) LOGOFF also terminates the communication connection between the user's network and Dialog, although the user may remain connected to the network for other purposes.

15.2.2 Target

In this mode, entered anytime after database selection, by issuing the TARGET command, Dialog allows the user to enter a "natural-language" query. Actually, it is simply a word list as we have suggested is often the case. The query is converted into a Boolean expression which consists of the query terms, less common words, ORed together. The retrieved set is then ranked according to the number of query terms found. A maximum of 50 records will be placed in the retrieval set. Figure 15.1 is a simple example of such a search, slightly simplified from the original. We may hit RETURN after a search to display results, or customize the display prior to executing it by choosing the customize option. The system will display the current defaults and provide a menu to allow us to modify them. As we can see, the presence of all required terms leads to a high ranking and the first position. The remaining documents, with only one query term in each, are ranked by the occurrence rate of that one term.

The set produced by a target search may be used as any other Dialog set, but it should be remembered that it is limited to 50 documents, and Boolean combinations with other sets will lose any value that the ranking of the documents provides. Also note that the user is not given the exact basis for ranking.

As we can see from the example in Fig. 15.1, this language option can be used by quite inexperienced searchers.

15.2.3 DIALOGweb–A Web Adaptation

The more traditional information retrieval services are now making their database searching facilities available by way of the Web. We can go to the Dialog site, the National Library of Medicine site, or the OCLC site and make use of their sophisticated search engines and authoritative databases. This is not a means to search for other Web sites, but a use of the Web to access services that provide more traditional information retrieval.

Dialog can be reached by telephone and modem, either directly or by commercial data packed network, using the DialogLink software communication package it provides, or by using this same software to establish an Internet connection. World Wide Web access is also available by way of a regular web browser.

?target
Input search terms separated by spaces (e.g., DOG CAT FOOD). You can
enhance your TARGET search with the following options:
  - PHRASES are enclosed in single quotes (e.g., 'DOG FOOD')
  - SYNONYMS are enclosed in parentheses (e.g., (DOG CANINE))
                        [an implied OR between terms]
  - SPELLING variations are indicated with a ? (e.g., DOG? to search DOG,
DOGS, ...)
  - Terms that MUST be present are flagged with an asterisk (e.g., DOG
*FOOD)   [a form of weighting on the term FOOD]
                . . .
?hedge trimming   [This is the query. The phrase is a bit of searcher's
                        jargon.]
Your TARGET search request will retrieve up to 50 of the statistically most
relevant records.
Searching ALL records
...Processing Complete
  Your search retrieved 50 records.

                        [User now asks to see records, showing only three
                        attributes, title, journal, and publication date.]

DIALOG-TARGET RESULTS (arranged by percent RELEVANCE)

------- Item: 1 ----------------------------------
Hedge Trimming and the Resurrection of the Controlled Vocabulary in Online
Searching.
  Online Review; v7 n6 p489-94 Dec 1983
  - Statistical Relevance: 99%
  - Term Frequency: HEDGE - 1 ; TRIMMING - 1

------- Item: 2 ----------------------------------
DIALOG(R)File   1:(c) format only 1998 The Dialog Corporation. All rts.
reserv.
  Carpentry Curriculum Guide. Construction Trades. Michigan Trade and
Industrial Education.
  [1984
  - Statistical Relevance: 32%
  - Term Frequency: HEDGE - 0 ; TRIMMING - 3

------- Item: 3 ----------------------------------
Hedging in Academic Writing: Some Theoretical Problems.
  English for Specific Purposes; v16 n4 p271-87 1997
  - Statistical Relevance: 26%
  - Term Frequency: HEDGE - 2 ; TRIMMING - 0

Figure 15.1
Dialog Target search: this shows the instructions given the user, a sample query (HEDGE TRIM-
MING), and selected portions of some of the records retrieved. The user may specify different
criteria for ranking than for retrieval. Reproduced courtesy of Dialog Corporation.

DIALOGweb offers Internet access to the regular Dialog search system
that allows the interaction just described, but also provides a Guided Search option (DialogWeb, 1998). The first page (Fig. 15.2) is a broad category display.

Guided Search

:::

Guided Search lets you search without Dialog commands. Click a search category and options, then fill out the search form. Guided Search will select the databases and enter commands for you.

Choose a category

- News & Media
- Business & Finance
- Intellectual Property
- Government & Regulations

- Technology
- Energy & Environment
- Medicine
- Pharmaceuticals

- Chemicals
- Food & Agriculture
- Social Sciences
- Reference

Expand Categories

Figure 15.2
Dialog Guided Search—broad category display: this panel shows the initial display of subject categories. Underlined phrases denote links to more detailed displays. We assume the user has selected News & Media, shown in the next figure. Reproduced courtesy of Dialog Corporation.

Clicking on one such category (NEWS & MEDIA in the figure) results in the more detailed display shown in Fig. 15.3. Clicking on a low-level category results in a display of a category-specific search form, that shown here in Fig. 15.4 being one for full text searching in magazines. Searches entered here result in sets of documents whose text can then be displayed. These sets are retained for modification. Fig. 15.5 shows the display summarizing results of the search. The next step would be to display the records.

News & Media

:::

Media Fulltext

- Magazines Fulltext
- Newsletters Fulltext
- Newswires Worldwide
- Press Releases
- World Reporter
- Worldwide News Bundle
  See also:
- Medical Journals Fulltext
- Consumer Reports Fulltext

Newspapers Fulltext

- Newspapers - U.S. & International

More News

- Company News
- Industry & Product News
- People in the News
- Regulatory News

Figure 15.3
Dialog Guided Search—detailed category display for guided search: the category News & Media is expanded to the subcategories shown, and may be yet further subdivided. Again, underlining indicates categories that may be selected for further detail. We assume Magazines Fulltext. Reproduced courtesy of Dialog Corporation.

Magazines Fulltext

Search by Words in Title	[ ]
Search the Entire Text	[electronic commerce]
Search by Magazine	[time]
Search by Author	[ ]
Focus by Year	[1997] ▼ To [1998] ▼
Focus by Exact Date	[Month] ▼ [Date] ▼ [Year] ▼ To [Month] ▼ [Date] ▼ [Year] ▼
	[Search] [Clear]

Figure 15.4
Dialog Guided Search—Magazines Fulltext display: we have now reached the point where the searcher must supply search terms, in this case ELECTRONIC COMMERCE as a subject, to appear anywhere in the text, TIME as the name of the magazine to be searched, and 1997–1998 as the year. Each of the ▼ symbols indicates that a menu of specifics, such as names of month, can be displayed on request. Reproduced courtesy of Dialog Corporation.

15.3

AltaVista

One of the most popular of the World Wide Web search engines, Alta Vista, like Dialog, offers more than one level of command language to suit different users' needs. Provided by Digital Equipment Corporation, now merged

>>>CURRENT1 STARTED
Dialog Response

Search History
Database Details

Set	Term Searched	Items	
S1	(ELECTRONIC(1N)COMMERCE) AND JN="TIME"	7	Display
S2	S1/FULLTEXT	7	Display
S3	RD (unique items)	7	Display
S4	Sort S3/ALL/PD,D	7	Display

Format
[Free] ▼

#Records
[10]

Figure 15.5
Dialog Guided Search—search history display: this search has retrieved seven items which may now be displayed to the user on request. Although the date restriction does not appear in this summary, it has affected the items retrieved. RD is a command to remove duplicates, and SORT puts the retrieved records in descending order by date. Reproduced courtesy of Dialog Corporation.

into Compaq Computer Corporation (www.altavista.com), it provides powerful advanced search capabilities, as well as a characteristic simple search interface.
AltaVista, like most Web search engines, will allowed the entry of only one set
definition to be in use at a time and does not retain the retrieved sets of previous searchers for reference in new queries. But the searcher may edit an existing
query, or re-enter from scratch. As with all retrieval systems, we often want the
ability to retrieve relevant material while suppressing the nonrelevant. On the
Web, unfortunately, we have no way to know which or how many sites are
relevant to any search. Thus, we can never be sure that we have good recall.
However, it is unlikely that a user would want to use the Web to find every site
on a particular subject. To achieve a high recall search, we would need to OR
together a large number of the terms matching those extracted by most search
engines since the use of controlled vocabularies is rare on the Web, and certainly
not consistent across sites when it is present. Most search engines build their index by scanning site pages word by word. Some scan only titles. Hence, the
searcher may have to try a large number of alternative words or spellings, which
risks retrieving a large number of irrelevant documents. Thus the real practical
problem in Web topical search is precision not recall. A review of search engine
capabilities and design may be found in Schwartz (1998).

The classic method of increasing precision is to require that multiple terms
appear in the same document, or in this case, site. This means ANDing terms
together on the assumption that each must be present for relevance to be established. This can be done by using phrases, but this solution will not be available
across the Web. It can also be done at the time of search by using a Boolean AND
operation on sets of sites associated with particular terms in an index. AltaVista
(as we will see in Section 15.3.2), and most other Web search engines, will permit this technique and will explain how to carry it out on an advanced search
syntax page. Increasing precision can be done even more effectively by requiring that words extracted from text appear a certain number of words before or
after one another in the text considered. AltaVista uses the NEAR operator for
this purpose. Traditionally this has been the most effective way of increasing
precision in free text systems. Before reviewing the advanced AltaVista features
we will review the default searching template.

15.3.1 Default Query Entry Form

In its typical entry form the AltaVista engine expects a user to type a word
or phrase or a question in natural language, and then click SEARCH or press the
ENTER key. To *require* that the word appear in all retrieved records, attach a
"+" to the beginning of the word. Otherwise, selection may be based on the
appearance of any of the query words. Negation can be indicated by a "−"

before a term, i.e., this term should *not* appear. An exact phrase may be entered enclosed in quotes, e.g., "EXACT PHRASE" would only retrieve documents in which those two words appear in the indicated positions relative to one another. All entered words will be considered search terms except for those appearing on a stop list.

The use of certain key words followed by a colon identifies attributes of certain HTML tags. This is rather like the use of field qualifiers in traditional IR systems. Here are some examples.

ANCHOR: <TEXT>, where <TEXT> is any word or phrase, will find that text only if it is in the anchor of a hyperlink.

APPLET: <CLASS>, where <CLASS> is any Java applet name, will locate pages using that applet.

DOMAIN: <DOMAINNAME>, where <DOMAINNAME> is the last portion of the URL, e.g., ORG, or COM, will limit a search to pages within that domain.

HOST: <NAME>, where <NAME> is the URL for a specific computer, will limit hit pages to those on that machine.

IMAGE: <FILENAME> will limit searches to pages which have images with a particular file.

LINK: <URLTEXT> will find pages which have links to the specified URL.

TEXT: <TEXT> limits the search to pages where the string in TEXT appears outside of links, URLs, and image tags.

TITLE: <TEXT> requires the text to be in the title tag.

URL: <TEXT> requires the text to be in the URL, in the host name, path, or filename in other words.

The DOMAIN and URL keys allow for searching the Web for sites only a portion of whose complete address or URL is known. The equivalent in telephone directory searching would be to allow searching for anyone living at number 365 of any street, or anyone in a given city and state. These, of course, would only be meaningful if combined with other information. AltaVista also allows limits to pages of a particular language by way of a selection list on the search form.

Use of lower case eliminates case sensitivity. Capitals in a search string are assumed to be required. An asterisk (*) is a multicharacter right-truncation symbol. AltaVista ignores punctuation except to interpret it, along with blank space, as a separator for words. Another typical search engine feature present in AltaVista is a document ranking scheme which will normally select the union of sites with query terms present, and then rank those sites on the basis of the number of such terms in each site's text, as we saw above in Dialog Target.

In other engines this may be a simple term appearance ranking, or in some a complex weighting algorithm may be used.

15.3.2 Advanced Search Form

If there is a need to find documents within a certain range of dates or to do some complex Boolean searching in the vein of the traditional IR system, AltaVista offers advanced search mode. The operators AND (&), OR (|), AND NOT (!), and NEAR (~) are recognized and available for use if the advanced search form is selected for entry. NEAR returns pages with both its arguments present and within 10 words of one another. Two entry fields for date ranges appear on the advanced search variant, in which dates in the form of two-number days, three-letter months, and two-number years, e.g., 21/MAR/96, may be entered to indicate both a starting and stopping date. This range selects upon the last modified dates of pages retrieved.

The Boolean queries are entered in their own search box on the advanced template. In advanced search, no ranking is imposed by AltaVista on retrieved pages unless words are listed in the separate ranking box on the search form which would have been used to enter the search on the regular form. Such words need not appear as Boolean search terms and their presence will be used to organize the display list generated by the Boolean expression in the other box.

Some search engine providers choose to index only the sites they feel are sound. There are over a hundred search engines active, although some consolidation of the players seems likely over time. The striking features of all of them are more problems caused by the database than by the search software. These are the general lack of ability to insure the accuracy and authority of what is found, and, strangely, a possible lack of currency of information in that some sites are updated infrequently if at all. AltaVista, and many others, do not evaluate sites in any way. Table 15.1 shows the results of several variations on a search for the subject INFORMATION RETRIEVAL using both the default and Boolean forms. Also shown are the number of hits for each query and they are listed in descending order of this number.

15.4

Northern Light Technology

One new entity, Northern Light Technology LLC (http://www. northernlight.com/), offers not just Web access through its search engine, but also searching of what it calls special collections. These are papers in a broad set of periodicals, both academic and popular, since 1995. The search results in

Table 15.1

Variations on queries to AltaVista

Query	Result
INFORMATION	'NO MATCHES FOUND'
INFORMATION RETRIEVAL	389,210
RETRIEVAL	389,217
RETRIEVAL OF INFORMATION	389,217
RANKING ALGORITHMS FOR THE	
RECORDS IN INFORMATION RETRIEVAL	978,952
INFORMATION (B)	31,134,183
INFORMATION OR RETRIEVAL (B)	31,227,132
INFORMATION AND RETRIEVAL (B)	360,165
INFORMATION NEAR RETRIEVAL (B)	180,536
"INFORMATION RETRIEVAL"	87,545

Note: These queries were all run on the same day. If repeated on a different day the figures would be different. Those queries without infixes were
sent using the default form. INFORMATION is treated by AltaVista as a common word. If used alone, it reports that no matches were found. If used in
conjunction with RETRIEVAL the result is the same as if RETRIEVAL alone
were used. When used as the sole term in a Boolean query (marked B), we
got over 30 million hits—but not zero. There is a slight difference between
the numbers of hits for RETRIEVAL OF INFORMATION and INFORMA-
TION RETRIEVAL, indicating an inconsistency in treating common words
also produces large numbers of hits. INFORMATION OR RETRIEVAL gets
a large number, but AND and NEAR do better, but even the highly restrictive "INFORMATION RETRIEVAL" presents the searcher with a formidable
browsing task. This is more an indication of the effects of the magnitude of
the World Wide Web than of any problem with AltaVista.

a typical search engine display which links to a bibliographic citation. Northern Light has agreements with the publishers of these journals and will supply
online full text of located papers for a fee. It is thus both a typical Web-based
search engine and a Web-based traditional information retrieval system. Access
of this sort, to carefully constructed collections with some authority, may well
be the future of Web searching for academic research.

15.5

The *Canadian Encyclopedia* and X-Portal™

Encyclopedias present a different search environment than do general purpose IR systems. The major differences in terms of content are volume of material to be searched, the authority or credibility of the text, and the fact that
the database is relatively stable, unlike most IR systems whose databases are in a

constant state of flux. Services such as Dialog, Lexis/Nexis, and MEDLINE deal with databases containing millions of records, while encyclopedias have articles numbered only in the thousands. Unless the searcher is an expert in the field of the search, the authority of the encyclopedia is generally accepted, while on the Web the fact that an article pertains to the query is not sufficient grounds to treat it as authoritative.

We present here a description of one of the search systems available with the *Canadian Encyclopedia* and an extension of the concepts used in that system to a new, full Web-searching IR system.

15.5.1 The Encyclopedia

Encyclopedia searchers are not normally looking for everything on a subject and they know it, while general searchers may be under the delusion that they can find everything or the few most important items. Encyclopedia articles, while written by experts, will not use only technical jargon, but will also include ordinary language as well, considerably simplifying the searcher's problem when searching for unfamiliar material.

One of the search techniques available (*1998 Canadian*, 1998; Kaufman, 1998) is called *smart search*. The user writes a short description of the subject matter of interest. While it is common to write this in correct syntactic English, it is not necessary. The words are not dealt with syntactically, but distance between words does matter. In this way the *smart search* differs from Dialog Target or AltaVista.

When the disc containing a new edition of the encyclopedia is developed, words are conflated or stemmed, word frequencies are counted, and a matrix of word co-occurrences is compiled, showing how often any two words occur together in the same article or sentence. Query words can then be associated with other words using the same root or with other words that often co-occur, even if not used in the query. (See Section 9.5.) This results in what we may call the *enhanced query*.

Next, the words of the enhanced query are individually assigned weights, following the principle of inverse term frequency (Salton and McGill, 1983, p. 63; Section 9.4.2), whereby terms are weighted highly if they occur with high frequency in some articles, but not uniformly so in all articles. The query words, related words that *smart search* has found, and associated weights are available for display to the user, as the *tuner*. In the tuner display, each word is followed by a scale, simply labelled as going from − to +, but which may be interpreted as a weight ranging from 0 to 1. A pointer shows the approximate weight assigned by the system. The user is free to vary any of these by using the mouse to move the pointer in either direction along the scale. When this is completed or the option to modify it is not taken, the search is begun. After a search, the user may return to the starting point and review and possibly modify the tuner.

Associated words are those found as a result of conflation or frequency of co-occurrence.

Another way to form a query is to extract a contiguous segment of text from a retrieved article and use it as the statement of the next query. This, in effect, is saying, "Get me more like this."

Articles are weighted, using a combination of factors. One factor is the frequency of occurrence of enhanced query terms in an article. Another, called the *topology*, considers several aspects of the placement of terms with respect to each other in the article. Roughly put, two terms are deemed to contribute more to the subject matter, hence should have higher weights, if they occur near each other in both the query and the article. Thus, if WORD and FREQUENCY occur in the same sentence, that is deemed more significant than if they were separated by 10 sentences. Finally, the system considers the number of query term types appearing in the article, rather than the number of tokens of terms that appear. To use an extreme example, if an article consisted only of the same word repeated 300 times (i.e., one type but many tokens of this type) and this were a query term it might carry a lower weight than an article in which 8 out of 10 query term types occurred 5 times each, for a total of 40 occurrences.

Once articles are weighted, their titles are displayed in descending order of weight. Upon scanning this list or sampling some of the articles, the user may return to the query and adjust it by adding new terms or deleting others. Altogether, *smart search* makes use of query words, words matching truncated or conflated versions of query words, word frequencies, and word co-occurrence frequencies. It weights them by frequency and proximity. The tuner is recomputed and the search process is repeated.

This procedure makes some demands on a user for time and patience. If these qualities are present, they are amply rewarded because they enable a search to scan a wide range of articles, to present suggestions for new query terms to the user, and to enable the user, by adjusting weights, to sharpen a query. None of these is so easily available in conventional search systems.

Again, this search procedure differs from that used with huge databases because of the stability and manageable size of the database. The result is an opportunity for greater user ability to fine-tune a search than has traditionally been available with other types of retrieval systems.

15.5.2 X-Portal™

This is a new system, brought to market only in late 1998. It is based on the techniques used with the *Canadian Encyclopedia* but offers a user two options.

One is to search any or all of 22 reference works, including, for example, the *Columbia Encyclopedia* and *American Heritage Dictionary*, as well as other almanacs, atlases, etc. The second option is to direct a search to the World Wide Web.

If applied to the Web, X-Portal™ searches its basic set of reference works from which it can find words associated with the user's query words. In a search for the name of the first prime minister of Canada, the system added the words DOMINION and MACDONALD to the query. (John A. MacDonald was the first prime minister of the then Dominion of Canada.) At this point the user can see a synopsis of the subject matter as presented in one or more of the reference works, normally a far more meaningful text than the abstracts given by Web search engines. The search can now be extended by invoking several of the major Web search engines, about which more below. X-Portal takes the top few items from each such search. These will have been ranked by the search engine's own ranking algorithm. The selected items are then ranked by X-Portal's ranking algorithm. The final result is a set of items from a number of sources, produced much faster than if the user had to invoke each search engine separately, and with all retrieved items combined into a single ranked list, improved by the use of associated words in the query.

The list of Web sites to be used for searching is under user control. Some of the most popular are displayed in a menu from which the user can reject any proffered sites and add any of his or her own choosing. The system functions as a gateway to other systems but enhances their utility.

In use, X-Portal offers a solution to some of the most vexing problems of Web searching: the retrieval of far too many documents, lack of positive help in finding helpful search terms other than those used in the query, the difficulty of combining retrieved sets from more than one source, and the time required to search more than one source.

15.6

Summary

After many years of ignoring methods that were developed in research by Salton and others, commercial systems are now using advanced searching methods that allow for use of natural language or something close to it, as well as recognizing specific attributes in a document. Making use of word association techniques enables an IRS to improve an original query. The World Wide Web still suffers from a general lack of record structure, that is, the ability for a search program to recognize an attribute value and select accordingly.

16

Measurement and Evaluation

Basics of Measurement

A *measurement* is a comparison of a quantity with a standard. A traditional example is the meter, originally defined as one ten-millionth of the distance from the equator to the North Pole. For many years the official standard was a metal bar maintained at a controlled temperature and atmospheric pressure at the International Bureau of Weights and Measures in Sèvres, France. The practical definition of a meter was a length equal to the length of this bar. In more modern times the meter was redefined as 1,650,763.73 times the wavelength of one spectral line of an isotope of the element krypton.

A *metric* is a defined quantity or quality that can be measured, but in common usage *measure* may refer to either the metric, the process of determining its value, or the value, itself. A *variable* is an attribute of some entity whose value can vary and whose values may be measures. It may be numeric (length) or alphabetic (name). Length is a metric and is one attribute of a table top, measured by comparing the longer dimension of the table with a meter stick that is close enough to the standard so that any difference is of no importance for the application of the measurement being made. In the measurement of physical objects, the variables or attributes are fairly well known and generally accepted by the scientific and technological communities, although there are still differences in the way the basic set of metrics may be defined. The basic physical quantities are length, time, mass, temperature, electric current, and light intensity (Physical measurement, 1971). All other physical measures can be derived from these. Speed, for example, is length divided by time. Even cost is most often expressed in monetary terms once representative of weight of certain metals.

In information retrieval, as in most human activities, we do not have the equivalents of these physical measures. What measures we may have tend to lack precise definition (measurement of human intelligence, for example) or method of measurement. As we shall see, there is no universally accepted way to measure the relevance of a text to a query (another text). We often measure cost and time of a search, but find that cost of *what* and time of *what* are answered differently by different observers.

The term *evaluation* may mean the same as *measurement* or may be used to refer to a composite metric applicable to a system as a whole, but experimenters often use different definitions or boundaries of the system being evaluated. To speak of evaluation of an information retrieval system is not meaningful without further definition.

We can divide information retrieval measures into three broad categories: *performance, outcome, and environment.* Measures of performance are descriptive of what happens during the use of an information retrieval system. Measures of outcome are descriptive of the results obtained. Environmental measures include information about human users or operators of systems, the systems themselves, and information in the databases being searched. *Evaluation* can be applied to any or all. When we speak of evaluating a system, it is essential to specify what aspects are of interest and to be certain that the meaning of *system* is clearly understood in the particular context.

We must remember that we are discussing information retrieval systems and these are often treated as the purely mechanical components of a system. By analogy, and in full recognition that analogies are not perfect, consider the evaluation of a chisel intended to be used by sculptors. There are certain purely mechanical aspects that can be measured: length of the tool, width of the cutting edge, hardness, and sharpness of the edge. Are these enough to predict performance using the chisel? Do we not need also to evaluate the user? The type of stone to be carved? We can go some part of the way by asking recognized artists their opinions of the chisel and of competing ones as well. We can ask a range of users, from top-flight artists to neophytes, what they think. We *cannot* say that, because this chisel has desirable mechanical properties and performs well in the hands of an expert, it will always generate true art. Evaluation of a tool can only measure potential in general, use by a particular individual, or use by a group of users of known characteristics.

Let us review the major *components* that may be measured or affect measurement of an IRS. Some works covering the subject in greater detail are Boyce *et al.* (1994), Losee (1990), Salton (1989), Tague-Sutcliffe (1995, 1996), and van Rijsbergen (1979). A broader review of system evaluation is found in Harter and Hert (1998).

16.1.1 The Data Manager

Consider the illustrations in Chapter 1. At the heart of an IRS there is a computer program called the *data manager* that searches for records containing precisely specified attribute values or makes equally precisely specified changes in the content or structure of a file. This program does not interpret. Its values are provided by another program which we have called the *query manager*. The data manager does not make errors except through faulty programming or computer malfunction. If asked to find the numbers of those records containing the string abc, it will do so exactly. It is left to another person or program to decide to what extent ABC is an appropriate search term. The performance of the data manager is usually measured in terms of speed of execution and memory space required by the file structures. These combine with usage of other computer components to provide a measure of the cost of use.

16.1.2 The Query Manager

The query manager may perform either or both of two major functions: *query interpretation* of input and *record* or *data evaluation* of output. A query manager used in conjunction with the traditional languages such as those of Dialog or MEDLINE actually does almost no real interpretation and no evaluation. Users specify attributes and values, create sets, and combine them with precise Boolean algebraic statements. But even these interpreters deal with sometimes complex or ambiguous syntax and can on one hand accept commands which do not represent what the user actually intended and on the other hand reject commands that are close to, but not exactly, correct. For example, a Dialog user might type the sequence E S2 AND S3, having struck the E key instead of the nearby S key. This makes it an EXPAND command instead of the intended SELECT. But Dialog will treat this as a valid EXPAND command and search in the inverted file for the string S2 AND S3, a string very unlikely to occur in a record but highly likely to occur in a SELECT statement. On the other hand the statement D 6-TI-1,3 looks reasonable and is unambiguous to the human reader but violates a formal rule and will be rejected. It should have used / instead of -.

Other query managers are required to interpret natural-language expressions and they may do this more or less "well." There are no established criteria for goodness of interpretation. Query managers may decide what to retrieve, evaluate retrieved records in order to rank them, or retrieve related records according to a definition of *related* that is not known to the searcher. Hence, we would like to be able to measure the performance of a query interpreter because it affects the performance of any larger system of which it is a part.

16.1.3 The Query Composition Process

Backing up one step, the query is written by an end user, the person with the information need, or an intermediary who interprets the need. In either case, we can say that the user's information need is translated into a query. This process may be entirely mental, in the mind of the user, or it may be the result of oral or written interaction between the user and an intermediary.

Is this step part of the operation of an information retrieval system? If we do not explicitly include it, then poor performance on the part of the user in understanding his or her information need or in explaining the need to an intermediary, or poor performance on the part of an intermediary in translating the need statement into query language may be attributed to poor performance on the part of the IRS. On the other hand, to include these preliminary processes in an evaluation requires either that we be able to measure the translation process or that we apply an overall measure to the entire translation–retrieval process. In the latter case, we may then be unable to identify the cause of any less than desirable overall system performance.

16.1.4 Deriving the Information Need

Now, back up one more step and recall that an information need exists because of a lack of information on the part of the user in the context of his or her environment. How is that lack of information transformed into a recognized information need? The ASK may be centered on the lack of a cure for AIDS, but a reasonably knowledgeable person knows better than to search a database using the expression CURE FOR AIDS. Since a cure is not known, the information needed by a person doing research on a cure presumably has to do with the nature of the disease, its causes, or its progress in the human body. Again, lack of skill could result in trying to formulate queries based on an inaccurate information need statement. In that case, the outcome of the resulting searches could hardly satisfy the ASK. Drucker (1998) reminds us that the need of management is for conceptual understanding, not mere data. That applies as well to scientists.

16.1.5 The Database

Picture an experiment designed to measure performance of an IRS but in which a laboratory aide is given the wrong database name to use with experimental subjects. This results in virtually no satisfactory outcomes. Is the system at fault? The only way to avoid ascribing poor database "performance" (lack of desired content) to the system is to include the database within the boundaries of the system to be evaluated or to separately verify that the database does have an adequate amount of information on subjects used in an evaluation study. We may have to consider not only content, but structure and scope as well.

In Chapter 1 we discussed the following conditions or steps in database design and production, almost any of which could affect the outcome of a search:

The user's need for information
Translation or expression of the need
Formulation of a search strategy
Formulation of a query
Computer processing of the query
Decision to create a database
Decision on the scope of the collection
Decision on the design of records
Selection of the actual items for inclusion
Creation of the content of individual records
Magnitude of the database
Data entry
Query processing
Data management

Given this number of factors and steps, the question of the system boundaries is a very practical one. Without a careful statement of what these boundaries are, the publication of measures of performance or outcome has little meaning.

16.1.6 Users

We referred to the key role of users in formulating queries. They also play a central role in evaluating outcome by deciding what is relevant to a query or useful and what is not. A key question for anyone undertaking to evaluate a system is whether the user or the intermediary is part of the system being evaluated. If so, then statistical controls must be introduced on the selection of users who participate in an evaluation study and on their contribution to the aspects of the system being evaluated.

16.2

Relevance, Value, and Utility

Central to most attempts to measure information retrieval outcome is the concept of *relevance*. Several meanings of this word are possible (Bookstein, 1979; W. S. Cooper, 1971; Saracevic, 1975; Schamber *et al.*, 1988, 1990; Wilson, 1973; and Froelich, 1994, which is a complete journal issue on the subject) but the two most common cluster around the concepts of *subject relatedness* of a record to a query and *value* or *utility* of a record to a user. Relevance is used to measure the outcome of a search. If each record retrieved in response to a query is evaluated as to its relevance then the resulting set of values becomes the basic data upon which the outcome of the system is based, regardless of what definition of *system* is used.

Actually, the two primary meanings of relevance can be used as almost entirely separate measures. The first gauges the closeness of retrieved documents to queries on the basis of the subject matter or other specified attributes of the record. The second gauges the value or utility of each document to the user who posed the query.

16.2.1   Relevance as Relatedness

The relatedness measure is often applied by someone other than the end user of the information: possibly by the intermediary, if one is used, or by independent judges who are expert in the subject matter of the database and presumably can tell whether documents "should" have been retrieved or not for the query in question. We put the quotation marks around *should* because the determination of whether a document is relevant to a query depends, at least to some extent, on how the person with the information need interprets the question and on that person's prior knowledge of information related to the query. There is no fixed definition of what *should* be retrieved.

An important issue in measuring relatedness is whether two documents can be said to be related, or the extent of their relationship measured, outside the context of a real person's real information need, which is a function of that person's state of mind.

Note also that subject is not the only basis for a search. The concept of relevance as relatedness must be extended to other attributes such as author or corporate source or whatever it is about a record that makes it interesting to the searcher.

16.2.2   Aspects of Value

There are many ways to interpret the value of an item (Hall, 1962). *Market value* is what the item can be exchanged for. *Imputed value* is an expected or anticipated value, but not one actually resulting from market forces. *Intrinsic value* is a personalized sense of value, likely to vary from person to person. Market value is essentially the price of an item sold in the market. Imputed values are used sometimes to set a price of an item never before brought to market. Price is not necessarily determined by cost to produce. Intrinsic value is often seen in lost-and-found advertisements, expressed as, "of great sentimental value."

Database producers place a market value, or price, on their commodities: records. Database distributors or search services place a value on their service: the use of their computers and software. A compact disk distributor markets a combination of records and software. The user of an information retrieval system, even if a reseller of the records, is likely to assign different values than the producer. This person's imputed value may differ from market value. The end user, or buyer of these products and services, is likely to assign an intrinsic value and to have to decide whether the intrinsic value was at least as high as the market value.

We can look at intrinsic value in terms such as *uniqueness, timeliness*, or *veracity*. One reason to pay for information is that it is unique—with this information, only *I* know the race is fixed, or only *I* know how to make this product. A complementary view is to value information to *avoid* being uniquely *un*informed—the only one who does not know the prices are changing next week. Timeliness is relative. It is sometimes not too valuable to know stock prices as of yesterday and they may be useless if more than a few minutes old. Veracity, as a determinant of value, should need no explanation.

It is often said that information is a unique commodity in that, after it is sold, the seller still has it. Stock does not deplete as a result of a sale. In that case, is information subject to the usual market controls of supply and demand? It appears that market value, to some extent, depends on the number of users who hold the information, not on the inventory available to the seller. To be the only holder of certain financial information would be valuable indeed to a securities trader. As other traders acquire the same information, its value decreases, not because the supply decreases but because its uniqueness decreases. An Ontario court once ruled (Potter, 1988) that an attempted theft of an employees' mailing list from an employer was not a crime because the information would be still held by its owner and would still be usable. But, theft of military classified information or industrial trade secrets can be a crime because what is lost is not merely the pages of text, but the uniqueness or limitation on access.

16.2.3 Relevance as Utility

Perhaps the best way to illustrate the difference between relatedness and value in information retrieval is to assume that a query retrieves a highly subject-relevant document with which the searcher is already quite familiar. In terms of relatedness, this document ranks highly. In terms of usefulness to the user, its value is zero because it brings no new information.

Because the relatedness measure cannot assess how well the results of a search actually satisfy a user's need, many people feel that utility is the ultimate measure. Both are useful. First, the difference between an end user's ratings of relevance (based on utility) and an intermediary's (based on subject-relatedness) may be a useful measure of how well the user is able to express the need or how well the intermediary is able to elicit it. Second, relatedness is virtually the only way to measure the performance of a query interpreter program, which cannot "know" what is in the mind of the individual user but can find records related to the query. All that it is reasonable to ask of this program is that it find related documents; it cannot be blamed for the fact that a user may already be familiar with a given record or has unstated additional conditions in mind.

16.2.4 Retaining Two Separate Measures

Rather than try to resolve which of these two (or conceivably more) definitions is "correct," they are best both retained, for they measure different attributes and their usefulness dominates different aspects of the total process of converting an ASK into useful information. Figure 16.1 shows the sequence of transformations from ASK to retrieved records: ASK to information need, need to query, query to search parameters, and search parameters to retrieved records. By our definition of the role of the data manager, the conversion of search parameters into retrieved records requires no evaluation other than those of time and memory use or checking for program errors. The more common

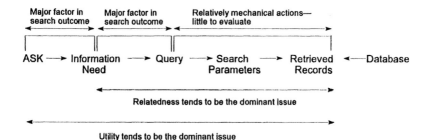

Figure 16.1

Steps from ASK to retrieved records: evaluation may take place over any sequence of these steps. Between the written query and the retrieved records there is little to evaluate, assuming the query interpreter plays no major role. That is, exactly those records specified will be retrieved. If we include the translation from information need to query, and include the database content in our consideration, relatedness is the major factor. If we include the original impetus to ask the question, then utility is likely the major factor.

evaluations of of IR systems consider only the steps between information need statement or query and retrieval of records, and evaluate outcome in terms of subject relatedness of records to what is assumed wanted. To measure utility, the achievement of which is the ultimate purpose of a search, it is necessary to go all the way back to the ASK and consider the reason the search was done.

Relatedness can be said to measure the strength of the relationship between an information need and a retrieved text, under the assumption of the previous paragraph that the query is stated in a language not subject to any significant amount of transformation by the query interpreter. Anyone reasonably knowledgable of the subject matter of the search should be able to render a competent judgment: the user, an intermediary, or a third-party judge. Thus, relatedness tends to be the dominant or most important measure in dealing with the information need-to-retrieved-records portion of the retrieval process. Relatedness can be measured, or approximated, by use of such functions as the cosine coefficient (Section 9.6.1).

Utility, under these assumptions, can be said to measure the relationship between the ASK and the retrieved records. Because the ASK is almost never explicit, for all practical purposes this relationship can only be measured by someone who understands such variables as the user's problem and state of knowledge, resources available, and pressures to perform. There may be no one, including the user if we accept that users may have an imperfect understanding of their own needs, who has all this knowledge. It is certainly rare that an intermediary or third-party judge will have it. Yet, utility is the most important measure in evaluating the complete process from ASK to records.

Relatedness will normally have a higher value than the *utility* measure because in most cases records must be related in order to be valuable. But this is not a law and it ignores the somewhat unexpected effects of browsing (Marchionini, 1995, pp. 102–138). It is not uncommon for a person searching for one item of information to find something valuable but not related to the search at hand, or to find, as a result of the search, that information exists which was not previously known and which changes what the user now wants. Such items are of high value but possibly of low relatedness to the original need or query. We should not consider such findings entirely random. One of the great benefits of searching in an old-fashioned, book-laden library is that once we find ourselves in the general area of the material we are looking for, we often find material we never thought to ask for. One of the risks of database searching is that IRSs do not encourage random browsing. Thus, the user is less likely to retrieve unexpected but valuable information.

The difference between the two types of relevance measure can be used as a measure of effectiveness of translation of the ASK into need and the need into a query. If users are finding related records of little value, this probably indicates that either the ASK has not been effectively converted to an information need statement or that the need has not been effectively converted into a query. Ineffective conversion of an ASK or of a need statement into a query may be caused by the user not making clear what is already known. Using this difference as a metric results in measuring not the IRS but its user.

If the query language is of the type to require interpretation by the query interpreter, as is the case with natural language, then formulation of the query can be considered a two-stage process: the first, writing the natural-language statement (conversion of need into query); the second, converting the query into search parameters. The query interpreter's effectiveness can be evaluated only relative to the input to it. Once again, if the user or user–human-intermediary combination cannot adequately represent the ASK then we can hardly attribute to the query interpreter any responsibility for failure to achieve results of value.

16.2.5 The Relevance Measurement Scale

Regardless of the definition used, relevance is usually measured either on a binary scale—relevant or not relevant—or on a Likert scale (Anderson, Basilevski, and Hun, 1983, pp. 231–287), which involves the assessor picking from among an ordered set of labelled choices descriptive of the relevance, or a value anywhere in the range [0, 1]. The Likert values are typically on an interval scale of two, three, five, or seven points, representing such judgments as NOT RELEVANT, SOMEWHAT RELEVANT, or HIGHLY RELEVANT, or essentially the same values with intermediate points interspersed among them. Tang, Vevea, and Shaw (1999) attempt to identify the optimal size of such a scale and find that evaluator confidence in the scale rises rapidly as number of choices increase from two, but begins to decrease after six. The mean of the number of scale points they observed was 7.5, which conforms nicely with many researchers' preference for a seven-point scale. An overall measure of relevance of a retrieved set is normally the average of the individual document relevance measures.

16.2.6 Taking the Measurements

Most of us know that, for physical measurements, the instruments used must be calibrated and the conditions of use controlled. We know that our body weight varies with time of day and clothing worn and that a variation of several pounds when measuring with someone else's scales may mean nothing because the two instruments are not calibrated in the same way. We know that air temperature measured at an airport 20 miles from a metropolitan area will differ from a similar measurement taken at the same time in the center of the city because of the heat generated by the city. Even in measures of social phenomena we are used to making calibrations and adjustments. A low unemployment rate during the Christmas season is not necessarily a cause for optimism because this is traditionally a period of high employment and the figure must be *seasonally adjusted*. Similarly, there is a need to consider the circumstances under which relevance measures are taken: what instruments (persons or computer programs) are making the measurements, when are the measurements taken, in what context (e.g., what other documents are under consideration at the time), and what definition and scale of relevance are being used. Any system evaluation must take these questions into account, and any report of an evaluation should describe the controls used. Further, some individuals tend to rate everything high and some low. We rarely "calibrate" our judges.

Consider some typical situations in which relevance is measured in retrieval experiments or evaluations.

1. An intermediary, working on behalf of an end user, assesses relevance on the basis of the relatedness of subject or other attributes of retrieved documents and the query. Normally, the intermediary has no basis for assessing the value of the material to the user. The assumption has to be made that the user's goal, at least at this stage of his or her quest for information, is to find related material. Intermediaries typically *do* have experience in making such judgments. The intermediary, as the one who formulated the query, is part of the system that produces the results being evaluated, and is therefore not impartial.

2. An independent assessor looks at the formal statements of information need written in natural language, looks at the retrieved records, and then determines which records *should* have been retrieved, assigning to these a high relevance rating. Sometimes, in experimental environments, these assessors know well what is in the database and can judge how many records should have been retrieved but were not. Independent assessors are usually selected on the basis of their subject matter expertise, so that their judgments of subject relatedness are as reliable as can reasonably be obtained. What they do not consider is the user and the user's state of knowledge. They judge only subject relatedness, not value.

3. The user does the assessing regardless of whether the query and strategy were formulated by the intermediary or the user. Published research reports rarely state which meaning of relevance users are instructed to employ nor do they report if users were asked which meaning they assumed. This means that the impartial observer does not necessarily know what attributes were measured. We tend to assume that end users will assess on the basis of utility unless otherwise directed, but others may feel differently.

16.2.7   Questions about Relevance as a Measure

A number of studies (Eisenberg, 1988; Eisenberg and Barry, 1988; Muzzano, 1997; Tiamiyu and Ajiferuke, 1988) have shown that context affects relevance judgments. Two hypothetical examples illustrate the point. Assume a query on a subject retrieves a single record which the user rates rather high, say 5 or 6 on a scale of 7. The user then revises the query and retrieves a set of 10 records, including once again the original one. Several of the new records are of much greater perceived value than the original. Will the user now give the same or a lower value to the original record? Probably lower. On the other hand, suppose a query yields 10 records, none of which are rated high. More searching finds nothing as good as the original 10. Will they achieve a higher rating in the user's mind, now that they appear to be the best possible? If the relevance assessments are made a year after the original query was posed, the user may have learned much about the subject and much new material may have been published. Will the ratings of a year ago remain constant? Should they?

Here are some excerpts of the opinion of Don Swanson (1988) on the subject. (Although we agree with the opinions expressed, they remain *opinion*.)

> An information need cannot be fully expressed as a search request that is independent of... pre-supposition of context—context that itself is impossible to describe fully, for it includes among other things the requester's own background of knowledge.

> A document cannot be considered relevant to an information need independently of all other documents that the requester may take into account.

> It is never possible to verify whether all documents relevant to any request have been found. . . .

The last sentence of this quote may not be true in the case of small, experimental databases, but it is surely true in the case of today's megarecord databases. Other studies on this topic include Barry (1997) and Barry and Schamber (1998).

16.3
Measures Based on Relevance

Relevance, by any definition, has the merit of appearing to be the most important concept in assessing the outcome of an information retrieval operation. In most actual evaluations it is used as the basis for three composite measures, two commonly and one rarely used. They are *precision*, *recall*, and *efficiency* or *effectiveness*. The formal definitions are due to Kent, Berry, Leuhrs, and

	Relevant	Not Relevant
Retrieved	a	b
Not Retrieved	c	d

Figure 16.2
Partitioning of a database according to segments retrieved or not and relevant or not: segment *a* represents records both retrieved and relevant, *c* those relevant but not retrieved.

Perry (1955) based on our ability to partition the entire database into relevant and irrelevant records and into retrieved and not retrieved records, according to the scheme shown in Fig. 16.2, due to Swets (1969).

16.3.1 Precision (*P*)

Precision measures the ratio of relevant to total material retrieved by a query or set of queries. Its inverse or complement (result of subtraction from 1) is a measure of the amount of work left to be done to extract only relevant records from the last set retrieved. A high value of *P* means little work left; a low value implies much work still to be done.

Precision or the *precision ratio* is defined as the ratio of number of relevant records retrieved to total number of records retrieved, or

$$P = \frac{a}{a+b} = \frac{|Ret \cap Rel|}{|Ret|}, \tag{16.1}$$

where *Ret* is the set of retrieved records and *Rel* the set of relevant records and | | indicates the number of elements in a set.

This form of the definition, (16.1) is based on the binary scale of relevance measurement. If an interval scale is used then each record has a score S_i ranging from zero to the maximum scale value S_{max}. Thus, the form is

$$P = \sum_{i=1}^{a+b} \frac{S_i}{(a+b)S_{max}}. \tag{16.2}$$

The numerator in (16.2) is the sum of the scores of retrieved records (whereas *a* is the count) and the denominator is the maximum possible total score, over all records retrieved.

Precision is calculated from relevance which is, in turn, typically measured by asking the user, intermediary, or third-party judge to assess the relevance of each record retrieved after a search. Mechanically, it is relatively easy to do, normally requiring only a paper form or computer-asked question and demanding little of the observer's time, especially if the assessor is the intermediary or end user, who would presumably be reading the records in any case.

16.3.2   Recall (R)

This metric is the ratio of the number of relevant records retrieved to the number of relevant records present in the file. A high value implies that nearly all relevant records were found by the query. A low value means that a large proportion of relevant records were not retrieved. The formal definition of *recall* or the *recall ratio* is the ratio of number of relevant records retrieved to number of relevant records in the file:

$$R = \frac{a}{a + c} = \frac{|Ret \cap Rel|}{|Rel|} \tag{16.3}$$

and the form for a nonbinary scale is

$$R = \sum_{i=1}^{a+c} \frac{RL_i}{(a + c)S_{\max}}, \tag{16.4}$$

where RL_i is the relevance of record i. Computation of recall is an entirely different matter from computing P. The end user or intermediary cannot *know* what relevant records were not retrieved, as Swanson pointed out. An extra effort must be made by an assessor to approximate what the intermediation–query process did not find. One method of doing this is to work with the final version of a query and systematically work to broaden it by such means as converting Boolean ANDs to ORs, truncating terms or moving up within hierarchical classification structures. Then the records retrieved by the broadened query must be evaluated, ideally by the same end user or intermediary originally involved. An alternative approach is to use the database expert, someone who either knows the contents of the database well (possible with small, experimental databases, impractical with million-record databases) and can judge from memory or from his or her own queries the totality of what might have been recovered.

16.3.3   Relationship of *Recall* and *Precision*

Experimental work (Cleverdon and Keen, 1966) shows that there tends to be a relationship between values of P and R. Usually, when a query has been

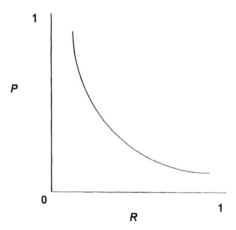

Figure 16.3

Typical relationship between precision and recall: if we have a low value of recall, the usual solution is to broaden the search, which typically results in a lower value of precision. Similarly, if precision is low, a more restrictive query is called for, which would decrease recall.

processed and results obtained, the query can then be modified in such a way as to improve either recall or precision, but each at the expense of the other. Or, if we measure R and P over a number of results of different queries we would see that high P implies low R and vice versa, more or less as shown in Fig. 16.3.

This relationship, which is mentioned frequently in the information retrieval literature, can be misleading. *Neither R nor P depends on the other, although it appears from the graph that P depends on R. Actually, they are jointly dependent on how the retrieval was carried out and the relevance values assigned.*

Such a relationship seems to say that it is not possible to get both high P and high R. Yet that may be a goal of the searcher and it may be obtainable. Certainly, if we were to compare results from two groups of searchers, one highly skilled and one much less so, we would expect the highly skilled group to be able to do better on both measures than the less skilled ones, the differences perhaps showing up as in Fig. 16.4. The highest skilled group should be able to get both higher precision and higher recall than those of lesser skills.

Here again we stress the importance of specifying the boundaries of the system before taking and using the measures. If searcher skill is included as a variable, then we might still see a form of the inverse relationship between P and R but the value ranges of both may be broader.

It would seem desirable to have a single measure of merit that indicates the extent to which all relevant and only relevant records were retrieved. Or, this could be considered a metric of the ability of a system, however defined, to

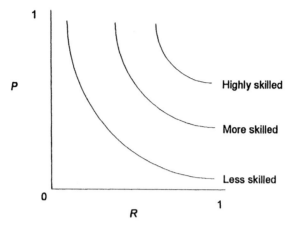

Figure 16.4

Relationship between precision, recall and user skill: while there may be an inverse relationship between precision and recall, the values of these variables may both depend heavily on such factors as the skill of the user. A highly skilled person may be able to achieve high values of both P and R.

convert input (the information need statement) into the theoretical optimum output. One form of a theoretical optimum would be ($P = 1$, $R = 1$). Another could be P and R goals set by a user. Yet another might be separate P and R values based, respectively, on relatedness and utility. Then a measure of comparison of such a goal with actual accomplishment might be taken as a measure of the *effectiveness* or *efficiency* of this overall system.

16.3.4   Overall Effectiveness Measures Based on R and P

Recall and precision are the most commonly used measures for evaluation of overall retrieval outcome. To what extent do they represent outcome from the point of view of a user or of a person or organization paying for system use? Regrettably, end users rarely state their goals in R–P terms and, we suspect, most are unable or unwilling to do so, probably from insufficient training in information retrieval to understand what the measures mean to them. At the conclusion of a sequence of iterations of a search, resulting in certain R and P values, it should always be possible to do one more iteration, if necessary selecting only relevant records, from the best set so far retrieved, by using known titles or accession numbers, to arrive at a value of $P = 1$. Hence, precision may be nothing more than a measure of how important a searcher feels it is to achieve an all-relevant result, or to reduce the amount of work left to be done to zero.

There have been several composite measures proposed (by Heine, 1973; by Meadow, 1973, p. 165; and by Vickery, described in van Rijsbergen, 1979, p. 175) all based on the assumption that the ideal outcome of a search or series of searches is a recall and a precision value of 1.0—retrieval of all relevant records and only relevant records.

Three such measures are

$$Eff_1 = 1 - \frac{\sqrt{((1-P)^2 + (1-R^2))}}{\sqrt{2}} \qquad \text{(Meadow)}, \qquad (16.5)$$

$$Eff_{2,s} = 1 - \frac{1}{1/P_s + 1/R_s - 1} \qquad \text{(Heine)}, \qquad (16.6)$$

$$Eff_3 = 1 - \frac{1}{2/P + 2/R - 3} \qquad \text{(Vickery)}. \qquad (16.7)$$

In each case P and R are in the range $[0, 1]$ and the resulting measure also ranges from 0 to 1. In Heine's measure, R_s and P_s are recall and precision for a single search, s. Then $Eff_{2,s}$ measures the outcome of a single search. Eff_1 and Eff_3 were intended to represent the average performance of an IRS over a number of searches, hence the P and R values are *averages* over all these searches.

Tiamiyu and Ajiferuke (1988) pointed out that "the relevance of a document is a function of both its own informational merit as well as the context created by the other documents seen and evaluated by the user..." which is consistent with Swanson (Section 16.2.7). They went on to state that "the effect... any document can have on the total relevance function [of a set] is either to increase it or leave it unchanged." This supports their contention that a measure of overall result is needed, rather than one that summarizes a set of individual record measures, as if independent of each other. Eisenberg (1988) and others have shown that the order of presentation of records affects the judgment of relevance by the user.

Let us again resort to a hypothetical situation in a further attempt to explore the usefulness of the measure.

Suppose a newspaper reporter is interested in writing an article on the effects of acid rain on the production of maple sugar. A query to an agricultural, environmental, or energy database might yield 5000 hits. Such a user might have said, at the outset, that he was interested in everything on the subject, never realizing how many items that could lead to. A little browsing might indicate that all the items were subject-relevant to the expressed need—a discouraging prospect. If he is able, the user will modify the search, now perhaps realizing that a numeric goal, the number he is willing to read, is in order. Suppose further that the set is finally reduced to 10 and that only 3 of them are really useful, but that, on careful consideration, it appears that they will provide all the information needed.

After the second cycle, the user has a value for a (retrieved, relevant) of 3, for b (relevant, not retrieved) of 7, and for c (relevant, not retrieved this time) of 5000. (Or, $|Ret| = 10$, $|Rel| = 5000$, $|Ret \cap Rel| = 3$.) P has the value 0.3, and R is $3/5000$, or 0.0006. Has this been a good search? Has the retrieval system, however defined, performed well? By the usual standards of published works on retrieval system performance, these scores have to be considered poor, even very poor. But the user who, in a few minutes, finds three articles that will enable him to complete his own work may be ecstatically happy.

Suppose the 3 good records out of 10 had instead been 3 out of 100 or even 3 out of 1000. More work would be required of the user and his evaluation of the system might well have been much lower, even if the same records were ultimately the ones retrieved. On the other hand, with one more iteration of the search, the 3-out-of-10 version could presumably have been made into a 3-out-of-3 search, with perfect precision. The situation seems muddled at best. For this reason, some research workers feel that the best way to evaluate is to ask the user for an overall evaluation, not a record-by-record evaluation. Possibly, the community in which the user works might be asked to evaluate that person's performance, although the practical difficulties of this should be obvious. Doyle (1963) pointed out that "the 'most relevant subset' is not only an individual matter for the searcher, dependent on time and circumstances of his searching foray, but also that the feedback he gets is quite capable of changing his idea of what he wants as well as changing his way of expression."

Katzer (1998) points out that, when storage and communication were expensive, retrieval services catered to the needs of people who needed correct answers, and assumed such existed. Today, retrieval systems serve populations who work in fields in which it is recognized that there is no "right" answer, or are required to provide citations whether or not actually used (certain students), or simply emphasize ease of acquisition. For such people, it may not matter if the best citations are found (even if they exist) or, if it does matter, there is usually an opportunity to remedy the situation later, frequently the case in management.

This raises the question of whether it is the purpose of an IRS to retrieve information relevant to an information need or to find those documents that satisfy the criteria that were requested, what was literally stated in the query. This, in turn, emphasizes the importance of the prequery work to define the need, develop a strategy, and formulate the query and also emphasizes the distinction between the IRS and the complete system consisting of user, intermediary, database, *and* IRS.

We can only conclude that we have yet to develop a satisfactory measure of the outcome of the performance of an information retrieval system and, in fact, yet to develop a definition of what we mean by satisfactory performance. The measures discussed so far and to be discussed below are still of some interest. Suggesting that some be treated with skepticism does not mean suggesting they never be used.

16.4
Measures of Process

While precision and recall are the most-used measures of retrieval systems, there are others. One set of them measures various aspects of the manner in which the process is carried out, without consideration of how the outcome is judged. While these do not combine readily into a single measure of merit for the overall system, individually they can provide useful insights to system or user performance (Boyce *et al.*, 1994; Fenichel, 1981; Fidel, 1987; Harter, 1986; Wang and Meadow, 1991). In some cases they are difficult to quantify but can be useful even if described only qualitatively. The main use of such measures has been to classify users, to be able to state that people with certain characteristics, such as experience or discipline speciality, tend to perform in certain ways. A related use would be to characterize the current user of a system as an aid for the program to know how to respond, for example, to treat the user as a novice or as an experienced searcher.

16.4.1 Query Translation

If the user's statement of need is translated into a query by an intermediary, or if the programmed query interpreter determines the logic, form, or selection of terms to be used as search parameters, or if the record evaluator ranks the outcome, how well is this done? This might be measured on a Likert scale by showing the user the translated version of his or her need statement and asking for a rating of the translation. Saracevic and Kantor (1988) and Jansen, Spink, Bateman, and Saracevic (1998) have done some investigation of measurement of questions.

16.4.2 Errors in a Query Statement

Here we mean actual, detectable errors of spelling, syntax, or other usage which would cause a command to be rejected by an IRS or lead to a null or irrelevant set (Fenichel, 1981; Penniman and Dominick, 1980; Yuan, 1997). Since errors made are not necessarily errors retained (the user can re-enter correctly) this should be used with caution, but it can be helpful especially in designing error messages, training materials, and help systems.

16.4.3 Average Time per Command or per User Decision

This measure can be used to assess users, for example, to distinguish between experienced and inexperienced users, but also to identify problem areas in human–computer communication. If there is a question or menu that seems to take an inordinate amount of time for most users to deal with, this is more an indication of poor system design than of poor user performance (Yuan, 1997). This attribute is measuring decisiveness or knowledge of the system in use, or both. There have been studies (Fenichel, 1981) in which such variables have shown no significant difference between experienced and inexperienced users, contrary to intuition, but this may be because the tasks were not difficult enough to bring out the differences.

16.4.4 Elapsed Time of a Search

Once again, we would expect experienced users to perform searches more quickly than inexperienced users. But this measure can be confounded with system response speed and with the difficulty of the problem at hand.

16.4.5 Number of Commands or Steps in a Search

This variable is not independent of the previous ones. If we know the number of commands used and their average time, we know elapsed time. Which combination to use depends on ease and means by which data are collected. Differences have been noticed in what might be termed institutional style, say where a library might require its employees to use simple forms of queries to keep costs down.

16.4.6 Cost of a Search

Given any metric of outcome, it is usually desirable to consider how much it costs to achieve a given value of that measure. Direct cost, the price of a search, is among the easiest of the variables to compute because it is normally given to the user by the search service. Indirect costs include the time of the intermediary which can be measured by the elapsed time attribute, but there are also costs of training, equipment purchase, maintenance, diversion of personnel from other tasks, etc. Vickery (1961) pointed out that "C. W. Cleverdon has urged that 'the only practicable method of comparing various systems is on the basis of their economic efficiency.... [T]he important matter is to find which system will give the required level of efficiency at the lowest cost.'"

16.4.7 Size of Final Set Formed

This is a rather weak measure, but there is some evidence and much thinking that set size is used by some searchers as a criterion to decide when to end a search. Users intuitively feel that an appropriately small but nonzero set size is right. This logic has some validity. If a set has 5000 records, the searcher is unlikely to want them all; hence a change in query formulation is necessary. It is the converse of this that can delude the searcher—the assumption that a "good" size implies a good outcome. Set size might be more useful if combined with other measures, for example, the time it took to reach an acceptable set size acceptable to the user.

Blair (1980) defined a user's *futility point* as "the number of retrieved documents the inquirer would be willing to *begin* browsing through." Note that this is a document count, not a ratio such as P or $1 - P$. Bates (1984) pointed out both the fallacy of assuming that there exists a set of just the "right" size for any search and, conversely, that a set of the "right" size is the right set.

16.4.8 Number of Records Reviewed by the User

This is another measure that is more descriptive of the user than of the system. It can detect a user who (1) is too impatient to sample enough records upon which to base a decision on how to modify the search, (2) is unwilling to sample any records until he or she is able to make the set size small enough to permit reading *all* of them, or (3) will sample too many, wasting money with no real increase in useful information.

16.4.9 Patterns of Language Use

There is a family of as yet incompletely developed measures of how a given user or group of like users employ the language of an IRS, whether command language, response to menus, or natural language. Examples of measures are:

The *relative frequency of usage of various commands, words, or options*—in any language, users will rarely use *all* the symbols available. Which ones are used? By what kinds of searchers? With what relative frequency?

The *relative frequency of sequences of commands*—this is the equivalent to looking for common sequences of words in natural language. Such sequences, with their associated probabilities of occurrence, can provide insight to a user's understanding of a system and can enable designers to create or modify commands and syntax to meet user behavior patterns. As a simple example, if most users display from the most recently created set, it might be of benefit to use this set number as a default in a display command.

Measures of the frequency distributions—most of us learn to characterize a set of data according to its mean, median, or standard deviation. But we have no collected data on command frequency distribution which would provide a quick basis for comparison between distributions.

Use of command and command sequence frequencies has enabled researchers to distinguish between groups of users, hence to give some insight into their performance. Measurement of the distribution treated as a whole was pioneered much earlier but never widely used in information retrieval studies.

Tables 16.1 and 16.2 show some examples of possible use of frequency distribution data. M. D. Cooper (1983) studied the use of the MEDLINE database by a group of trained searchers and compiled a frequency distribution (Table 16.1) for occurrences of individual commands by these searchers. This shows the number of times various commands were used, grouped by command type. Table 16.2 shows the same data in inverse frequency order. By itself, such a distribution shows primarily what was *not* used, but it can be used to compare with similar data to indicate differences in command usage by different groups, perhaps differentiated by type of training or length of experience.

Penniman (1975a, 1975b) and Chapman (1981) have used not only individual command frequencies, but the relative frequencies of occurrence of *strings of commands* to differentiate the performance of different user groups. Again, the main value of such data may be to help system designers or instructors understand how people actually use the system or to detect differences in the way that different groups use the system.

Zipf and others (Mandelbrot, 1953; Meadow *et al.*, 1993; Zipf, 1949) have introduced parameters of the frequency distribution of a sample of words in a text, or commands in a search, to characterize the overall behavior, rather than simply distinguish between them. Briefly, if a frequency distribution of commands is put in frequency order, i.e., most frequent first, down to least

Table 16.1

Cooper's command frequency data for MEDLINE: Commands are listed in the left-hand column in approximately the order in which types of commands are used. Administrative commands are grouped at the end. These may occur anywhere.

Command type	Frequency	Description
LOGIN	6759	Begin search
FILE	6304	Select database (= Dialog BEGIN)
NEIGHBOR	432	Inverted file search (= Dialog EXPAND)
TREE	112	Show portion of subject heading tree (occurs in Dialog EXPAND)
SEARCH STMT	93123	Form set, no explicit command required. (= Dialog SELECT)
SENSEARCH	103	Form of proximity search
STRINGSEARCH	225	Form set, using CONTAIN (no Dialog equivalent)
TITLESEARCH	6301	Search for a word in title (Dialog uses TI suffix)
MESHNO	14	Search for a Med. Subject Heading
SUBHEADS APPLY	505	Specialized command related to subject headings
PRINT	36069	Display search results (Dialog TYPE or DISPLAY
Disconnect	3671	Not a command, automatically invoked LOGOFF
STOP	6236	Terminate a search session (= Dialog LOGOFF)
EXPLAIN	59	Elaborate last message
NEWS	380	Asks for administrative news of system
HELP	7	Asks for information about system
OFFSEARCH	1806	Asks to perform this search offline (later, saving charges)
TIME	340	Asks for time used so far
USERS	94	Asks for number of users currently online

frequent, and a rank is assigned to each command, then the relationship between rank and frequency is

$$f = k(r + m)^b. \tag{16.8}$$

If we use the logarithms of f and r, the resulting curve is usually nearly a straight

Table 16.2

Cooper's command frequency data in frequency order:
The data of Figure 16.5a are shown in descending order
of frequency of occurrence

Command type	Frequency
SEARCH STMT	93123
PRINT	36069
LOGIN	6759
FILE	6304
TITLESEARCH	6301
STOP	6236
DISCONNECT	3671
OFFSEARCH	1806
SUBHEADS APPLY	505
NEIGHBOR	432
NEWS	380
TIME	340
STRINGSEARCH	225
TREE	112
SENSEARCH	103
USERS	94
EXPLAIN	59
MESHNO	14
HELP	7

line (Fig. 16.5), where b measures its slope (always negative) and m the extent to which the actual distribution deviates from a straight line. Earlier, in Fig. 9.1, we showed an example of this relationship for a specific, rather small document. Not enough work has been done as this is written to be sure how useful these parameters may be for information retrieval.

16.5
Measures of Outcome

In a sense, the ultimate test of a retrieval system is its ability to produce desired *outcome*, or the extent to which the user is satisfied with the results. What the user does as a result of use of the system is unfortunately nearly impossible to measure. Perhaps the highest measure we might strive for is to assess the performance of an organization based on its employees' use of a retrieval service, but there is no known, reliable way to do this.

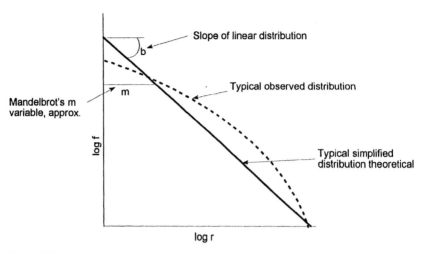

Figure 16.5

Geometry of the Zipf-Mandlebrot distribution—this shows the typical curve resulting from plotting the frequency of occurrence of words against their rank, both in logarithmic form. The heavy line represents Zipf's Law, $f = kr^{-1}$. The dashed line is closer to actual observations made on large English language texts. Mandlebrot's function, $f = k(r + m)^{-b}$, fits the observations better. In this case, b is the slope of the fitted line and m is approximately the value of the rank at which the observed and computed values cross.

Because we have so little to base a metric on, in spite of its importance, outcome measurement has been largely limited to variations on relevance measurement. This can be done by asking users to rate the overall outcome, or to rate individual records then use the average value. The measures used are *precision, recall, efficiency,* and *overall user evaluation.*

An alternative to direct user assessment of relevance is to use the user's action upon retrieval, or opinions of others. A user's willingness to order a copy of a document referred to in a retrieved record, or to print it offline or download it, is reasonably good direct evidence of valuation. Hence a high weight can be assigned any document ordered in full text, possibly a lesser value for any ordered printed offline, and a lower weight if a record was viewed but not ordered in any fashion. Since there may be other sources for documents than ordering through the retrieval system the validity of this form of measure is questionable, although mechanically easily obtained.

Another alternative, for bibliographic or law databases, is to use the opinions of others in a field, as represented by the number of citations to any given item. This can be ascertained by reference to another file, such as the *Science Citation Index, Social Science Citation Index,* or any of a host of legal citation journals.

Variations include checking for citations to the author—evaluating the author instead of the specific work. (See Chapter 12 on mapping.)

However relevance is measured or calculated, the following are variations in how such information may be used.

16.5.1 Precision

Defined in Section 16.3.1, precision is often used as one of the two principal measures of outcome.

16.5.2 Recall

The second of the most frequently used measures of outcome is recall, defined in Section 16.3.2.

16.5.3 Efficiency

As defined in Section 16.3.4 efficiency is not commonly used (Yannakoudakis, Ayres, and Huggil, 1990), but should be capable of conveying more information than do precision and recall, taken separately, because it recognizes that precision and recall are interdependent and it measures the extent to which a set of recall–precision values differ from their combined maximum achievable values.

16.5.4 Overall User Evaluation

In our opinion, this is the most useful of the current measures if the objective is overall assessment of an information retrieval process. It can be recorded by asking individual users to evaluate outcome immediately following a retrieval task, or it can be recorded by using the *focus group* method of inviting a group of representative users to discuss their experiences with a system. Such an approach does not yield statistical results but can yield deep insights to user reactions, ultimately perhaps what system designers and operational managers most need.

Regretfully, too much reliance on user opinion may cause the evaluation to be biased by factors not directly related to the IRS—anything that affects the user's state of mind at the time of search and evaluation. These factors may include job pressure to get the "right" answer (which could mean either get the "true" answer or the answer the organization has already committed itself to), time or cost constraints, or frustration or embarrassment at not knowing how to use the IRS well.

16.6
Measures of Environment

As with almost any measurements involving humans, it is necessary to consider the environment in which tasks are carried out and measurements taken. There is, for example, the motivation of persons performing searches. Are they students required to do this as part of a class? Volunteers recruited to do a few searches in return for a payment? Serious researchers looking for information important to their work? It matters. How knowledgeable are they in the subject field? Are they high school students searching a point of law? Lawyers preparing a case for appeal? Are we using the best database for the testing involved? Do the persons doing the searching understand exactly what is being asked of them? Do all the persons who will be asked to make judgments tend to use the evaluations scales the same way; that is, do they show the same mean and standard deviation of judgments rendered?

These kinds of questions are often difficult to answer. Simply trying to assure that all persons participating in a controlled test of user performance have the same or similar degrees of motivation to succeed can affect the outcome of an experiment. But any experimenter should consider them.

16.6.1 Database Record Selection

How many records are in the database? What is the overlap in coverage with other, related databases? Low overlap with possibly related databases indicates uniqueness of content and suggests, but does not prove, high potential value. What known records are missing? What information, even if not explicitly identifiable as records that should have been present, seems to be missing? That is, even if we cannot identify actual records that should be in the database, a searcher may find no coverage of certain expected subjects or other attributes (Boyce *et al.*, 1994, pp. 156–163; Fidel, 1987, pp. 33–33).

16.6.2 Record Content

What attributes have been selected by the database producer to describe the entity that is the subject of the record? How accurate, reliable, or timely are they?

16.6.3 Measures of Users

There is a large and growing literature on users and their characteristics, behavior, or performance in using information retrieval systems, but since our emphasis is on the operation of the systems, we shall limit our comments on user measurements.

Typically, when research has been done on users there are two classes of variables: user characteristics and performance measures. User characteristics have included measures such as age, gender, major field of study, language spoken, experience in various aspects of computing or librarianship, and their mental models of retrieval systems. Also, as noted above, it would help to consider motivation of those asked to make judgments and their use of measurement scales as approaches to calibration of the measuring instruments. Are they grade escalators? Hard markers?

Performance measures have included elapsed time to complete a task, rate of issuance of commands, number of errors made, recall and precision ratios of a retrieved set, and number of records retrieved that were also retrieved by a control group. See, for example, Boyce *et al.* (1994) and Dillon (1997), the latter a complete issue of a journal on the subject.

16.7

Conclusion

The measurement of the information retrieval process is a relatively new undertaking. Our approach has been to point out that it includes not merely a measurement of a machine's activity, what we call the IRS, but also of human behavior in searching, assisting others to search, and in creating a database. The machine side is easy and meaningful to measure—time, cost, even precision and recall if taken as measures of the IRS—but the human side has remained elusive. It is perhaps well to remember that information retrieval is a *human* activity that will not easily yield its mysteries to simplified, machine-oriented measurement.

We conclude with the words of Lauren Doyle (1963), written over 30 years ago. "[I]n the long run, for the best satisfaction of the searcher, as well as for the satisfaction of all concerned, we must also study the human side of the interface, and study especially both sides of the interaction. . . . 'Relevance' will serve its purpose, but will decline as the realization slowly comes that an individual's information need is so complex that it cannot be accurately stated in a simple request."

Bibliography

The 1998 Canadian & World Encyclopedia. (1998). McClelland & Stewart, Toronto.

AECMA Simplified English. (1995). (AECMA Document PSC-85-16598). Association européenne des constructeurs de matériel aérospatial, Brussels.

Anderson, A. B., Basilevsky, A., and Hun, D. P. J. (1983). Measurement theory and techniques. In *Handbook of Survey Research* (P. H. Ro *et al.* eds), pp. 231–287. Academic Press, San Diego.

"Andy Capp" (1989). *Toronto Star*, 26 September 1989. (Quotation reprinted with special permission of North American Syndicate, Inc.)

Angione, P. V. (1975). On the equivalence of Boolean and weighted searching based on the convertibility of query forms. *Journal of the American Society for Information Science* **26**(2), 112–124.

Auleta, K. (1998). The last sure thing. *The New Yorker* **LXXIV**(34), 9 Nov. 40–47.

Auster, E. (1990). *The Online Searcher*. Neal-Schuman, New York.

Bagley, P. R. (1951). Electronic digital machines for high-speed information searching. Thesis presented to Department of Electrical Engineering, MIT.

Bar Hillel, Y. (1959). The mechanization of literature searching. In *National Physical Laboratory: Proceedings of a Symposium on the Mechanisation of Thought Processes*, pp. 791–807. H. M. S. Stationery Office, London.

Barlow, H., and Morgenstern, S. (1976). *A Dictionary of Opera and Song Themes* (rev. ed.). Crown, New York.

Barry, C. L. (1994). User defined relevance criteria: An exploratory study. *Journal of the American Society for Information Science* **45**(3), 149–159.

Barry, C. L. (1997). A preliminary examination of clues to relevance and criteria within document representation. In *Proceedings of the American Society for Information Science 56th Annual Meeting* (S. Bonzi, ed.), pp. 81–87. Learned Information, Medford, NJ.

Barry, C. L., and Schamber, L. (1998). Users' criteria for relevance evaluation: A cross-situational comparison. *Information Processing and Management* **34**(2/3), 219–236.

Bates, M. J. (1979). Information search. *Journal of the American Society for Information Science* **30**(4), 205–214.

Bates, M. J. (1984). The fallacy of the perfect thirty item online search. *RQ* **24**(1)4, 43–50.

Bates, M. J. (1989). The design of browsing and berrypicking techniques for the online search interface. *Online Review* **13**(5), 407–424.

Batory, D. S., and Gotlieb, C. C. (1982). A unifying model of physical databases. *Association for Computing Machinery Transactions on Database Systems* **8**(2), 509–539.

Becker, J., and Hayes, R. M. (1963). *Information Storage and Retrieval: Tools, Elements, Theories*. Wiley, New York.

Belkin, N. J. (1980). Anomalous states of knowledge as a basis for information retrieval. *Canadian Journal of Information Science* **5**, 133–143.

Belkin, N. J., and Robertson, S. E. (1976). Information science and the phenomenon of information. *Journal of the American Society for Information Science* **27**(4), 197–204.

Benson, J. A., and Weinberg, B. H. (1988). *Gateway Software and Natural Language Interfaces: Options for Online Searching*. Pierian Press, Ann Arbor.

Berners-Lee, T. (1996). WWW: Past, present and future. *Computer* **29**(10), 69–77.

Blair, D. C. (1980). Searching biases in large interactive document retrieval systems. *Journal of the American Society for Information Science* **31**(4), 271–277.

Blair, D. C. (1990). *Language and Representation in Information Retrieval*. Elsevier Science, Amsterdam/New York.

Blair, D. C., and Maron, M. E. (1985). An evaluation of retrieval effectiveness for a full-text document retrieval system. *Communications of the Association for Computing Machinery* **28**(3), 280–299.

Bollmann-Sdora, P., and Raghavan, V. V. (1993). On the delusiveness of adopting a common space for modeling IR objects: Are queries documents? *Journal of the American Society for Information Science* **44**(10) December, 579–587.

Bonner, R. E. (1964). On some clustering techniques. *IBM Journal of Research* 22–32.

Bookstein, A. (1979). Relevance. *Journal of the American Society for Information Science* **30**(5), 269–273.

Bookstein, A. (1983). Outline of a general probabilistic retrieval model. *Journal of Documentation* **39**(2), 63–72.

Bookstein, A. (1985). Probability and fuzzy set applications to information retrieval. In *Annual Review of Information Science and Technology* (M. E. Williams, ed.), Vol. 20. Knowledge Industry Publications, White Plains, NY.

Boole, G. (1854). *An Investigation of the Laws of Thought*. Macmillan, London. (Reprinted by Dover, NY, in 1958.)

Bourne, C. P. (1963). *Methods of Information Handling*. Wiley, New York.

Boyce, B. R., and Kraft, D. H. (1985). Principles and theories in information science. In *Annual Review of Information Science and Technology* (M. E. Williams, ed.), Vol. 20, pp. 153–178. Knowledge Industry Publications, White Plains, NY.

Boyce, B. R., Meadow, C.T., and Kraft, D. H. (1994). *Measurement in Information Science*. Academic Press, San Diego.

Bracken, R. H., and Tillit, H. E. (1957). Information searching with the 701 calculator. *Journal of the Association for Computing Machinery* **4**(2), 131–136.

A Brief Guide to DIALOG Searching. (1976). Lockheed Information Services, Palo Alto, CA.

Brookes, B. C. (1980). The foundations of information science. Part 1. Philosophical aspects. *Journal of Information Science* **2**(3–4), 125–133.

Buell, D. A. (1985). A problem in information retrieval with fuzzy sets. *Journal of the American Society for Information Science* **36**(6), 398–401.

Bush, V. (1945). As we may think. *Atlantic Monthly* **176**(1), 101–108.

Cardenas, A. F. (1985). *Data Base Management Systems*. Allyn and Bacon, Boston.

Casey, R. S., Perry, J. W., Berry, M. M., and Kent, A. (1958). *Punched Cards, Their Applications to Science and Industry*. Reinhold, New York.

Chapman, J. L. (1981). A state transition analysis of online information seeking behavior. *Journal of the American Society for Information Science* **32**(5), 107–116.

Chen, P. P. (1976). The entity-relation model—towards a unified view of data. *Association for Computing Machinery Transactions on Database Systems* **1**(1) January, 9–36.

Cherry, C. (1957). *On Human Communication, a Review, a Survey, and a Criticism* (1st ed.). MIT Press, Cambridge, MA, and Wiley, New York.

Chomsky, N. (1965). *Aspects of the Theory of Syntax*. MIT Press, Cambridge, MA.

Clausewitz, K. von (1943). *On War*. The Modern Library, New York.

Cleverdon, C., and Keen, M. (1966). *Factors Affecting the Performance of Indexing Systems*, Vol. 2. ASLIB, Cranfield Research Project, Bedford, UK.

Cleverdon, C. W., and Thorne, R. G. (1954). *A Brief Experiment with the Uniterm System of Coordinate Indexing for the Cataloging of Structural Data*. (RAE Library Memorandum #7, AD 35004). Royal Aircraft Establishment, Farnborough, UK.

Cochrane, P. A. (1981). Study of events and tasks in the search interviews before online searching. In *Proceedings of the 2nd National Online Meeting*, pp. 133–147. New York, March 24–26.

Codd, E. F. (1970). A relational model of data for large shared data banks. *Communications of the Association for Computing Machinery* **13**(6), 377–387.

Committee on Government Operations, United States Senate (1960). *Documentation, Indexing, and Retrieval of Scientific Information* (Senate Doc. 113, 88th Congress) U.S. Government Printing Office, Washington, D.C.

Condon, E. U. (1928). Statistics of vocabulary. *Science* **1733**, 300.

Cooper, M. D. (1983). Usage patterns of an online search system. *Journal of the American Society for Information Science* **31**(5), 343–349.

Cooper, W. S. (1970). The potential usefulness of catalog access points other than author, title, and subject. *Journal of the American Society for Information Science* **21**(1), 112–127.

Cooper, W. S. (1971). A definition of relevance for information retrieval. *Information Storage and Retrieval* **7**, 19–37.

Croft, W. B. (1982). An overview of information systems. *Information Technology: Research and Development* **1**(1), 73–96.

Croft, W. B., and Thompson, R. H. (1987). I^{3}R: A new approach to the design of document retrieval systems. *Journal of the American Society for Information Science* **38**(6), 389–404.

Date, C. J. (1983). *An Introduction Database Systems*, Vol. 2. Addison-Wesley, Reading, MA.

Date, C. J. (1985). *An Introduction to Database Systems*, Vol. 1 (4th ed.). Addison-Wesley, Reading, MA.

de Stricker, U., and Dysart, J. 1. (1989). *Business Online, A Canadian Guide*, pp. 35–40. Wiley, Toronto.

Dewey, G. (1923). *Relative Frequency of English Speech Sounds*. Harvard Univ. Press, Cambridge, MA.

DialogWeb (1998). http://www.dialogWeb.com/topics/ds/ and http://www.dialogWeb.com/forms/ds/.

Dijkstra, E. W. (1989). On the cruelty of teaching computer science. *Communications of the Association for Computing Machinery* **32**(12). (A special issue devoted entirely to the subject of user studies.)

Dillon, A., ed. (1997). Current research in human-computer interaction. *Journal of the American Society for Information Science* **48**(11).

Doszkocs, T. E. (1983a). CITE-NLM: Natural language searching in an online catalog. *Information Technology and Libraries* **2**(4), 364–380.

Doszkocs, T. E. (1983b). From research to application: The CITE natural language information retrieval system. In *Research and Development in Information Retrieval*, Springer Lecture Notes in Computer Science, Vol. 146. Springer-Verlag, Berlin.

Downie, J. S. (1997). Informetrics and music information retrieval. In *Communication and Information in Context: Technology and the Professions. Proceedings of the 25th Annual Conference of the Canadian Association for Information Science*. Canadian Association for Information Science, Toronto.

Doyle, L. B. (1963). Is relevance an adequate criterion in retrieval system evaluation? In *American Documentation Institute, 26th Annual Meeting*, pp. 199–200. Washington, ADI, D.C.

Drucker, P. F. (1998). The next information revolution. *Forbes ASAP* 24 Aug. (www.forbes.com/asap/98/0824/046.htm.)

The Dublin Core (1998). http://purl.org/DC/index.htm.

Duggan, A. (1940). *God and My Right*. Faber and Faber, London.

Edmundson, H. P., and Wyllys, R. E. (1961). Automatic abstracting and indexing—sources and recommendations. *Communications of the Association for Computing Machinery* 4(5), 226–234.

Ei Thesaurus. (1993). CCM Information Corp., New York.

Eisenberg, M. B. (1988). Measuring relevance judgment. *Information Processing and Management* 24(4), 373–389.

Eisenberg, M. B., and Barry, C. L. (1988). Order effects. A study of the possible influence of presentation order on user judgement of document relevance. *Journal of the American Society for Information Science* 39(5), 293–300.

Eliot, T. S. (1937). Choruses from "The Rock." In *Collected Poems*. Faber and Faber, London.

Encyclopedia of Library and Information Science, Vol. 4. (1970). (A. Kent, and H. Lancour, eds.). Dekker, New York.

Englebart, D. C. (1963). A conceptual framework for the augmentation of man's intellect. In *Vistas in Information Handling* (P. D. Howerton, and D. C. Weeks, eds.), Vol. 1. Spartan Books, Washington, D.C.

Englebart, D. C., and English, W. K. (1968). A research center for augmenting human intellect. In *Proceedings of the 1968 Fall Joint Computer Conference*, pp. 395–410. AFIPS Press, Montvale, NJ.

Faloutsos, C., and Christodoulakis, S. (1984). Signature files: An access method for documents and its analytical performance evaluation. *Association for Computing Machinery Transactions on Office Information Systems*, 2(4), 267–288.

Fenichel, C. (1981). Online searching: Measures that discriminate among users with different types of experiences. *Journal of the American Society for Information Science* 32(1), 23–32.

Fidel, R. (1987). *Database Design for Information Retrieval, a Conceptual Approach*. Wiley, New York.

Forsyth, R. (1984). The architecture of expert systems. In *Expert Systems: Principles and Case Studies* (R. Forsyth, ed.), p. 10. Chapman and Hall, London/New York.

Fox, C. (1990). A stop list for general text. *SIGIR Forum* 20(12), 19–35.

Fox, C., Frakes, W., and Gandel, P. (1988). Foundational issues in knowledge-based information systems. *The Canadian Journal of Information Science* 13(3/4), 90–102.

Frakes, W. B., and Baeza-Yates, R., eds. (1992). *Information Retrieval: Data Structures & Algorithms*. Prentice Hall, Englewood Cliffs, NJ.

Froelich, T., ed. (1994). *Relevance research. Journal of the American Society for Information Science* 45(3). (A special issue devoted entirely to the subject of relevance.)

Garg, A. K., and Gotlieb, C. C. (1986). Order-preserving key transformation. *Association for Computing Machinery Transactions on Database Systems* 1(2), 213–234.

Gassaway, L. A. (1997). Library reserve collections from paper to electronic collections. In *Growing Pains: Adopting Copyright for Libraries, Education, and Society* (L. Gassaway, ed.), pp. 125–149. Fred B. Rothman & Co., Littleton, CO.

Giles, C. A., Brooks, A. A., Doszkocs, T., and Hummel, D. J. (1976). *A Computerized Scheme for Duplicate Checking of Bibliographic Databases* (ORNL CSD-5). Oak Ridge National Laboratory, Oak Ridge, TN.

Goldfarb, C. F. (1990). *The SGML Handbook*. Clarendon, Oxford.

Graham, I. S. (1995). *HTML Sourcebook*. Wiley, New York.

Gull, C. D. (1956). Seven years of work on the organization of materials in the special library. *American Documentation* 7, 320–329.

Hall, A. D. (1962). *A Methodology for Systems Engineering*, pp. 253–255. Van Nostrand, Princeton.

Harter, S. P. (1986). *Online Information Retrieval Concepts, Principles, and Techniques*, pp. 153–165. Academic Press, San Diego.

Harter, S. P., and Hert, C. A. (1998). Evaluation of information retrieval systems: Approaches, issues, and methods. In *Annual Review of Information Science and Technology* (M. E. Williams, ed.), Vol. 32, pp. 3–94. Information Today, Medford, NJ.

Hawkins, D. (1989). In search of ideal information pricing. *Online* 13(2), 15–30.

Hayakawa, S. I. (1939). *Language in Thought and Action*. Harcourt, Brace & World, New York.

Heine, M. H. (1973). Distance between sets as an objective measure of retrieval effectiveness. *Information Storage and Retrieval* **9**, 181–198.

Herner, S. (1984). Brief history of information science. *Journal of the American Society for Information Science* **35**(3), 157–163.

Hickey, T. B., and Rypka, D. J. (1979). Automatic detection of duplicate monographic records. *Journal of Library Automation* **12**(2), 125–142.

Hildreth, C. R. (1983). To Boolean or not to Boolean. *Information Technology and Libraries* **2**(3), 235–237.

Humphreys, B. L., and Lindberg, D. A. B. (1993). The UMLS project: Making the conceptual connection between users and the information they need. *Bulletin of the American Library Association* **81**(2), 170–177.

Ingwerson, P. (1984). A cognitive view of three selected online search facilities. *Online Review* **8**(5), 465–492.

Janes, J. W. (1989). The application of search theory to information science. In *Proceedings of the 52nd Annual Meeting, American Society for Information Science*, 9. Learned Information, Medford, NJ.

Jansen, B. J., and Spink, A., Bateman, J., and Saracevic, T. (1998). Real life information retrieval: a study of user queries on the Web. *SIGIR Forum* **32**(1), 5–17.

Johnson, E. D. (1970). *History of Libraries in the Western World* (2nd ed.). Scarecrow Press, Metuchen, NJ.

Katzer, J. (1998). Personal communication.

Kaufman, I. (1998). Personal communication.

Kearsley, G. (1988). Design and implementation of online help systems. In *Conference on Human Factors in Computing Systems*, ACM/SIGCHI. Washington, D.C., May 1988.

Kent, A., Berry, M. M., Leuhrs, F. U., and Perry, J. W. (1955). Machine literature searching VII. Operational criteria for designing information retrieval systems. *American Documentation* **6**(2), 93–101.

Kessel, B., and DeLucia, A. (1959). A specialized library index search computer. In *Proceedings of the 1959 Western Joint Computer Conference*. Inst. of Radio Engineers, New York.

Kleinrock, L. (1961). Information flow in large communication nets. *RLE Quarterly Progress Report*, July.

Knott, G. D. (1975). Hashing functions. *Computer Journal* **18**(3), 265–278.

Knuth, D. E. (1973). *The Art of Computer Programming*, Vol. 3. *Sorting and Searching*. Addison-Wesley, Reading, MA.

Kochen, M. (1974). *Principles of Information Retrieval*. Melville, Los Angeles.

Korfhage, R. R. (1997). *Information Storage and Retrieval*. Wiley, New York.

Korth, H. F., and Silberschatz, A. (1986). *Database System Concepts*. McGraw-Hill, New York.

Kraft, D. H., and Buell, D. A. (1983). Fuzzy sets and generalized Boolean retrieval systems. *International Journal of Man-Machine Studies* **19**, 45–56.

Lancaster, F. W. (1968). *Information Retrieval Systems: Characteristics, Testing, and Evaluation* (2nd ed.). Wiley, New York.

Lee, J. A. N., Fano, R. M., Scherr, A. L., Corbato, F. J., and Vyssotsky, V. A. (1992). Project MAC (time-sharing computer project). *IEEE Annals of the History of Computing* **14**(2), 9–13.

Lefkovitz, D. (1969). *File Structures for On-Line Systems*. Spartan Books, New York.

Leimkuhler, F. F. (1968). A literature search and file organization model. *American Documentation* **19**, 131–136.

Levy, L. R. (1987). Launching electronic information services for end-users: The AT&T experience. In *Proceedings of the 8th National Online Meeting*, pp. 273–280. Learned Information, Medford, NJ.

Library of Congress Subject Headings (21st ed.) (1998). Subject Cataloguing Division, Library of Congress, Washington, D.C.

Licklider, J. C. R. (1960). Man–machine symbiosis. *IRS Transactions on Human Factors in Electronics* **HFE-1**(1), 4–11.

Liddy, E. (1990). Anaphora in natural language processing and information retrieval. *Information Processing and Management* **26**(1), 39–52.

Liddy, E. D., Paik, W., Yu, E. S., and McKenna, M. (1995). Document retrieval using linguistic knowledge. In *RAIO 94 Proceedings*. Rockefeller University, New York.

Litman, J. (1997). New copyright paradigms. In *Growing Pains: Adopting Copyright for Libraries, Education, and Society* (L. Gassaway, ed.), pp. 63–84. Fred B. Rothman & Co., Littleton, CO.

Losee, R. (1990). *The Science of Information*. Academic Press, San Diego.

Lovins, J. B. (1968). Developing of a stemming algorithm. *Mechanical Translation and Computational Linguistics* **11**(1, 2) March, 11–31.

Luhn, H. P. (1958). The automatic creation of literature abstracts. *IBM Journal of Research* **2**(4), 159–165.

Mallery, D. (1987). Genscan! *DEC Professional* **6**(4), 106–111.

Mandelbrot, B. (1953). An informational theory of the statistical structure of language. In *Communication Theory* (W. Jackson, ed.), pp. 486–502. Butterworths Scientific, London.

Marchionini, G. (1995). *Information Seeking in Electronic Environments*. Cambridge Univ. Press, Cambridge, UK.

Marchionini, G., Lin, X., and Dwiggins, S. (1990). Effects of search and subject expertise on information seeking in a hypertext environment. In *Proceedings of the 53rd American Society for Information Science Annual Meeting* (D. Henderson, ed.), pp. 129–142. Learned Information, Medford, NJ.

Marcus, R. S. (1982). *Investigation of Computer-Aided Document Search Strategies.* (Report LIDS-R-1233). Massachusetts Institute of Technology, Cambridge, MA.

Marcus, R. S. and the CONIT Project Staff (1987a). *The CONIT Guide*. Version 1. Laboratory for Information Decision and Systems, Massachusetts Institute of Technology, Cambridge, MA.

Marcus, R. S. and the CONIT Project Staff (1987b). *The CONIT Manual*. Version 7. Laboratory for Information Decision and Systems, Massachusetts Institute of Technology, Cambridge, MA.

Maron, M. E., Kuhns, and J. L. (1960). On relevance, probabilistic indexing and information retrieval. *Journal of the Association for Computing Machinery* **7**(3), 216–244.

Marshall, J. G. (1990). Database search services: A quality assurance approach. In *Q. A. Quality Assurance in Libraries: The Health Care Sector* (M. H. Taylor, and T. Wilson, eds.), pp. 85–100. Canadian Library Association/The Library Association, Ottawa.

McGraw-Hill Encyclopedia of Science and Technology, Vol. 5. (1971). McGraw-Hill, New York.

Meadow, C. T. (1973). *The Analysis of Information Systems* (2nd ed.). Melville, Los Angeles. (p. 165.)

Meadow, C. T. (1979). Information science and scientists in 2001. *Journal of Information Science* **1**(4), 217–222.

Meadow, C. T. (1988). OAKDEC, a program for studying the effect on users of a procedural expert system for database searching. *Information Processing and Management* **24**(4), 449–457.

Meadow, C. T., and Cochrane, P. A. (1981). *Basics of Online Searching*. Wiley, New York.

Meadow, C. T., Marchionini, G., and Cherry, J. (1994). Speculations on the measurement and use of user characteristics in information retrieval experimentation. *Canadian Journal of Information and Library Science* **19**(4), 1–22.

Meadow, C. T., Wang, J., and Stamboulie, M. (1993). An analysis of Zipf–Mandelbrot language measures and their application to artificial languages. *Journal of Information Science* **19**, 247–258.

Meadow, C. T., and Yuan, W. (1997). Measuring the impact of information: Defining the concepts. *Information Processing and Management* **33**(6), 697–714.

Meadow, C. T., Cerny, B. A., Borgman, C. L., and Case, D. O. (1989). Online access to knowledge: system design. *Journal of the American Society for Information Science* **40**(2), 86–98.

Meadow, C. T., Loranger, M., and Olander, B. (1985). An experiment to identify decision points in online searching. In *Proceedings of the 13th Annual CAIS Conference*, Montreal, 1985, pp. 12–22. Canadian Association for Information Science, Toronto.

Medical Subject Headings. (1987). National Library of Medicine, Bethesda, MD.

Menou, M. J. (1995). The impact of information II. Concepts of information and its value. *Information Processing and Management* **31**(4), 479–490.

Mettler, M., and Norby, F. (1995). TREC routing experiments with the TRW/Parcel Fast Data Finder. *Information Processing and Management* **31**(3), 379–384.

Miller, G. A. (1995). WordNet: A lexical database for English. *Communications of the Association for Computing Machinery* **38**(11), 39–41.

Miyamoto, S. (1990). *Fuzzy Sets in Information Retrieval and Cluster Analysis*. Kluwer Academic, Boston.

Mooers, C. N. (1951). Coding, information retrieval, and the Rapid Selector. *American Documentation* **1**, 225–229.

Morris, C. W. (1946). *Signs, Language, and Behavior*. Prentice Hall, New York.

Morse, P. M. (1970). Search theory and browsing. *The Library Quarterly* **40**(1) January, 391–408.

Mosteller, F., and Wallace, D. L. (1963). Inference in an authorship problem. *Journal of the American Statistical Association* **53**(302), 275–309.

Muzzano, S. (1997). Relevance: The whole history. *Journal of the American Society for Information Science* **48**(9), 810–832.

Nance, J. W., and Lathrope, J. W. (1968). *System Design Specifications: General Purpose ORBIT* (TM-DA-20/000/00). System Development Corporation, Santa Monica, CA.

National Library of Medicine. (1998). *UMLS Knowledge Sources* (9th ed.). (http://www.nlm.gov/research/umls/UNLSDOC. HTML.)

Nelson, T. H. (1965). The hypertext. In *Proceedings of the World Documentation Federation*.

Nelson, T. H. (1981). *Literary Machines*. Nelson, Swarthmore, RA.

Nelson, T. H. (1988). Unifying tomorrow's hypermedia. In *Online Information 88. 12th International Online Information Meeting*, Vol. 1, pp. 1–7.

Nitecki, J. Z. (1985). The concept of information–knowledge continuum. *Journal of Library History* **20**(4), 387–407.

Noreault, T., Koll, M. B., and McGill, M. (1977). Automatic ranked input from Boolean searches in SIRE. *Journal of the American Society for Information Science* **28**(6), 333–341.

Noreault, T., McGill, M., and Koll, M. B. (1981). A performance evaluation of similarity measures, document term weighting schemes, and representation in a Boolean environment. In *Information Retrieval Research* (R. N. Oddy, ed.), pp. 57–76. Butterworths, London.

Ojala, M. (1986). Views on end-user searching. *Journal of the American Society for Information Science* **37**(4), 197–203.

O'Leary, M. (1988). Price versus value for online data. *Online* **12**(2), 26–30.

Paice, C. D. (1990). Another sternmer. *SIGIR Forum* **24**(3), 56–61.

Paice, C. D. (1991). Constructing literature abstracts by computer: Techniques and prospects. *Information Processing and Management* **26**(1), 171–186.

Parsaye, K., Chigell, M., Khoshafran, S., and Wong, H. (1989). *Intelligent Databases, Object Oriented, Deductive Hypermedia Technologies*. Wiley, New York.

Parsons, D. (1975). *The Directory of Tunes and Musical Themes*. Spencer Brown, Cambridge, MA.

Penniman, W. D. (1975a). *Rhythms of dialogue in human-computer communication*. Ph. D. dissertation. The Ohio State University, Columbus.

Penniman, W. D. (1975b). A stochastic process analysis of on-line behavior. *Proceedings of the American Society for Information Science 38th Annual Meeting*. pp. 167–168. *American Society for Information Science*, Washington, D.C.

Penniman, W. D., and Dominick, W. (1980). Monitoring and evaluation of online information system usage. *Information Processing and Management* **16**, 17–35.

Perry, J. W., Kent, A., and Berry, M. M. (1956). *Machine Literature Searching*. Western Reserve Univ. Press, Cleveland, and Interscience, New York.

Physical measurement. (1971). *McGraw-Hill Encyclopedia of Science and Technology*, Vol. 10, pp. 226–232. McGraw-Hill, New York.

Potter, R. B. (1988). If someone steals a secret, has theft been committed? Toronto, *The Globe and Mail*, September 22, p. A7.

Rasmussen, E. M. (1997). Indexing images. In *Annual Review of Information Science and Technology* (M. E. Williams, ed.), Vol. 32, pp. 169–196. Information Today, Medford, NJ.

Records, Computers, and the Rights of Citizens. (1973). Report of the Secretary's Advisory Committee on Automated Personal Data Systems. U.S. Department of Health, Education, and Welfare, Washington, D.C. (See Secretary Advisory Committee, 1973.)

Ro, J. S. (1988). An evaluation of the applicability of ranking algorithms to improve the effectiveness of full-text retrieval. II. On the effectiveness of ranking algorithms on full-text retrieval. *Journal of the American Society for Information Science* **39**(3), 147–160.

Robertson, S. E. (1977). The probability ranking principle in IR. *Journal of Documentation* **33**(4), 294–304.

Robertson, S. E., Thompson, C. L., Macaskill, M. J., and Bovey, J. D. (1986). Weighting, ranking, and relevance feedback in a front-end system. *Journal of Information Science* **12**(1/2), 71–75.

Robertson, S. E., Walker, S., and Beaulieu, M. (1997). Laboratory experiments with Okapi: Participation in the TREC programme. *Journal of Documentation* **53**(1), 20–34.

Sachs, W. M. (1976). An approach to associative retrieval through the theory of fuzzy sets. *Journal of the American Society for Information Science* **27**(2), 85–87.

Salton, G. (1980). The SMART system 1961–1976: Experiments in dynamic document processing. In *Encyclopedia of Library and Information Science* (A. Kent, H. Lancour, and W. Z. Lazri, eds.), Vol. 28, pp. 1–35. Dekker, New York.

Salton, G. (1989). *Automatic Text Processing*. Addison-Wesley, Reading, MA.

Salton, G., and McGill, M. J. (1983). *An Introduction to Modern Information Retrieval*. McGraw-Hill, New York.

Samstag-Schnook, U., and Meadow, C. T. (1993). PBS: An economical natural-language query interpreter. *Journal of the American Society for Information Science* **44**(5), 265–272.

Samuelson, A. L. (1959). Some studies in machine learning using the game of checkers. *IBM Journal of Research* **3**(3), 210–229.

Saracevic, T. (1975). Relevance: A review of and a framework for the thinking on the notion in information science. *Journal of the American Society for Information Science* **26**(4), 321–343.

Saracevic, T., and Kantor, P. (1988). A study of information seeking and retrieving, III. Searchers, searches, and overlap. *Journal of the American Society for Information Science* **39**(3), 197–216.

Savage, G. S., and Pemberton, J. K. (1978). SCISEARCH on DIALOG. *Database* **1**(1), 50–67.

Sawyer, D. C. (1995). *Sawyer's Survival Guide for Information Brokers*. Burwell Enterprises, Houston, TX.

Schamber, L., Eisenberg, M. B., and Nilan, M. S. (1988). Relevance: A search for a definition. In *Proc. 51st Annual Meeting, American Society for Information Science*. (C. L. Borgman and E. Y. H. Pai, eds.), pp. 164–168. Learned Information, Medford, NJ.

Schamber, L., Eisenberg, M. B., and Nilan, M. S. (1990). A re-examination of relevance: Toward a dynamic situational definition. *Information Processing and Management* **26**(6), 755–776.

Schwartz, C. (1998). Web search engines. *Journal of the American Society of Information Science* **49**(11), 973–982.

The Science of Fingerprints. (1979). U.S. Department of Justice, Federal Bureau of Investigation, Washington, D.C.

Secretary's Advisory Committee on Automated Personal Data Systems. (1973). *Records, Computers, and the Rights of Citizens* (DHEW PW (OS)). U.S. Department of Health, Education, and Welfare, Washington, D.C.

Shannon, C. E., and Weaver, W. (1959). *The Mathematical Theory of Communication*. Univ. of Illinois Press, Urbana, IL.

Shera, J. H., Kent, A., and Perry, J. W., eds., (1957). *Documentation in Action*. Reinhold, New York.

Shneiderman, B. (1986). Designing menu selection systems. *Journal of the American Society for Information Science* **37**(2), 57.

Shneiderman, B. (1987). *Designing the User Interface: Strategies for Effective Human–Computer Interaction*. Addison-Wesley, Reading, MA.

Shneiderman, B., and Kearsely, G. (1989). *Hypertext Hands On! An Introduction to a New Way of Organizing and Accessing Information*. Addison-Wesley, Reading, MA.

Shreider, Yu. A. (1970). On the semantic characteristics of information. In *Introduction to Information Science* (T. Saracevic, ed.), pp. 24–32. Bowker, New York.

Sievert, M. C. (1996). Full-text retrieval. *Journal of the American Society for Information Science* **47**(4). (A special issue devoted entirely to the subject of full-text searching.)

Sievert, M. C., and Andrews, M. J. (1991). Indexing consistency in Information Science Abstracts. *Journal of the American Society for Information Science* **42**(1), 1–6.

Soergel, D. (1985). *Organizing Information, Principles of Data Base and Retrieval Systems*. Academic Press, San Diego.

Spark Jones, K. (1995). Reflections on TREC. *Information Processing and Management* **31**(3), 291–314.

Squires, S. J. (1993). Access to biomedical information: The Unified Medical Language System. *Library Trends* **42**(1), 127–151.

Srinivasan, P. (1989). Intelligent information retrieval using rough set approximations. *Information Processing and Management* **25**(4), 347–361.

Standish, T. A. (1980). *Data Structure Techniques*. Addison Wesley, Reading, MA.

Steuart, B. W. (1990). *The Soundex Reference Guide*. Precision Indexing, Bountiful, UT.

Successful Searching on Dialog. (1998). Dialog Corporation, Palo Alto, CA. (Available at http://library. dialog. com/essentials.html.)

Swanson, D. R. (1979). Libraries and the growth of knowledge. *Library Quarterly* **49**(1), 3–25.

Swanson, D. R. (1988). Historical note: Information retrieval and the future of an illusion. *Journal of the American Society for Information Science* **39**(2), 92.

Swets, J. A. (1969). Effectiveness of information retrieval methods. *American Documentation* **20**(1), 72–89.

Tague-Sutcliffe, J. (1995). *Measuring Information*. Academic Press, San Diego.

Tague-Sutcliffe, J., ed. (1996). Evaluation of information retrieval systems. *Journal of the American Society for Information Science* **47**(1). (A special issue devoted entirely to the subject of system evaluation.)

Tang, R., Vevea, J., and Shaw, W. M., Jr. (1999). Toward the identification of the optimal number of relevance categories. *Journal of the American Society for Information Science* **50**(3), #–#.

Taube, M., ed. (1953–1965). *Studies in Coordinate Indexing*, Vol. 1–6. Documentation, Inc., Washington, D.C.

Taylor, R. S. (1968). Question negotiation and information seeking in libraries. *College and Research Libraries* **29**(3), 178–194.

Teskey, F. N. (1989). User models and world models for data, information, and knowledge. *Information Processing and Management* **25**(1), 7–14.

Thesaurus of ERIC Descriptors. (1995). (13th ed.). Oryx Press, Phoenix, AZ.

Tiamiyu, M. A., and Ajiferuke, I. Y. (1988). A total relevance and document interaction effects model for the evaluation of information retrieval processes. *Information Processing and Management* **24**(4), 391–404.

Tremblay, J.-P., and Sorenson, P. G. (1985). *An Introduction to Data Structures with Applications.* McGraw-Hill, New York.

Tucker, A. B., Jr. (1979). *Text Processing: Algorithms, Languages, and Applications.* Academic Press, New York.

Turtle, H., and Croft, W. B. (1990). Inference networks for document retrieval. In *Proceedings of the Thirteenth International Conference on Research and Development in Information Retrieval* (J. L. Vidick, ed.), pp. 1–24. Accoc. Comp. Mach., New York.

van Rijsbergen, C. J. (1979). *Information Retrieval* (2nd ed.). Butterworths, London.

van Rijsbergen, C. J. (1986). A new retrieval framework for information retrieval. In *Proceedings of the 9th International SIGIR Conference on Research and Development in Information Retrieval,* pp. 194–200. Assoc. Comput. Mach., New York.

Vickery, A., and Brooks, H. M. (1987). Plexus: The expert system for referral. *Information Processing and Management* **23**(2), 99–118.

Vickery, B. C. (1961). *On Retrieval System Theory,* p. 160. Butterworths, London.

Wang, J., and Meadow, C. T. (1991). Measuring user performance in online searching: A preliminary report. *Canadian Journal of Information Science* **16**(2), 28–39.

Warner, A. S. (1987). *Mind Your Own Business: A Guide for Information Entrepreneurs.* Neal-Schuman, New York.

Warnken, K. (1981). *The Information Brokers: How to Start and Operate Your Own Fee-Based Service.* R. R. Bowker, New York.

Webster's New World Dictionary of the American Language. (1962). World, Cleveland.

Weibel, S. (1997). The Dublin Core: A simple content description model for electronic resources. *Bulletin of the American Society for Information Science* **24**(1), 9–11.

Weinberg, A. M., and the President's Science Advisory Committee (1963). *Science, Government, and Information: The Responsibilities of the Technical Community and the Government in the Transfer of Information.* U.S. Government Printing Office, Washington, D.C.

Wente, V. A. (1971). NASA/RECON and user interface considerations. In *Interactive Bibliographic Search: The User/Computer Interface* (D. F. Walker, ed.), pp. 95–104. AFIPS Press, Montvale, NJ.

Westin, A. F. (1976). *Computers, Health Records, and Citizen Rights.* Petrocelli Books, New York.

Weyer, S. (1989). Questing for the 'Dao': DowQuest and intelligent text retrieval. *ONLINE* **13**(5), 39–45.

Wiederhold, G. (1987). *File Organization for Database Design.* McGraw-Hill, New York.

Whitehorn, J. C., and Zipf, G. K. (1943). Schizophrenic language. *Archives of Neurological Psychiatry* **49**, 831–851.

Williams, J. H. (1963). A discriminant method for automatically classifying documents. In *Proceedings of the Fall Joint Computer Conference.* AFIPS Press, Montvale, NJ.

Williams, P. (1984). Model for an expert system for automated information retrieval. In *8th International Online Information Meeting, London 1984,* pp. 139–149. Learned Information, Oxford.

Wilson, P. (1973). Situational relevance. *Information Storage and Retrieval* **9**, 457–471.

Yannakoudakis, E. J., Ayres, F. H., and Huggil, J. A. W. (1990). Matching of citations between non-standard databases. *Journal of the American Society for Information Science* **41**(8), 599–610.

Yovits, M. C., Foulk, C. R., and Rose, L. L. (1981). Information flow and analysis: Theory, simulations and experiments. Part 1. Basic theoretical and conceptual development. *Journal of the American Society for Information Science* **32**(3), 187–210.

Yu, K., Hsu, S., and Otsubo, P. (1984). The Fast Data Finder—an architecture for very high speed data search and dissemination. In *IEEE 1984 International Conference on Data Engineering*, pp. 167–174. IEEE Computer Society Press, Silver Spring, MD.

Yuan, W. (1997). End-user searching behavior in information retrieval: A longitudinal study. *Journal of the American Society for Information Science* **48**(3), 218–234.

Yule, G. U. (1944). *The Statistical Study of Literary Vocabulary*. Cambridge Univ. Press, Cambridge, MA.

Zadeh, L. (1965). Fuzzy sets. *Information and Control*, **8**, 338–353.

Zakon, R. H. (1997). Hobbes' Internet timeline. (Found at http://info.isoc.org/guest/zakon/Internet/History/HIT.html.)

Zipf, G. K. (1949). *Human Behavior and the Principle of Least Effort*, pp. 22–27. Addison-Wesley, Cambridge, MA.

Recommended Reading

Chowdhury, G. G. (1999). *Introduction to Modern Information Retrieval*. Library Association Publishing, London.

Debons, A., Home, E., and Cronenweth, S. (1988). *Information Science: An Integrated View*. Hall, Boston.

Fenichel, C. H., and Hogan, T. H. (1990). *Online Searching: A Primer* (3rd ed.). Learned Information, Marlton, NJ.

Hawkins, D. T. Online Information Retrieval Bibliography. (This has been updated and published annually in *Online Review* since 1976.)

Korfhage, R. R. (1997). *Information Storage and Retrieval*. Wiley, New York.

Salton, G. (1989). *Automatic Text Processing*. Addison-Wesley, Reading, MA.

Spark Jones, K. (1981). *Information Retrieval Experiment*. Butterworths, London.

Vickery, B., and Vickery, A. (1987). *Information Science in Theory and Practice*. Butterworths, London.

Zakon, R. H. (1993). Hobbes' Internet timeline. (Found at http://info.isoc.org/guest/zakon/Internet/History/HIT.html.)

Index

Library and Information Science

(Continued from page ii)

Lois Swan Jones and Sarah Scott Gibson
Art Libraries and Information Services

Nancy Jones Pruett
Scientific and Technical Libraries: Functions and Management
Volume 1 and Volume 2

Peter Judge and Brenda Gerrie
Small Bibliographic Databases

Dorothy B. Lilley and Ronald W. Trice
A History of Information Sciences 1945–1985

Elaine Svenonius
The Conceptual Foundations of Descriptive Cataloging

Robert M. Losee, Jr.
The Science of Information: Measurement and Applications

Irene P. Godden
Library Technical Services: Operations and Management,
Second Edition

Donald H. Kraft and Bert R. Boyce
Operations Research for Libraries and Information Agencies:
Techniques for the Evaluation of Management Decision
Alternatives

James Cabeceiras
The Multimedia Library: Materials Selection and Use, Second
Edition

Charles T. Meadow
Text Information Retrieval Systems, First Edition

Robert M. Losee, Jr., and Karen A. Worley
Research and Evaluation for Information Professionals

Carmel Maguire, Edward J. Kazlauskas, and Anthony D. Weir
Information Services for Innovative Organizations